THE MILITARY-INDUSTRIAL COMPLEX

THE MILITARY-INDUSTRIAL COMPLEX

CARROLL W. PURSELL, Jr.

University of California at Santa Barbara

HARPER & ROW, PUBLISHERS
NEW YORK EVANSTON SAN FRANCISCO LONDON

CONTENTS

List of Appendices

viii   LIST OF APPENDICES

Preface

The military-industrial complex can be defined as "an informal and changing coalition of groups with vested psychological, moral, and material interests in the continuous development and maintenance of high levels of weaponry, in preservation of colonial markets and in military-strategic conceptions of international affairs."[1] The groups include such diverse persons as congressmen, labor leaders, corporation executives, church spokesmen, university professors, and professional soldiers, along with the host of followers and families dependent upon them. At the center of the complex (though not entirely defining it) is the unique relationship between the Pentagon as buyer and the war industries as seller.

The critical matter is whether these groups tend to act in concert to reinforce each other, or whether they are countervailing forces, tending to keep each other in check. In other words, does the traditional American political reliance on the balance of special interests really work in this case to check tyranny, or has this special interest coalesced to the point where it can, to a dangerous degree, operate free of effective restraint from other interests.

The documents which follow were selected to cast light on this problem. Some scholarly and some polemical, they are arranged in a roughly chronological order to emphasize the need to understand the problem in its historical context. Unfortunately, historians have only recently begun to study the various pieces of the story, so that its history cannot yet be written in the detail and with the confidence one would prefer. Nevertheless the effort at historical understanding must be made, for it is one of the ways in which the problem can be understood and dealt with.

[1] Marc Pilisuk and Thomas Hayden, "Is There a Military Industrial Complex Which Prevents Peace?: Consensus and Countervailing Power in Pluralistic Systems," *Journal of Social Issues*, XXI (July 1965), 103.

At the same time, the documents themselves give a solidity and specificity to the investigation, which can transcend the too often vague and ritualistic rhetoric in which the discussion is usually cast. A number of appendices, in addition to tables within the text, give still more data to the student embarked upon a research topic or simply trying to understand and evaluate the judgments made in the documents and accompanying notes.

The historical Introduction is both incomplete and tentative. The scholarly articles and books upon which it is based, however, and which are cited in the accompanying notes, have laid the groundwork for future understanding of how the military-industrial complex developed into its present form.

Carroll W. Pursell, Jr.
Santa Barbara, Calif.
23 December 1971

INTRODUCTION

It is generally assumed, or hoped, that in the United States various special interests act as countervailing forces—that they tend to counteract or modify each other in a way that prevents the tyranny of any one of them. There has been, during the past decade, an increasing concern that in the area of what is called "national defense" such countervailing forces have given way to a constellation of interests that work to reinforce rather than hold each other in check. This has usually been called the "military-industrial complex," a term taken from President Dwight D. Eisenhower's farewell address to the nation in 1961. The fear is that a community of interest has developed among some corporations, military officers, civilian bureaucrats, labor leaders, scientists and others, which tends increasingly to dictate the dimension and direction of both foreign and domestic policies.

Although the origins of the military-industrial complex customarily are traced to the Korean War, or at the earliest to World War II, most of its salient features (military domination of the federal budget, armed adventures and interventions abroad, political influence of prominent military officers, etc.) date from the very origins of the nation. Nevertheless, it appears more fruitful to seek the modern roots of the complex in the Progressive reforms of the federal government made during the first two decades of this century. The problem of the military-industrial complex is only a special case of the more general problem of the maldistribution of wealth (and therefore of political influence) from which the country suffers. The Welfare State which has been elaborated upon by successive Administrations since Theodore Roosevelt's Presidency, carries within it the institutional and ideological seeds of the military-industrial complex.

THE LIBERAL CORPORATE STATE

Whatever else was accomplished during the Progressive era, it was the period during which the controllers of America's largest economic interests learned to work with and use the federal government to regulate and stabilize the nation's economy in their own behalf. American business, especially big business, sought to adapt governmental machinery for the new role of applying continuous administrative control over the most important aspects of society. The day when Congress ruled by discrete pieces of politically inspired legislation, and big business looked to its own ability to dominate and shape the market, was clearly ended because that system failed so signally to insure prosperity and growth in the modern industrial age.[1]

Two sets of reforms were necessary: Within the government, power had to be shifted from the Congress to the Presidency, and new administrative agencies had to be established which could exercise discretion over broad reaches of the economy. Within the business community, the ideology of liberalism had to predominate over that of laissez faire. Irresponsible and individualistic business-men had to be overriden by new, modern, liberal spokesmen who were aware of social problems and the need for government intervention. Instead of resisting federal regulation and the unionization of labor, enlightened businessmen must cooperate with and, so far as possible, guide these institutions into "responsible" channels. Such groups as the National Civic Federation pioneered the cooperative approach: As one historian has written, "in addition to keeping social questions out of the arena of public debate, this approach started with the assumption that problems were essentially technical, that the framework of the political economy need only be rationalized and that 'experts' applying their skills in the assumed common interest could best do the job."[2]

WORLD WAR I

World War I provided the great test of the new liberal state. The coming of war presented two major problems for President Woodrow Wilson. He had both to mobilize American resources (manpower, raw materials, productive plant, finance) and build a war machine in a very short time, and, of course, to win the cooperation (or at least neutralize the opposition) of such diverse groups as business, labor, agriculture, and political opponents. These needs fit precisely the liberal ideology of corporate leaders. The coordination of disparate economic and political elements, under the leadership of disinterested experts, seemed to be a task for which big business interests were manifestly prepared.

As yet the federal government lacked the massive bureaucratic necessities to launch a war mobilization. The United States Chamber of Commerce, among other groups, had been far ahead of the government (military as well as civil) in calling for industrial mobilization. Now, the government turned to business for

[1] See particularly James Weinstein, *The Corporate Ideal in the Liberal State*, 1900-1918 (Boston, 1968).

[2] *Ibid.*, p. 31. For an analysis of how this worked out in the field of natural resources, see James Penick, *Progressive Politics of Conservation: The Ballinger-Pinchot Affair* (Chicago, 1968) and Samuel P. Hays, *Conservation and the Gospel of Efficiency: The Progressive Conservation Movement, 1890-1920* (Cambridge, 1959).

the skills and leadership it needed. Between April 1916 and June 1919, the army pumped $14.5 billion into the economy, and many businessmen realized that such sums, if not carefully controlled, could badly disrupt the nation's industrial structure.

It was the military during World War I which resisted coordination. Too confused and busy to try to dominate the civilian economy, the military at the same time refused to surrender its traditional right to buy supplies. The army insisted that because procurement and strategy were intimately linked contracting should not be given over to a civilian agency. In this determination they were backed up by Secretary of War Newton D. Baker, who had no desire to see government activities so inflated that they could not be cut back at the end of the war. The confusion of supply was so great that at last the War Industries Board (WIB), staffed by dollar-a-year men on temporary loan from their own corporation, was beefed up and Bernard Baruch was placed in charge. Although the WIB was never given absolute authority over munitions (as did happen in other nations), belated reforms within the military did make it possible for civilian businessmen to run the procurement program while the army maintained formal authority over supply.[3]

Not surprisingly, the industrialists who controlled the WIB wanted also to influence the demobilization that came after the Armistice in November 1918. Two goals of big business were espoused by the WIB: first a continuation of price controls to prevent a drastic deflation, and second, the weakening of antitrust legislation to allow various industries to cooperate to maintain high prices without government support. President Wilson did not support these goals and instead dissolved the WIB. Partly because they knew that they had little congressional support, and partly because they failed to get unanimous support even from the business community, WIB members allowed the matter to lapse.[4]

The wartime mobilization experiment had been a huge success. Military supply services had been reorganized to conform to the more rational organization of private industry, and many happy bonds had been forged between business and the military. The prewar trend toward industrial self-regulation had been strengthened, and the antitrust tradition weakened. Both socialism and anarchy had been avoided by an emergency system which had, in fact, strengthened the large corporations and seriously weakened possible countervailing forces such as the union movement or the Socialist Party. America had become a world power and many leaders, both within the military

[3]See Paul A. C. Koistinen, "The 'Military-Industrial Complex' in Historical Perspective: World War I," *Business History Review*, 41 (Winter 1967), 378-403; Daniel R. Beaver, "Newton D. Baker and the Genesis of the War Industries Board, 1917-1918," *Journal of American History*, 52 (June 1965), 43-58; and Robert D. Cuff, "A 'Dollar-a-Year Man' in Government: George N. Peek and the War Industries Board," *Business History Review*, 41 (Winter 1967), 404-420.
[4]Robert F. Himmelberg, "The War Industries Board and the Antitrust Question in November 1918," *Journal of American History*, 52 (June 1965), 59-74.

and from industry, had become convinced that in the future, successful military machines could operate only from a strong and coordinated industrial base.

INTERWAR YEARS

The successful projection of the prewar liberal state into the postwar decade is attributable to the sophistication of the leading businessmen, the favorable world position of the United States in terms of trade, finance, and manufacturing, and the virtual lack of any strong opposition from other segments of society.[5] Attempts to perpetuate the specific climate of cooperation between industrial and military leaders were not always successful, but the relationship was never allowed to slip back to the prewar condition of ignorance and hostility.

Preparedness (in terms of manpower and industrial capacity as well as weapons) was sponsored by such groups as the soon defunct National Security League. From 1914 to 1919 this group, financed by many of the same liberal business leaders who were prominent in the National Civic Federation, advocated such programs as universal military training: It would, said General Pershing, help educate the masses against "the anarchistic or bolshevik proposals of numerous agitators."[6] The same sort of work was carried on by the Navy League of the United States, which had been organized in 1902. Worried that military spending was tied, as one historian has put it, to "politics, log rolling, pork-barreling, geographic prejudice, economic interest, everything, that is, except the national interest," the Navy League sought to act as a civilian lobby for a Big Navy policy.[7] Throughout the interwar years it worked closely (although not always successfully) with Big Navy congressmen to build up the fleet and issued periodic warnings against falling behind the menacing British Navy.

The activities of such preparedness advocates and the failure of the disarmament conferences of the interwar years, a growing disillusionment with the consequences of World War I and the multiplying signs of renewed hostilities, all combined to nurture a growing demand for neutrality, both by the general public and in Congress. The neutralists' highwater mark was the Senate Munitions Inquiry of 1934-1936, better known as the Nye investigations. In an attempt to discover and expose the machinations of the "merchants of death," the committee gathered evidence from the files and personnel of fifty companies involved in the arms trade. Although no secret conspiracy was ever proved, there was evidence aplenty of vast profits and interlocking directorates both within and without the government.[8]

[5]Weinstein, *op. cit.*, pp. 253-254.
[6]Robert D. Ward, "The Origin and Activities of the National Security League, 1914-1919," *Mississippi Valley Historical Review*, 47 (June 1960), 51-65.
[7]Armin Rappaport, *The Navy League of the United States* (Detroit, 1962), p. 29.
[8]See John E. Wiltz, *In Search of Peace: The Senate Munitions Inquiry, 1934-36* (Baton Rouge, 1963).

Both before and after the Nye investigations, industry and the War Department continued to plan for the mobilization of the nation's economy in preparation for another war. Industrial executives now moved freely not only in and out of the civilian agencies of government, but into the military as well. By 1931 about 14,000 had received reserve commissions and were directly responsible for industry-military liaison.[9] Given the facts that the military still was responsible for defining and supplying their needs for materiel, and that the nation's large corporations operated largely outside the limits of democratic control, it was inevitable that such relationships should develop. World War I had brought the military into the already flourishing community of interest and cooperation between business and the civilian branches of the government. Given the thesis that the United States must be ready for a renewal of world war, industrial mobilization was an inevitable part of military concern and military planning an important part of industry's future.

WORLD WAR II

In 1940, for the second time within a generation, the United States began to mobilize for war. The elaborate plans laid by military and industrial leaders proved not to be useful in detail, but the spirit behind them was triumphant. Despite antipathy for his Administration among big businessmen, Franklin D. Roosevelt respected and needed the aid of business in his mobilization plans. Both the Office of Production Management and the War Production Board (WPB), which was set up in 1942, were dominated by dollar-a-year men who worked closely and comfortably with military leaders.

In this war as in the last, mobilizers were as much concerned with not disturbing established competitive patterns as they were with maximizing production. Having failed (and perhaps not even tried) to break the power of big business during the depression, the President now accepted the nation's economic structure as a given and merely sought to build upon it. As he said, he was sending Dr. New Deal away and was now consulting Dr. Win-the-War. The basic decision was to defeat fascism; the second (but no less strongly held) decision was that the war should not be used or allowed to disrupt the power of big business. It was no accident, for example, that General Motors sent its president to be production chief of the WPB, and that General Motors also received a greater dollar value of prime contracts than any other American corporation. This was the result not of a conspiracy, but of the basic decision to fit the war program to the existing economic structure. If the structure was undemocratic and maladjusted, the war program would inevitably share these same defects—and it did.

After a decade of fighting economic privilege at home and fascism abroad, control over the American economy was even more concentrated at the end of

[9]Paul A. C. Koistinen, "The Industrial-Military Complex in Historical Perspective: The Interwar Years," *Journal of American History*, 56 (March 1970), 827.

the war than it had been at the beginning. Prime contracts both for research and for production had been concentrated in the largest civilian institutions, and subcontracting had done little to share the wealth with smaller firms and colleges. Suggestions to make the war effort more democratic were brushed aside as divisive and disruptive: It was clearly unpatriotic to talk of reform in the midst of a total war with fascism.[10]

President Roosevelt was profoundly disinterested in the domestic aspects of the war, and preferred to concentrate on the needs of maintaining Allied harmony and the grand designs of strategy. One of the few agencies that attempted to oversee the entire home-front effort was the Senate Special Committee to Investigate the National Defense Program, chaired by Harry Truman of Missouri.[11] The committee prodded the civilian mobilization chiefs to exert more authority, worked to maintain civilian dominance over military pretensions, and exposed numerous examples of fraud and excessive profiteering. Like the Nye Committee, however, it never traced these problems back to the nation's fundamental economic structure.

RECONVERSION

As the war drew to a close, the problem of reconversion provided new grounds for controversy. Through its domination of such agencies as the WPB, big business had been able to give itself the vast majority of prime contracts (the top 30 corporations got one-half the dollar value, the top 100 got two-thirds); small business either lived off the small amount of subcontracting or found activities that involved neither war contracts nor strategic materials and manpower. The danger was that if materials and manpower were made "too" available to them before the war was over, the small companies could begin to fill pent-up civilian needs while the big corporations were still busy with war work, thus undermining to some extent their prewar domination of the consumer-goods industry.

Once again, big business and the military saw eye to eye. The military wanted no letup in the war effort, and the large corporations wanted no controls lifted until the war was over.[12] In the summer of 1945 President Truman failed to support either the consumer-oriented Office of Price Administration (OPA) or the Smaller War Plants Corporation. Attempts to maintain price and wage

[10]Useful material on this problem may be gotten from Barton J. Bernstein, "America in War and Peace: The Test of Liberalism," *Towards A New Past*, ed. Barton J. Bernstein (New York, 1968), pp. 289-321; Bruce Catton, *War Lords of Washington* (New York, 1948); I. F. Stone, *Business As Usual: The First Year of Defense* (New York, 1941); and *Economic Concentration and World War II*, Report of the Smaller War Plants Corporation to the Special Committee to Study Problems of American Small Business, U.S. Senate, 79th Cong., 2d sess. (1946).

[11]See Donald H. Riddle, *The Truman Committee: A Study in Congressional Responsibility* (New Brunswick, 1964).

[12]Barton J. Bernstein, "The Debate on Industrial Reconversion: The Protection of Oligopoly and Military Control of the Economy," *American Journal of Economics and Sociology,* 26 (April 1967), 159-172.

controls failed, and reconversion was so planned that the largest contractors once again managed to implement their already decisive positions of power.[13]

The results of World War II domestically were analogous to the results of World War I. Big business, already dominant in the peacetime economy, had been allowed to organize the war effort in such a way that their power was enhanced. In both wars, possible opponents from the labor movement or the general ranks of social reform were brought in as either window-dressing or as subordinate partners in the grand patriotic effort. Power and prestige were shared by business and a renascent military, pulled up from the doldrums of peacetime disregard. In both wars, the American economy, unlike that of any other major industrial nation, was vastly strengthened, not (like that of Great Britain or the Soviet Union) laid prostrate.

The major difference was that the nation did not revert to the isolationism sought by an uncertain and disillusioned United States after World War I. It was universally agreed that we would continue to play a decisive military role in international affairs. A peaceful world secure for trade was henceforth to be guaranteed by a standing military establishment backed up by a war economy prepared to offer massive support to foreign interventions. After World War I the economy had been boldly international, but public opinion had kept the government timidly aloof from most international cooperative actions. In 1945 the flag stood ready to support trade.

THE COLD WAR

Like big business, the military began planning during the war for its peacetime activities. The 1930s had been a poor time for the army and navy. Never had they received such a small share of the federal budget, nor faced such hostility on the part of the general public. As a result, according to the military, Germany and Japan had been allowed to arm themselves unobstructed, and at Pearl Harbor the United States had been once again caught off guard with an inadequate military establishment. Career officers joined with leaders in other sectors of society in vowing that such unpreparedness would never again happen. After World War II, the United States must keep itself prepared for any military eventuality. There was debate over details (would the American people tolerate a peacetime draft, or perhaps even universal military training?), but the general intent received wide support.

No military service stood to gain as much as the air force. A subordinate branch of the army before the war, the air force had parlayed its strategic bombing mission into a popular appeal which held out the promise at long last of independent status. In 1943, largely without the support or participation of any civilian leaders, the air force, along with the army and navy, began to plan

[13]Barton J. Bernstein, "The Removal of War Production Board Controls on Business, 1944-1946," *Business History Review*, 39 (Summer 1965), 243-260.

for peace.[14] With relentless logic untempered by political guidance, the air force began to lay its plans for separate status. The only mission justifying independence was strategic bombing, so this was preached as the new gospel and was greatly strengthened by the advent of nuclear bombs. Drawing upon President Roosevelt's idea of multilateral Big Power peace-keeping (rather than true collective security), the air force moved from a goal (autonomy) to a doctrine (strategic bombing), to a budgetary goal (at least one-third of the military budget), to a likely maximum personnel (400,000 men), to a number of air wings sufficient for that many men, to foreign bases adequate to deploy so many airplanes, to a potential enemy adequate to justify such a force in being (the Soviet Union).[15] As subsequent events were to reveal, the air force was remarkably successful in achieving all of its postwar goals.

Another military objective was postwar unification of the services. During the winter of 1941-1942 the Joint Chiefs of Staff was established; during the war they effectively bypassed the civilian Secretaries of War and the Navy. Like the State Department, they suffered from President Roosevelt's tendency to handle important wartime matters (military and diplomatic) himself with a few personal advisers. Now with only the navy dissenting, the military leaders sought postwar unification as a means of gaining strength in the fight for budgets and as a way of perpetuating the wartime dominance of military over civilian leaders.[16] Beginning in 1945 the army and navy fought this issue in the Congress, and in the summer of 1947, within weeks after the adoption of the Marshall Plan and the Truman Doctrine for intervention in Greece and Turkey, Congress established a new Department of Defense, formalized the Joint Chiefs of Staff, established the National Security Council, and set up the Central Intelligence Agency.

The reform left power largely in the hands of the several services, and the new Secretary of Defense, James Forrestal, had little influence on the individual branches. His staff, for example, was limited by statute to four "special assistants" and a few dozen other top administrative personnel in his own office. Then, in 1949, 1953, and 1958, a series of reorganizations gradually broke down the power of the services and strengthened that of the Secretary of Defense. By the end of the Eisenhower Administration the Secretary had gained virtually complete control over his department and was served by fifteen assistant secretaries, nearly 4,000 other administrative personnel, and a very powerful Chairman of the Joint Chiefs of Staff.[17]

[14]On the danger of such lack of civilian leadership, see William Appleman Williams, "Officers and Gentlemen," *New York Review of Books*, 16 (May 6, 1971), 3-4, 6-8.
[15]Perry McCoy Smith, *The Air Force Plans for Peace, 1943-1945* (Baltimore, 1970) is a very important book which may be supplemented with Vincent Davis, *Postwar Defense Policy and the U.S. Navy, 1943-1946* (Chapel Hill, 1966).
[16]Demetrios Caraley, *The Politics of Military Unification: A Study of Conflict and the Policy Process* (New York, 1966).
[17]*Ibid.*, pp. 284-285.

During the immediately postwar years, a number of other lessons drawn from the war were being applied. Pearl Harbor had caught the nation dangerously short of certain strategic materials such as rare metals. In part this was the result of poor planning, in part of industry's desire to protect monopoly-based scarcity. In 1946 Congress passed a Stockpiling Act designed to reform the Strategic Materials Act of 1939, which had so badly failed. The United States was a net importer of all metals but vanadium and molybdenum, and one-third of the 100 metals in use came largely from other lands. Over the years this program of stockpiling moved from military to civilian control, its national security function was distorted by domestic needs, it became isolated from other developments in defense policy, and the number of stockpiles increased. By 1964, for example, the nation had stockpiled 180,187,374 pounds of castor oil, or 158,187,374 pounds in *excess* of the stockpile objective.[18]

Such scandals were made possible, in part, by a continuing disagreement over the type of war that would be fought in the future. The Truman Administration never decided. Nuclear and thermonuclear weapons were developed and stockpiled, and the Strategic Air Command was built up in anticipation of a nuclear exchange with the Soviet Union. At the same time, there was a continued adherence to the idea that battles were won in the nation's shops and factories rather than at the front. By the time of Dwight D. Eisenhower's inauguration, it was obvious that the two concepts were incompatible. In case of a nuclear exchange, there would be no shops and factories, no need for stockpiles of castor oil.

The tendency to think in terms of the presumed lessons of World War II was strengthened by the concept of Red Fascism, which argued that the Soviet Union was little different from prewar Germany, presenting the same threat of world domination and to be dealt with as we had failed to deal with Hitler—by refusing to appease its lust for power. The United States had never really been friendly to the Soviet Union. In 1918 we had joined with allies to invade Russia with the hope of destroying the Soviet government, and when that failed we had refused to extend diplomatic recognition to Moscow until 1933. The Hitler-Stalin pact of 1939 had reinforced the idea that fascism, whether communist or Nazi, was evil and dangerous. The brief wartime alliance of 1941-1945 was marked by recurring disagreements and mutual distrust, which Roosevelt did his best to ignore, smooth over, or postpone until after the defeat of the Axis.[19]

The concept of Red Fascism served well as the core of a rapidly elaborated ideological attack on communism during the postwar years. Any number of sermons, novels, motion pictures, congressional speeches, school programs, and

[18] Glenn H. Snyder, *Stockpiling Strategic Materials: Politics and National Defense* (San Francisco, 1966).
[19] Les K. Alder and Thomas G. Paterson, "Red Fascism: The Merger of Nazi Germany and Soviet Russia in the American Image of Totalitarianism, 1930s-1950s," *American Historical Review*, 75 (April 1970), 1046-1064.

union pep talks drove home in baroque detail that we were engaged in a war—no less real for being undeclared—which must inevitably prove fatal to one or both of the contesting parties. The McCarthy Era, given birth by the loyalty programs and ideological overkill of the Truman Administration, saw the creation of what has been called a "garrison state"—one in which war and the preparation for war colors and distorts all other national purposes and values.[20]

THE KENNEDY YEARS

When in his Farewell Address President Eisenhower warned of the military-industrial complex, he spoke carefully in terms of the future, of what might possibly happen should the nation not be aware of the danger to its fundamental freedoms. In fact, he had already felt much of the weight of the complex during the last years of his own Administration.

During the immediate postwar years, as the liberal historian Eric Goldman has written:

> . . . Two critically important questions were pressing to be
> answered. One of the questions concerned affairs inside the
> United States: would America continue, through extensions of
> the welfare state and of welfare capitalism and through a
> variety of other techniques, the economic and social revolution
> which had marked the previous decades? The other question
> concerned foreign affairs: would the United States keep
> moving along the path marked out in the early Truman years,
> a path suggested by the words "containment" and
> "co-existence" and one which represented a sharp departure
> from deep-seated American traditions?[21]

The election of Eisenhower and his aggressively anti-New Deal associates in the Republican Party cast new doubt on the answers to these questions. As it turned out, Eisenhower was a liberal very much in the mainstream of the previous half century of American reform, and all but the most uncompromising party theoreticians could see the economic gains nestled within otherwise objectionable welfare programs.[22] By the end of the fifties, it was apparent that even the Republican Party had been won over to support of the Welfare State at home and abroad.

Two complimentary policies of the Eisenhower years were, however, of particular concern from the perspective of the military-industrial complex. On

[20]Richard M. Freeland, *The Truman Doctrine and the Origins of McCarthyism* (New York, 1972).
[21]Eric F. Goldman, *The Crucial Decade—and After: America, 1945-1960* (New York, 1960), p. vi.
[22]For example, see Thomas V. DiBacco, "American Business and Foreign Aid: The Eisenhower Years," *Business History Review*, 41 (Spring 1967), 21-35.

the one hand, the Administration was philosophically (and politically) committed to working for a balanced budget. Deficit spending, even for arms, nagged at the Republican conscience. At the same time, having resolved the strategic ambivalence of the Truman years, a commitment to nuclear ("massive") retaliation allowed the Republicans to cut back on military aspirations that did not fit into the scenario of nuclear exchange. The infantry was eclipsed by the Strategic Air Command. Perhaps only a President who was himself a military chieftain could have withstood as well as he did the inevitable pressures from a disappointed Pentagon.

Opposition from corporate liberals was not so easily suppressed, especially when they found their authentic voice within the Democratic Party. Culminating in John F. Kennedy's effective (although, as it turned out, erroneous) claims of a missile gap during the 1960 Presidential campaign, the Democrats launched a sustained attack on both the fiscal and stategic aspects of Eisenhower's security policy. In July 1958, for example, the Committee for Economic Development (in some ways a midcentury counterpart of the progressive National Civic Federation) published a study, *The Problem of National Security*, which called for both higher defense spending and a more "flexible response capability." Both proposals were later embodied in the New Frontier's Keynesian fiscal policy and activist foreign policy.[23]

The other great innovation of the Kennedy years, of course, was the logical culmination of Defense Department reorganizations in the career of Robert S. McNamara. Called by his many admirers "the first Secretary of Defense," McNamara and his Whiz Kids made a massive attack on service parochialism and autonomy through their application of systems analysis to defense needs. Late in his tenure McNamara also spoke of the danger of the military-industrial complex, but the potential effectiveness of his solutions—integrity and management—was questionable.

How fundamental these reforms were is still the subject of debate. The record of the TFX (F-111) fighter-bomber casts doubt upon the efficacy of the new system. At the other extreme, the economist Seymour Melman has found the discontinuity so fundamental as to mark the end of the complex and the birth of what he calls Pentagon Capitalism. In part the McNamara revolution suffers from the characteristic tendency of such progressive reforms to obscure even while they ratify the power of vested interests. In more than one case of similar reform, the illusion of disinterested experts applying the scientific method to solve social problems had turned out to do more violence to the public interest than to the special interests they were designed to thwart.

In part also the confusion arises from the attempt to discover which component of the complex—the military, the industrialists, the civilian

[23]Compare with Chamber of Commerce of the United States, *The Economics of Defense Spending*, A Report by the Committee on Economic Policy (Washington, D.C., February 1965).

government officials—is ascendent at any given time because, as in any complex, their interests are not always and at all points identical. Generals from the air force and the infantry do not always see eye to eye, nor do the boards of directors of Lockheed and General Electric, nor the Secretaries of State and Defense. When labor unions, university laboratories, the communications media, and church groups are added, the confusion as well as the viability of the complex is compounded.

A knowledge not only of the dimensions but also of the history of the military-industrial complex makes it clear that it is merely a special (although increasingly important) facet of the liberal corporate state, the roots of which go back to the reforms of the Progressive Era and the New Deal. This Welfare State, as it came to be called after World War II, encompasses not only the familiar doles to the defective and delinquent classes of American society, but even more importantly the whole structure of foreign and domestic aid to business. The two policies of welfare at home and Cold War abroad were intimately connected, and provided the fertile seedbed for a thousand subsidies and guarantees, encouragements and protections. It is within this context that the problem must be studied—and hopefully solved.

I. THE MILITARY-INDUSTRIAL COMPLEX IN THEORY AND FACT

A major point of confusion over the military-industrial complex is whether such a thing exists. Critics of the complex are often at a handicap because they are unable to do more than cite a few misdeeds, or point to a handful of interconnections which seem inappropriate, even though no actual illegal acts are alleged. In other words, without a theoretical framework some critics are driven to implying what they cannot prove, and then perhaps even denying explicitly whay they have charged implicitly.

Defenders of the complex find this lack of a theoretical framework useful, and resort to one of their own in denying any impropriety. Thus "complex" is usually translated to mean "conspiracy," and great sport is made of people who are still so naive as to believe in devils. The issue is reduced to the simple one of personal wrongdoing, and it becomes impossible to prove that any one congressman or corporation president — each a pillar of respectability — is personally engaged in illegal activities.

The key to understanding the complex is to see it as a system, and to realize that it is only as a part of this system that the individual examples of its operations make any sense at all. Moreover, the system was put together by specific men and institutions to achieve certain specific purposes: It is neither inevitable nor universal. Recently, scholars from several different disciplines have attempted to clarify the theory of the complex and look closely at its operations.

1. THE WARFARE STATE: HISTORY OF A CONCEPT

Keith L. Nelson

The fear that government, military, and business leaders desire war for their own advantages can be traced back into the dim origins of civilized man. The historian Keith L. Nelson has provided us with a detailed review of the development of this persistent idea. To say that the concept always has been with us is not, of course, to denigrate its importance or accuracy in describing a real and threatening facet of modern life in America. As Nelson concludes, we have hardly begun to ask the questions that may eventually provide answers to one of the most persistent and currently demanding problems of national existence.

An accusation is abroad in the land which, if unfamiliar until recently, is far from as unprecedented as is often supposed. Not surprisingly, perhaps, the assertion that political, military, and industrial interests are conniving to perpetuate crisis is frequently taken today to be a new phenomenon and, like the "complex" it purports to attack, the product of an extraordinary "cold war" situation. Yet charges of this kind, either in whole or in part, have many times been heard before in other contexts, and in words strikingly similar to those in use at present.

This essay is intended to point up the considerable history of such ideas and

Source: © 1971 by the Pacific Coast Branch, American Historical Association. Reprinted from *Pacific Historical Review*, Volume 40, Number 2, pp. 127-143, by permission of the Branch.

their developing interrelationships. Thus, the focus is primarily upon the concepts themselves and not upon the forces that shaped them nor upon the objective reality of what observers thought they saw. In pursuing this emphasis, I desire in no way to denigrate the importance or the seriousness of the sociostructural changes which were and are occurring, but simply to assist the further definition of a field in which there has been an astonishing lack of dependable scholarly work.[1] At any rate, it is assumed that, once in existence, ideas or myths can have considerable causal power in their own right, and are therefore worthy in themselves of extensive examination. Moreover, it is hoped that an analysis of what men believed about reality may give us new hints as to what was actually going on outside their minds.

One last point of introduction: Fred J. Cook's term, the "warfare state,"[2] has been employed here to stand in a general sense for contemporary suspicions, not in order to limit ourselves to the definition of the problem he presents, but simply because his phrase encompasses, more easily than any other, the tripartite nature of the coalition which is feared. Nevertheless, any one of several related and current descriptions could have been used, including Marcus Raskin's "national security state," Juan Bosch's "Pentagonism," Murray Weidenbaum's "defense-space complex," or the best known of all, Dwight D. Eisenhower's "military-industrial complex."[3] The only weakness of the last term is its lack of a third adjective to represent the "governmental" factor, which in most statements of the case is so obviously involved.[4]

Distrust of the politician, soldier, and businessman as they relate to war, then, is nothing new. From the beginnings of history, these have been the individuals considered most vulnerable to its attractions, particularly in those cultures where power has been somewhat decentralized and where one or another group could upset the balance or utilize a crisis to gain advantage. Fear of the ruler and his war-making inclinations is evident as far back as Aristotle and Polybius and appears in its modern form with the rise of liberalism and such thinkers as John Locke, Immanuel Kant, and Thomas Paine.[5] Fear of the warrior, or the military, is also found in the ancient world and becomes clearly visible again in the seventeenth and eighteenth centuries, when the development of standing armies provoked the precautions of the English and American bills of rights as well as warnings from Jean Jacques Rousseau, Thomas Jefferson, and others.[6] Fear that the merchant might find affinity with war makes its appearance with Aristophanes but waits for its modern champions until the time of Karl Marx and the socialist writers who followed him.[7] All of these traditions (and the real dangers), of course, have waxed and waned depending upon the place and time. And just as a history of the Christian church could conceivably be built around the alternating ascendancy of Father, Son, and Holy Ghost, so the development of Western reform in modern times might be explained in terms of the successive dominance of political, military, and economic fears.

Yet the thought that two or more of the suspected groups might combine themselves for the sake of war was not unheard of. Especially in the decades before the world wars of this century, as the heat of passions rose and as armaments races accelerated, a tendency grew to see forces coalescing which may have stood to benefit from a continuation of the tension. To what extent such mergings of interest really did take place is difficult to estimate on the basis of present studies. Perhaps the image was largely a function of the emotional temperature, or perhaps not. Possibly the socioeconomic and political pluralism which characterized the Western states was breaking down during these eras, and those individuals who were most fearful of its loss tended to perceive its going first.

Let me return, however, to the three distinct traditions (anti-political, anti-military, anti-economic), bringing them down through time, pointing up certain shifts in meaning which have occurred, and illustrating the routes by which the ideas have both come together and yet survived. Each of these fears is very much alive today and, as we shall see, even in merging with others often remains dominant within the new complex of thought. Indeed, assessing the relative weight of the component anxieties is a useful way to separate and relate the various accusations about the warfare state which are being made today.

As has been noted, fear that the ruler might lead the nation into war for his own ends has a history which dates back to the origins of organized society. It was a prime motive in the modern movement toward limited government and ultimately toward republicanism (for, as Tom Paine said, "What is the history of all monarchical governments but a disgustful picture of human wretchedness, and the accidental respite of a few years' repose? . . . War is their trade, plunder and revenue their objects. While such governments continue, peace has not the absolute security of a day"[8]). Yet even popular elections did not remove the root of the concern, as Abraham Lincoln testified at the time of President James Polk's indiscretions before the Mexican War:

> The provision of the Constitution giving the war-making power to Congress was dictated, as I understand it, by the following reasons: Kings had always been involving and impoverishing their people in wars, pretending generally, if not always, that the good of the people was the object. This our [Constitutional] convention understood to be the most oppressive of all kingly oppressions, and they resolved to so frame the Constitution that no one man should hold the power of bringing this oppression upon us.[9]

In our own day we have witnessed a continuation of this anxiety in such American developments as congressional criticism of Woodrow Wilson's maintaining troops abroad after World War I,[10] widespread charges in the 1940s that Franklin D. Roosevelt had "lied us into war,"[11] and recent chafing at the relinquishment of power to the executive in the Formosa Straits Resolution and the Tonkin Gulf Resolution.[12] In fact, in the period between the world wars there were considerable efforts made to take the matter of war and peace out of the hands of government entirely, a design perhaps most obvious in the referendum requirement of the proposed Ludlow Amendment (1938).

Anti-militarism, too, builds on a long and proud tradition, stretching back in England to the age of Cromwell and on the continent at least as far as the Enlightenment. Rousseau described armies as "the pest which depopulated Europe" and Kant thought them dangerous because "they threaten other states continually with war by their readiness to appear always ready for war; they incite states to excel in the number of armed men, to which no limit is set; and when by the costs it involves, peace becomes even more burdensome than a short war, armies themselves furnish the reason for aggressive war in order to get rid of this burden."[13] Dread of unnecessary war and fear that, as George Mason put it, "once a standing army is established in any country, the people lose their liberty"[14] were the primary reasons for the longstanding American insistence on civilian dominance over the military and on a leading role for the militia,[15] policies which found their parallels abroad, particularly in Britain. Though anti-militarism fell off in the nineteenth century under the impact of industrialization and Social Darwinism, it experienced a vigorous rebirth in the 1890s in response to rising navalism, jingoism, and imperialism.[16] The Dreyfus case in France and socialist pacifism generally were strong indications of a new hostility towards the army,[17] and following the world wars continuing distrust was revealed in such developments as American opposition to Universal Military Training, the worldwide movement for disarmament in the 1920s, and Allied decisions to ban the German and Japanese military establishments after 1945.[18]

In turning to our third line of thought—that which fears the business man as provocateur—one cannot resist quoting Aristophanes' fervent prayer that, "If any merchant, selling spears or shields, would fain have battles to improve his trade, may he be seized by thieves and eat raw barley"![19] In this case also there is a venerable tradition, but a tradition which remained largely in eclipse during the long bourgeois climb to predominance in Europe. As a matter of fact, in the early nineteenth century Auguste Comte and others were so impressed with the potential of industrialization that they came to see history as a unilinear movement from the "military" society of the past to the "industrial" society of the future, with the two types representing the polar extremes of social organization.[20] This was the view of Herbert Spencer, too, who contended that "with an increasing ratio of industrialism . . . there has been . . . a strengthening assertion of individuality . . . [and with it] a growing respect for the individualities of others."[21] A similar perspective was reflected later in the work of William Graham Sumner, Norman Angell, Thorstein Veblen, and Joseph Schumpeter.[22] It required the belligerent national expansionism of the 1880s and 1890s before even socialist intellectuals could develop that critique of the capitalist's role in international conflict at which Marx himself had hinted.[23] These were the years in which the Second International began to protest the "militarism" of the owning classes,[24] and it was in 1902 that J. A. Hobson, in his classic attack on imperialism, made the matter emphatically clear:

> Our economic analysis has disclosed the fact that it is only the interests of competing cliques of business men—investors, contractors, export manu-

facturers, and certain professional classes—that are antagonistic; that these cliques, usurping the authority and voice of the people, use the public resources to push their private interests, and spend the blood and money of the people in this vast and disastrous military game, feigning national antagonisms which have no basis in reality.[25]

Since Hobson's day this set of charges has never really been disproved, and has recurred from time to time not only in Soviet attacks against the West, but also during the Anglo-American munitions investigations of the 1930s and on the occasion of Allied attempts to break up German and Japanese industrial monopolies after World War II.[26]

With the rising international tension of 1900-1917, it was to be expected that all three of the traditional fears—the political, military, and economic—would come more and more into prominence. In Europe, where socialists were carrying the principal burden of reform, it was naturally the capitalists who were most frequently blamed (when other nations were *not*) for rampant "militarism."[27] In America, on the other hand, where the middle class was at the heart of both progressivism and the peace movement, it was the ruler and the soldier who were usually held responsible.[28] Yet there were many shades of opinion on both sides of the Atlantic. Kaiser Wilhelm was criticized in Germany (and elsewhere), just as Theodore Roosevelt was called to task at home for "his constant encouragement of the military spirit."[29] And in 1913, 120,000 Frenchmen demonstrated against the three-year army service bill, in seeming agreement with an American who asserted that "It is because the nations of the Old World have given themselves so largely to the guidance of military experts that modern civilization finds itself so handicapped and plagued."[30] Meanwhile, other Americans were attacking the "powder trust" with much the same spirit that George Bernard Shaw had revealed in *Major Barbara* when the armament maker Undershaft told his audience, "You will make war when it suits us and keep peace when it doesn't. . . . When I want anything to keep my dividends up, you will call out the police and the military."[31]

Moreover, particularly after 1910, as crisis appeared imminent, it began to seem to many that the villains in the story were linking forces. "We are in the hands of an organization of crooks," cried Lord Welby in the British Parliament early in 1914. "They are politicians, generals, manufacturers of armaments and journalists. All of them are anxious for unlimited expenditure, and go on inventing scares to terrify the public."[32] A few weeks later, the Socialist MP Philip Snowden spoke out to document these charges "to the hilt," taking particular care to point up the considerable personal investment by members of the government in armaments firms, and the way in which retired generals and admirals were being hired by arms contractors because they (the military officers) "knew the ropes."[33] "In every country and across every border," contended the English liberal, H. N. Brailsford, "there is a powerful group of capitalists, closely allied to the fighting services, firmly entrenched in society, and well served by politicians and journalists, whose business it is to exploit the rivalries and jealousies of nations."[34] Allegations such as these, to be sure, became less common in Britain after war had been declared,[35] but it is interesting to note with what eagerness the conservatives adopted them for use against the enemy, who was quickly demonized in the shape of Kaiser, Krupp, and Tirpitz.[36] In the interim, as the preparedness controversy raged in the United States, American radicals picked up the cry against the international alliance of "the generals and the Krupps, Armstrongs, and Du Ponts."[37]

Even so, the war came and went, and peace brought a return to more pluralist perspectives. In Paris in 1919 the Americans wrote a provision into the League Covenant requiring members to "agree that the manufacture by private enterprise of munitions and implements of war is open to grave objections,"[38] and in the next few years the League of Nations took up the question of controlling armaments firms.[39] At the same time, on the popular level, the politician and the soldier were each subjected to considerable criticism. French statesmen, for example, were severely pummeled in the British and American press for refusing to disarm,[40] while the establishment of a publicity bureau in the United States War Department in 1926 led to charges that "in scores of ways the military are entering our civil life, arrogating to themselves . . . a vigorous leadership they were never meant to have."[41]

Then, with the end of the decade, the onset of the Depression, and the breakdown of stability, the mood of the matter changed again, and the industrialist became the paramount "warmonger." Indeed, growing economic radicalism and fear of future conflict led to a deluge of books attacking munitions makers which was not to be equaled in volume until the comparable inundation of the 1960s.[42] The titles can give only some indication of the fury: *The Bloody International; Death and Profits; Patriotism Limited; Enemies of Peace; The Bloody Traffic; Iron, Blood and Profits;* and *Merchants of Death.*[43] The charges being brought, in most cases, were the same: that the weapons manufacturers were organized in interlocking directorates, that they equipped nations indiscriminately (including enemies of their own), that they made unheard of profits, that they fomented war scares in order to maximize sales, that they corrupted the press and governments for their own ends, that they worked in close cooperation with patriotic societies, and that their intrigues were largely responsible both for the world war and more recent conflicts. Here and there among these writings were also hints of accusation against different "guilty" parties (for example, against "governments driven by the economic crisis" which "work hand in hand with armament manufacturers";[44] and against military officers who upon retirement pass "into the service of armament firms"[45]), but it was clearly the capitalists who bore the major portion of the blame.

There were competitive if less vocal schools of thought in the 1930s, however, which emphasized the danger of war from other directions. Among these, the anti-political and anti-military interpretations were ably represented, both being heavily influenced by what was then occurring in Germany, Japan, and Russia. In the conservative polemic *Democratic Despotism,* for instance, Rauol Desvernine warned that Roosevelt's New Deal was fast on its way to becoming like those dictatorships abroad which "strive to consolidate their power by building up in the minds of their people the bugaboo of danger from other nations."[46] And Sinclair Lewis, in his novel *It Can't Happen Here,* depicted a cabinet officer in a future, fascist America arguing that whereas "once . . . governments had merely let themselves slide into a war, thanking Providence for having provided a conflict as a febrifuge against internal discontent, . . . in this age of deliberate, planned propaganda, a really modern government . . . must figure out what brand of war they [sic] had to sell and plan the selling-campaign consciously."[47] On the military side, Charles Beard in *The Navy: Defense or Portent* worried about preventing "army and navy bureaucrats" from pushing the country into a foreign policy of "brag and bluster."[48] And Harold Lasswell looked even further into the future in his article, "Sino-Japanese Crisis: The Garrison State versus the Civilian State," unveiling a vision which has profoundly distrubed and influenced students of war down to the present day. Voicing the severest doubts about the ability of civilian institutions to survive prolonged international crisis, Lasswell hypothesized that the "business state" of the present would gradually give way to a "garrison state" in which the "specialists on violence," that is, the military commanders, would have mastered and subordinated businessmen, party leaders, government officials, and the nation at large.[49]

Once again, the closer war actually came, the more those who tended to blame interest groups for this saw their enemies coalescing. Accusing the admirals and diplomats of wanting to build a "super-navy" and attacking the President for refusing to specify policy, the *Nation's* editor, Oswald Garrison Villard, was frank to admit fear that paring down the armed forces would require "the over-ruling of a tremendously powerful military and naval machine and its lobby, plus the unnumerable elements which profit by a huge Army and Navy."[50] Similarly, John T. Flynn decried the "liberal idealists . . . , old-time Republican reactionaries, professional militarists, and political junkers" who were ganging up with businessmen to create a war industry which "you cannot demobilize . . . and you will have to keep on inventing reasons for. . . ."[51] The *New Republic* expressed its great concern at some of the "hysterical suggestions" being made, which if followed, it believed, could eventuate in a "capitalist-military oligarchy."[52]

World War II itself, while dampening such pessimism, did allow these ideas to survive or appear in other guises. By the end of the struggle Charles E. Wilson, vice-chairman of the War Production Board (and later Eisenhower's Secretary of Defense), was so impressed by the experience of mobilization that he urged a group of high-ranking officers and businessmen to guard against future Pearl Harbors by embarking on a program of "full [peace-time] preparedness according to a continuing plan." "The burden," he said, "is on all of us to integrate our respective activities—political, military, and industrial—because we are in world politics to stay, whether we like it or not."[53] It was shortly before this that James Forrestal, the Secretary of the Navy, had organized several large war contractors into the National Security Industrial Association, ostensibly with the same objective in mind.[54]

Yet, surprisingly, the intensity of the Cold War which followed was not severe enough for combinations of this kind to prosper or for concern about them to develop. Fear as such was not extinguished, to be sure, but the eagerness with which American industry reconverted to civilian production after V-J Day, together with the sudden prominence of military men in the early Truman administration, apparently broke up both the image and reality of the warfare state in its tripartite sense. At least the fact is that for almost a decade after 1945, while conservatives institutionalized their longstanding misgivings about the presidency in the 22nd Amendment (ratified, interestingly enough, in a sudden rush only three months after the Chinese crossed the Yalu),[55] the uneasiness of the Left regarding domestic "warmongering" was centered primarily on the armed forces. Harold Lasswell's concepts became the order of the day, especially in the form which he had given to them in those postwar extensions of his thesis that he called the "garrison-prison state" and the "garrison-police state."[56] Perhaps the most vivid presentation of such ideas was to be found in George Orwell's gruesome novel, *1984*,[57] but their presence was unmistakable in numerous editorials and articles which lamented the growing prestige of the defense establishment, its hold over public and congressional opinion, and its influence in high-level decision-making.[58] "The military are getting the bit in their teeth," contended Hanson Baldwin in 1947, and "there is considerable evidence that their objective is absolute preparedness in time of peace, an objective which has led all nations which have sought it to the garrison state, bankruptcy, and ruin."[59] Five years later Supreme Court Justice William O. Douglas was quite typical in insisting that the greatest threat to democracy lay in trusting "the military clique that spreads [itself] slowly throughout the government, expanding its hold."[60]

Not until the middle 1950s and America's unexpected failure to reduce its post-Korean military expenditures did critics of the situation begin to enlarge upon their explanations once again. A striking series of articles in the *Nation* by Matthew Josephson both signalled the change and helped to usher in the return to accusations of merging interests.[61] Josephson was quickly followed, however, by an even more effective spokesman for this point of view in C. Wright Mills, a Columbia University sociologist whose book, *The Power Elite* (1956), was to become one of the classic attacks upon pluralist thought in the United States. Briefly, Mills' assertion was that since World War II the "decisive political relevance" of the military leadership had thrust it into the ranks of the corporate and political elites which, in his view, had long dominated American society. "American capitalism is now in considerable part a military capitalism," he wrote, "and the most important relation of the big corporation to the state rests on the coincidence of interests between military and corporate needs, as defined by [the] warlords and corporate rich. . . . Of the three types of circle that compose the power elite today, it is the military that has benefited the most in its enhanced power. . . . It is the professional politician who has lost the most."[62]

Since 1956, and especially since Eisenhower's famous warning of 1961, there has been a steady growth of concern and publication regarding the dangers to peace from coalescing interest groups. Eisenhower, of course, differed from Mills both in ignoring the governmental aspect of the problem and in treating the whole thing as largely in the future,[63] but there have been others before and after him who lean more directly on Mills, including Fred J. Cook (*The Warfare State,* 1962), Irwin Suall (*The American Ultras,* 1962), and Victor Perlo (*Militarism and Industry,* 1963).[64] Less elitist and less radical than these authors, but equally troubled by political-military-industrial "cooperation," are Julius Duscha (*Arms, Money and Politics,* 1964), H. L. Nieburg (*In the Name of Science,* 1966), John Kenneth Galbraith (*The New Industrial State,* 1967, *How to Control the Military,* 1969), and Ralph Lapp (*The Weapons Culture,* 1968).[65] Nieburg, in a sense, speaks for all when he writes:

> For almost three decades the nation's resources have been commanded by military needs, and political and economic power have been consolidated behind defense priorities. What was initially sustained by emergency has been normalized through a cabal of vested interests. . . . The so-called military-industrial complex is not a conspiracy but rather a culmination of historical trends. It is a fact of contemporary public life that is eating the heart out of our society, reducing potential for real economic and social growth and eroding the foundation of democratic pluralism.[66]

A wide variety of other diagnoses are also being propounded. There remain those pluralists who, while sensing danger, see it deriving primarily from one sector of society, as Arthur Schlesinger apparently does in his recent attack upon the "warrior class" in *The Crisis of Confidence.*[67] There are those observers, too, who, accepting the major outlines of the warfare state, tend to view one or another of the leading groups as predominant within it. Jack Raymond (*Power at the Pentagon,* 1964), for example, fears "civilian militarists" in Washington,[68] while John Swomley (*The Military Establishment,* 1964) is more suspicious of the military itself,[69] and Tristam Coffin (*The Armed Society,* 1964) and G. William Domhoff (*Who Rules America?,* 1967) argue that the generals have been "co-opted" by the corporate rich.[70] Some critics assent to the military-industrial complex only to extend it with an "academic" or "scientific" or even "labor" factor,[71] taking an approach which harks back to another part of Eisenhower's farewell admonition ("We must also be alert to the . . . danger that public policy could . . . become the captive of a scientific-technological elite") and pushes in the direction of making an accusation against American society as a whole, such as those formulated by Marc Pilisuk and Thomas Hayden in their article, "Is There a Military Industrial Complex Which Prevents Peace?" (1965) and in the anonymous, deadly hoax entitled *Report from Iron Mountain* (1967).[72] Meanwhile, there are still a few optimistic liberals like Kenneth Boulding, an economist who thinks that disarmament could be accomplished with relative ease and finds little evidence "that . . . the private sector of the war industry in any way dominates defense decisions."[73] There are also increasing numbers of conservatives who are willing to admit that a military-industrial link exists, but who deny collusion within it and who perceive the relationship as an "essential element of our national survival."[74] There are even authors who suggest that the warfare state is an international development, with the American situation having its counterpart today in the Soviet Union[75]—a theory which serves to remind us just how parochial many of our recent critics have tended to become.[76]

Thus, the warfare state as an accusation has a long and varied history. Its three constituent traditions, which hold ruler, soldier, and merchant responsible for war, wind back their separate paths through many centuries. And the merging of these notions into fear that such men may combine against the peace dates back at least as far as 1910.

Such a perspective should be helpful in the questions that it raises. What role *have* various groups (or functional types) played in the bringing on of wars? And why have certain groups been blamed? And by whom? In what ways does pluralism really suffer in a crisis situation? And can declining pluralism engender combinations of interests which then are in some sense peculiarly prone to war? Did the nations of the West become warfare states in the years before 1914? Or before 1939? Or before 1971? Or were and are these ideas largely myths, compounded out of psychological necessity, or for use as instruments of social change? The research and writing to answer queries such as these is begging to be done.

FOOTNOTES

[1] There is, e.g., a real need for study of the recurring peace movement in America and Europe, especially in the latter, where pacifism has become somewhat obscured by its strategic alliance with socialism. The secondary literature includes relatively little beyond the following: Roland Bainton, *Christian Attitudes Toward War and Peace* (New York, 1960), Kurt von Raumer, *Ewiger Friede: Friedensrufe und Friedenspläne seit der Renaissance* (Freiburg, 1953), Elizabeth Souleyman, *The Vision of World Peace in 17th and 18th Century France* (New York, 1941), Christina Phelps, *The Anglo American Peace Movement in the Mid-Nineteenth Century* (New York, 1930), Merle Curti, *The American Peace Crusade, 1815-60* (Durham, N.C., 1929), Curti, *Peace or War: The American Struggle, 1636-1936* (Boston, 1936), Peter Brock, *Pacifism in the United States from the Colonial Era to the First World War* (Princeton, 1968), John K. Nelson, *The Peace Prophets: American Pacifist Thought, 1919-1941* (Chapel Hill, 1969), Laurence Wittner, *Rebels Against War: The American Peace Movement, 1941-1960* (New York, 1969), Christopher Driver, *The Disarmers* (London, 1964), David Boulton, *Voices from the Crowd against the H bomb* (London, 1964, and Norman Moss, *Men Who Play God* (New York, 1967). Also relevant and particularly interesting for their comparative approach are Kenneth N. Waltz, *Man, The State and War: A Theoretical Analysis* (New York, 1959) and Donald A. Wells, *The War Myth* (New York, 1967).

For analysis of the sociostructural changes which were and are taking place, one is largely dependent, beyond those works cited in this essay, upon general diplomatic, military, and economic histories. Yet there are a number of notable volumes, including Eckart Kehr, *Schlachtflottenbau und Parteipolitik, 1894-1901* (Berlin, 1930), Oron James Hale, *Publicity and Diplomacy with Special Reference to England and Germany, 1890-1914* (Charlottesville, 1940), Gerhard Ritter, *Staatskunst und Kriegshandwerk: Das Problem des Militarismus in Deutschland* (4 vols., Munich, 1954-1968), Aaron Wildavsky, *The Politics of the Budetary Process* (Boston, 1964), Roger Bolton, *Defense Purchases and Regional Growth* (Washington, 1966), William L. Baldwin, *The Structure of the Defense Market, 1955-1964* (Durham, N.C., 1967), and Vincent Davis, *The Admirals' Lobby* (Chapel Hill, 1967). See also Clive Trebicock, "Legends of the British Armament Industry, 1890-1914," *Journal of Contemporary History,* V (1970), 3-19, and Paul A. C. Koistenen, "The 'Industrial-Military Complex' in Historical Perspective: The InterWar Years," *Journal of American History,* LVI (1970), 819-839.

[2]Fred J. Cook, *The Warfare State* (New York, 1962).

[3]"A National Security State," *The Progressive,* XXXIII (July 1969), 5-6; Juan Bosch, *Pentagonism: A Substitute for Imperialism* (New York, 1968); Murray L. Weidenbaum, "The Defense-Space Complex: Impact on Whom?" *Challenge,* XIII (April 1965), 43-46; Dwight D. Eisenhower, "Farewell Address," *New York Times,* Jan. 18, 1961, p. 22.

[4]Note a similar point of view in Michael D. Reagan, "The Business and Defense Services Administration, 1953-57," *Western Political Quarterly,* XIV (1961), 569-586; Peter d'A. Jones, "The Military-Industrial Complex, 1952-64," in H. H. Quint et al., eds., *Main Problems in American History* (2 vols., New York, 1965), II, 370-383; and Walter Adams, "The Military-Industrial Complex and the New Industrial State," *American Economic Review,* LVIII (1968), 652-665.

[5]Aristotle, *The Politics* (London, 1923), bk. VIII, chap. XI; Polybius, *History* (in Kurt von Fritz, *The Theory of the Mixed Constitution in Antiquity* [New York, 1954]), bk. VI, sec. XIV; John Locke, *Of Civil Government: The Second Treatise* (1690), in Peter Laslett, ed., *John Locke: Two Treatises of Government* (Cambridge, 1967), secs. 88, 94-95, 134, 147-149, 221-222; Immanuel Kant, *Eternal Peace* (1795), in Carl J. Friedrich, *Inevitable Peace* (Cambridge, Mass., 1948), sec. 2, art. 1; Thomas Paine, *The Rights of Man* (1791), in Moncure Conway, ed., *The Writings of Thomas Paine* (4 vols., New York, 1967), II, part 2, introduction. For a helpful commentary, see David Rapoport, "Praetorianism: Government without Consensus" (Ph.D. dissertation, University of California, Berkeley, 1960).

[6]Aristotle, *Politics,* bk. III, chap. XVI, bk, IV, chap. XIV, and bk. VIII, chap VI; Aristophanes, *The Peace* (Cambridge, Mass., 1924), lines 440-445; Jean Jacques Rousseau, "Considerations on the Government of Poland" (completed, 1772), in Frederick Watkins, ed., *Rousseau: Political Writings* (Edinburg, 1953), chap. 12; Thomas Jefferson Memorial Association, *The Writings of Thomas Jefferson* (20 vols., Washington, 1905), II, 242, IV, 218, X, 365, XIII, 261, and XIV, 261.

[7]Aristophanes, *Peace,* lines 446-448; Karl Marx and Friedrich Engels, *The Communist Manifesto* (1848), (Chicago, 1946), 39; Karl Liebknecht, *Militarism and Anti Militarism* (1907), (Glasgow, *ca.* 1917), 1-21; Rosa Luxemburg, *The Accumulation of Capital* (1913), (London, 1951), 454-467; G. Zinoviev and V. I. Lenin, *Socialism and War* (1915), in V. I. Lenin, *Collected Works* (23 vols., New York, 1927-1945), XVIII, 214-258. It is worth noting that socialist writers never claimed that there was anything specifically capitalistic about militarism, but only that, in the current economic stage of Western nations, capitalism was responsible for bringing on armaments and war.

[8]Paine, *Rights of Man,* II, Introduction.

[9]John G. Nicolay and John Hay, *Complete Works of Abraham Lincoln* (12 vols., New York, 1905), I, 111-112.

[10]E.g., Peter D. Filene, *Americans and the Soviet Experiment, 1917-33* (Cambridge, Mass., 1967), 51.

[11]The phrase was coined by Congresswoman Clare Booth Luce in 1944 (*New York Times,* *Oct. 14, 1944, p. 9*). For a further example of this point of view, see William Henry Chamberlin, *"The Bankruptcy of a Policy,"* in Harry Elmer Barnes, ed., *Perpetual War for Perpetual Peace* (Caldwell, Idaho, 1953), 489.

[12]Eric F. Goldman, *The Tragedy of Lyndon Johnson* (New York, 1969), 410-411.

[13]Alfred Vagts, *A History of Militarism, Civilian and Military* (rev. ed.; New York, 1959), 76-77.

[14]"The Military Peril; The Virginia Convention," in Russell F. Weigley, ed., *The American Military: Readings in the History of the Military in American Society* (Reading, Mass., 1969), 63.

[15]For discussion, see Arthur A. Ekirch, Jr., *The Civilian and the Military* (New York, 1956); Samuel P. Huntington, *The Soldier and the State* (Cambridge, Mass., 1957); and Marcus Cunliffe, *Soldiers and Civilians: The Martial Spirit in America, 1775-1865* (Boston, 1969).

[16]Ekirch, *Civilian and Military,* 124-139; Curti, *Peace or War,* 136-165. For examples of the primary literature, see Edward Berwick, "American Militarism," *Century*, XLVII (1893), 316-317; A. B. Ronne, "The Spirit of Militarism," *Popular Science Monthly*, XLVII (1895), 234-239; Joseph Dana Miller, "Militarism or Manhood," *Arena*, XXIV (1900), 379-392; Urbain Gohier, "The Danger of Militarism," *The Independent*, LII (1900), 233-236; and Gustave Hervé "Anti-Militarism in France," *ibid.*, LIV (1904), 2170-2173.

[17]David Thomson, *Democracy in France* (London, 1946), 147-161. See also Liebknecht, *Militarism,* 89-136.

[18]See L. B. Wheildon, "Militarization," *Editorial Research Report* (May 1948); Robert H. Ferrell, *Peace in Their Time: The Origins of the Kellogg-Briand Pact* (New Haven, 1952); John W. Wheeler-Bennett, *The Reduction of Armaments* (London, 1925); Wheeler-Bennett, *Disarmament and Security Since Locarno* (London, 1932); William E. Rappard, *The Quest for Peace Since the World War* (Cambridge, Mass., 1940); Lucius D. Clay, *Decision in Germany* (Garden City, N.Y., 1950), 17; and William J. Sebald, *With MacArthur in Japan* (New York, 1965), 79-83.

[19]Aristophanes, *Peace,* lines 446-448.

[20]Raymond Aron, "War and Industrial Society," in Leon Bramson and George W. Goethals, eds., *War: Studies from Psychology, Sociology, Anthropology* (New York, 1964), 352-359; Huntington, *Soldier and State,* 222-226.

[21]Herbert Spencer, "The Military and the Industrial Society," in Bramson and Goethals, *War,* 308.

[22]William Graham Sumner, *War and Other Essays* (New Haven, 1911), 13, 28-30; Norman Angell, *The Great Illusion* (New York, 1910), 198-221; Thorstein Veblen, *An Inquiry into the Nature of Peace and the Terms of Its Perpetuation* (New York, 1917), 196-200; and Joseph Schumpeter, *Imperialism [and] Social Classes* (New York, 1951), 92-96. For an earlier example of Spencer's influence, see Ronne, cited above. Note also Edmund Silberner, *The Problem of War in Nineteenth Century Economic Thought* (Princeton, 1946), passim.

[23]Marx and Engels, *Communist Manifesto,* 39.

[24]Julius Braunthal, *History of the International* (2 vols., New York, 1967), I, 325-329.

[25]J. A. Hobson, *Imperialism: A Study* (London, 1902), 127.

[26]See John E. Wiltz, *In Search of Peace: The Senate Munitions Inquiry, 1934-36* (Baton Rouge, 1963); J. D. Scott, *Vickers: A History* (London, 1962), 238-256; Clay, *Decision,* 325-334; Sebald, *With MacArthur,* 87-89.

[27]For evidence of this, see Braunthal, *International,* I, 329-348; Carl E. Schorske, *German Social Democracy, 1905-1917* (Cambridge, Mass., 1955), 66-87, 241-250; Harvey Goldberg, *The Life of Jean Jaurès* (Madison, 1962), 417-457; and Arthur Marwick, *Britain in the Century of Total War* (London, 1968), 50-51. The primary literature includes such writings as Guglielmo Ferrero, *Il Militarismo* (Milan, 1898); Liebknecht, *Militarism*; Luxemburg, *Capital*; Francis McCullagh, *Syndicates for War* (Boston, 1911); and Francis Delaisi, "Le

Patriotisme des plaques blindées," *La Paix par le Droit,* XXIV (1913), 65-74, 129-138, 286-296.

[28]Curti, *Peace or War,* 196-227. See also Julius Moritzen, *The Peace Movement of America* (New York, 1912); and Marie Louise Degen, *The History of the Woman's Peace Party* (Baltimore, 1939). For examples of the primary literature, see E. H. Crosby, *Swords and Plowshares* (New York, 1902); Crosby, *The Absurdities of Militarism* (Boston, 1907); Charles E. Jefferson, "Some Fallacies of Militarism," *The Independent,* LXIV (1908), 457-460; Jefferson, "The Delusion of Militarism," *Atlantic Monthly,* CIII (1909), 379-388; A. C. Coolidge, *The Scoundrel of Militarism* (Worcester, 1911); and Peter Ainslie, *The Scourge of Militarism* (New York, 1914).

[29] Michael Balfour, *The Kaiser and His Times* (Boston, 1964), 241-302; "A Parting Glance at Roosevelt," *Nation,* LXXXVIII (1909), 240-241.

[30]Michael Curtis, *Three Against the Third Republic: Sorel, Barres, and Maurras* (Princeton, 1959), 43; D. W. Brogan, *The Development of Modern France, 1870-1939* (2 vols., New York, 1966), II, 428-431; the quotation is from Jefferson, "Some Fallacies," 460.

[31] E. g., William H. S. Stevens, *The Powder Trust, 1872-1912* (Philadelphia, 1912); Charles Edward Russell, "For Patriotism and Profits," *Pearson's Magazine,* XXX (1913), 545-556. See also the statements of Senator Robert La Follette on February 12, 1915, in the *Cong. Rec.,* 63 Cong., 3 sess., 3632-3633; and the remarks of Representative Clyde H. Tavenner on December 15, 1915, in the *Cong. Rec.,* 64 Cong., 1 sess., 272-293; the latter were later amplified and published as *The World-Wide War Trust* (Washington, 1916). The quotation is from George Bernard Shaw, *Major Barbara* (London, 1905), Act III.

[32]George Seldes, *Iron, Blood and Profits* (New York, 1934), 333. The reference is to the citation of these remarks in Phillip Snowden's later speech.

[33]Seldes, *Iron, Blood and Profits,* 333-340; Philip Viscount Snowden, *An Autobiography* (2 vols., London, 1934), I, 244-251. Snowden admits to having been heavily dependent on the research of J. T. Walton Newbold, who makes similar charges in *The War Trust Exposed* (London, 1914). So does George H. Perris in *The War Traders: An Exposure* (London, 1914).

[34]Henry Noel Brailsford, *The War of Steel and Gold: A Study of the Armed Peace* (London, 1914), 92-93.

[35]Radical criticism did continue to appear, however, with such publications at H. Robertson Murray, *Krupp's and the International Armaments Ring* (London, 1914); Union of Democratic Control, *The International Industry of War* (London, 1915); and J. T. Walton Newbold, *How Europe Armed for War* (London, 1916). For a helpful bibliography of this period, see John Mez, *Peace Literature of the War* (New York, 1916).

[36]See Irene Cooper Willis, *England's Holy War* (New York, 1928), 86-134. One could, perhaps, advance the theory that, as long as conservatives were in power, they tended to see *abroad* what radicals saw both *at home and abroad.*

[37]Lucia Ames Mead, "America's Danger and Opportunity," *Survey,* XXXV (1915), 90. See, in addition, Charles E. Jefferson, "Military Preparedness as a Peril to Democracy," *The Annals,* LXVI (1916), 228-236; Arthur Capper, "The West and Preparedness," *The Independent,* LXXXV (1916), 49-50; Allan L. Benson, *Inviting War to America* (New York, 1916), 8, 23-25; and David Starr Jordan, *War and Waste* (Garden City, N.Y., 1918), 102-104. Yet Scott Nearing, in *The Menace of Militarism* (New York, 1917), 9-17, was still inclined to blame the capitalists almost exclusively. For a recent examination of what actually occurred to American business, government, and the military *after* 1917, see Paul A. C. Koistenen, "The Industrial-Military Complex in Historical Perspective: World War I," *Business History Review,* XLI (1967), 378-403. There is a parallel study for Germany entitled *Total War and Compulsory Labor: A Study of the Military-Industrial Complex in Germany during World War I,* by Robert B. Armeson (The Hague, 1964).

[38]Covenant of the League of Nations, Art. VIII, sec. 5. See also Manley O. Hudson, "Private Enterprise and Public War," *New Republic*, XXVIII (Nov. 16, 1921, supplement), 26-30; and Scott, *Vickers*, 238-241.

[39]Ralph H. Stimson, *The War System* (Washington, 1933), 9-14; C. D. Judd, *Traffic in Armaments* (Dallas, 1934), 13-20. As part of its effort, the League published *A Statistical Yearbook of the Trade in Arms and Ammunition* (Geneva, 1925-1945).

[40]Selig Adler *The Isolationist Impulse* (New York, 1957), 144.

[41]H. A. Overstreet, "Militarizing Our Minds," *The World Tomorrow*, IX (1926), 144; Harry F. Ward, "Free Speech for the Army," *New Republic*, LI (1927), 194-196.

[42]For the best bibliography available, see H. C. Engelbrecht and F. C. Hanighen, *Merchants of Death* (New York, 1934), 285-296.

[43]Otto Lehmann-Russbueldt, *Die blütige Internationale der Rüstungsindustrie* (Hamburg, 1929; translated as *War for Profits*, New York, 1930); Seymour Waldman, *Death and Profits: A Study of the War Policies Commission* (New York, 1932); Union of Democratic Control, *Patriotism Limited: An Exposure of the War Machine* (London, 1933); George A Drew, *Enemies of Peace: An Exposé of Armament Manufacturers* (Toronto, 1933); A. Fenner Brockway, *The Bloody Traffic* (London, 1933); Seldes, *Iron, Blood and Profits*; and Engelbrecht and Hanighen, *Merchants of Death*.

[44]Union of Democratic Control, *Patriotism Limited*, 5.

[45]Union of Democratic Control, *The Secret International: Armament Firms at Work* (London, 1933), 29. In this regard, note also the findings of the Nye Committee, as discussed in Koistenen, "The InterWar Years," 831-833.

[46]Raoul E. Desvernine, *Democratic Despotism* (New York, 1936), 87.

[47]Sinclair Lewis, *It Can't Happen Here: A Novel* (Garden City, N.Y., 1945), 418-419. During this period the American Right tended to fear that a war would assist the Left in establishing a collectivist dictatorship, while the Left suspected that belligerency would have just the opposite result, strengthening the Right to the point of making fascism possible.

[48]Charles A. Beard, *The Navy: Defense or Portent?* (New York, 1932), 13.

[49]Harold D. Laswell, "Sino-Japanese Crisis: The Garrison State versus the Civilian State," *China Quarterly*, II (1937), 643-649. The influence of Herbert Spencer is particularly evident in this article, although, of course, Lasswell tended to see history as flowing in exactly the opposite direction.

[50]Oswald Garrison Villard, *Our Military Chaos: The Truth About Defense* (New York, 1939), 105-115. Villard had been somewhat more traditional in his anti-militarism earlier in the 1930s, and he was to return to that position after World War II. For his earlier attitudes, see Villards, "We Militarize," *Atlantic Monthly*, CLVII (1936), 138-149, and, for his later, note Villard, *How America is Being Militarized* (New York, 1947).

[51]John T. Flynn, "The Armament Bandwagon," *New Republic*, XCVIII (1939), 121-123. Among others who saw a similar danger were Maurice A. Hallgren, "War," in Harold E. Stearns, ed., *America Now* (New York, 1938); Eugene Staley, "Power Economy Versus Welfare Economy," *The Annals*, CXCVIII (1938), 9-14; and George Soule, "After the New Deal: The New Political Landscape," *New Republic*, XCIX (1939), 35-38. After World War II Flynn's views were to become much more conservative, but even in his classic attack on "creeping socialism," *The Road Ahead* (New York, 1949), he would argue against becoming dependent upon "a 'war' economy" (see p. 8). That such criticism as Villard's and Flynn's had an impact on the Roosevelt administration is attested by the President's sudden abandonment in late 1939 of the newly appointed War Resources Board (WRB); for this, see Koistenen, "The InterWar Years," 836-838.

[52]"The Way to Prepare," *New Republic*, CII (1940), 715-716.

[53]*New York Times*, Jan. 20, 1944, p. 1 ff. The *First* World War, apparently, had inspired similar reactions on the part of *German* conservatives; see, for example, A. T. Lauterbach, "Militarism in the Western World," *Journal of the History of Ideas*, V (1944), 474-477.

[54]John W. Swomley, Jr., *The Military Establishment* (Boston, 1964), 101. See also Bruce

Catton, *The War Lords of Washington* (New York, 1948), 211, 313; Barton J. Bernstein, "The Debate on Industrial Reconversion: The Protection of Oligopoly and Military Control of the Economy," *American Journal of Economics and Sociology,* XXVI (1967), 159-172; and Paul Goodman, "A Causerie at the Military Industrial," *New York Review of Books,* IX (Nov. 23, 1967), 14-19. Note, as well, Perry McCoy Smith, *The Air Force Plans for Peace, 1943-1954* (Baltimore, 1969).

[55]Donald A. Morgan, *Congress and the Constitution: A Study of Responsibility* (Cambridge, Mass., 1966), 226-245.

[56]See Harold D. Lasswell, "The Garrison State," *American Journal of Sociology,* XLVI (1941), 455-468; Lasswell, "The Universal Peril: Perpetual Crisis and the Garrison-Prison State," in Lyman Bryson *et al.,* eds., *Perspectives on a Troubled Decade* (New York, 1950); Lasswell, *National Security and Individual Freedom* (New York, 1950); and Lasswell, "Does the Garrison State Threaten Civil Rights?" *The Annals,* CCLXXV (1951), 111-116. Note also Lasswell, "The Garrison State Hypothesis Today," in Samuel P. Huntington, ed., *Changing Patterns of Military Politics* (New York, 1962), 51-70.

[57]George Orwell, *1984* (New York, 1948), 417-419.

[58]For example, "A Militarized America," *Christian Century,* LXIII (1946), 390-391; Lewis Mumford, "Social Effects," *Air Affairs,* I (1947), 370-382; Committee for Economic Development, "The Threat of a Garrison State," *American Affairs,* XII (1950), 114-120. An interesting embellishment on Lasswell's argument is provided by Louis Smith in "The Garrison State: Offspring of the Cold War," *Nation,* CLXXVII (1953), 461-464. Smith is really more concerned about the politician than about the military.

[59]Hanson W. Baldwin, "The Military Move In," *Harper's,* CXCV (1947), 481-489.

[60]William O. Douglas, "Should We Fear the Military?" *Look,* XVI (March 11, 1952), 34. One striking exception to the trend was Henry A. Wallace, who blamed both "Big Brass" and "Big Gold" for the Cold War; note, especially, his "Whipped Up Hysteria," *New Republic,* CXVIII (March 29, 1948), 10, and his "Farewell and Hail!," *New Republic,* CXIX (July 19, 1948), 14-18. Another untypical voice was that of Ray Jackson, who, in "Aspects of American Militarism," *Contemporary Issues,* I (Summer 1948), 19-24, expressed the fear that "certain sections of industry have an interest" in helping the military achieve "domestic Spartanisation."

[61]Matthew Josephson, "The Big Guns," *Nation,* CLXXXII (1956), 30-33, 50-52, and 69-72.

[62]C. Wright Mills, *The Power Elite* (New York, 1956), 276. Note, for discussion, G. William Domhoff and Hoyt B. Ballard, eds., *C. Wright Mills and the Power Elite* (Boston, 1968).

[63]See, in this regard, Arnold M. Rose, *The Power Structure: Political Process in American Society* (New York, 1967), 26-39.

[64]Cook, *The Warfare State*; Irwin Suall, *The American Ultras: The Extreme Right and the Military-Industrial Complex* (New York, 1962); Victor Perlo, *Militarism and Industry: Arms Profiteering in the Missile Age* (New York, 1963).

[65]Julius Duscha, *Arms, Money, and Politics* (New York, 1964); H. L. Nieburg, *In the Name of Science* (Chicago, 1966); John Kenneth Galbraith, *The New Industrial State* (Boston, 1967); Galbraith, *How to Control the Military* (New York, 1969); Ralph E. Lapp, *The Weapons Culture* (New York, 1968).

[66]Nieburg, *Science,* 380-381.

[67]Arthur M. Schlesinger, Jr., *The Crisis of Confidence: Ideas, Power, and Violence in America* (Boston, 1969), 165-174.

[68]Jack Raymond, *Power at the Pentagon* (New York, 1964), 319-334. Raymond focuses on the Department of Defense, but certain other writers find the most sinister of these "civilian militarists" in the Central Intelligence Agency. See, e.g., David Wise and Thomas B. Ross, *The Invisible Government* (New York, 1964), 3-6, 350-352; and the editorial entitled "American Militarism," *New Republic,* CLX (April 12, 1969), 7-9.

[69]Swomley, cited above. Swomley seems to have gravitated recently toward a more "balanced" view of the warfare state, as indicated in his "Economic Basis of the Cold War,"

Christian Century, LXXXV (1968), 581-585. Yet there are still many Americans who believe that the military is the leading partner; e.g., David M. Shoup, "The New American Militarism," *Atlantic Monthly,* CCXXIII (April, 1969), 51-56.

[70]Tristam Coffin, *The Passion of the Hawks* (also published as *The Armed Society,* both, New York, 1964); G. William Domhoff, *Who Rules America?* (Englewood Cliffs, N.J., 1967), 115-131. Gabriel Kolko agrees with Coffin and Domhoff in *The Roots of American Foreign Policy: An Analysis of Power and Purpose* (Boston, 1969), 30-37.

[71]Note, for instance, Sidney Lens, *The Military-Industrial Complex* (Philadelphia, and Kansas City, Mo., 1970). See also Eugene J. McCarthy, "The Powers of the Pentagon," *Saturday Review,* LI (Dec. 21, 1968), 8-10; Michael T. Klare, "Science for the Pentagon: The Secret Thinkers," *Nation,* CCVI (1968), 503-504; and Eric Sevareid, "American Militarism; What Is It Doing To Us?" *Look,* XXXIII (Aug. 12, 1969), 14-16 Sevareid speaks of a "military-industrial-academic-labor union-congressional complex."

[72]Marc Pilisuk and Thomas Hayden, "Is There a Military Industrial Complex Which Prevents Peace? Consensus and Countervailing Power in Pluralistic Systems," *Journal of Social Issues,* XXI (Jan. 1965), 67-117; anonymous, *Report from Iron Mountain* (New York, 1967).

[73]Kenneth Boulding, "The Role of the War Industry in International Conflict," *Journal of Social Issues,* XXII (Jan. 1967), 54-55. This is not to say that Boulding in any sense endorses America's vast defense expenditures, a fact that he makes very clear in the interesting symposium edited by Erwin Knoll and Judith McFadden, *American Militarism 1970* (New York, 1969), 89-95.

[74]E. g. Vice Admiral J. B. Colwell, "Nation Needs Military Industrial Link to Survive," *Los Angeles Times,* July 20, 1969, sec. G, p. 3; or Senator Barry Goldwater, who claims that the ultimate aim of the military-industrial complex is "peace in our time, regardless of the aggressive, militaristic image that the left-wing is attempting to give it." *Cong. Rec.,* 91 Cong., I sess., 3719-3721.

[75]E. g., William Hyland and Richard Shryock, in *The Fall of Kruschchev* (New York, 1968), 176, write of certain Soviet politicians finding kindred souls among the "military-heavy industry clique"; and I. F. Stone, in "The Test Ban Comedy," *New York Review of Books,* XIV (May 7, 1970), 17, asserts, in regard to the reception of the test ban treaty by America and Russia, that "In both capitals there was a military-industrial complex, buttressed by the same paranoia and cave-man instinct." See also Richard Armstrong, "Military Industrial Complex: Russian Style," *Fortune,* LXXX (Aug. 1, 1969), 84-87, 122-126.

[76]Admittedly, representatives of the New Left have often been willing to lump the Soviet Union and United States together as "two of a kind" (for a very much qualified illustration of this, see, e.g., Herbert Marcuse, *One Dimensional Man: Studies in the Ideology of Advanced Industrial Society* [Boston, 1964], 48-55), but astonishingly little of the literature attacking the warfare state has been informed by this perspective. It would seem that, while the nature of the Cold War (involving, so to speak, only one real power on each side) has deprived both liberals and socialists of a certain comparative dimension, the critique of the farther Left has become too radical to inspire comparative analysis of this specific problem.

2. THE INDUSTRIAL-MILITARY COMPLEX IN HISTORICAL PERSPECTIVE: THE INTERWAR YEARS

Paul A. C. Koistinen

The historian Paul A. C. Koistinen, basing his work on records in the federal archives, has meticulously traced the origins of the military-industrial complex back to World War I. As this analysis clearly demonstrates, there is a great deal of historical continuity between the pre- and post-World War II years. One way in which to understand what is happening today is to be aware of what has happened in the past. While some may draw the conclusion that the complex is perhaps an inevitable consequence of unchangeable conditions, others will draw comfort from the realization that in attacking the complex they are maintaining a long tradition of democratic struggle against institutions which threaten freedom.

Scholars and journalists have limited their analyses of the "industrial-military complex" to the years of World War II and the Cold War.[1] This focus is quite natural, for it is during this period that the multibillion-dollar war and defense budgets have had the most dramatic effects upon the nation's institutional structure. Nevertheless, to neglect the years prior to 1940 greatly limits an understanding of the "complex" which has resulted from the military's

Source: Paul A. C. Koistinen, "The 'Industrial-Military Complex' in Historical Perspective: The Interwar Years," *Journal of American History*, LVI (March 1970), 819-839. Reprinted by permission.

expanded role in the federal government and its elaborate ties with the industrial community.

The "industrial-military complex" of World War II and after is an outgrowth of economic mobilization for World War I, of interwar planning by the armed forces and the business community for future emergencies, and of defense spending during the 1920s and 1930s. Almost all practices currently ascribed to the "complex" arose before 1940.

During World War I, as during World War II, federal agencies, largely controlled by industry and the military, regulated the economy. World War I differed from World War II, however, in that the army, the largest wartime military service, was a reluctant participant in the civilian mobilization agencies. Relatively isolated within the federal government and the nation before hostilities, the army was suspicious of, and hostile toward, civilian institutions. It was also unprepared for the enormous wartime responsibilities. Congress and the Wilson administration had to force the army to integrate its personnel into the War Industries Board (WIB). This integration was essential for coordinating army procurement with the Board's regulatory functions in order to maintain a stable economy.

After the war, Congress authorized the army to plan for procurement and economic mobilization in order to insure its preparation for future hostilities. The navy also joined the planning process. The interwar planning was guided by thousands of industrialists, and by the late 1930s the armed services were not only prepared for wartime operations but also in full agreement with prominent industrial elements on plans for economic mobilization. Those plans, based on World War I mobilization, provided the guidelines for regulating the World War II economy.

Interwar planning was inseparable from defense spending. Many of the businessmen who participated in the planning were associated with firms that were actual or potential military contractors. Despite the relatively small defense budgets of the 1920s and 1930s, the pattern of industrial-military relations during those years foreshadows in many striking ways what developed after World War II.

The American economy was mobilized for World War I by federal agencies devised and staffed primarily by businessmen.[2] In the Army Appropriations Act of August 1916, Congress provided for a Council of National Defense, which consisted of six cabinet members, to serve as the President's advisory body on industrial mobilization. It was assisted by a National Defense Advisory Commission (NDAC), composed largely of businessmen serving for a dollar-a-year or without compensation; most of the members surrendered neither their positions nor incomes as private citizens. When the nation declared war, NDAC assumed responsibility for mobilizing the economy. In July 1917 a more effective mobilization agency, WIB, took over NDAC functions; the former agency, like the latter, was controlled by business elements. Until March 1918, neither NDAC nor WIB had legal authority to enforce its decisions; both were subordinate to the Council of National Defense, and it could only advise the President.

During 1917, businessmen perfected the mobilization agencies and devised the means for curtailing civilian production and converting industry to meet governmental needs. In addition, they developed price, priority, allocation, and other economic controls. By the end of the year, WIB had created the organization and the controls essential for regulating a wartime economy.

Through WIB, industry largely regulated itself during World War I. Key to WIB's operations were major subdivisions called commodity committees, which served under the chairman and his lieutenants. These committees, which made policy for and administered the various industries, were staffed by businessmen who often came from the industries they directed. Assisting the commodity committees were war service committees which were trade associations or councils elected by the national industries. Since the war service committees were neither organized nor financed by the government, they officially only "advised" the commodity committees. But in practice the commodity committees relied heavily upon industry representatives to formulate and execute all policy decisions.

Even without legal authority to enforce its decisions, WIB had industry's cooperation because businessmen dominated it. Industry's cooperation, however, was not enough to maintain a stable wartime economy. WIB required some control over procurement by the war and navy departments and other agencies. Throughout 1917 it attempted to coordinate procurement with its own operations in order to prevent the various departments and agencies from competing among themselves and to insure uniform prices and the distribution of contracts according to availability of facilities, resources, and transportation. Economic stability depended upon such coordination, since wartime demand always exceeded supply. With only advisory powers, WIB relied upon the procurement agencies' voluntary cooperation. While most of these proved to be reasonably cooperative, the war department—the largest, most powerful procurement agency—undermined WIB's regulatory efforts by acting independently and purchasing billions of dollars worth of munitions. As a result, industrial plants in the Northeast were overloaded with contracts; prices skyrocketed; critical shortages of fuel, power, and raw materials developed; and the railway and shipping systems became hopelessly congested.

The war department was both unwilling and unable to cooperate with WIB—unwilling, because it feared that the civilian agency would try to take over army procurement functions; unable, because the department could not control its own supply operations, let alone coordinate them with WIB. As many as eight supply bureaus, such as the Quartermaster Corps and the Ordnance Department, purchased independently for the army. Competing with one another and other purchasing agencies, the bureaus let contracts indiscriminately, commandeered facilities without plan, and hoarded supplies. Cooperation between WIB and the war department was also thwarted by the fact that WIB was organized along commodity lines while the army's supply network was structured by function (such as ordnance and quartermaster). Before army procurement could be coordinated with WIB, the war department had first to accept the need for cooperating with the civilian mobilization agency and then to centralize its supply network along commodity lines. For months, the department would do neither, not only because it was suspicious of WIB but also because it was torn by internal dissension.

In theory, the war department was under the centralized control of the chief of staff, aided by the General Staff. Serving as the secretary of war's principal military adviser, the chief of staff supervised the entire army, including the supply bureaus as well as the combat troops. This system never worked in practice. The bureaus resisted control by the chief of staff. Conflict between the General Staff and the bureaus rent the war department before the war; it paralyzed the department during hostilities.

Unable to regulate the economy without war department cooperation, WIB during 1917 sought the authority to impose its will on the department. But Secretary of War Newton D. Baker, reflecting army suspicion of the Board, squelched the efforts to give it more than advisory powers. He managed to do so because he served as chairman of the Council of National Defense, under which WIB functioned, and as Woodrow Wilson's chief adviser on industrial mobilization.

By the winter of 1917-1918, with WIB stalemated by the war department and the latter virtually collapsing under burgeoning munitions requirements, the economy had become critically dislocated. The business community and Congress demanded that the crisis should be resolved by placing military procurement under a civilian munitions ministry. Adamantly opposed to such a drastic remedy, Wilson headed off the critics in March 1918 by separating WIB from the Council of National Defense and placing it directly under his control. He granted it broad powers for regulating the economy, including a measure of authority over the procurement agencies. To avoid losing control of procurement and to facilitate coordination with WIB, the war department also began reforming its supply system. In December 1917, the department began to consolidate the bureaus into one agency under General Staff control. The new organization was structured to match WIB's commodity committee system.

From March 1918, the strengthened WIB, under the chairmanship of Bernard M. Baruch, effectively used the organization and economic controls developed over the past year to regulate the economy. Procurement was coordinated with WIB activities by integrating war department representatives and those of the other purchasing agencies into WIB. Once the department reorganized its system and adopted a cooperative attitude, members of the army commodity committees joined WIB committees and shared equally in making decisions. Working together, industrial and military personnel learned that WIB could function for their mutual interests. Through WIB's operations, the foundation for the "industrial-military complex" was laid.

The collaboration of industry and the military continued during the 1920s and 1930s and took the form of procurement and economic planning for future wars. This planning was authorized by Congress in the National Defense Act of 1920, which reorganized the war department's system of supply and procurement. To insure that the army did not disrupt economic mobilization in a future emergency, the act placed the supply bureaus under an assistant secretary of war. It was assumed that he would be an industrialist. The assistant secretary would supervise the bureaus and, through planning, prepare them for wartime procurement. Since the assistant secretary was made the chief of staff's equal, the secretary of war had two principal advisers instead of one, as had been the case before 1920.[3]

Congress based the legislation upon the recommendations of Assistant Secretary of War Benedict Crowell, various industrial consultants, several bureau chiefs, and other military personnel. Crowell, a Cleveland businessman who had been involved in military procurement since 1916, believed that World War I demonstrated that industrial production was as important to military success as were tactics and strategy. He felt that supply and procurement must receive the same emphasis in war department affairs as did the traditional military functions. That would not take place, he maintained, under the old system in which the chief of staff, aided by the General Staff, served as the secretary of war's principal adviser. The General Staff would neglect supply and procurement because it knew little about those subjects. Only by placing the bureaus under a qualified civilian who was equal to the chief of staff, he argued, would the army be prepared for future hostilities.[4] Crowell and his associates intended that the assistant secretary of war should plan only for army procurement. Congress went further. The National Defense Act empowered the assistant secretary, though in an ambiguous way, to plan for an entire wartime economy. Why Congress authorized the more comprehensive planning is obscure.

J. Mayhew Wainwright, the first assistant secretary of war under the act, set up an Office of the Assistant Secretary of War (OASW) with personnel drawn from the bureaus. In 1922 an Army-Navy Munitions Board was created in order to include the navy in the planning and to coordinate the supply systems of the two services. And, in 1924 the war department supply planners organized an Army Industrial College to facilitate their work.[5]

At first, OASW concentrated upon wartime military procurement, but it soon became obvious that this planning was futile without also planning for economic mobilization.[6] Though authorized to draft such plans, war department officials, civilian and military alike, hesitated to assume what they considered to be civilian responsibilities. It took the influence of Baruch to convince the war department that economic planning was not exclusively a civilian matter. After World War I, he and other architects of wartime mobilization insisted that the nation's security depended upon constant preparation for war. They favored joint industry-military planning for economic mobilization in order to avoid confusion and delay.[7] Baruch pleaded with the department to draw up full-scale plans for mobilization based on World War I.[8] After years of hesitation, OASW began to plan for economic mobilization as well as procurement. Under Baruch's critical eye, the supply planners between 1929 and 1931 drafted the first official economic blueprint for war – the "Industrial Mobilization Plan" of 1930.[9]

This plan amounted to little more than a proposal for using the methods of World War I to regulate a wartime economy. The key to OASW's blueprint was a War Resources Administration. Comparable to the War Industries Board, the War Resources Administration would rely upon a commodity committee-war service committee system for economic control. The military services would also organize their procurement networks along commodity lines and integrate their personnel into the War Resources Administration. In a future war, the economy would be mobilized by new federal agencies largely dominated by industrial and military personnel.[10] In 1933, 1936, and 1939, the war department published revised editions of the plan. With each revision, the proposed mobilization apparatus was simplified and patterned more explicitly after the World War I model.[11]

The fact that the war department wrote the 1930 plan is of the greatest significance. After ten years of planning, OASW recognized that modern warfare required a totally planned economy; the armed services would have to adapt themselves to the civilian mobilization agencies during hostilities. The Industrial Mobilization Plan did not mean, however, that the army as a whole had accepted the new conditions of warfare. Before that could take place, the supply planners had to convert the chief of staff and the General Staff to their point of view. Throughout the 1920s and into the 1930s, the army's command structure refused to recognize that supply and procurement set limits for tactics and strategy; and the General Staff's war plans provided for raising and fielding an army at rates that exceeded the economy's capacity. The General Staff insisted that supply had to adjust to strategy. OASW and the supply bureaus adamantly opposed such thinking. Both the economy and the military mission, they argued, would be threatened.[12] The admonition went unheeded for years.

The General Staff turned a deaf ear to OASW because, knowing little about procurement, it could not gauge the effects of industrialized warfare on the army or the economy and, therefore, continued to view civilian and military responsibilities as if they were unrelated. In addition, the General Staff and OASW were rivals for power· The General Staff resented the 1920 reorganization which deprived it of control of the bureaus. It was intent upon keeping the supply side of the department subordinate to itself. If the General Staff granted the importance of supply and procurement in military affairs, it would strengthen the hand of its rival. Relations between the two groups in the war department became so embittered in the 1920s that communication broke down almost completely. In the 1930s, however, the strife began to wane. As relations improved, the General Staff gradually became more receptive to OASW ideas.[13]

A major turning point occurred in 1935-1936, when General Malin Craig became chief of staff and Harry W. Woodring, secretary of war. Woodring, who had served as assistant secretary of war from 1933 to 1936, was convinced of the need for practical war plans. Craig agreed. Under their combined influence, the General Staff's Mobilization Plan of 1933 was scrapped and the Protective Mobilization Plan drawn up and perfected between 1936 and 1939. It was the first war plan based on the nation's industrial potential.[14] A radical change had taken place in the thinking of the army's command structure. It had finally accepted army dependence on the civilian economy in order to fulfill the military mission. Woodring observed: "I believe the reduction of our mobilization program to sensible workable proportions to be one of the highest attainments of the War Department since the World War."[15]

OASW planning naturally led to numerous war department contacts with the business community. Thousands of industrialists, most of whom had participated in wartime mobilization, guided and assisted the department's efforts in various ways. When the Army Industrial College was organized, it had an Advisory Board graced with such prominent business figures as Baruch, Elbert H. Gary, and Walter Gifford. The various procurement districts also set up civilian advisory boards composed of army contractors to review the department's supply operations. In 1925 the department organized a Business Council, which included members from the nation's largest corporations, to help introduce modern business techniques into army operations and to familiarize the industrialists with army procurement and planning methods.[16]

Most contacts between the war department and industry involved representatives from trade associations and interested corporation executives. Often these men were or became reserve officers assigned to OASW. By 1931 about 14,000 individuals served in such a capacity. They aided in the drafting of procurement and mobilization plans and sought to further cooperative relations between the military and business.[17]

Mixed motives explain industry's participation in war department planning.[18] Firms contracting with the army obviously welcomed the opportunity of working closely with OASW in order to secure or advance their special interests. Some business elements assisted the army so that they could identify their products or materials with national defense in order to enhance their chances for tariff protection, government assistance, or other special privileges. Also, their firms received free publicity of a "patriotic" nature. But reasons other than immediate economic concerns must be considered in assessing industry's role in army planning. Industrial preparedness became almost an ideological crusade for some business executives after the war. That was the case with Baruch and his coterie; with Howard E. Coffin, a prominent industrialist and leading participant in wartime mobilization; and with businessmen associated with the American Legion.[19] They participated in army planning as a means of preparing the nation for war. The business community in general was not so disposed. Without being committed to industrial preparedness *per se,* many businessmen were willing to assist in the planning at the war department's request because it helped the department to adjust its structure and thinking to modern warfare.

The general trend of the interwar political economy is also significant for measuring the response of business to army planning. World War I greatly strengthened the cooperative ethic within the business community and between it and the government. Before World War II, both business and the government experimented with official and unofficial attempts at economic control through industrial cooperation. The National Recovery Administration was only the most formal example. The army's economic planning accurately reflected this cooperative trend.[20] For that reason, among others, the planning received the endorsement of interested businessmen.

OASW did not confine itself simply to planning for industrial mobilization. It also sought legislative authority for implementing the "Industrial Mobilization Plan" in an emergency.

During the 1920s the department's drive for industrial preparedness was carried on in conjunction with the American Legion. The Legion rank and file seethed with resentment about alleged wartime profiteering and the unequal burden shouldered by the fighting forces. In order to remove the promise of riches as an inducement to war and to distribute the burdens of warfare more equitably, the returning veterans demanded a total draft of manpower and capital in any future emergency. Ironically, the Legion's peace movement, which originated in dissent over the economics of World War I, was ultimately converted into support for the "Industrial Mobilization Plan" based on the wartime model. Legion leadership and its special relationship with the war department explains why. Substantial business elements and former military officers dominated Legion affairs; throughout the 1920s the secretaries and assistant secretaries of war were usually active Legionnaires. When acting on the proposal for a total draft that was favored by the rank and file, the Legion leaders turned to the war department for assistance. In 1922, OASW drafted for the Legion a bill that in general terms would have granted the President almost unlimited authority over the nation's human and economic resources in the event of war.[21] The Legion consistently referred to the bill as a "universal draft," as a measure for promoting peace, and as a proposal for "equalizing wartime burdens." That was scarcely the case. The bill was so vague that it could be used for many different purposes. Its grant of authority was so great and its power so general that it could sanction a presidential dictatorship. Once the economic planning of OASW was fully underway, the war department and the Legion leadership clearly intended the bill to be a general grant of authority for implementing the "Industrial Mobilization Plan."

Beginning in 1922, the Legion-sponsored bill was repeatedly introduced in Congress. Despite Legion lobbying and war department support, each Congress sidetracked the proposed legislation. Unable to get its bill through Congress, the Legion asked for a bipartisan commission to study and recommend policies for industrial mobilization. An active campaign by congressmen who were also Legionnaires soon led to action. By a joint resolution in June 1930, Congress created the War Policies Commission (WPC), which consisted of eight congressmen and six cabinet members. Six of the fourteen commissioners were Legionnaries. The Commission was to study and make recommendations for equalizing war burdens and preventing war profiteering, and it was to formulate "policies to be pursued in event of war."[22]

WPC, like the Legion's drive for a "universal draft," quickly became a means for futhering military preparation.[23] Because the war department dominated the proceedings, WPC emphasized how to mobilize the economy for war and not how to equalize war burdens and eliminate war profits. Secretary of War Patrick J. Hurley, an active Legionnaire, served as WPC's chairman. WPC's staff came almost exclusively from the war department. The department's presentation of its 1930 "Industrial Mobilization Plan" and Baruch's testimony on the economics of World War I were the highlights of WPC's public hearings. After extended deliberations, WPC, with only one dissenting vote, directly endorsed the department's planning and indirectly endorsed the "Industrial Mobilization Plan."[24] WPC efforts were more impressive as an attempt to popularize and legitimize department planning than as a serious study of wartime economics.

Despite a friendly Commission, the department was unable to drum up much overt support for its plans. In addition to the department itself, the principal advocates of the planning before WPC were the American Legion and some wartime mobilization leaders like Baruch, Gifford, and Coffin.[25] The business community in general was either unconcerned about or unwilling to commit itself publicly on issues involving economic mobilization. Of the thousands of business-men participating in the army planning, only a few came forward to testify.

Although support for department planning was weak, the opposition was vociferous. Witnesses like Norman Thomas, several congressmen, and spokesmen for some peace societies and humanitarian groups were hostile to WPC and the department's plans. Some advocates of peace detected inherent dangers in the department's work. According to their analyses, the promise of wartime riches, while not a major cause of war, was a contributing one that had to be eliminated. The army's plans would not do this. Moreover, the opponents feared that the industrial-military ties resulting from department planning could endanger the nation's future.[26] But the critics—among them a member of WPC, Representative Ross A. Collins of Mississippi—were weak on analysis. Their critique of the department's plans and planning was often nebulous, contradic-tory, or incomplete. Seymour Waldman, a journalist covering the hearings, articulated more clearly and precisely what appeared to alarm Collins and some witnesses before WPC:

> The hearings revealed a gigantic machine, whose intricate parts touch the entire nation, which is being constructed by the War Department and industrial magnates for use in the event of war . . . . They reveal the dangers inherent in a militarization of industry, an industrialization of the military forces, or a combination of the two. . . .
> I would feel rewarded and gratified if this book should be the precursor of a much needed diagnosis of the whole problem, a study of the interlocking of our war mechanism and our economic system. . . . Such a work . . . is imperative if we are to be effective in preventing more national and international bloodshed.[27]

Opposition to the department's plans and proposed legislation for implementing them increased after WPC's hearings as the peace and isolationist movement gained in strength.[28] The most formidable challenge came from the Senate's so-called Nye Committee. In addition to the munitions makers, the Nye Committee's purview included economic mobilization for World War I, interwar military procurement policies, and the "Industrial Mobilization Plan." In a fragmentary manner, the Committee disclosed the dynamics of an emerging "industrial-military complex." The elements were presented in the Committee hearings and reports, but they were not fitted together. Senator Gerald P. Nye and his colleagues still saw only through a glass darkly.[29]

The Nye Committee clearly perceived that industrialized warfare created qualitatively new and ominous problems for the nation. To fight a modern war, even to prepare for one, eroded the barriers between private and public, civilian and military institutions. The Committee observed that during hostilities "[p]ractically every important industry in the country is necessary for the supply of the armed forces." "[E]ven in time of peace," the Committee reported, "the line of demarkation between the munitions industry and other industries is not clear and fixed."[30]

From its investigation of interwar defense spending the Committee established that various industries depended upon military contracts for profitable operations and that the military services depended upon them for developing and producing weapons. There were many prime examples. Shipbuilding indirectly included "the steel companies, the electrical manufacturing groups, the boiler producers, the instrument people," and "the biggest banking interests in the Nation." Du Pont and other munitions producers were virtual adjuncts of the war department. Industrialists and military leaders regarded their interests as mutual. Industry favored and worked for increased military appropriations; the armed services granted industry special favors, encouraged monopoly where it served their interests, financed research, and, despite legislation to the contrary, displayed little concern about profit restraints.[31] Committee members were shocked to find that the war and navy departments, and even the commerce and state departments at times, cooperated with munitions firms in a manner that compromised national policies for disarmament, arms limitation, arms sales, and arms embargoes.[32] The fact that Public Works Administration funds, intended to stimulate industrial recovery, went to the armed services and that some businessmen favored defense spending as an antidote to the depression also disturbed Nye and his colleagues.[33]

The Nye Committee found a web of personal as well as contractual ties binding industrial-military elements. Retired army and navy officers often joined firms contracting with the services. Frequently, officials of corporations supplying the armed services became reserve officers. A society like the Army Ordnance Association, organized in 1919, combined in its membership actual or potential military contractors and retired and active army officers. The Association lobbied for the army, participated in the industrial mobilization planning, and attempted to influence war department policies and the selection and promotion of personnel.[34]

The Nye Committee carefully avoided charges of conspiracy. It pointed out that plausible reasons existed for what was done and stated that it was not drawing a one-to-one correlation between expenditures for defense and the causation of war.[35] Nevertheless, argued the Committee,

> any close associations between munitions and supply companies . . . and the service departments . . . , of the kind that existed in Germany before the World War, constitutes an unhealthy alliance in that it brings into being a self-interested political power which operates in the name of patriotism and satisfies interests which are, in large part, purely selfish, and that such associations are an inevitable part of militarism, and are to be avoided in peacetime at all costs.[36]

In order to check the growth of an "unhealthy alliance," a majority of the Committee favored nationalizing the munitions facilities. Congress never seriously considered the proposal. Upon the advice of the Roosevelt administration, Congress even refused to strengthen regulations governing military procurement as the Committee minority recommended.[37]

The army's economic planning for war also disturbed the Nye Committee. The planning, argued the Committee, assured that industry and the military would function more effectively as a team than they had in World War I; but, because the "Industrial Mobilization Plan" was patterned after wartime methods, it would not eliminate the "economic evils of war." According to the Committee's analysis, World War I mobilization was accompanied by "shameless profiteering" and extravagant waste. The war left a legacy of inflation, debt, and increased concentration of economic power. Similar results would occur in a future war if industry, in conjunction with the armed services, virtually regulated itself.[38]

In order to secure the nation's economic future and to remove the promise of riches as an inducement to war, the Nye Committee maintained that wartime "economic evils" had to be eliminated. That required radical changes in the economic system during hostilities, not the preservation of the status quo as proposed by the "Industrial Mobilization Plan." The profit motive and the prerogatives of private property would have to be modified. To accomplish that purpose, the Committee supported legislation drafted under the direction of John T. Flynn. In an emergency, profits would be limited to 3 percent and personal annual income to $10,000. No individual with direct or indirect interests in an industry could serve in a government capacity involving that industry. Moreover, the President would be granted vast authority over the economy to the point of conscripting capital and management if necessary.[39] Although vague at many points, the Flynn legislation amounted to a proposal for state capitalism during wartime with the industrial managers removed from the seats of power.

The war department opposed the Committee's major recommendations. It viewed with alarm any taxation proposals that threatened production. It maintained that conscripting management would not work and insisted that economic mobilization was impossible without the assistance of managers of the industries to be regulated.[40] Baruch responded to the proposed bill with undisguised hostility. Attempting to change the economic system during a war, he argued, was an invitation to disaster.[41]

In its most impressive reports, the Nye Committee curiously agreed with both the war department and Baruch. The Committee's support of the Flynn proposals ignored its own findings. Without constitutional amendments that could be "far worse than the situation of profiteering in a national emergency," the Flynn legislation could not be enforced. The Committee recognized that, even if the bill and the necessary amendments were adopted, they would probably be repealed or ignored in an emergency. The only men qualified to administer a wartime economy were industrialists themselves. It was inconceivable that they would attempt to enforce laws they considered detrimental to the economy and to the war effort.[42]

The Flynn bill was introduced into Congress in 1935. For a time, Franklin D. Roosevelt seemed disposed toward the bill. Ultimately, he joined Baruch, the war department, and, with reservations, the Legion in backing competing legislation that would have granted the President authority for mobilizing the economy, but with few safeguards against abuse. That bill would have sanctioned what the "Industrial Mobilization Plan" proposed. The administration let it be known that it, too, believed that curtailing the profit motive during a war would jeopardize any mobilzation program. No legislation was passed.[43]

After the Nye Committee investigation, the nation knew more about the political economy of warfare; but short of avoiding war and excessive spending for defense, there was no viable way to prevent close and compromising relations between business and the armed services. Military spending in the American industrial system inevitably drew industrial and military elements together, and the threat of an "unhealthy alliance" was always present.

War department planning entered its final and most important phase after the Nye Committee investigation. With the approach of war and the growing American preparedness movement, the department launched a drive for the appointment of a joint industry-military board to review and ultimately to implement the "Industrial Mobilization Plan."

The proposal for a joint board originated with civilians who were concerned about a major flaw in the "Industrial Mobilization Plan." Because of a continuing distrust of civilian institutions, the army determined to dominate the wartime mobilization agencies. To insure that OASW plans were realistic and to keep the nation ready for war, Baruch and others repeatedly recommended that industrialists officially meet each year with the war department. They would review the department's plans and prepare themselves for the eventuality of official duty.[44]

The war department resisted suggestions for officially sharing its planning authority with industrialists until Louis Johnson, a past American Legion commander, became assistant secretary of war in June 1937. With international relations deteriorating, Johnson was determined to prepare both the army and the nation for war. He arranged for Baruch, some former WIB members, and younger talent to serve as an advisory board to OASW.[45] For Johnson, that was the first essential step for instituting the "Industrial Mobilization Plan." But the President refused to sanction the scheme.[46] Despite the setback, Johnson was determined to create an advisory board. He was stealthily maneuvering to achieve that end in mid-1939,[47] when Roosevelt, fearing that war was imminent and that the nation might become involved,[48] authorized Johnson to set up a mobilization advisory group called the War Resources Board (WRB). Roosevelt chose Edward R. Stettinius, Jr., of the United States Steel Corporation as chairman and left the selection of other members to the war department. With Stettinius serving as an intermediary, Johnson, Acting Secretary of the Navy Charles Edison, Army Chief of Staff George Marshall, and two senior members of OASW selected the others. In addition to Stettinius, WRB included Gifford, president of American Telephone and Telegraph; John Lee Pratt of General Motors Corporation; Robert E. Wood, chairman of Sears, Roebuck, and Company; Karl T. Compton of the Massachusetts Institute of Technology; and Harold G. Moulton, president of the Brookings Institute. The membership was cleared with the President.[49] Why Baruch was excluded is still unclear. He was described as being "sore as hell" about being passed over.[50] WRB did not get his blessing until his close associate, John Hancock, was appointed to it in September. Hancock played a prominent role in WRB proceedings.

Assistant Secretary of War Johnson announced to the nation that WRB would review the "Industrial Mobilization Plan" of 1939, revise it if necessary, and implement it in an emergency.[51] Key to the plan was the War Resources Administration, organized along commodity committee-war service committee lines with military representatives integrated into it. Unlike earlier plans, the 1939 edition moderated proposed military influence in the civilian agencies.[52]

Working hand in hand with the armed services, WRB, while still reviewing the "Industrial Mobilization Plan," began preparing to institute it. In sharp contrast to its attitude toward WPC, the business community was eager to cooperate with WRB. The National Association of Manufacturers and the United States Chamber of Commerce rushed forward to volunteer their services. Through conferences with these organizations, former WIB members, the commerce department, and other private and public sources, WRB drew up an industrial who's who to staff the War Resources Administration and also made provisions for the use of war service committees.[53] The most daring move was a memorandum drafted for the President's signature that would have granted the WRB and the Army-Navy Munitions Board authority to mobilize the economy and that instructed all government agencies to cooperate with those two boards.[54]

Roosevelt suddenly cut the ground from under WRB shortly after its creation because the war scare had waned and because of widespread opposition within the administration and the nation to it. Liberal Democrats were aghast at the dominant position held by the major banking and industrial interests in WRB. They identified Stettinius, Gifford, and Pratt with J. P. Morgan. The anti-Morgan banking elements on Wall Street who were sympathetic to the administration were bitterly disappointed. Labor and agriculture were irate over their exclusion.[55]

The President waited until WRB had completed reviewing the "Industrial Mobilization Plan" and had submitted a final report in November 1939 before dismissing it. In its final report, WRB indirectly endorsed the war department plan and fully accepted its basic assumptions. A wartime economy should be regulated by federal agencies largely controlled by industry and the military services. In circumscribed terms, WRB recommended the suspension of the antitrust laws and also suggested that domestic reform would be a casualty of a mobilized economy. It further proposed that the Army-Navy Munitions Board, through consultation with industry, continue to explore the yet unresolved issues of industrial mobilization. It concluded by offering its advisory services for the future.[56] Roosevelt thanked WRB members and never called on them again.[57]

WRB's fate did not negate the years of planning. Because of this planning, the war department adjusted to emergency conditions during World War II with relative ease. In the late 1930s the department began a gradual transition from planning for, to participating in, a mobilization program. Starting in 1937-1938, Congress, after years of departmental advocacy, authorized educational orders and the stockpiling of essential and strategic raw materials and slowly modified peacetime restraints on military contracting.[58] As the army and military budgets grew, OASW expanded its staff and activities proportionately until the mobilization stage was reached in 1940-1941. Writing in mid-1940, Assistant Secretary of War Johnson observed: "Without the benefit of plans perfected by 20 years of study the successful and timely execution of this [expanded munitions] program would have been virtually impossible."[59]

When the war department began the transition to mobilization in 1937-1938, it also launched the drive for implementing the "Industrial Mobilization Plan"; it had been convinced by the years of planning that civilian mobilization agencies were essential for fulfilling the military mission. During 1940-1941, the Army-Navy Munitions Board played a more active role in mobilizing the economy than the army plans had envisaged. But that was the case principally because the civilian agencies were weak. After WRB's demise, the Roosevelt administration relied upon the resuscitated NDAC and other agencies that were totally inadequate for mobilization. War department officials were in the vanguard of those working for more effective civilian agencies until the creation in early 1942 of the War Production Board.

Throughout the years 1940-1941, the war department, and the navy department as well, sided with industry on most major policies involving economic mobilization. After war was declared, the nation's largest corporations and the armed forces ultimately dominated the War Production Board through an alliance of mutual interests.[60] Though officially rejected in 1939, the principal proposals concurred in by WRB and the military were adopted during World War II. As foreseen by the Nye Committee and others, relations between the business community and the armed services during World War I and the interwar period prepared the way for the full-blown "industrial-military complex" of World War II and the Cold War years.

FOOTNOTES

[1] For example, see C. Wright Mills, *The Power Elite* (New York, 1956), 212; Walter Millis, *Arms and Men: A Study in American Military History* (New York, 1956), 306-307; Fred J. Cook, *The Warfare State* (New York, 1962), 41-65; Jack Raymond, *Power at the Pentagon* (New York, 1964), 167; H. L. Nieburg, *In the Name of Science* (Chicago, 1966), vii-viii, 184-185.

[2] Paul A. C. Koistinen, "The 'Industrial-Military Complex' in Historical Perspective: World War I," *Business History Review*, XLI (Winter 1967), 378-403. Further research by the author in the papers of Woodrow Wilson, Newton D. Baker, James W. Wadsworth, Jr., George W. Goethals, and Bernard M. Baruch and in commerce department records has not significantly modified the conclusions reached in the essay on World War I.

[3] *U.S. Statutes at Large,* XLI (1921), Part 1, pp. 762-765.

[4] "Reorganization of the Army," Senate, *Hearings before the Subcommittee of the Committee on Military Affairs,* 66 Cong., 2 Sess., 1919, pp. 1760-1777; "Army Reorganization," House, *Hearings before the Committee on Military Affairs,* 66 Cong., 1 Sess., 1919-1920, pp. 1801-1835; Charles Saltzman, "Reminiscences of the Battle of Washington," Nov. 26, 1935, File No. 020/2/113.1, Planning Branch (PB), Assistant Secretary of War (ASW), Office of the Secretary of War, RG 107 (National Archives); Benedict Crowell and Robert F. Wilson, *The Armies of Industry* (New Haven, 1921), 8-19. See also E. O. Saunders, "National Defense Act—Legislative History of Industrial Mobilization Clauses," Oct. 11, 1923, File No. 628, PB ASW Office of the Secretary of War; A. H. Moran, "Legislative History of the General Staff Corps and the Assistant Secretary of War," Feb. 14, 1928, File No. 46, *ibid.*; Troyer S. Anderson, "Introduction to the History of the Under Secretary of War's Office," 1947, Office of the Chief of Military History, Washington, D.C.; Harry B. Yoshpe, "Economic Mobilization Planning Between Two World Wars," *Military Affairs,* XV (Winter 1951), 199-204, XVI (Summer 1952), 71-83.

[5] Harold W. Thatcher, *Planning for Industrial Mobilization, 1920-1940* (Washington, D.C., 1943), 16, 24-25, 42-43.

[6] J. Mayhew Wainwright to President, Aug. 29, 1940, PPF 1678, Franklin D. Roosevelt Papers (Franklin D. Roosevelt Library, Hyde Park, N.Y.); War Department, *Report of the Secretary of War to the President, 1925* (Washington, 1925), 27-28; War Department, *Report of the Secretary of War to the President, 1926* (Washington, 1926), 30-31; War Department, *Report of the Secretary of War to the President, 1927* (Washington, 1927), 25, 27, 29-35; War Department, *Report of the Secretary of War to the President, 1928* (Washington, 1928), 16-18, 50-58. See also Marvin A. Kreidberg and Merton G. Henry, *History of Military Mobilization in the United States Army, 1775-1945* (Washington, 1955), 502-507; Erna Risch, *The Quartermaster Corps: Organization, Supply, and Services* (2 vols., Washington, 1953), I, 56-57, 208-210, 243-252, 323-329.

[7]Bernard M. Baruch, *American Industry in the War: A Report of the War Industries Board (March 1921)* (New York, 1941), 7-8, 36, 102-104; Crowell and Wilson, *Armies of Industry,* 18-19; Grosvenor B. Clarkson, *Industrial America in the World War: The Strategy Behind the Lines, 1917-1918* (New York, 1923), 483-484; "Final Report of the Chairman of the United States War Industries Board to the President of the United States, February, 1919," Senate, Special Committee Investigating the Munitions Industry, *Senate Committee Print No. 3,* 74 Cong., 1 Sess., 1935, pp. 44-52; "Reorganization of the Army," 371-372, 432-441; United States Council of National Defense, *Third Annual Report, Fiscal Year Ended June 30, 1919* (Washington, D.C., 1919), 16-17; United States Council of National Defense, *Fourth Annual Report, Fiscal Year Ended June 30, 1920* (Washington, D.C., 1920), 3-108.

[8]Bernard M. Baruch, Speeches Delivered at the Army War College, Jan. 15, Dec. 2, 1925, Dec. 14, 1926, File No. 011.2, Records of the War Production Board, RG 179 (National Archives); John W. Weeks to Chairman, House Military Affairs Committee, Feb. 9, 1923, File No. 374, PB ASW Office of the Secretary of War; Baruch to Dwight F. Davis, March 6, 1923, Dec. 11, 1924, June 6, 1925; Baruch to Weeks, Jan. 22, 1923; Baruch to H. E. Ely, Feb. 20, Oct. 29, 1925; Ely to Baruch, Oct. 30, 1925, Bernard M. Baruch Papers (Princeton University Library). Harry B. Yoshpe, "Bernard Baruch: Civilian Godfather of the Military M-Day Plan," *Military Affairs,* XXX (Spring 1965), 1-15.

[9]"Plan for Governmental Organization For War," Nov. 12, 1929, File No. 109, PB ASW Office of the Secretary of War (Baruch's comments are written on the Plan); George Van Horn Mosely to Baruch, Jan. 9, Feb. 1, 13, 1930; Baruch to Moseley, Feb. 4, 18, 1930, Baruch Papers.

[10]"Industrial Mobilization Plan," 1930 ("IMP"), File No. 110, PB ASW Office of the Secretary of War. In "IMP," 1939, the major mobilization agency was called the War Resources Administration.

[11]"IMP," 1933, File No. 112, PB ASW Office of the Secretary of War; "IMP," 1936, File No. 120, *ibid.*; "IMP," 1939, File No. 334/117.3, *ibid.*

[12]Kreidberg and Henry, *History of Military Mobilization,* 382-461, 502-503; War Department, *Report of the Secretary . . . 1928,* pp. 56-57; War Department, *Report of the Secretary of War to the President, 1935* (Washington, 1935), 36; Constance McLaughlin Green, Harry C. Thomson, and Peter C. Roots, *The Ordnance Department: Planning Munitions for War* (Washington, 1955), 51-54.

[13]Paul A. C. Koistinen, "The Hammer and the Sword: Labor, the Military, and Industrial Mobilization, 1920-1945" (doctoral dissertation, University of California, Berkeley, 1964), 15-16, 24-27; War Department, *Report of the Secretary . . . 1927,* p. 38; War Department, *Report of the Secretary . . . 1928,* p. 58; Kreidberg and Henry, *History of Military Mobilization,* 382-461, 502-503.

[14]Kreidberg and Henry, *History of Military Mobilization,* 382-461, 466-492, 502-503; Otto L. Nelson, Jr., *National Security And The General Staff* (Washington, 1946), 303-307; Mark S. Watson, *Chief of Staff: Prewar Plans and Preparations* (Washington, 1950), 78, 81-84.

[15]War Department, *Report of the Secretary of War to the President, 1938* (Washington, 1938), 1.

[16]War Department, *Report of the Secretary . . . 1925,* p. 27; War Department, *Report of the Secretary . . . 1926,* pp. 30-31; War Department, *Report of the Secretary . . . 1927,* pp. 28, 34, 39; War Department, *Report of the Secretary of War to the President, 1929* (Washington, 1929), 35-65; Senate, *Hearings Before the Special Committee Investigating the Munitions Industry,* 73-74 Congs. (40 parts, Washington, 1934-1943), Part 15, pp. 3623-3626, Part 16, pp. 3996-4022; Thatcher, *Planning for Industrial Mobilization,* 26; Green, Thomson, and Roots, *Ordnance Department,* 26-27, 36-37, 54-55; Harry C. Thomson and Lida Mayo, *The Ordnance Department: Procurement and Supply* (Washington, 1960), 13.

[17]EFK memo, [circa] Feb. 1922, File No. 46, H. B. Ferguson to Planning Branch, Dec. 12, 1924, File No. 44, PB ASW Office of the Secretary of War; War Department, *Report of the Secretary . . . 1925,* p. 27; War Department, *Report of the Secretary . . . 1927,* pp. 31-33; War Department, *Report of the Secretary . . . 1928,* p. 53; War Department, *Report of the Secretary of War to the President, 1932* (Washington, 1932), 34-35; U.S. War Policies Commission, "Hearings," *House Doc.,* 72 Cong., 1 Sess., No. 163 (Serial 9538), 188.

[18]War Department, *Report of the Secretary . . . 1926,* p. 30; War Department, *Report of the Secretary . . . 1927,* pp. 28, 38; War Department, *Report of the Secretary . . . 1928,* pp. 15, 51, 57; War Department, *Report of the Secretary . . . 1929,* pp. 35-65; War Department, *Report of the Secretary of War to the President, 1931* (Washington, 1931), 26; War Department, *Report of the Secretary . . . 1932,* p. 32; War Department, *Report of the Secretary of War to the President, 1934* (Washington, 1934), 31; War Department, *Report of the Secretary . . . 1938,* p. 21; Koistinen, "Hammer and the Sword," 16, 19-21, 29-30, 58-59, 61-62, 71-77; War Policies Commission, "Hearings," 258-265; Thatcher, *Planning for Industrial Mobilization,* 128-129; Green, Thomson, and Roots, *Ordnance Department,* 54-57; Thomson and Mayo, *Ordnance Department,* 22; Dulany Terrett, *The Signal Corps: The Emergency (To December 1941)* (Washington, 1956), 58-69.

[19]Concerning Howard E. Coffin, see Koistinen, " 'Industrial-Military Complex,' " 381-382, and Coffin's correspondence with the Hoover and Roosevelt administrations, File No. 92819, General Correspondence, Office of the Secretary of Commerce, RG 40 (National Archives). Coffin to Stephen Early, Dec. 21, 1936, OF 172, Roosevelt Papers.

[20]The War Department's participation in NRA resulted directly from ASW planning. See Senate, *Hearings Before the Special Committee Investigating the Munitions Industry,* Part 17, pp. 4292-4293, 4319-4320, 4444-4445.

[21]D. John Markey to Weeks, Feb. 1, 1922, File No. 62, PB ASW Office of the Secretary of War; correspondence concerning the Legion-war department bill, File No. 560, *ibid.*; "Mobilization of Manpower and Industrial Resources, Legislative History," Feb. 18, 1937, File No. 010/178, *ibid.*; Thatcher, *Planning for Industrial Mobilization,* 100-109; Marcus Duffield, *King Legion* (New York, 1931), 4-12, 109-115, 129-145; Justin Gray with Victor H. Bernstein, *The Inside Story of the Legion* (New York, 1948), 44-70, 87-92. See also Roscoe Baker, *The American Legion and American Foreign Policy* (New York, 1954); Richard Seelye Jones, *A History of the American Legion* (Indianapolis, 1946). The Legion affiliations of the war department officials can be traced through the above volumes.

[22]War Policies Commission, "Report to the President," *House Doc.,* 72 Cong., 1 Sess., No. 163 (Serial 9538), vi.

[23]In addition to the hearings and reports of the War Policies Commission collection, see War Policies Commission Files No. 1-211, PB ASW Office of the Secretary of War.

[24]"Message from the President . . . Transmitting . . . the Final Recommendation of the Commission," *House Doc.,* 72 Cong., 1 Sess., No. 264 (Serial 9549), 2-5. See also War Policies Commission, "Documents by War Policies Commission," *House Doc.,* 72 Cong., 1 Sess., No 271 (Serial 9549), 1-71.

[25]War Policies Commission, "Hearings," 7-72, 85-113, 121-144, 169-190, 218-221, 252-265, 288-323, 481-488, 776-790, 794-836, 854-875.

[26]*Ibid.,* 20-24, 66-71, 73-85, 93-94, 119-121, 136-140, 186-189, 258-265, 272-273, 279-280, 323-350, 380-385, 489-502, 535-687, 722-776, 850-854; Seymour Waldman, *Death and Profits: A Study of the War Policies Commission* (New York, 1932), 91, 131-134.

[27]Waldman, *Death and Profits,* v-vii. See also *ibid.,* 71, 147-156.

[28]File No. 049.12/175, 381/116.4b, PB ASW Office of the Secretary of War; Kreidberg and Henry, *History of Military Mobilization,* 516, 518, 529-531, 538-540; Rose M. Stein, *M-Day: The First Day of War* (New York, 1936).

[29]The Nye Committee findings, although not all of its recommendations, received the unanimous endorsement of all members.

[30]"Report on War Department Bills S.1716-S.1722 Relating to Industrial Mobilization in Wartime," *Senate Report,* 74 Cong., 2 Sess., No. 944, Part 4 (Serial 9884), 7. See also "Report of the Special Committee on Investigation of the Munitions Industry," *Senate Report,* 74 Cong., 2 Sess., No. 944, Part 3 (Serial 9983), 3.

[31]"Preliminary Report of the Special Committee on Investigation of the Munitions Industry," *Senate Report,* 74 Cong., 1 Sess., No. 944, Part 1 (Serial 9881) 1-8, 15-343, 384-389; "Report . . . on Investigation of the Munitions Industry," No. 944, Part 3, 159-204; "Report on Government Manufacture of Munitions by the Special Committee on Investigation of the Munitions Industry," *Senate Report,* 74 Cong., 2 Sess., No. 944, Part 7 (Serial 9987), 1-13.

[32]"Report . . . on Investigation of the Munitions Industry," No. 944, Part 3, pp. 3-12, 15-17, 159-204; Wayne S. Cole, *Senator Gerald P. Nye and American Foreign Relations* (Minneapolis, 1962), 76, 79-81; John E. Wiltz, *In Search of Peace: The Senate Munitions Inquiry, 1934-36* (Baton Rouge, 1963), 81.

[33]Senate, *Hearings Before the Special Committee Investigating the Munitions Industry,* Part 37, pp. 12409-12437, 12502-12526, 12766; "Report . . . on Investigation of the Munitions Industry," No. 944, Part 3, pp. 204-207; Wiltz, *In Search of Peace,* 116.

[34]"Preliminary Report . . . on Investigation of the Munitions Industry," No. 944, Part 1, pp. 220-221; "Report . . . on Investigation of the Munitions Industry," No. 944, Part 3, pp. 10-11, 159-217; Senate, *Hearings Before the Special Committee Investigating the Munitions Industry,* Part 36, pp. 11972-12043; Part 37, pp. 12399-123443, 12501-12528, 12766. Concern existed about military contractors employing retired officers before World War I. "To Increase the Efficiency of the Military Establishment of the United States," House, *Hearings before the Committee on Military Affairs,* 64 Cong., 1 Sess., 1916, pp. 540-542, 1147-1148, 1153-1155; "Army Appropriations Bill, [Fiscal] 1917," House, *Hearings before the Committee on Military Affairs,* 64 Cong., 1 Sess., 1916, pp. 848-850.

[35]"Preliminary Report . . . on Investigation of the Munitions Industry," No. 944, Part 1, p. 222; "Report . . . on Investigation of the Munitions Industry," No. 944, Part 3, p. 8; Cole, *Senator Gerald P. Nye,* 95-96; Wiltz, *In Search of Peace,* 224-227.

[36]"Report . . . on Investigation of the Munitions Industry," No. 944, Part 3, p. 12.

[37]*Ibid.,* 15-17; "Preliminary Report . . . on Investigation of the Munitions Industry," No. 944, Part 1, pp. 11-14; "Report on Government Manufacture of Munitions . . . ," No. 944, Part 7, pp. 1-123; Wiltz, *In Search of Peace,* 91-98, 115-116.

[38]"Preliminary Report . . . on Investigation of the Munitions Industry," No. 944, Part 1, pp. 345-389; "Report on War Department Bills S.1716-S.1722 . . . ," 74 Cong., 2 Sess., No. 944, Part 4, p. 1-46 (direct quotations, 7, 11), 57-61; "Report on Government Manufacture of Munitions . . . ," No. 944, Part 7, pp. 3-64; "To Prevent Profiteering in War," *Senate Report,* 74 Cong., 1 Sess., No. 577 (Serial 9879), 9-20. See also Senate, *Hearings Before the Special Committee Investigating the Munitions Industry,* Parts 13, 14, 15, 16, 17, 21, 22, 24, 36, 37. The Nye Committee was less critical of World War I military procurement practices than an earlier investigation by the so-called Graham Committee. See "War Expenditures," House, *Hearings before the Select Committee on Expenditure in the War Department,* 66 Cong., 1 Sess., Vol. 3, 1921 (Serial 1), [Reports of Committee] ; *ibid.,* Vol. 1, 1921 (Serial 1); *ibid.,* 1920 (Serial 3).

[39]"To Prevent Profiteering in War," No. 577, pp. 1-9, 20-35. See also Senate, *Hearings Before the Special Committee Investigating the Munitions Industry,* Part 22, pp. 6179-6257, 6425-6429, 6643-6648, Part 24, pp. 7087-7112.

[40]Memo on conference on HR 5529, May 24, 1935, File No. 1401, PB ASW Office of the Secretary of War; Planning Branch Orientation Conference, Oct. 27, 1936, pp. 11-12, File No. 010/178.1A, *ibid.;* "IMP," 1936, pp. 99-113, File No. 120, *ibid.*

[41]Senate, *Hearings Before the Special Committee Investigating the Munitions Industry,* Part 22, pp. 6623-6643. See also *ibid.,* 6259-6423.

[42]"Preliminary Report on Wartime Taxation and Price Control," *Senate Report,* 74 Cong., 1 Sess., No. 944, Part 2 (Serial 9882), 1-164 (direct quotation, 3); "Report on War Department Bills S.1716-S.1722 . . . ," No. 944, Part 4, pp. 1-46.

[43]Wiltz, *In Search of Peace,* 119-122, 131-146. For some relevant data on the administration and the Nye Committee, see OF 178, 1934-1935, OF 1672, PPF 1820, Roosevelt Papers.

[44]"Plan for Governmental Organization for War," Nov. 12, 1929, File No. 109, PB ASW Office of the Secretary of War; "IMP," 1936, pp. 14-21, 34-35, File No. 120, *ibid.*; Assistant Secretary of War and Navy to Joint Board and memo of C. T. Harris and W. S. Farber, July 19, 1934, File No. 112, *ibid.*; W. A. Buck to Harry B. Jordan, April 4, 1936, File No. 1401, *ibid.*; H. K. Rutherford at John Hancock Lecture, "Mobilization of Industry," May 27, 1938, File No. 352/109.1, *ibid.*; War Policy Commission, "Hearings," 38, 55-56, 169-190, 288-309, 481-488, 776-790, 854-856; Senate, *Hearings Before the Special Committee Investigating the Munitions Industry,* Part 22, pp. 6281-6282; Thatcher, *Planning for Industrial Mobilization,* 84-91; Kreidberg and Henry, *History of Military Mobilization,* 507-508, 530.

[45]Louis Johnson to Baruch, Sept. 19, 1937, File No. 381/116.4b, PB ASW Office of the Secretary of War; War Department, *Report of the Secretary of War to the President, 1937* (Washington, 1937), 21-25; War Department, *Report of the Secretary . . . 1938,* pp. 19-25; War Department, *Report of the Secretary of War to the President, 1939* (Washington, 1939), 15-20.

[46]Roosevelt to Johnson in Johnson to Roosevelt, Oct. 23, 1937, OF 813, Roosevelt Papers.

[47]Johnson to Roosevelt, Aug. 9, 1939, OF 25, *ibid.*; Charles Hines to John Hancock, July 1, Aug. 11, 1939, Hancock to Hines, July 7, 1939, File No. MB-223-23.1, Records of the Joint Army and Navy Boards and Committees, RG 225 (National Archives); Johnson to Crowell, Aug. 9, 1939, File No. 011/27c, Records of the War Production Board.

[48]Charles W. Wiltse to James W. Fesler, July 19, 1946, File No. 011.2, Records of the War Production Board; "Industrial Mobilization Plan," Senate, *Hearings Before the Special Committee Investigating the National Defense Program,* 80 Cong., 1 Sess., 1948, Part 42, pp. 25662-25669.

[49]War Resources Board (WRB) Minutes, Aug. 17, 1939, pp. 1-2, File No. 011.25, Records of the War Production Board; Wiltse to Fesler, July 19, 1946, File No. 011/2, *ibid.*

[50]Memo. Re: "War Industries [sic] Board," undated, PPF 702, Roosevelt Papers.

[51]Joint Release, war and navy departments, Aug. 17, 1939, WRB Minutes, File No. 011.25, Records of the War Production Board.

[52]"IMP," 1939, File No. 334/117.3, PB ASW Office of the Secretary of War.

[53]WRB Minutes, Aug. 17, 1939, p. 2, Aug. 23-25, 1939, pp. 1, 3-4, Aug. 29-31, 1939, pp. 1-3, Sept. 9, 1939, pp. 1-2, Sept. 13-14, 1939, pp. 1-4, File No. 011.25, Records of the War Production Board; Memo of A. B. Anderson, Sept. 1, 1939, *ibid.*; Rutherford to Edward R. Stettinius, Jr., Sept. 4, 1939, *ibid.*; Wiltse to Fesler, July 19, 1939, File No. 011.2, *ibid.* For the fourteen-page list of the names of individuals selected to staff the mobilization agencies, see File No. 011.27c, *ibid.*

[54]WRB Minutes, Sept. 6, 1939, p. 1, File No. 011.25, Records of the War Production Board. Memo, acting secretary of war and navy to President, Sept. 6, 1939; "Memorandum for Departments and Executive Agencies, Federal Government," from the President, File No. 334/117.3, PB ASW Office of the Secretary of War. These documents were never sent out.

[55]WRB Minutes, Aug. 29-31, 1939, pp. 1-2, Sept. 13-14, 1939, p. 3, File No. 001.25, Records of the War Production Board; Memo. Re: "War Industries [sic] Board," PPF 702, Roosevelt Papers. See also OF 3759, 1939, PPF 5344, PPF 702-H, OF 200XXX, Roosevelt Papers; File No. 011.25, File No. 011.27c, Records of the War Production Board. See also Harold L. Ickes, *The Secret Diary of Harold L. Ickes* (3 vols., New York, 1953-1954), II,

710, 716-720; Albert A. Blum, "Birth and Death of the M-Day Plan," Harold Stein, ed., *American Civil-Military Decisions: A Book of Case Studies* (University, Ala., 1963), 61-96; Eliot Janeway, *The Struggle for Survival: A Chronicle of Economic Mobilization in World War II* (New Haven, 1951), 47-71.

[56]"Report of the War Resources Board," Oct. 13, 1939, File No. 334.117.3, PB ASW Office of the Secretary of War. The Army-Navy Munitions Board (ANMB) was reorganized and strengthened in 1931-1932, and the "IMP" was published by ANMB even though OASW continued to do most of the work.

[57]President to Stettinius and others, Nov. 24, 1939, File No. 370.26/110.B, *ibid.*

[58]Educational orders were intended to help industry and the army through the transitional phase from planning to mobilizing for war. Without the restrictions of competitive bidding, the army could award contracts to selected firms for the limited production of various munitions items. In that way, industry accumulated the tools and worked out the techniques for quantity production and the army tested its munitions designs and procurement plans. Educational orders were first introduced before World War I at the instigation of businessmen and public officials striving to prepare the nation for hostilities. For years after the war, Congress rejected bills authorizing educational orders. Before such legislation was passed in the late 1930s, however, the army interpreted the laws and regulations governing procurement in a way that allowed it to grant some educational orders to selected firms. During the 1930s, the businessmen in the Army Ordnance Association launched a drive for educational orders to help stimulate industrial recovery. See "Investigation of the War Department," Senate, *Hearings Before the Committee on Military Affairs,* 65 Cong., 2 Sess., 1917-1918, pp. 2268-2271; War Department, *Report of the Secretary . . . 1927,* pp. 36-38; War Department, *Report of the Secretary . . . 1928,* p. 57; War Department, *Report of the Secretary . . . 1929,* pp. 47-49, 53-65; War Department, *Report of the Secretary . . . 1932,* pp. 32-34; War Department, *Report of the Secretary . . . 1935,* pp. 34-35; War Department, *Report of the Secretary of War . . . 1938,* pp. 21-25; War Department, *Report of the Secretary . . . 1939,* pp. 15-22; War Department, *Report of the Secretary of War to the President, 1940* (Washington, 1940), 1-10; War Department, *Report of the Secretary of War to the President, 1941* (Washington, 1941), 21-46; Senate, *Hearings Before the Special Committee Investigating the Munitions Industry,* Part 37, pp. 12409-12437, 12502-12526, 12766; "Report . . . on Investigation of the Munitions Industry," No. 944, Part 3, pp. 204-207. See also R. Elberton Smith, *The Army and Economic Mobilization* (Washington, 1959), 61-65; Irvin Brinton Holley, Jr., *Buying Aircraft: Matériel Procurement for the Army Air Forces* (Washington, 1964), 6-193, Edwin H. Rutkowski, *The Politics of Military Aviation Procurement, 1925-1934: A Study in the Political Assertion of Consensual Values* (Columbus, 1966).

[59]War Department, *Report of the Secretary . . . 1940,* p. 10.

[60]Economic mobilization for World War II is treated extensively in Koistinen, "Hammer and the Sword," 553-831.

3. IS THERE A MILITARY-INDUSTRIAL COMPLEX?

Marc Pilisuk and Thomas Hayden

Historical interpretations, like any others, rely in part upon assumptions about what is or is not plausible (or possible) in social relations. A great deal of debate about the military-industrial complex revolves not around data concerning what is actually happening but rather around what is or is not theoretically possible. Thus, for some, facts about cost-overrides in defense contracts, retired military officers on corporate payrolls, and propaganda campaigns waged on behalf of weapons systems are less significant than the assumed pluralistic nature of American society — a pluralism that presumably prevents the parts from ever coming together into a whole.

Much of the historical (and other social science) research since World War II has tended to give American history what the Nixon Administration might call a low profile. Basic conflicts of interest have been denied and our rich diversity has been extolled only within the bounds of basic agreement over fundamentals. The radical sociologist C. Wright Mills insisted, somewhat unfashionably, that power elites not only exist but in fact control important sectors of American life. His seminal work, and that of his critics, is described and evaluated here by Marc Pilisuk and Thomas Hayden.

Source: Marc Pilisuk and Thomas Hayden, "Is There a Military Industrial Complex Which Prevents Peace?: Consensus and Countervailing Power in Pluralistic Systems," *Journal of Social Issues,* XXI, No. 3 (July 1965), 67-117. The complete essay is also reprinted in Perrucci and Pilisuk, *The Triple Revolution* (Boston: Little, Brown, 1968). Reprinted by permission.

INTRODUCTION

The term "military-industrial complex" is very much in the literature. If its most sinister depictions are correct, then the peace researcher who works with the hope that his research may actually improve chances for world peace is wasting his time. A research finding, like a bit of knowledge, is always double-edged in what it portends for application. The project which tells us the surest steps to peace, tells us with equal certainty the steps which must be by-passed if peace is shunned. If there exists an omnipotent elite, committed to militarism, then there is simply no basis for hope that voices for peace have gotten, or can get, an influential channel into inner policy circles. If, on the other hand, the pluralist thesis can be said to apply in full even to basic policy directions of preparedness for war or for peace, then some influential decision makers must be eagerly awaiting the research findings on paths to peace with intentions to press for their immediate application.

Because we agree with neither of the above positions, because we believe that most research workers in this area tend either to ignore or to over-rate the potential consequences of their work to peace, and because we feel that consideration of the conditions which dictate major directions of policy is essential for an evaluation of any contribution to peace research, we are bringing the concept of the "military-industrial complex" to both the microscope and the scalpel. The implications of this inquiry point to a research approach which does have relevance to the decision process and to the most central agencies of social change, and resistance to change, within American society.

THE NEW CONCERN

Not since the 30s has there been such a rash of attention to military-industrial power as there is today. Then, as now, the President himself raised the spectre of improper military influence. FDR, on the eve of a Senate investigation of the munitions industry, said flatly that the arms race was a "grave menace . . . due in no small measure to the uncontrolled activities of the manufacturers and merchants of the engines of destruction and it must be met by the concerted action of the people of all nations." (Raymond, 1964, p. 262; also Congressional Quarterly Weekly Report, 6, 1964, pp. 265-278.) While Dwight Eisenhower did not sound as militant as Roosevelt, and while he never adopted FDR's 1932 campaign pledge to "take the profits out of war," he did resume a popular tradition with his warning about the "unwarranted influence" of the military-industrial complex. It may be a significant measure of the times that one President could make such warnings in his very first campaign for office, while the other couched it among several other going-away remarks.

The 30s serve as a prelude to the 60s, too, in the area of congressional investigation of militarism. Then it was Senator Gerald P. Nye investigating the fabulous World War I profits of U.S. Steel and Hercules Powder and discovering, with horror, the instrumental role of munitions-makers and other commercial interests in beginning the war. Nye revealed, for example, that the American ambassador in London informed President Wilson in 1917 that probably "the only way of maintaining our pre-eminent trade position and averting a panic is by declaring war on Germany" (Raymond, p. 264). As Roosevelt was more aggressive than Eisenhower, so also were Nye, Borah and other popular Senators more aggressive than their present counterparts in the 60s. But, nevertheless, similar issues are now being raised in congressional committees. The most shocking of these may be found in the hearings of Senator John McClellen's committee on *Pyramiding of Profits and Costs in the Missile Procurement Program.* This report pointed out the likely danger that the government "can be placed in the unenviable position of reluctant acquiescence to the demands and conditions set by the contractor," and that "profits were pyramided on other profits without any relationship at all to the effort being expended by those making the profit." In what might have been front page scandal in any area but national defense, the committee documented two mechanisms by which millions upon millions of dollars of excess profit have been reaped by the defense industries. The mechanisms are: (a) claiming profits on work subcontracted to other firms (which in turn subcontract portions of their work to others and charge a profit on the sub-subcontracted work, too), and (b) overestimating the subcontracting costs (on incentive type contracts) thereby reaping huge profit rates by undercutting the original estimates. However, the contrast with the 30s is clear; Senator McClellen only wants to improve the efficiency of what he calls "these necessary monopolies." (U.S. Senate, Committee on Government Operations, report of the Permanent Subcommittee on Investigations, *Pyramiding of Profits and Costs in the Missile Procurement Program,* March 31, 1964.) A more far-reaching investigation, under the direction of Senator Clark, deals with the convertibility of the defense empire to civilian job-creating tasks. He claims that (1) the new defense emphasis on electronics and on research and development, and the monopolization of defense by a few companies and geographic areas, considerably reduces the potential effect of defense as an economic stabilizer; and (2) that certain firms, especially those in the aerospace industry, are suffering an overcapacity crisis that spurs them to insist on more missiles than the nation needs. (U.S. Senate, Committee on Labor and Public Welfare, report of the Subcommittee on Employment and Manpower, *Convertibility of Space and Defense Resources to Civilian Needs: A Search for New Employment Potentials,* 88th Congress, 2d Session, 1964.) Senator Clark's hearings, too, are mild in contrast to the 30s. Even milder, however, was the recent survey report of Senator Hubert Humphrey, who says it is "nonsense" to believe American industry is opposed to disarmament. (U.S. Senate, Committee on Senate Foreign Relations, Subcommittee on Disarmament, *The Economic Impact of Arms Control Agreements,* Congressional Record, October 5, 1962, pp. 2139-2194.)

Another measure of interest in military-industrial power is the number of popular and technical books dealing with the subject. In the 30s, the widely read books were Davenport's *Zaharoff, High Priest of War,* Engelbrecht and Haneghen's *Merchants of Death* and Selde's *Iron, Blood and Profits.* Two decades then passed before the work of C. Wright Mills began to attract broad attention to the subject of organized militarism. Including Mills' pioneering books, there have been at least 21 major books published in this area during the past several years. Many of them are by journalists (Cook, Coffin, Raymond, Swomley, Wise and Ross); some by economists (Benoit, Boulding, Melman, Peck, Perlo, Scherer); sociologists (Etzioni, Horowitz, Janowitz, Mills); political scientists (Meisel, Rogow); novelists (Bailey, Burdick, Knebel, Sutton); and at least one physical scientist (Lapp).

Whatever the objective referent, if any, of a "military-industrial complex" may be, it is undeniable that the concept occupies an important role in the political consciousness of many persons, on a scale without precedent since the 30s. It is a telling fact that the new literature, with the exceptions of Mills, Cook and Perlo, still lacks the bite of the old, and that the proposed solutions are quite "modest." In the 30s a typical popular solution, proposed by the Nye Committee but never implemented, was the nationalization of the munitions industries. By the 60s the reverse has happened; most military research, development, and production is done by private companies subsidized by the Federal government. The loci of military-political-industrial cooperation are so pervasive and frequent that it becomes a hair-splitting task to identify specifically any "merchants of death." Also, the scale of potential destruction has so increased, the nature of warfare strategy so changed, and the existence of the military in peacetime so accepted, that it seems quaint to associate defense contractors with bloody hands. Furthermore, the assumed threat of communist expansion has become the ultimate justification of the post-war military buildup, whereas in the past such buildups could be attributed more clearly to industrial profit and power motives. Probably reasons such as these explain both the long silence and the modest character of the current resurgence in discussion of these matters.

But these reasons account partially for the inadequacy of analysis as well. The question, "Does there exist a military-industrial complex which prevents peace?" at first seems debatable in straightforward yes-or-no terms. Indeed, it might have been answerable in the 20s or 30s but not in the post-war period. When there is permanent intermingling and coordination among military, industrial, and governmental elites, and whenever greater war-preparedness can be justified by reference to the communist movement, it becomes a much "stickier" question. Because it is sticky, the easiest conclusion to support is that a "complex" simply does not exist as an omnipresent obstacle to policy change. Indeed, this belief has become the accepted norm for "informed" discussion of interests vested in the perpetuation of military preparedness. The next most easily supported conclusion would be that we have become trapped in the hell-fires of militarism by a sinister but concealed elite of military-industrial leaders, which through its puppets, pulls the strings on every major policy decision. This latter theory is non-conformist, radical, and smacks too closely of classical conspiracy theory to be palatable to most scholars. Indeed, the dominant attitude (explicit or tacit) in most of the new literature is that there exists no military-industrial complex capable of preventing peace. It is claimed that the military-industrial complex operates as a sub-group within the limits of an essentially civilian society. In this view the complex is seen as making an interest-conscious equation of its own interests with those of the nation as a whole. But, it is argued, this tendency of power aggrandizement is checked by countervailing interest blocks in the society. Moreover, the "complex" is not seen as having a corrosive effect on democratic processes; even if it is conceded that military and technological expertise or well-financed public relations give the "complex" unusual privilege and visibility, this is no different, in principle, from certain other influential groups, all of which are limited by the web of constraints but comprise a pluralist society. Usually, it is added that the internal differences in the "complex" such as differences among the separate services or between the military and the industrial procurement sectors, tend to restrict further its ability to impose a policy "line" on the United States. These points of view appear in scattered form throughout the literature. A few examples are cited to demonstrate this.

Wise and Ross call their brilliantly-rich study of the CIA *The Invisible Government* without realizing the theoretical problems immediately raised by such a title. Does the CIA, and the broader "intelligence community" actually have the tools and, more importantly, the prerogatives of sovereignty (for its own operations) associated with the concept of "government"? If this is the case, then the conventional pluralist argument would be perforated decisively, because it rests on the assumption that no power centers are unaccountable to democratic review. The nature of the evidence used in the book, however, precludes an objective answer to this question. Using case studies primarily, although there also are chapters on the CIA structure, the authors are concerned with such issues as: the contradictions between sinister CIA practices and professed U.S. policy objectives; the tendency of the CIA to support only conservative or reactionary governments; the danger that the CIA can influence specific policy objectives of the U.S. government, as in the case of the U-2 interference with the 1960 Paris summit meeting; the progressive acceptance in America of subversive techniques as part of a "necessary Cold War strategy." But it is explicitly maintained that the "invisible government" is subordinate, at least so far, to the visible one in general as well as in nearly every specific case. At worst, it has an undefined "quasi-independent" status which should be brought under somewhat greater congressional and executive review (p. 352). Also, the authors suggest fewer statements of misinformation and "more discreet silence" by the government "in difficult circumstances" (p. 356). Accepting the broad lines of government policy, but realizing the dilemmas of such a stance, the authors conclude:

The secret intelligence machinery of the government can never be totally reconciled with the tradition of a free republic. But in a time of Cold War, the solution lies not in dismantling this machinery, but in bringing it under greater control. The resultant danger of exposure is far less than the danger of secret power. If we err as a society, let it be on the side of control (356).

New York Times reporter, Jack Raymond, is much less forboding in his *Power at the Pentagon,* but assumes the same framework of government control over the defense establishment. He goes further, however, to point that "the United States could embrace militarism under civilian as well as military auspices." With the same popular democratic values as Wise and Ross (the better journalists remain pugnaciously committed to the civil liberties), he believes that the traditional arguments against military dominance must be broadened to challenge civilian, or bureaucratic, dominance as well.

The military apparatus must not be an automated juggernaut whose operations we take for granted. We ought to raise hell with it constantly, ask questions, demand truthful answers. (334)

This point of view is reflected also in periodic statements by political leaders as disparate as Dwight Eisenhower and Hubert Humphrey. Eisenhower's speech, as mentioned, was instrumental in spurring and legitimizing later discussions. His point of view was that the military-industrial complex might exercise "unwarranted influence":

In the councils of government, we must guard against the acquisition of unwarranted influence, whether sought or unsought, by the military-industrial complex. The potential for the disastrous rise of misplaced power exists and will persist. . . . Only an alert and knowledgeable citizenry can compel the proper meshing of the huge industrial and military machinery of defense with our peaceful methods and goals, so that security and liberty may prosper together. (Eisenhower's Farewell Address)

Humphrey's Subcommittee report claimed that by and large U.S. industries not only could, but would be delighted to shift to full peacetime production of goods and services.[1] According to Humphrey, the military-industrial complex that President Eisenhower warned against "is one which appears to be centered in a few hands and in a few key places." Where Raymond attempted to use fragmentary evidence, mostly personal interviews and citations of particular instances, and Eisenhower cited no evidence at all, Humphrey is more like Wise and Ross in his attempt to generalize from studies of a "slice" of military-industrial organization. That is, even were we to accept his evidence as a valid representation of industrial reality, it still neglects the interrelation of industry with military and political interests. It isolates a part from the whole, then makes claims about the nature of the whole. While extremely interesting and useful, it takes the word of contractors as a valid measure of the desirability and feasibility of conversion. No doubt such words are critically important, but they constitute only a piece of objective reality. It is with such pieces that the existence of an obstructing elite is denied.

Disarmament and the American Economy, edited by Benoit and Boulding, is a collection of essays and studies by several separate individuals. That many of these individuals have connections in the worlds of defense, industry, and government probably reflects the degree to which these worlds command the intellectual resources of modern America. It is a book which received considerable attention in policy-making circles when it appeared last year. It is considerably more lenient in its interpretation of a military-industrial complex, merely pointing out that a few vested interests of long duration are among the structural obstacles to a disarmament pact. These obstacles, according to Emile Benoit, can be overcome rather easily by economic growth in sectors which could more lucratively employ those presently in defense-related work. Prosperity becomes the lubricant for change. But this approach glosses over the existence of propensities to place short-run security over long-run prosperity, and so avoids delineating the kind of political forces which might oppose economic change. As the authors themselves admit, their volume is abstracted from politics. In plainer fact, this abstracting process considerably dissolves any military-industrial complex which might exist. What is left is a pooh-poohing of the threat of a complex, plus the claim that increased overall demand, and therefore new employment opportunities, will make "structural adjustments" manageable:

> [The massive defense complex] does not mean that disarmament is impossible or that the possibilities of peace are threatened by the vested interests of an holy alliance of generals and war contractors. It does mean that to redefine the content of many defense jobs will be a far easier and more constructive solution than to abolish them. (291)

While the authors address themselves only to the question of what the economy can do if disarmament should somehow come about, they are obviously aware of the potential socio-political consequences of removing the threat of the more foreboding economic consequences of disarmament which have sometimes been suggested. Perhaps the authors assume that *only* through a new consensus, sweetened by economic opportunities, can there be a chance for disarmament. That, however, is allowing the problem of social change to be defined by the hope for disarmament. Such an approach may well be a utopian one, and tends to the pole opposite Wise and Ross among the believers in civilian control.

Easily the most well-researched book of this kind is *The Weapons Acquisition Process* by Peck and Scherer, both at Harvard Business School. This book is by and for persons with a sophisticated business viewpoint. After several hundred pages of detailed data and analysis, it concludes that the weapons acquisition process is honest and efficient. However, it too is relatively "above" the politics of the defense economy. Much politics, they find, is ritualistic, with "little impact at the operating levels where the source selection decision is made" (382). Where they believe politics do enter, for instance when competing producers of the Bomarc and Nike-Hercules take out full-page advertisements, they defend its practice. While President Eisenhower warned against the "munitions lobby," in the Bomarc-Nike-Hercules case Peck and Scherer believe that "selling" the Government is symptomatic of a healthy tendency.

> Both contractors and sponsoring agencies, which are often the contractors' allies, believe their weapons programs are essential to the national defense. If this sincerity does not come from pride in invention, it soon develops as a result of constantly living with the idea. This zeal serves a useful function, since it fortifies the participants' . . . personal contact with "the right people" and is an effective means of getting ideas accepted. Similarly, creating public demand for a program through advertising and feature articles is a way of winning over or bypassing balky decision-makers. (243)

This book thus explicitly defends the "advocates" who exaggerate their weapons' capabilities, "whatever the effect of this (military-industrial) complex upon grand strategy" (243).

Whether such salesmanship or advocacy is as ethical as it is effective is a question not raised in the Peck and Scherer book. One of our own interviews with the vice-president of a defense contracting firm specializing in Research and Development, sites the positive ethical value of developing and promoting strategic conceptions of military function (which include the use of the weapon system being worked upon). Such promotion is an absolutely essential buttress to the military services which are incapable of constructing their own strategic doctrines. The system manager concept, a concept used by some prime contractors to justify profit pyramiding, in testimony before the McClellen committee, seems to suggest that promotion of the concept of the entire weapon system is part of the contractor's service to the military and as such is not only ethical but deserving of compensation.

None of these denials of irresponsible military-industrial power marshall very significant evidence to support their views. There are examples given of specific conflicts between civilian and military groups which were lost by the military (e.g., the dropping of General Walker, the refusal to be first to break the moratorium on testing). There are examples given of heated divisions between the services over what military strategy should be pursued (the arguments over conventional warfare in the late 50s and the more recent RS 70 controversy). There are sociological studies which reveal underlying diversities within single corporations, between competing corporations, and within the demographic and institutional character of each branch of the armed services.[2] And, throughout, there are citations of American pluralism as an automatic check system against any elite group.[3]

At a more general level, these fragments of evidence point toward three grounds for denying that a military-industrial complex prevents peace:

1. it is held that the *scope* of decisions made by any interest group is quite narrow and cannot be said to govern anything so broad as foreign policy.

2. it is held that the "complex" is not *monolithic, not self-conscious,* and *not coordinated,* the presumed attributes of a ruling elite.

3. it is held that the military-industrial complex does not wield power if the term "power" is defined as the ability to realize its will even against the resistance of others and regardless of external conditions.

These formulations, to repeat, are made neither explicitly nor consistently in the new literature. But they crystallize the basic questions about definition which the new literature raises. Moreover, they are quite definitely the major contentions made by academic criticisms of power elite theory. The more widely read of these academic critics include Daniel Bell, Robert Dahl, and Talcott Parsons. Since their critiques are mainly directed at the work of C. Wright Mills, it is with Mills that we will begin to analyze the theories which claim there *is* a military-industrial complex blocking peace.

THE THESIS OF ELITE CONTROL

Mills is by far the most formidable exponent of the theory of a power elite. In his view, the period in America since World War II has been dominated by the ascendance of corporation and military elites to positions of institutional power. These "commanding heights" allow them to exercise control over the trends of the business cycle and international relations. The Cold War set the conditions which legitimize this ascendance, and the decline and incorporation of significant left-liberal movements, such as the CIO, symbolizes the end of opposition forces. The power elite monopolizes sovereignty, in that political initiative and control stem mainly from the top hierarchical levels of position and influence. Through the communications system the elite facilitates the growth of a politically indifferent mass society below the powerful institutions. This, according to the Mills argument, would explain why an observer finds widespread apathy. Only a small minority believes in actual participation in the larger decisions which affect their existence and only the ritual forms of "popular democracy" are practiced by the vast majority. Mills' argument addresses itself to the terms of the three basic issues we have designated, i.e., scope of decision power, awareness of common interest, and the definition of power exerted.

By *scope,* we are referring to the sphere of society over which an elite is presumed to exercise power. Mills argues that the scope of this elite is general, embracing all the decisions which in any way could be called vital (slump and boom, peace and war, etc.). He does not argue that *each* decision is directly determined, but rather that the political alternatives from which the "Deciders" choose are shaped and limited by the elite through its possession of all the large-scale institutions. By this kind of argument, Mills avoids the need to demonstrate how his elite is at work during each decision. He speaks instead in terms of institutions and resources. But the problem is that his basic evidence is of a rather negative kind. No major decisions have been made for 20 years contrary to the policies of anti-communism and corporate or military aggrandizement; *therefore* a power elite must be prevailing. Mills might have improved his claims about the scope of elite decisions by analysing a series of actual decisions in terms of the premises which were *not* debated. This could point to the mechanisms (implicit or explicit) which led to the exclusion of these premises from debate. By this and other means he might have found more satisfying evidence of the common, though perhaps tacit, presuppositions of seemingly disparate institutions. He then might have developed a framework analyzing "scope" on different levels. The scope of the Joint Chiefs of Staff, for instance, could be seen as limited, while at the same time the Joint Chiefs could be placed in a larger elite context having larger scope. Whether this could be shown awaits research of this kind. Until it is done, however, Mills theory of scope remains open to attack, but, conversely, is not subject to refutation.

Mills' theory also eludes the traditional requirements for inferring monolithic structure, i.e., consciousness of elite status, and coordination. The modern tradition of viewing elites in this way began with Mosca's *The Ruling Class* in a period when family units and inheritance systems were the basic means of conferring power. Mills departs from this influential tradition precisely because of his emphasis on institutions at the basic elements. If the military, political, and economic *institutional orders* involve a high coincidence of interest, then the groups composing the institutional orders need not be monolithic, conscious, and coordinated, yet still they can exercise elite power.[4] This means specifically that a military-industrial complex could exist as an expression of a certain fixed ideology (reflecting common institutional needs), yet be "composed" of an endless shuffle of specific groups. For instance, our tables show 82 companies have dropped out of the list of 100 top defense contractors, and only 36 "durables" have remained on the list in the years since 1940. In terms of industry, the percentage of contracts going to the automobile industry dropped from 25 percent in World War II to 4 percent in the missile age. At the same time, the aircraft companies went from 34 to 54 percent of all contracts, and the electronics industry from 9 to 28 percent (Peck and Scherer, 1962). Mills' most central argument is that this ebb-and-flow is not necessarily evidence for the pluralists. His stress is on the unities which underlie the procession of competition and change. The decision to change the technology of warfare was one which enabled one group to "overcome" another in an overall system to which both are fundamentally committed. Moreover, the decision issued from the laboratories and planning boards of the defense establishment and only superficially involved any role for public opinion. The case studies of weapons development by Peck and Scherer, in which politics is described as a marginal ritual, would certainly buttress Mills' point of view.

Making this institution analysis enables Mills to make interesting comments on his human actors. The integration of institutions means that hundreds of individuals become familiar with several roles: General, politician, lobbyist, defense contractor. These men are the power elite, but they need not know it. They conspire, but conspiracy is not absolutely essential to their maintenance. They mix together easily, but can remain in power even if they are mostly anonymous to each other. They make decisions, big and small, sometimes with the knowledge of others and sometimes not, which ultimately control all the significant action and resources of society.

Where this approach tends to fall short, is in its unclarity about how discontinuities arise. Is the military-industrial complex a feature of American society which can disappear and still leave the general social structure intact? Horst Brand has suggested a tension between financial companies and the defense industries because of the relatively few investment markets created by defense (1962). Others are beginning to challenge the traditional view that defense spending stimulates high demand and employment. Their claim is that the concentration of contracts in a few states, the monopolization of defense and space industry by the largest 75 or 100 corporations, the low multiplier effect of the new weapons, the declining numbers of blue-collar workers required, and other factors, make the defense economy more of a drag than a stimulant (Melman et al., 1963; Etzioni, 1964). Mills died before these trends became the subject of debate, but he might have pioneered in discussion of them if his analytic categories had differentiated more finely between various industries and interest groups in his power elite. His emphasis was almost entirely on the "need" for a "permanent war economy" just when that need was being questioned even among his elite.

However, this failure does not necessarily undermine the rest of Mills' analysis. His institutional analysis is still the best means of identifying a complex without calling it monolithic, conscious and coordinated. Had he differentiated more exactly he might have been able to describe various degrees of commitment to an arms race, a rightist ideology constricting the arena of meaningful debate, and other characteristics of a complex. This task remains to be done, and will be discussed at a later point.

Where Mills' theory is most awkward is in his assertions that the elite can, and does, make its decisions against the will of others and regardless of external conditions. This way of looking at power is inherited by Mills, and much of modern sociology, directly from Max Weber. What is attributed to the elite is a rather fantastic quality: literal omnipotence. Conversely, any group that is *not* able to realize its will even against the resistance of others is only "influential" but not an elite. Mills attempts to defend this viewpoint but, in essence, modifies it. He says he is describing a tendency, not a finalized state of affairs. This is a helpful device in explaining cracks in the monolith—for instance, the inability of the elite to establish a full corporate state against the will of small businessmen. However, it does not change the ultimate argument—that the power elite cannot become more than a tendency, cannot realize its actual self, unless it takes on the quality of omnipotence.

When power is defined as this kind of dominance, it is easily open to critical dispute. The conception of power depicts a vital and complex social system as essentially static, as having within it a set of stable governing components, with precharted interests which infiltrate and control every outpost of decision-authority. Thereby, internal accommodation is made necessary and significant change, aside from growth, becomes impossible. This conception goes beyond the idea of social or economic determinism. In fact, it defines a "closed social system." A "closed system" may be a dramatic image, but it is a forced one as well. Its defender sees events such as the rise of the labor movement essentially as a means of rationalizing modern capitalism. But true or false as this may be, did not the labor movement also constitute a "collective will" which the elite could not resist? An accommodation was reached, probably more on the side of capital than labor, but the very term "accommodation" implies the existence of more than one independent will. On a world scale, this becomes even more obvious. Certainly the rise of communism has not been through the will of capitalists, and Mills would be the first to agree. Nor does the elite fully control technological development; surely the process of invention has some independent, even if minor, place in the process of social change.

Mills' definition of power as dominance ironically serves the pluralist argument, rather than countering it. When power is defined so extremely, it becomes rather easy to claim that such power is curbed in the contemporary United States. The pluralists can say that Mills has conjured up a bogeyman to explain his own failure to realize his will. This is indeed what has been done in review after review of Mills' writings. A leading pluralist thinker, Edward Shils, says that Mills was too much influenced by Trotsky and Kafka:

> Power, although concentrated, is not so concentrated so powerful, or so permeative as Professor Mills seems to believe. . . . There have been years in Western history, e.g., in Germany during the last years of the Weimer Republic and under the Nazis when reality approximated this picture more closely. . . . But as a picture of Western societies, and not just as an ideal type of extreme possibilities which might be realized if so much else that is vital were lacking, it will not do. (Shils, 1961)

But is Mills' definition the only suitable one here? If it is, then the pluralists have won the debate. But if there is a way to designate an irresponsible elite without giving it omnipotence, then the debate may be recast at least.

This fundamental question is not answered in the other major books which affirm the existence of a military-industrial complex. Cook's *The Warfare State* and Perlo's *Militarism and Industry* are good examples of this literature which is theoretically inferior to Mills' perplexing account.

Cook's volume has been pilloried severely by deniers of the military-industrial complex. At least it has the merit of creating discussion by being one of the few dissenting books distributed widely on a commercial basis. It suffers, however, from many of the same unclarities typical of the deniers. Its title assumes a "warfare state" while its evidence, although rich, is only a compilation of incidents, pronouncements, and trends, lacking any framework for weighing and measuring. From his writing several hypothesis can be extracted about the "face of the Warfare State," all of them suggestive but none of them conclusive: (1) the Department of Defense owns more property than any other organization in the world:[5] (2) between 60 and 70 percent of the national budget is consistently allocated to defense or defense related expenditures: (3) the Military and Big Business join in an inevitable meeting of minds over billions of dollars in contracts the one has to order and the other to fulfill: (4) the 100 top corporations monopolize three-fourths of the contracts, 85 percent of them being awarded without competition; (5) as much as one-third of all production and service indirectly depends on defense; (6) business and other conservative groups, even though outside of the Defense establishment, benefit from the warfare emphasis because it keeps subordinate the welfare-state which is anathema to them (pp. 20-24, 162-202).

Cook's work, much more than Mills' is open to the counter-argument that no monolithic semi-conspiratorial elite exists. Even his definitions of vested interests are crude and presumed. Moreover, he suffers far more than Mills from a failure to differentiate between groups. For instance, there is nothing in his book (written in 1962) which would explain the economic drag of defense spending, which Cook perceptively observed in a *Nation* article, "The Coming Politics of Disarmament" in 1963. One year he wrote that Big Business was being fattened off war contracts, but the next year the "prolonged arms race has started, at last, to commit a form of economic hara-kiri." "Hara-kiri" does not happen spontaneously; it is a culmination of long-developing abnormalities. That Cook could not diagnose them before they became common in congressional testimony illustrates the lack of refinement in his 1962 analysis. Cook's failure lies in visualizing a monolith, which obscures the strains which promote new trends and configurations.

It is in this attention to strains that Perlo's book is useful. He draws interesting connections between the largest industrial corporations and the defense economy, finding that defense accounts for 12 percent of the profits of the 25 largest firms. He adds the factor of foreign investment as one which creates a further propensity in favor of a large defense system, and he calculates that military business and foreign investments combined total 40 percent of the aggregate profits among the top 25. He draws deeper connections between companies and the major financial groups controlling their assets.

This kind of analysis begins to reveal important disunities within the business community. For instance, it can be seen that the Rockefellers are increasing their direct military investments while maintaining their largest foreign holdings in extremely volatile Middle Eastern and Latin American companies. The Morgans are involved in domestic industries of a rather easy-to-convert type, and their main foreign holdings are in the "safer" European countries, although they too have "unsafe" mining interests in Latin America and Africa. The First National City Bank, while having large holdings in Latin American sugar and fruit, has a more technical relation to its associated firms than the stock-owner relation. The Mellons have sizeable oil holdings on Kuwait, but on the whole are less involved in defense than the other groups. The DuPonts, traditionally the major munitions makers, are "diversified" into the booming aerospace and plutonium industries, but their overseas holdings are heavily in Europe. Certain other groups with financial holdings, such as Young and Eaton interests in Cleveland, have almost no profit stake in defense or foreign investments. On the other hand, some of the new wealth in Los Angeles is deeply committed to the aerospace industry.

Perlo makes several differentiations of this sort, including the use of foreign-policy statements by leading industrial groups. But he does not have a way to predict under what conditions a given company would actively support economic shifts away from the arms race. These and other gaps, however, are not nearly as grave as his lack of analysis of other components of the military-industrial complex.[6] There is no attempt to include politicians, military groups and other forces in a "map" of the military-industrial complex which Perlo believes exists. This may be partly because of the book's intent, which is to document profiteering by arms contractors, but for whatever reason, the book is not theoretically edifying about the question we are posing. Nor does it refute the pluralist case. In fact, it contains just the kind of evidence that pluralist arguments currently employ to demonstrate the absence of a monolith.

REVISING THE CRITERIA FOR INFERRING POWER

After finding fault with so many books and divergent viewpoints, the most obvious conclusion is that current social theory is currently deficient in its explanation of power. We concur with one of Mills' severest critics, Daniel Bell, who at least agrees with Mills that most current analysis concentrates on the "intermediate sectors," e.g., parties, interest groups, formal structures, without attempting to view the underlying system of "renewable power independent of any momentary group of actors" (Bell, 1964). However, we have indicated that the only formidable analysis of the underlying system of renewable power, that of Mills, has profound shortcomings because of its definition of power. Therefore, before we can offer an answer of our own to the question, "Is there a military-industrial complex which blocks peace?," it is imperative to return to the question of power itself in American society.

We have agreed essentially with the pluralist claim that ruling-group models do not "fit" the American structure. We have classified Mills' model as that of a ruling-group because of his Weberian definition of power, but we have noted also that Mills successfully went beyond two traps common to elite theories, *viz.,* that the elite is total in the scope of its decisions, and that the elite is a coordinated monolith.

But we perhaps have not stressed sufficiently that the alternative case for pluralism is inadequate in its claim to describe the historical dynamics of American society. The point of our dissent from pluralism is over the doctrine of "counter-vailing power." This is the modern version of Adam Smith's economics and of the Madisonian or Federalism theory of checks-and-balances, adapted to the new circumstances of large-scale organization. Its evidence is composed of self-serving incidents and a faith in semi-mystical resources. For instance, in the sphere of political economy, it is argued that oligopoly contains automatic checking mechanisms against undue corporate growth, and that additionally, the factors of "public opinion" and "corporate conscience" are built-in limiting forces.[7] We believe that evidence in the field, however, suggests that oligopoly is a means of stabilizing an industrial sphere either through tacit agreements to follow price leadership or rigged agreements in the case of custom-made goods; that "public opinion" tends much more to be manipulated and apathetic than independently critical; that "corporate conscience" is less suitable as a description than Reagan's terms, "corporate arrogance."

To take the more immediate example of the military sphere, the pluralist claim is that the military is subordinate to broader, civilian interests. The first problem with the statement is the ambiguity of "civilian." Is it clear that military men are more "militaristic" than civilian men? To say so would be to deny the increasing trend of "white-collar militarism." The top strategists in the Department of Defense, the Central Intelligence Agency and the key advisory positions often are Ph.D.'s. In fact, "civilians" including McGeorge Bundy, Robert Kennedy, James Rostow and Robert McNamara are mainly responsible for the development of the only remaining "heroic" form of combat: counter-insurgency operations in the jungles of the underdeveloped countries. If "militarism"[8] has permeated this deeply into the "civilian" sphere, then the distinction between the terms becomes largely nominal. Meisel's description is imaginative and alluring:

> What we still honor with the name of peace is only the domestic aspect of a world-wide industrial mobilization let up at intervals by the explosions of a shooting war. . . . The industrial revolution in its class-struggle aspect is becoming externalized, projected upon the industrial field, that it is being relegated, so to speak, from barricade to barracks. . . . The armies, navies, and air forces of our time [are] the embodiment of the industrial revolution in its aggressive form (Meisel, 1962, pp. 157-158).

While the more traditional military men have not taken kindly to the takeover of military planning by civilian professors, the takeover has, none-the-less, gone far. More than 300 universities and non-profit research institutions supply civilian personnel to, and seek contracts from, the Department of Defense. Approximately half of these institutions were created specifically to do specialized strategic research. Probably the most influential of the lot of these civilian centers is the Rand Corporation.

Consistent with its Air Force origins, Rand's civilian army of almost 1,000 professional researchers and supporting personnel derives most of its support from Air Force Project Rand Studies. Rand charges the Air Force 6 percent of the estimated cost of the contracts which the Air Force farms out to private industry as a result of work done at Rand. This brings the Air Force contribution to Rand to over 80 percent where it has been for the past few years. When a large Ford Foundation Grant permitted Rand's reorganization in May of 1948, the organization was granted virtual autonomy from the Air Force and from Douglas Aviation which were its original parents. Such autonomy seemed necessary both to draw independent intellectuals into the establishment and to promote the image of objectivity in its research. The charter establishes a non-profit corporation to "further and promote scientific, educational and charitable purposes, all for the public welfare and security of the United States of America." The actual measure of Rand autonomy should not be taken solely from its dependence upon Air Force money. In actual practice, Rand scholars have differed with the Air Force and on issues quite important to the Air Force. The turns of the cold war strategies from massive retaliation through finite deterrence and limited war, through counter-force, and on into controlled response had never, until 1961 and 1962 involved major reductions in any type of weaponry other than the post Korean War automotive cutbacks. Automotives were, however, a largely civilian market industry. The first place where the strategic innovations served not only to rationalize existing weaponry (in the more specialized defense industry) or to call for accelerated development in additional areas, but also to call for "cost effectiveness" or cutting back in a favored weapon area, came at the expense of the Air Force. In short order the Skybolt and the RS 70 met their demise. For a time, Harvard economist Charles Hitch (then with Rand, now Defense Department comptroller) and perhaps the entire battalion of systems analysts at Rand were personally unpopular with Air Force brass. The Air Force was particularly incensed over the inclination and ability of Rand personnel to consult directly with the Defense Department and bypass the Air Force. Rand, incidentally, maintains a permanent Washington office with facilitates such confrontation. This is not exactly what Air Force spokesmen intend when they see Rand serving the function of giving "prestige type support for favored Air Force proposals to the Department of Defense and the Congress" (Friedman, 1963). The controversy shows that there is obviously no monolithic influence in defense policy. It shows also that civilian and military factions are involved and that, in this instance, even the combined influential interests of traditional Air Force leaders and industrial aircraft contractors could not hold sway over the civilian analysts. The case also illustrates the weakness of the pluralist argument. The controversy, involving sums of money exceeding the total requested for President Johnson's war on poverty, did not threaten to starve either the Air Force or the aircraft industries. Indeed, it was a controversy among family members all sharing the same source of income and the same assumptions regarding the need for maximal military strength in the cold war.

While Rand scientists played the role of civilian efficiency experts in this particular controversy, Rand experts have clearly played the role of military expansionists in civilian clothing at other times. Albert Wohlstetter and Herbert Dinerstein, Rand experts on military strategy and Soviet policy, deserve major credits for the creation of the mythical "missile gap" and for the equally unreal-preemptive war strategy for the Soviet Union during the period from Sputnik, in October of 1957, until the issue if inadequate military preparedness helped bring the New Frontier to Washington. Among the possible consequences of the U.S. missile buildup to overcome the mythical gap may well have been the Soviet resumption of nuclear tests in defiance of the moratorium, an act which completed a rung of the spiralling arms race which in turn nourishes all factions, civilian and military, who are engaged in military preparedness. We do not wish to labor the point that Rand experts have, at times, allowed the assumptions of their own ideology to form the basis of their rational analyses of Soviet capability and intentions. The point we wish to stress here is merely that the apparent flourishing of such civilian agencies as Rand (it earned over 20 million dollars in 1962 with all the earnings going into expansion and has already spawned the non-profit Systems Development Corporation with annual earnings exceeding 50 million dollars) is no reflection of countervailing power. The doctrine of controlled response under which the RS 70 fell was one which served the general aspirations of each of the separate services; of the Polaris and Minuteman stabile deterrent factions, of the brushfire or limited war proponents, guerrilla war and paramilitary operations advocates, and of the counterforce adherents. It is a doctrine of versatility intended to leave the widest range of military options for retaliation and escalation in U.S. hands. It can hardly be claimed as victory against military thought. The fighting may have been intense but the area of consensus between military and civilian factions was great.

The process of "civilianizing" the military is not restricted to the level of attitudes but extends to the arena of social interaction. Traditionally, the military has been a semi-caste quite apart from the mainstream of American life. But that changed with World War II; as Mills points out:

> Unless the military sat in on corporate decisions, they would not be sure that their programs would be carried out; and unless the corporation chieftains knew something of the war plans, they could not plan war production . . . the very organization of the economics of war made for the coincidence of interest and the political mingling among economic and military chiefs (Mills, 1965, p. 212).

One relatively early statement (January, 1944), by Charles E. Wilson, shows that the intermeshing of military and industrial leaders was, at least on the part of some, a self-conscious and policy-oriented enterprise. Wilson proposed a permanent war economy led by the Commander and Chief, and the War Department in cooperation with an industrial partner whose response and cooperation must be free from such political accusations as the "merchants of death" label. The program would not be a creature of emergency but rather an interminable measure to eliminate emergencies. "The role of Congress," Wilson added, "is limited to voting the funds" (Swomley, 1959). Now, twenty years later we can report a personal interview with a mid-western Congressman, a fourteen-year veteran, suggesting some truth to Wilson's projection.

It is not possible for a congressman to know, according to veteran Congressman George Meader, whether defense cutbacks are feasible. The whole area is very complicated and technical and congress has very few military experts in its membership or on its research staffs. When budget time comes about the Department of Defense sends literally hundreds of experts to report before committee hearings. We have to take the word of the people who know. This paraphrased statement regarding the rubber stamping of more than 60 percent of the national budget was made by a congressman who claims a perfect record in opposition to the growth of governmental bureaucracy and to federal spending. If we were to examine the dozen or so congressional "experts" to whom Congressman Meader makes reference we find among them a number of high ranking reserve officers and a number representing districts or states economically dependent upon either military bases, or defense contracts, or both.

The same kind of planning requirements for modern war forced an overlapping of politicians with military and businessmen. There too, the very nature of world war, and especially cold war, integrated military, political and economic concepts of strategy, making the military officer much more than a cog. A variety of recent studies demonstrate the outcome of these developments. The 1959 hearings and survey by the House Armed Services Subcommittee disclosed that over 1,400 retired officers with the rank of major or higher (including 261 of general or flag rank) were in the employ of the top 100 defense contractors (Hébert Subcommittee of the House Armed Services Committee, 1959). Coffin listed 74 Senators and Representatives with continuing status in the armed forces (Coffin, 1964). By 1957, 200 active (not reserve) generals or admirals were on assignment to "non-military" departments of the government or to international or interservice agencies. An added 1,300 colonels or naval officers of comparable rank, and 6,000 lower grade officers were similarly assigned (Swomley, 1959). Janowitz studied an historical sample of over 760 generals and admirals, administered questionnaires to about 600 current Pentagon staff officers, and interviewed 113 career officers. He found an "elite in transition" toward civilian and managerial habits: (1) the basis of authority and discipline is changing from authoritarian domination to greater reliance on manipulation, persuasion and group consensus; (2) the skill differential between civilians and soldiers is narrowing because of the need for technical specialties in the military; (3) officers are being recruited from a broader status and class base, reflecting the demand for more specialists; (4) the source of prestige recognition is hifting from military circles to the public at large; (5) this growth makes the officer define himself more and more as a political, rather than a technical, person with concerns about national security concepts and affairs (Janowitz, 1960, pp. 3-16, 442-452). These trends clearly demonstrate that the traditional American separation of military and civilian is outmoded. The new, blurred reality has not been successfully defined.

The main point here is that the pluralist argument relies on "counter-vailing forces" which are more mythical than real. The Wise and Ross book shows indisputably that at least during certain instances the Executive is not counter-vailing the CIA. Moreover, who is counter=vailing the "military-civilian" Executive centered in the Pentagon and the White House? What Knorr sees as a "peacefare state" counter-vailing the "warfare state" is merely its white-collar brother. The symbolic figure of the Arms Control and Disarmament Agency demonstrates this reality vividly. One side of the ACDA figure is a diplomat with tie and attaché case; the other side is a warrior dedicated to the pursuit of stabilizing control measures which might assure national advantages in a never ending cold war.

ACDA's narrow conception of its own role is as much a function of its internal quest for respectability as it is a matter of the prerogatives given it by a reluctant Congress. It has sought respectability not only in its apparent choice of essentially technical questions for study but also in its manner of study. One favored study technique is to collapse large socially significant questions into several questions answerable by short-term studies and suited for study by the grossly oversimplified techniques of policy appraisal employed by those same operations research corporations which serve, and live upon, defense contracts. These organizations have traditionally produced quick answers embedded in rationalistic models which ring with scientism and jargon. *Strategy and Conscience,* a powerfully written book by Anatol Rapoport, documents the manner in which the rationalist models employed in such strategic studies frequently conceal (often unknowingly) gross assumptions of the nature of the cold war. The point here is that if these are the same assumptions which necessitate a high level of military preparedness, then it matters little whether the studies are commissioned by civilian or military authorities.

CONSENSUS

All that counter-vailing power refers to is the relationship between groups who fundamentally accept "the American system" but who compete for advantages within it. The corporate executive wants higher profits, the laborer a higher wage. The President wants the final word on military strategies, the Chairman of the Joint Chiefs does not trust him with it. Boeing wants the contract, but General Dynamics is closer at the time to the Navy Secretary and the President, and so on: what is prevented by counter-vailing forces is the dominance of society by a group or clique or a party. But this process suggests a profoundly important point; that *the constant pattern in American society is the rise and fall of temporarily-irresponsible groups.* By temporary we mean that, outside of the largest industrial conglomerates,[9] the groups which wield significant power to influence policy decisions are not guaranteed stability. By irresponsible we mean that there are many activities within their scope which are essentially unaccountable in the democratic process. These groups are too uneven to be described with the shorthand term "class." Their personnel have many different characteristics (compare IBM executives and the Southern Dixiecrats) and their needs as groups are different enough to cause endless fights as, for example, small vs. big businesss. No one group or coalition of several groups can tyrannize the rest as is demonstrated, for example, in the changing status of the major financial groups, particularly the fast-rising Bank of America which has been built from the financial needs of the previously-neglected small consumer.

However, it is clear that these groups exist within consensus relationships of a more general and durable kind than their conflict relationships. This is true, first of all, of their social characteristics. The tables which follow combine data from Suzanne Keller's compilation of military, economic, political and diplomatic elite survey materials in *Beyond the Ruling Class* (1963) and from an exhaustive study of American elites contained in Warner et al., *The American Federal Executive* (1963). Data on elites vary slightly from study to study because of varying operational definitions of the elite population. However, the data selected here are fairly representative and refer exclusively to studies with major data collected within the decade of the fifties. (See tables.)

The relevant continuities represented in this data suggest an educated elite with an emphasis upon Protestant and business-oriented origins. Moreover, the data suggest inbreeding with business orientation in backgrounds likely to have been at least maintained, if not augmented, through marriage. The consistencies suggest orientations not unlike those which are to be found in examination of

Table 3.1 SOCIAL CHARACTERISTICS OF AMERICAN ELITES

Elite	Nativity percent foreign born	Rural-Urban percent urban born[1]	Religion percent Protestant	Education percent college grads.
Military	2%	30-40%[3]	90	73-98%[3]
Economic	6	65	85	61
Political	2	48	81	91
Diplomatic	4	66	60	81
U.S. adult males	7[2]	42[4]	65	7[2]

[1]Towns of 2500 or more.
[2]30 years of age and older.
[3]Taking the services separately.
[4]1910 U.S. Population.
The majority of foreign-born and second-generation come from Northwestern Europe. The proportion of foreign-born from these areas is significantly lower for the general male population.
The difference between "political" and "diplomatic" and "economic" indicated that Congress, in the 1950's was more conservative—especially in its small business and non-integrationist attitudes—than the federal executive or the corporation leaders. The sharp difference between "military" and the rest lumps military policymakers with lower level personnel, thus underemphasizing the new trend cited by Janowitz.

Table 3.2 FATHER'S OCCUPATION

	Civilian federal executives	Military executives	Business leaders	Total U.S. male pop. 1930
Unskilled laborer	4%	2%	5%	33%
Skilled laborer	17	12	10	15
White-collar (clerk or sales)	9	9	8	12
Foreman	5	5	3	2
Business owner	15	19	26	7
Business executive	15	15	23	3
Professional	19	18	14	4
Farm owner or manager	14	9	8	16
Farm tenant or worker	1	1	1	6
Other	1	1	2	2

editorial content of major business newspapers and weeklies and in more directly sampled assessments of elite opinions.[10]

The second evidence of consensus relationships, besides attitude and background data indicating a pro-business sympathy, would come from an examination of the *practice* of decision making. By analysis of such actual behavior we can understand which consensus attitudes are reflected in decision-making. Here, in retrospect, it is possible to discover the values and assumptions which are defended recurrently. This is at least a rough means of finding the boundaries of consensus relations. Often these boundaries are invisible because of the very infrequency with which they are tested. What are visible most of the time are the parameters of conflict relationships among different groups. These conflict relationships constitute the ingredients of experience which give individuals or groups their uniqueness and varieties, while the consensus relations constitute the common underpinnings of behavior. The tendency in social science has been to study decision-making in order to study group differences; we need to study decision-making also to understand group commonalities.

Were such studies done, our hypothesis would be that certain "core beliefs" are continuously unquestioned. One of these, undoubtedly, would be that efficacy is preferable to principle in foreign affairs. In practice, this means that violence is preferable to non-violence as a means of defense. A second is that private property is preferable to collective property. A third assumption is that the particular form of constitutional government, which is practiced within the United States is preferable to any other system of government. We refer to the preferred mode as limited parliamentary democracy, a system in which institutionalized forms of direct representation are carefully retained but with fundamental limitations placed upon the prerogatives of governing. Specifically included among the areas of limitation are many matters encroaching upon corporation property and state hegemony. While adherence to this form of government is conceivably the strongest of the domestic "core values," at least among business elites, it is probably the least strongly held of the three on the international scene. American relations with, and assistance for, authoritarian

Table 3.3 BUSINESS AND EXECUTIVE ORIGINS OF WIVES OF ELITES

	Political executives		Foreign-service executives		Military executives		Civilian federal executives		Business leaders	
	Father	Spouse's father	Father	Spouse's father	Father	Spouse's father	Father	Spouse's father	Father	Spouse's father
Minor executive	10%	10%	11%	11%	15%	12%	11%	11%	11%	7%
Major executive	6	5	9	9	5	7	4	4	15	8
Business owner	21	25	19	24	19	22	20	23	26	28
Professional	24	19	25	23	18	19	19	16	14	15
Military executive					9	11				

and semi-feudal regimes occurs exactly in those areas where the recipient regime is evaluated primarily upon the two former assumptions and given rather extensive leeway on the latter one.

The implications of these "core beliefs" for the social system are immense, for they justify the maintenance of our largest institutional structures: the military, the corporate economy, and a system of partisan politics which protects the concept of limited democracy. These institutions, in turn, may be seen as current agencies of the more basic social structure. We use the term "social structure" as Robert S. Lynd does as the stratification of people identified according to kinship, sex, age, division of labor, race, religion, or other factors which differentiate them in terms of role, status, access to resources, and power. According to Lynd:

> This structure established durable relations that hold groups of people together for certain purposes and separate them for others. Such social structures may persist over many generations. Its continuance depends upon its ability to cope with historical changes that involve absorption of new groupings and relations of men without fundamental change in the structure of the society of a kind that involves major transfer of power (Lynd, 1959).

The "renewable basis of power" in America at the present time underlies those institutional orders linked in consensus relationships: military defense of private property and parliamentary democracy. These institutional orders are not permanently secure, by definition. Their maintenance involves a continuous coping with new conditions, such as technological innovation and with the inherent instabilities of a social structure which arbitrarily classifies persons by role, status, access to resources, and power. The myriad groups composing these orders are even less secure because of their weak ability to command "coping resources," e.g., the service branches are less stable than the institution of the military, particular companies are less stable than the institutions of corporate property, political parties are less stable than the institution of parliamentary government.

In the United States there is no ruling group. Nor is there any easily discernible ruling institutional order, so meshed have the separate sources of elite power become. But there is a social structure which is organized to create and protect power centers with only partial accountability. In this definition of power we are avoiding the Weber-Mills meaning of *omnipotence* and the contrary pluralist definition of power as consistently *diffuse.* We are describing the current system as one of overall "minimal accountability" and "minimal consent." We mean that the role of democratic review, based on genuine popular consent, is made marginal and reactive. Elite groups are minimally accountable to publics and have a substantial, though by no means maximum, freedom to shape popular attitudes. The reverse of our system would be one in which democratic participation would be the orienting demand around which the social structure is organized.

Some will counter this case by saying that we are measuring "reality" against an "ideal," a technique which permits the conclusion that the social structure is undemocratic according to its distance from our utopian values. This is a convenient apology for the present system, of course. We think it possible, at least in theory, to develop measures of the undemocratic in democratic conditions, and place given social structures along a continuum. These measures, in rough form, might include such variables as economic security, education, legal guarantees, access to information, and participatory control over systems of economy, government, and jurisprudence.

The reasons for our concern with democratic process in an article questioning the power of a purported military-industrial complex are twofold. First, just as scientific method both legitimizes and promotes change in the world of knowledge, democratic method legitimizes and promotes change in the world of social institutions. Every society, regardless of how democratic, protects its core institutions in a web of widely shared values. But if the core institutions should be dictated by the requisites of military preparedness, then restrictions on the democratic process, i.e., restrictions in either mass opinion exchange (as by voluntary or imposed news management) or in decision-making bodies (as by selection of participants in a manner guaranteeing exclusion of certain positions), then such restrictions would be critical obstacles to peace.

Second, certain elements of democratic process are inimical to features of militarily oriented society, and the absence of these elements offers one type of evidence for a military-industrial complex even in the absence of a ruling elite. Secretary of Defense Robert McNamara made the point amply clear in his testimony in 1961 before the Senate Armed Services Committee:

> Why should we tell Russia that the Zeus development may not be satisfactory? What we ought to be saying is that we have the most perfect anti-ICBM system that the human mind will ever devise. Instead the public domain is already full of statements that the Zeus may not be satisfactory, that it has deficiencies. I think it is absurd to release that level of information. (Military Procurement Authorization Fiscal Year 1962)

Under subsequent questioning McNamara attempted to clarify his statement that he only wished to delude Russian, not American, citizens about U.S. might. Just how this might be done was not explained.

A long established tradition exists for "executive privilege" which permits the President to refuse to release information when, in his opinion, it would be damaging to the national interest. Under modern conditions responsibility for handling information of a strategic nature is shared among military, industrial, and executive agencies. The discretion regarding when to withhold what information must also be shared. Moreover, the existence of a perpetual danger makes the justification, "in this time of national crisis" suitable to every occasion in which secrecy must be justified. McNamara's statement cited above referred not to a crisis in Cuba or Viet Nam but rather to the perpetual state of cold war crisis. And since the decision about what is to be released and when, is subject to just such management the media became dependent upon the agencies for timely leaks and major stories. This not only adds an aura of omniscience to the agencies, but gives these same agencies the power to reward "good" journalists and punish the critical ones.

The issues involved in the question of news management involve more than the elements of control available to the President, the State Department, the Department of Defense, the Central Intelligence Agency, the Atomic Energy Commission or any of the major prime contractors of defense contracts. Outright control of news flow is probably less pervasive than voluntary acquiescence to the objectives of these prominent institutions of our society. Nobody has to tell the wire services when to release a story on the bearded dictator of our hemisphere or the purported brutality of Ho Chi Minh. A frequent model, the personified devil image of an enemy, has become a press tradition. In addition to a sizeable quantity of radio and television programming and spot time purchased directly by the Pentagon, an amount of service, valued at $6 million by *Variety,* is donated annually by the networks and by public relations agencies for various military shows (Swomley, 1959). Again, the pluralistic shell of an independent press or broadcasting media is left hollow by the absence of a counter-vailing social force of any significant power.

The absence of a counter-vailing force for peace cannot, we have claimed, be demonstrated by an absence of conflicting interests among powerful sectors of American society. Indeed, such conflicts are ever-present examples of American pluralism. Demonstrating the absence of a discussion of the shared premises, among the most potent sectors of society, would go far in highlighting the area of forced or acquiescent consensus. But even the absence of debate could not complete the case unless we can show how the accepted premises are inconsistent with requisites of a viable peace-time social system. It is to this question: of the compatibility of the unquestioned assumptions of American society with conditions of peace, that we now turn. The "core beliefs" which we listed as unchallenged by any potent locus of institutionalized power are:

1. Efficacy is preferable to principle in foreign affairs (thus military means are chosen over non-violent means);

2. Private property is preferable to public property; and

3. Limited parliamentary democracy is preferable to any other system of government.

What characteristics of a continuing world system devoid of military conflict fly in the face of these assumptions?

We identify three conditions for enduring peace which clash with one or more of the core beliefs. These are: (1) the requirements for programming an orderly transition and the subsequent maintenance of a non-defense economy within a highly automated and relatively affluent society; (2) the conditions for peaceful settlement of internal disputes within underdeveloped countries and between alien nations and commercial interests; and (3) the conditions under which disparities in living standards between have and have-not nations can be handled with minimum violence.

If one pools available projections regarding the offset programs, especially regional and local offset programs, necessary to maintain economic well-being in the face of disarmament in this country, the programs will highlight two important features. One is the lag time in industrial conversion. The second is the need for coordination in the timing and spacing of programs. One cannot reinvest in new home building in an area which has just been deserted by its major industry and left a ghost town. The short-term and long-term offset values of new hospitals and educational facilities will differ in the building and the utilization stages and regional offset programs have demonstrable interregional effects (Reiner, 1964). Plans requiring worker mobility on a large scale will require a central bank for storing job information and a smooth system for its dissemination. Such coordination will require a degree of centralization of controls beyond the realm which our assumption regarding primacy of private property would permit.

Gross intransigence can be expected on this issue. Shortly after Sperry Rand on Long Island was forced to make major cutbacks of its professional and engineering staff to adapt to the termination of certain defense contracts, the union approached Sperry's management with the prospect of collaborating in efforts to commence contingency plans for diversification. The response, by Carl A. Frische, President of Sperry Gyroscope, a division of Sperry Rand, remains a classic. There must be no "government-controlled mechanisms under the hood of the economy." He suggested, with regard to such planning, that "we let Russia continue with that." (*Long Island Sunday Press,* February 23, 1964.) Sperry is an old-timer in defense production. Its board of directors average several years older than the more avant garde board of directors of, say, General Dynamics. But the prospect of contingency planning will be no more warmly welcomed in the newer aeroframe industry (which is only 60 percent convertible to needs of a peace-time society), (McDonagh and Zimmerman, 1964). Private planning, by an individual firm for its own future does occur, but, without coordinated plans, the time forecast for market conditions remains smaller than the lag time for major retooling. A lag time of from six to ten years would not be atypical before plans by a somewhat over-specialized defense contractor could result in retooling for production in a peace-time market. In the meantime, technological innovations, governmental fiscal or regulatory policies, shifts in consumer preferences, or the decisions by other firms to enter that same market could well make the market vanish. Moreover, the example of defense firms which have attempted even the smaller step toward diversification presents a picture which has not been entirely promising (Fearon and Hook, 1964). Indeed, one of several reasons for the failures in this endeavor has been that marketing skills necessary to compete in a private enterprise economy have been lost by those industrial giants who have been managing with a sales force of one or two retired generals to deal with the firm's only customer. Even if the path of successful conversion by some firms were to serve as the model for all individual attempts, the collective result would be poor. To avoid a financially disastrous glutting of limited markets some coordinated planning will be needed.

The intransigence regarding public or collaborative planning occurs against a backdrop of a soon-to-be increasing army of unemployed youth and aged, as well as regional armies of unemployed victims of automation. Whether one thinks of work in traditional job market terms or as anything worthwhile that a person can do with his life, work (and some means of livelihood) will have to be found for these people. There is much work to be done in community services, education, public health, and recreation, but this is people work, not product work. The lack of a countervailing force prevents the major reallocation of human and economic resources from the sector defined as preferable by the most potent institutions of society. One point must be stressed. We are not saying that limited planning to cushion the impact of arms reduction is impossible. Indeed, it is going on and with the apparent blessing of the Department of Defense (Barber, 1963). We are saying that the type of accommodation needed by a cutback of $9 billion in R&D and $16 billion in military procurement requires a type of preparation not consistent with the unchallenged assumptions.

Even the existence of facilities for coordinated planning does not, to be sure, guarantee the success of such planning. Bureaucratic institutions, designed as they may be for coordination and control, do set up internal resistance to the very coordination they seek to achieve. The mechanisms for handling these bureaucratic intransigencies usually rely upon such techniques as bringing participants into the process of formulating the decisions which will affect their own behavior. We can conceive of no system of coordinated conversion planning which could function without full and motivated cooperation from the major corporations, the larger unions, and representatives of smaller business and industry. Unfortunately, it is just as difficult to conceive of a system which would assure this necessary level of participation and cooperation. This same argument cuts deeper still when we speak of the millions of separate individuals in the "other America" whose lives would be increasingly "administered" with the type of centralized planning needed to offset a defense economy. The job assignment which requires moving, the vocational retraining program, the development of housing projects to meet minimal standards, educational enrichment programs, all of the programs which are conceived by middle-class white America for racially mixed low income groups, face the same difficulty in execution of plans. Without direct participation in the formulation of the programs, the target populations are less likely to participate in the programs and more likely to continue feelings of alienation from the social system which looks upon them as an unfortunate problem rather than as contributing members. Considering the need for active participation in real decisions, every step of coordinated planning carries with it the responsibility for an equal step in the direction of participatory democracy. This means that the voice of the unemployed urban worker may have to be heard, not only on city council meetings which discuss policy on the control of rats in his dwelling, but also on decisions about where a particular major corporation will be relocated and where the major resource allocations of the country will be invested. That such decision participation would run counter to the consensus on the items of limited parliamentary democracy and private property is exactly the point we wish to make.

Just as the theoretical offset plans can be traced to the sources of power with which they conflict, so too can the theoretical plans for international governing and peace-keeping operations be shown to conflict with the unquestioned beliefs. U.S. consent to international jurisdiction in the settlement of claims deriving from the nationalization of American overseas holdings or the removal of U.S. military installations is almost inconceivable. Moreover, the mode of American relations to less-developed countries is so much a part of the operations of those American institutions which base their existence upon interminable conflict with Communism that the contingency in which the U.S. might have to face the question of international jurisdiction in these areas seems unreal. Offers to mediate, with Cuba by Mexico, with North Viet Nam by France, are bluntly rejected. Acceptance of such offers would have called into question not one but all three of the assumptions in the core system. International jurisdictional authority could institutionalize a means to call the beliefs into question. It is for this reason (but perhaps most directly because of our preference for forceful means) that American preoccupation in those negotiations regarding the extension of international control which have taken place, deal almost exclusively with controls in the area of weaponry and police operations and not at all in the areas of political or social justice.[11]

The acceptance of complete international authority even in the area of weaponry poses certain inconsistencies with the preferred "core beliefs." Non-violent settlement of Asian-African area conflicts would be slow and ineffective in protecting American interests. The elimination, however, of military preparedness, both for projected crises and for their potential escalation, requires a faith in alternate means of resolution. The phasing of the American plan for general and complete disarmament is one which says in effect: prove that the alternatives are as efficient as our arms in protection of our interests and then we disarm. In the short term, however, the effectiveness of force always looks greater.

The state of world peace contains certain conditions imposed by the fact that people now compare themselves with persons who have more of the benefits of industrialization than they themselves. Such comparative reference groups serve to increase the demand for rapid change. While modern communications heighten the pressures imposed by such comparisons, the actual disparities revealed in comparison speak for violence. Population growth rates, often as high as three percent, promise population doubling within a single generation in countries least able to provide for their members. The absolute number of illiterates as well as the absolute number of persons starving is greater now than ever before in history. Foreign aid barely offsets the disparity between declining prices paid for the prime commodities exported by underdeveloped countries and rising prices paid for the finished products imported into these countries (Horowitz, 1962). All schemes for tight centralized planning employed by these countries to accrue and disperse scarce capital by rational means are blocked by the unchallenged assumptions on private property and limited parliamentary democracy. A recent restatement of the principle came in the report of General Lucius Clay's committee on foreign aid. The report stated that the U.S. should not assist foreign governments "in projects establishing government owned industrial and commercial enterprises which compete with existing private endeavors." When Congressman Broomfield's amendment on foreign aid resulted in cancellation of a U.S. promise to India to build a steel mill in Bokaro, Broomfield stated the case succinctly: "The main issue is private enterprise vs. state socialism." (*The Atlantic,* September, 1964, p. 6.) Moreover, preference for forceful solutions assures that the capital now invested in preparedness will not be allocated in a gross way to the needs of underdeveloped countries. Instead, the manifest crises periodically erupting in violence justify further the need for reliance upon military preparedness.

We agree fully with an analysis by Lowi (1964) distinguishing types of decisions for which elite-like forces seem to appear and hold control (redistributive) and other types in which pluralist powers battle for their respective interests (distributive). In the latter type the pie is large and the fights are over who gets how much. Factional strife within and among military industrial and political forces in our country are largely of this nature. In redistributive decisions, the factions coalesce, for the pie itself is threatened. We have been arguing that the transition to peace is a process of redistributive decision.

Is there, then, a military-industrial complex which prevents peace? The answer is inextricably imbedded into the mainstream of American institutions and mores. Our concept is not that American society contains a ruling military-industrial complex. Our concept is more nearly that American society *is* a military-industrial complex. It can accommodate a wide range of factional interests from those concerned with the production or utilization of a particular weapon to those enraptured with the mystique of optimal global strategies. It can accommodate those with rabid desires to advance toward the brink and into limitless intensification of the arms race. It can even accommodate those who wish either to prevent war or to limit the destructiveness of war through the gradual achievement of arms control and disarmament agreements. What it cannot accommodate is the type of radical departures needed to produce enduring peace.

The requirements of a social system geared to peace, as well as the requirements for making a transition to such a social system, share a pattern of resource distribution which is different from the one the world now has. Moreover, these requirements for peace are, in significant measure, inconsistent with constraints set by the more enduring convergencies among power structures in the United States. The same is true whether one speaks of allocation of material or of intellectual resources. Both are geared to the protection of the premises rather than to avenues of change. We are not saying that war is inevitable or that the changes cannot be made. We are saying that the American political, military, and industrial system operates with certain built-in stabilizers which resist a change in the system. If there is to be peace, as opposed to detente or temporary absence of war, marked changes will be needed. Whether this society can or will accommodate to such changes is a question which is fundamentally different from the questions posed by most studies conventionally grouped under the rubric of peace research. One difference which marks the question of capacity to accommodate is in the theoretical conception or model of the cold war which is assumed. And a second distinction lies in the manner in which the end product of the research may be suited to meet the social forces (as apart from the intellectual arguments) which promote long-term changes in policy.

FOOTNOTES

Research relevant to this paper was made possible by a series of small grants from the Christopher Reynolds Foundation, The Society for Psychological Study of Social Issue, The Institute for Policy Studies, and the University of Michigan Phoenix Memorial Project. Appreciation is also due to Michael Locker and Anatol Rapoport for review and assistance with the manuscript and to the University of Michigan's Mental Health Research Institute and Center for Research on Conflict Resolution for the use of facilities.
[1]Senator Humphrey's investigation consisted of an inquiry sent by mail to a sample of major industrial defense contractors asking about their willingness to shift to non-defense areas if cutbacks were necessitated by progress toward arms reduction. For some unexplicable reason the results were classified but the Senator's statement indicated apparent readiness to make the shift.
[2]See Janowitz for a good sociological study of interservice differences.
[3]For the thesis that a "peacefare state" counterweighs the "warfare state," see Klaus Knorr's review of Fred J. Cook in the *Journal of Conflict Resolution,* VII, 4 (December 1963). The

"pluralist position," which usually is that the social system has semi-automatic checking mechanisms against tyranny, appears as basic in discussions not only of the military, but of economics and politics as well. See Robert Dahl, *Who Governs?;* John K. Galbraith, *American Capitalism;* Seymour Martin Lipset, *Political Man;* Talcott Parsons, *The Social System.*

[4]See James H. Meisel, *The Myth of the Ruling Class,* for the best available discussion of this innovation in theorizing about elites.

[5]Swomley (1964) accounts for Department of Defense holdings equivalent in size to eight states of the U.S.A. Kenneth Boulding, including personnel as well as property criteria, calls the Department of Defense the world's third largest socialist state. (Personal discussion, 1963.)

[6]In an earlier book, *The Empire of High Finance* (1957), he documented the close relations of the major financial groups and the political executive. He did not, however, carry this analysis to congressmen and senators, nor did he offer sufficient comparative evidence to demonstrate a long-term pattern.

[7]For this argument, see A. A. Berle, *The Twentieth Century Capitalist Revolution* and J. K. Galbraith, *American Capitalism.* For sound criticisms, but without sound alternatives, see Mills' and Perlo's books. Also see Michael Reagan, *The Managed Economy* (1963) and Berland Nossiter, *The Mythmakers* (1964) for other refutations of the counter-vailing power thesis.

[8]We are defining the term as "primary reliance on coercive means, particularly violence or the threat of violence, to deal with social problems."

[9]The term used in recent hearings by Senator Philip A. Hart refers to industrial organizations like Textron, which have holdings in every major sector of American industry.

[10]For some interesting work bearing upon the attitudes of business and military elites see Angell, 1964; Bauer et al., 1963; Eells and Walton, 1961; and Singer, 1964.

[11]An objective account of the major negotiations related to disarmament which have taken place may be found in Frye (1963)

4. THE MILITARY-INDUSTRIAL COMPLEX AND THE NEW INDUSTRIAL STATE

Walter Adams

One of the most exciting and useful concepts to come from economists in recent years is John Kenneth Galbraith's description of the new industrial state. Walter Adams uses Galbraith's formulation as a vantage point from which to analyze the military-industrial complex. Galbraith's work is, in some ways, a continuation of the post-World War II scholarship that postulates a smooth (perhaps almost inevitable) evolution of modern forms, all taking place within a framework of consensus. Adams takes particular pains to emphasize that the military-industrial complex, far from being the product of automatic forces, is the result of deliberate economic choices, made for the specific benefit of particular people and institutions.

In *The New Industrial State*,[1] Galbraith finds that the giant corporation has achieved such dominance of American industry that it can control its environment and immunize itself from the discipline of all exogenous control mechanisms—especially the competitive market. Through separation of ownership from management, it has emancipated itself from the control of stockholders. By reinvestment of profits, it has eliminated the influence of the

Source: Walter Adams, "The Military-Industrial Complex and the New Industrial State," *American Economic Review*, LVIII (May 1968), 652-665. Reprinted by permission.

financier and the capital market. By brainwashing its clientele, it has insulated itself from consumer sovereignty. By possession of market power, it has come to dominate both suppliers and customers. By judicious identification with, and manipulation of, the state, it has achieved autonomy from government control. Whatever it cannot do for itself to assure survival and growth, a compliant government does on its behalf—assuring the maintenance of full employment; eliminating the risk of and subsidizing the investment in research and development; and assuring the supply of scientific and technical skills required by the modern technostructure. In return for this privileged autonomy, the industrial giant performs society's planning function. And this, according to Galbraith, is inevitable because technological imperatives dictate it. The market is dead, we are told; and there is no good reason to regret its passing.

This blueprint for technocracy, private socialism, and the corporate state suffers from three fundamental defects. First, it rests on the unproved premise that corporate giantism is an inevitable product of technological determinism. Second, it rests on the increasingly more dubious assumption that industrial and political power are confined to separate, distinct, and hermetically sealed compartments. Finally, it offers no policy guidance, and ignores the crucial questions of responsibility and accountability. If industrial giants, freed from all traditional checks and balances, are to perform society's planning function, what standards shall they use and what assurance is there of an automatic convergence between private and public advantage? What are the safeguards—other than the intellectual in politics—against arbitrary abuse of power, capricious, or defective decision making? Must society legitimize a self-sustaining, self-serving, self-justifying, and self-perpetuating industrial oligarchy as the price for efficiency and progress?

In this paper, I shall eschew a dreary and repetitive recital of the voluminous evidence that negates the Galbraith version of a crude technological determinism.[2] I shall also spare the reader any comments on the virtues of private planning—the proposition that what is good for General Motors is good for the country. Instead, I shall offer an alternative (and, hopefully, more realistic) explanation of the current levels of industrial concentration, in general, and the military-industrial complex, in particular.

I

My hypothesis—the obverse of Galbraith's—holds that industrial concentration is not the inevitable outgrowth of economic and technical forces, nor the product of spontaneous generation or natural selection. In this era of big government, concentration is often the result of unwise, man-made, discriminatory, privilege-creating governmental action. Defense contracts, R and D support, patent policy, tax privileges, stockpiling arrangements, tariffs and quotas, subsidies, etc., have far from a neutral effect on our industrial structure. In all these institutional arrangements, government plays a crucial, if not decisive, role.[3] Government, working through and in alliance with "private enterprise," becomes the keystone in an edifice of neomercantilism and industrial feudalism. In the process, the institutional fabric of society is transformed from economic capitalism to political capitalism.

My hypothesis is best explained in Schumpeterian power terms. According to Schumpeter, the capitalist process was rooted, not in classical price competition, but rather "the competition from the new commodity, the new technology, the new source of supply, the new type of organization—competition which commands a decisive cost or quality advantage and which strikes not at the margin of the profits and outputs of existing firms but at their very foundations and their very lives."[4] The very essence of capitalism, according to Schumpeter, was the "perennial gale of creative destruction" in which existing power positions and entrenched advantage were constantly displaced by new organizations and new power complexes. This gale of creative destruction was to be not only the harbinger of progress but also the built-in safeguard against the vices of monopoly and privilege.

What was obvious to Schumpeter and other analysts of economic power was also apparent to those who might suffer from the gales of change. They quickly and instinctively understood that storm shelters had to be built to protect themselves against this destructive force. The mechanism which was of undoubted public benefit carried with it exorbitant private costs. And, since private storm shelters in the form of cartels and monopolies were either unlawful, unfeasible, or inadequate, they turned increasingly to government for succor and support. By manipulation of the state for private ends, the possessors of entrenched power found the most felicitous instrument for insulating themselves against, and immunizing themselves from, the Schumpeterian gale.

It requires no exaggeration to argue that modern technology and the inherent dynamism of Schumpeterian competition are such that, in the absence of governmental interference and protection, some of the bulwarks of concentrated power could be successfully eroded. Government policy toward the petroleum industry is a case in point. Under the antitrust laws, it is a per se offense for private firms to fix prices or allocate markets, yet in the name of conservation the government does for the oil companies what they could not legally do for themselves. The process is familiar. The Bureau of Mines in the Department of Interior publishes monthly estimates of the market demand for petroleum (at current prices, of course). Under the Interstate Oil Compact, approved by Congress, these estimates are broken down into quotas for each of the oil producing states which, in turn, through various prorationing devices, allocate "allowable production" to individual wells. Oil produced in violation of these prorationing regulations is branded as "hot oil," and the federal government prohibits its shipment in interstate commerce. Also, to buttress this government sanctioned cartel against potential competition, oil imports by sea are limited to slightly more than one million barrels a day. Finally, to top off these indirect subsidies with more visible favors and to provide the proper incentives for an industry crucial to the national defense, the government authorizes oil companies to charge off a 27½ percent depletion allowance against their gross income. In all, the industry has been estimated to receive special favors of $3.5

billion (according to Milton Friedman)[5] and $4.0 billion (according to Morris Aldelman)[6]—in addition to having a government sanctioned cartel provide the underpinning for its control of markets and prices.

Another case in point is the military-industrial complex, where the morganatic alliance between government and business is even clearer, bolder, and more positive. Here government not only permits and facilitates the entrenchment of private power but serves as its fountainhead. It creates and institutionalizes power concentrations which tend to breed on themselves and to defy public control. The scenario of events should be familiar. The "mad momentum" of an international weapons race militates toward large defense expenditures (currently at an annual rate of $75 billion). This generates a demand, not only for traditional, commercial, shelf items like food, clothing, fuel, and ammunition, but also for the development and production of sophisticated weaponry. Lacking a network of government-owned arsenals, such as produced the shot and cannon in the days of American innocence, or having dismantled the arsenals it did have, the government is forced to buy what it no longer can make. It becomes a monopsonistic buyer of products which are not yet designed or for which production experience is lacking. It buys at prices for which there is little precedent and hardly any yardsticks. It deals with contractors, a large percentage of whose business is locked into supplying defense, space, or atomic energy needs. It confronts powerful oligopolists in a market where technical capability rather than price is the controlling variable—in an atmosphere shrouded by multilateral uncertainty and constant warnings about imminent aggression. In the process, government becomes almost totally dependent on the chosen instruments, i.e., creatures of its own making, for effectuating public policy.[7] Lacking any viable in-house capabilities, competitive yardsticks, or the potential for institutional competition, the government becomes—in the extreme—subservient to the private and special interests whose entrenched power bears the governmental seal.

This unique buyer-seller relationship, which defies analysis by conventional economic tools, lies at the root of the military-industrial complex and the new power configurations generated by it. The complex is not a conspiracy between the "merchants of death" and a band of lusty generals, but a natural coalition of interest groups with an economic, political, or professional stake in defense and space. It includes the armed services, the industrial contractors who produce for them, the labor unions that represent their workers, the lobbyists who tout their wares in the name of "free enterprise" and "national security," and the legislators who, for reasons of pork or patriotism, vote the sizable funds to underwrite the show. Every time the Congress authorizes a military appropriation, it creates a new constituency (i.e., propaganda machine) with a vested interest in its perpetuation and aggrandizement. Thus, the current proposal for an anti-ballistic-missile system, the "thin" variety of which would cost $5 billion and the "thick" variety $40 billion, and which would probably be obsolete by the time it was completed, has been estimated to involve 28 private contractors, with plants located in 42 states (i.e., 84 senators), and 172 congressional districts. Given the political reality of such situations and the economic power of the constituencies involved, there is little hope that an interaction of special interest groups will somehow cancel each other out and that there will emerge some compromise which serves the public interest. There is little assurance that the corporal's guard of auditors in the General Accounting Office or Galbraith's scientific-professional elite or a handful of disinterested university analysts will constitute a dependable and adequate force of countervailing power. The danger remains that the "conjunction of an immense military establishment and a large arms industry," against which President Eisenhower warned, will become a Frankenstein threatening to control the contract state which brought it into being. The danger persists that power will be coalescing, not countervailing—that the political cloakroom will displace the economic market place.

It would be facile to conclude that the military-industrial complex and the new industrial state represent a price which society must pay—and inevitably so—because of national defense considerations or because of technological inexorability. But this would be to miss the point—to ignore the crucial political component in the institutional arrangements at issue. The military-industrial complex is only a special case illustrating the power problems inherent in the new industrial state. Both are created, protected, privileged, and subsidized by the state. Both represent a form of private socialism—a type of social planning through fragmented, special-interest chosen instruments operating in the "private" sector. Both represent a blending of private economic power and public political power. Both are reminiscent of the Elizabethan monopoly system and its abuse, corruption, favoritism, waste, and inefficiency—an *imperium in imperio*, without demonstrable public benefits, and without any built-in safeguards for the public interest. In sum, to the extent that they are creatures of political power and not the product of natural evolution, there is nothing inevitable about their survival and nothing inevitable about the public policies which spawn and preserve them.

II

Let us examine these public policies which lie at the base of the new industrial state, and particularly the military-industrial complex.

Defense and Space Contracts. These contracts, typically awarded on a negotiated rather than a competitive bid basis and as much the result of political as economic bargaining, convert the private contractor into a quasi-governmental, mercantilist corporation, maintained in a privileged position by "royal" franchise. The attendant abuses, especially the creation of entrenched power positions, are not inconsiderable.

In 1965, the U.S. Comptroller General, an Eisenhower appointee, highlighted the following characteristics of the contract system before a congressional committee:

1. excessive prices in relation to available pricing information,
2. acceptance and payment by the government for defective equipment,
3. charges to the government for costs applicable to contractors' commercial work,

4. contractors' use of government-owned facilities for commercial work for extended periods without payment of rent to the government,

5. duplicate billings to the government,

6. unreasonable or excessive costs, and

7. excessive progress payments held by contractors without payment of interest thereon.[8]

To this list could be added the procurement of items that were not needed, or in adequate supply elsewhere in the armed services, or were in fact being sold as surplus by the buying agency; indirect procurement through the prime contractor rather than direct purchase from the actual manufacturer—at far lower prices and without the pyramiding of overhead and profits; awarding of sole-source contracts for which the contractor had no special competency; the refusal by firms with overall systems responsibility to break out components for competitive bidding, or to furnish specifications for such bidding;[9] and finally, according to the Comptroller General, "excessive prices resulting from the failure of the agencies to request, or the contractors to furnish, current, accurate, and complete pricing data or from the failure to adequately evaluate such data when negotiating prices".[10] In quantitative terms, according to a summary of GAO studies covering the period from May, 1963, to May, 1964, there was ascertainable waste of $500 million in a 5 percent sample of procurements.[11]

Perhaps it is unavoidable that in the procurement of complicated weapons systems, where uncertainty is pervasive and precedents are unavailable, cost estimates will be unduly inflated. As Peck and Scherer found in their study of twelve major weapon system development programs, actual costs exceeded predicted costs by 3.2 times on the average, with a range of actual versus predicted costs of from 70 to 700 percent.[12] Recent prediction errors in the F-111 and Apollo programs, Scherer reports, are of the same order of magnitude.

One can sympathize with the contracting officers negotiating for complex and sophisticated weapons technology and still agree with the McClellan Committee's conclusion that the government should not abdicate its responsibilities for program management, nor delegate these responsibilities to private contractors, if it wants to avoid avoidable abuses and flagrant overcharges: "Even the most reputable and ethical contractor is placed in the conflicting position of managing a program where the feasibility, technical, and economic decisions which should be made by the customer-Government are made by the producer-contractor," the Committee observed with charitable understatement. "The absence of competition, coupled with the urgency to get the program underway, removes normal safeguards against large profits and weakens the Government's negotiating position."[13]

On the other hand, one must understand the reluctance to endanger the national security because of excessive delays caused by punctillious bookkeeping. As Charles G. Dawes told a congressional committee investigating World War I procurement scandals:

> Sure we paid. We didn't dicker. Why, man alive, we had to win the war. We would have paid horse prices for sheep if sheep could have pulled artillery to the front. Oh, it's all right now to say we bought too much vinegar and too many cold chisels, but we saved the civilization of the world. Damn it all, the business of an army is to win the war, not to quibble around with a lot of cheap buying. Hell and Maria, we weren't trying to keep a set of books, we were trying to win the war![14]

Government R and D and Patents. The awarding of government R and D contracts—and the disposition of patent rights thereunder—is another technique of creating, privileging, subsidizing, and entrenching private power. Again, this is a matter of man-made policy, not institutional inevitability.

The importance of federal policy in this area derives from a number of characteristics of federally financed research. Since World War II, the government has generally paid for roughly 65 percent of the nation's research and development, but performed only 15 percent of the work. Two agencies, the Department of Defense and NASA, account for about 80 percent of the government's R and D outlays. The lion's share of these outlays is concentrated in a few industries, notably aerospace, electronics, and communications. The concentration of R and D contracts is even greater than that of production contracts. There is high correlation between companies receiving R and D contracts and those receiving production contracts. Finally, the benefits of military R and D tend to spill over into civilian markets.[15]

The typical R and D contract, it should be noted, is a riskless cost-plus-fixed-fee venture. It usually protects the contractor against increases in labor and materials costs; it provides him with working capital in the form of periodic progress payments; it allows him to use government plant and equipment; in addition, it guarantees him a fee up to 15 percent of the estimated cost. Nevertheless, some contractors demand additional incentives. With the arrogance characteristic of all privilege recipients, they want to extend and compound such privilege. "We recognize," says the vice-president of the Electronics Industries Association, a prime beneficiary of government-financed R and D, "that the ownership of a patent is a valuable property right entitled to protection against seizure by the Government without just compensation."[16] In this view, the patent is a right, not a privilege voluntarily bestowed by the government to effectuate a public purpose. By a curious perversion of logic, it becomes a vested privilege to which the private contractor is entitled and of which he is not supposed to be deprived without "just" compensation.

Characteristically, both the Department of Defense and NASA have accepted this argument for privilege creation and made it the cornerstone of their patent policies. The principle at issue requires little adumbration. Allowing a contractor to retain patents on research financed by and performed for the government, as Wassily Leontief points out, "is no more reasonable or economically sound than to bestow on contractors, who build a road financed by public funds, the right to collect tolls from the cars that will eventually use it"[17]—or the right to close the road altogether. It is tantamount to socializing the financial support for research while permitting private monopolization of its benefits. Moreover, as Admiral Rickover observed, firms receiving R and D contracts "are relatively few huge corporate entities already possessing great concentrated economic power. They are not ailing segments of the economy in need of public aid or subsidy. Nor are there any real reasons to offer patent give-aways in order to induce them to accept Defense Department research grants or contracts. . . . To claim that agencies cannot get firms to sign such contracts unless patent rights are given away strikes me as fanciful nonsense."[18]

Stockpiling of Strategic and Critical Materials. This is an "ever normal granary" program, ostensibly designed to enable the United States to fight a war of specified duration, determined by the strategic assumptions of the Joint Chiefs of Staff. In reality, it is a price support program, the details of which are buried in secret government files and the "primary purpose" of which is to subsidize selected mining interests in the name of national security.[19] That, at least, was the conclusion of the exhaustive hearings conducted by the Symington Subcommittee of the Senate Armed Services Committee which examined the origin and growth of the national stockpile, the Defense Production Act inventory, and supplemental stockpile, which by 1961 had involved the expenditure $8.9 billion.[20]

These were the specific findings of the Symington Subcommittee:

1. Stockpile objectives were constantly manipulated to increase purchases regardless of national security needs. Thus, starting in 1954, "to justify further purchases of lead and zinc, when use of the old formula or requirements versus supplies did not permit additional buying, basic strategic assumptions were changed, and two objectives for each material were established. Under this new concept, the basic objective was determined under the usual method, but a new objective—the maximum objective—was arrived at by disallowing all supplies of a material from overseas. This had the effect, in many instances, of doubling the amount of a material that had to be stockpiled. It was then discovered, however, that even this new system would not permit additional purchases of lead and zinc in the amounts needed to maintain higher prices for lead and zinc. Resort was then had to the arbitrary one-year rule. Under this rule objectives were set at one year's consumption of the total national economy during a normal year without regard to what our requirements and supplies were."[21] In the case of some ores and minerals, an arbitrary six-month rule was adopted.

2. The buying programs to develop a domestic supply of certain ores, said the Committee, "can only be described as a failure. . . . Much of the material purchased was not needed. A substantial part of these ores did not meet the specifications of the stockpile. Nor was any domestic mobilization base

established by these purchases as is indicated by the fact that when the purchases stopped production stopped as well."[22] Moreover, contrary to expectations, most of the expenditures did not go to small business but to well-established mining companies; 86.7 percent of the tungsten purchases, for example, were made from the ten largest producers.

3. The price support level of some materials, like tungsten, e.g., were set two or three times above world prices, thus allowing the contractors windfall profits by buying at low world prices and supplying the stockpile at artificially exorbitant prices.[23]

4. Premium prices were often paid to contractors on the assumption that it would be necessary for the contractor to incur substantial capital expenditures to perform under the contract. Yet the government was denied the right under these contracts to check whether the capital expenditures had in fact been made, or to inspect the contractor's book to ascertain his production costs, or to renegotiate the price if the anticipated high costs were not realized.[24]

5. When market prices for some materials, like copper, e.g., rose above the contractual stockpile price, producers were permitted to divert deliveries from the stockpile to private industry—without sharing this windfall with the government.[25]

6. When the Joint Chiefs of Staff changed their strategic assumptions from a five-year war to a three-year war, the stockpile administrators waited for two years before implementing the change. Felix Wormser, Assistant Secretary of the Interior for Minerals Resources, who before and after his government service was vice-president of the nation's largest lead producer (St. Joseph Lead Co.), protested that such a change would constitute "a breach of faith with the mining industry."[26]

7. Disposals of excess supplies were resisted strenuously, and only in tin and rubber were any large-scale sales made. "It is significant," the Symington Committee noted wryly, "that there are no producers of natural rubber and tin in the United States and this could well account for the fact that the only two large disposals have been in these materials."[27]

The point need not be belabored. The rules for operating the national stockpiles as articulated by the industries concerned and their protagonists in government are fairly simple: The government must accumulate reserves against the most unthinkable eventualities. It must buy these materials at prices industry considers remunerative, regardless of world market conditions. This subsidy must be adequate to enable industry to operate profitably until such time as its services are required for mobilization in time of war. Finally, regardless of the available stocks, no disposal must ever be made from the stockpile. Such sales would not only endanger national security but also disturb market conditions and hence constitute unwarranted government interference with free enterprise.

Alienation of the Public Domain. To achieve or solidify their control over prices and markets, the giants of American industry cannot rely on the imperatives of modern technology. On the contrary, they must live in constant fear of the "creative destruction" wrought by new technology; and they must always be alert to the potential competition of substitute products and processes. Even more important, they must fight to contain, neutralize, and sterilize the "institutional" competition of the public domain which threatens to impose an intolerable regulatory yardstick on their operations. TVA is an embarrassment to the electric power monopoly, the communication satellite to AT&T dominance, navy shipyards to the shipbuilding cartel, and the Army's Redstone Arsenal and Jet Propulsion Laboratory to the condottieri of aerospace. Pressure must be exerted, therefore, to dismantle such operations, or to circumscribe their competitive viability, or to sell their facilities to private enterprise—in a manner which does not disturb the existing power structure and indeed might even entrench it more solidly. Here, again, governmental cooperation is required for implementation of this grand strategy, and this is a matter of political decision, not technological or economic inevitability.

The disposal of government-owned plants at the end of World War II underscores the nature of the power struggle and the availability of public policy alternatives.[28] In aluminum, the disposal program was a qualified success; Alcoa's prewar monopoly was broken, Kaiser and Reynolds sprung like Minerva from Jupiter's brow, and the aluminum industry was converted into a triopoly. Synthetic nitrogen production was also deconcentrated by the infusion of additional sellers. In steel, by contrast, the disposal program served to entrench and extend oligopoly dominance; the Geneva Steel plant, built at a cost of $202.4 million, was sold to the United States Steel Corporation for $47.5 million, and enabled U.S. Steel to increase its regional control over the Pacific Coast and Mountain States market from 17.3 to a commanding 39 percent. In synthetic rubber, the wartime operation of the government plants gave a handful of large firms enormous patent and know-how advantages for the postwar period, and the subsequent disposal program resulted in the sale of twenty-five plants to three firms controlling 47 percent of the industry's capacity.

More recent is the controversy over the disposition of the government's oil shale lands, located in the Rocky Mountain States, and estimated to contain two trillion barrels of oil (i.e., six times the known oil reserves of the entire world).[29] It illustrates the public policy options which are available to influence the structure of markets and to cope with existing power concentrations. At issue are the ground rules to be established for the control and development of a resource valued at $2.5 to $3.5 trillion.[30]

The petroleum industry's plan, according to one of its spokesmen, is to create "an economic climate equivalent to that provided [for] crude oil." Under its plan, the oil companies would be allowed to carve out homestead-like leases from the public lands and would be eligible for the customary subsidy of 27½[%] depletion allowance in return for their development efforts. Shell Oil has already proposed to lease a "homestead" that would cover its refining requirements (at present rates) for the next 660 years; Sinclair has entered its more modest request for a tract that would fill its needs for 226 years; Humble's request would provide for the next 54 years; and Continental's for the next 27 years.[31] The desire to gain control of a potentially competitive resource is not coupled with any guarantee to produce from it; and if production should take place, it would be subject to the oligopolistic rationality of the oil majors, restrained from undue competitiveness by government proration regulations.

Opponents of this plan, notably John K. Galbraith, argue that this "would be a free ride to monopoly for the big companies. Unless safeguards ... are carefully spelled out what would happen is that few of the majors would get these reserves as their reward. An eventual position in the basins would be their payoff. This would be in addition to the lands that they already own in most cases. Were there development, the processes for recovering the shale would then presumably be patented by them and reserved to them."[32] Obviously there are policy alternatives, including *inter alia* TVA- and COMSAT-like arrangements. "Certainly," as Senator Hart, chairman of the Senate Antitrust Subcommittee put it, "the development of oil shale reserves should offer a unique opportunity for new sources of competition to penetrate the petroleum industry. And that opportunity depends substantially on Government policy."[33]

International Trade Barriers. No system based on protection, privilege, and subsidy is safe without barriers to foreign competition. Its beneficiaries recognize the rough validity of the Mancunian assumption that "free international trade is the best antimonopoly policy and the best guarantee for the maintenance of a healthy degree of free competition." Action is, therefore, necessary to protect domestic restrictionism against erosion and subversion from abroad. And governmental action is the most reliable technique available.

The steel industry, in its current clamor for tariffs and/or quotas, illustrates the rationale of (what *Barron's* calls) the "protection racket" (Oct. 18, 1967). Roger Blough, congenitally unable to resist the ludicrous, observes that "obviously there are many things in life that should and must be protected. For example, millions of our people—and a number of government agencies—are laudably striving to protect certain vanishing forms of wildlife that are threatened with extinction; and one may reasonably wonder, I suppose, how far down the road to oblivion some of our major industries must go before they are deemed to merit similar concern."[34] To this, the president of the American Iron & Steel Institutes adds the ominous warning that "a first-class power with global responsibilities cannot afford to rely for any important part of its needs on overseas sources of steel thousands of miles away. There is the constant danger that these sources may be cut off at a critical moment."[35] Finally, the United Steel Workers of America, upon whom Galbraith once relied as a source of countervailing power, and not to be outdone in their concern for the public interest and national security, lend their voice and not inconsiderable political influence to the fight for a quota law to limit steel imports.[36]

What is at stake, of course, is the steel industry's right to preserve its administered price structure, to remain the catalyst of seller's inflation, to impose periodic price squeezes on independent fabricators, to price itself out of world export markets, to encourage the growth of substitute materials, and to persist in its technological lethargy.[37] Specifically, the industry needs government help to validate its investment in "40 million tons of the wrong capacity—the open hearth furnace" which it built in the 1950's. This capacity, as *Fortune* points out, was "obsolete when it was built" and the industry by installing it "prepared itself for dying."[38] This is the $800 million blunder, the cost of which the industry would like to shift to the public by obtaining government protection from foreign competition.

The point need not be stressed. Tariffs, quotas, "anti-dumping" statutes, "Buy American" regulations, and similar devices are not only a tax on domestic consumers and a subsidy to sheltered industries, but the capstone of any policy to protect entrenched economic power. They are a crucial facet of the *Realpolitik* designed to preserve the discipline of a nation's *Ordnungswirtschaft.*

III

In conclusion, we may note that the problem at hand is not one of technological determinism which would militate toward fatalistic acceptance of the *status quo.* Nor is it rooted in the ineffectiveness of what Galbraith calls the charade of antitrust. Instead, it is largely a political problem of governmental creation, protection, and subsidization of private privilege. If this diagnosis is indeed correct, then public policy alternatives are available and a reasonably competitive market is more than a utopian policy objective.

Let me offer two general policy recommendations:

1. Most important is government noninterference in markets which in the absence of such interference would be workably competitive. In the words of Adam Smith, it may be difficult to "prevent people of the same trade from sometimes assembling together," but government "ought to do nothing to facilitate such assemblies; much less to render them necessary." While assuring effective enforcement of the antitrust laws, government should abjure the role of the mercantilist state in sanctioning and legitimizing private privilege. One can only speculate on the quantitative benefits of such measures as the abolition of tariffs in concetrated industries, the deregulation of surface transportation from ICC control, or the elimination of the honeycomb of governmental supports for the petroleum price and power structure.

2. In those areas where competition cannot be allowed full sway or where government cannot avoid active participation in the economic game, the basic guidelines point to preserving the maximum amount of power decentralization feasible. This may require positive encouragement of institutional competition from whatever source available and, at the very least, the preservation of effective yardsticks by which to measure and control monopoly performance. In the national defense sector, for example, government must rebuild and preserve its in-house competence for R and D, systems engineering and management, and contract evaluation As the Bell Report of 1962 concluded, "there are certain [management] functions which should under no circumstances be contracted

out."[39] Basic policy and program decisions respecting the research and development effort—relating to "the types of work to be undertaken, when, by whom, and at what cost—must be made by full-time Government officials. Such officials must also be able to supervise the execution of work undertaken, and to evaluate the results."[40] In short, the government cannot surrender the yardsticks essential for the discharge of its responsibilities to the public.[41] And the public must recognize that the servants of the military-industrial state cannot be allowed to become its masters—either in the name of "free enterprise" or under the guise of promoting the "national security."

What I have said here is not likely to please those who rationalize the *status quo* by invoking some deterministic inevitability. I do not claim that what I have said is particularly new or startling. I do believe, however, that it is true and that, as Dr. Johnson said, men need not so much to be informed as reminded.

FOOTNOTES

[1]John K. Galbraith, *The New Industrial State* (Boston, 1967).

[2]U.S. Senate Select Committee on Small Business, *Planning, Regulation, and Competition, Hearings,* 90th Cong., 1st Sess., 1963, pp. 11-27, 53-66. [See also] U.S. Senate Subcommittee on Antitrust and Monopoly, *Economic Concentration, Hearings,* Parts 3 and 6, (Washington, 1965 and 1967).

[3]Walter Adams and Horace M. Gray, *Monopoly in America: The Government as Promoter* (New York, 1955).

[4]Joseph A. Schumpeter, *Capitalism, Socialism, and Democracy* (New York, 1942).

[5]Milton Friedman, "Oil and the Middle East," *Newsweek,* June 26, 1967.

[6]Morris A. Adelman, "Efficiency of Resource Use in Crude Petroleum: Abstract," *A.E.R.,* May 1964.

[7]David E. Bell, "Report to the President on Government R & D Contracting," Apr., 1962, printed in House Committee on Government Operations, *Systems Development and Management, Hearings,* Part 1, Appendix I, 87th Cong., 2d Sess., 1962, pp. 191-337. [See also] Clark R. Mollenkoff, *The Pentagon* (New York, 1967) and H. L. Nieburg, *In the Name of Science* (Chicago, 1966).

[8]U.S. House Committee on Government Operations, *Comtroller General Reports to Congress on Audits of Defense Contracts, Hearings,* 89th Cong., 1st Sess., 1965, p. 46.

[9]*Ibid.* [See also] U.S. Joint Economic Committee, *Background Materials on Economic Impact of Federal Procurement,* Washington, various years 1964-1967; appendices contain lists and digests of General Accounting Office reports on defense activities to Congress.

[10]U.S. House Committee on Government Operations, *Comptroller General Reports to Congress on Audits of Defense Contracts,* p. 46.

[11]Nieburg, *op. cit.,* p. 269.

[12]Merton J. Peck and Frederic M. Scherer, *The Weapons Acquisition Process: An Economic Analysis* (Harvard Bus. Sch. Div. of Res., 1962).

[13]U.S. Senate Committee on Government Operations, *Pyramiding of Profits and Costs in the Missile Procurement Program, Report No. 970,* 88th Cong., 2d Sess., 1964.

[14]Mollenkoff, *op. cit.,* pp. 53-54.

[15]Richard J. Barber, *The Politics of Research* (Washington, 1966), pp. 71-90.

[16]U.S. Senate Select Committee on Small Business, *Planning . . . ,* p. 132.

[17]U.S. Senate Select Committee on Small Business, *Economic Aspects . . . ,* p. 234.

[18]Nieburg, *op. cit.,* p. 294.

[19]U.S. Senate Committee on Armed Services, Draft Report of the National Stockpile and

Naval Petroleum Reserves Subcommittee, *Inquiry into the Strategic and Critical Material Stockpiles of the United States,* 88th Cong., 1st Sess., 1963, pp. 36-45.

[20]*Ibid.,* p. 4.

[21]*Ibid.,* pp. 4-5.

[22]*Ibid.,* pp. 8-9, 66.

[23]*Ibid.,* pp. 69-71.

[24]*Ibid.,* pp. 68-69.

[25]*Ibid.,* 49-54.

[26]*Ibid.,* p. 25.

[27]*Ibid.,* p. 28.

[28]Adams and Gray, *op. cit.,* pp. 117-141.

[29]U.S. Senate Subcommittee on Antitrust and Monopoly, *Competitive Aspects of Oil Shale Development, Hearings,* Part I, 90th Cong., 1st Sess., 1967, pp. 106-107.

[30]*Ibid.,* pp. 403, 407.

[31]*Ibid.,* p. 455.

[32]*Ibid.,* p. 22.

[33]*Ibid.,* p. 3.

[34]Roger M. Blough, "Progress Is Not Our Most Imported Product," Address at the Annual Meeting of the Indiana Manufacturers Association, Indianapolis, Nov. 16, 1967.

[36]U.S. Senate Committee on Finance, *Import Quota Legislation, Hearings,* Part 2, 90th Cong., 1st Sess., 1967, p. 830.

[37]*Ibid.,* pp. 888-896.

[38]*Ibid.,* p. 855.

[39]*Bell, op. cit.,* p. 213.

[40]*Ibid.,* pp. 214-215.

[41]Nieburg, *op. cit.,* pp. 334-350.

II. ORIGINS OF THE MILITARY-INDUSTRIAL COMPLEX

One danger of ignoring history is that without it we lack perspective in dealing with current problems. At the same time, one danger of knowing history is that the causes of events might seem lost in the misty past and their effects always to have been with us. The first can lead to radically inappropriate responses, the second to no action at all.

For the generation now in power in the United States, the World War II was the great discontinuity. It is the point at which this nation presumably ceased being isolationist and took up its world responsibilities. It is the point at which we acquired a large standing army in contravention of our traditions, but in response to our new obligations. It was, in short, the great watershed of our times.

It is somewhat easier for those either older or younger to appreciate the continuities in American history — the fact that the Roosevelt years owed much to the past and broke with it somewhat less than contemporaries either feared or hoped. In fact one might argue that the World War I, despite its short duration, was more of a turning point than World War II. At any rate, it is clear that the corporate liberalism so characteristic of the Progressive Era, as well as the Welfare State developed during the New Deal years, formed the context within which the military-industrial complex was hatched and incubated.

5. AMERICAN INDUSTRY IN THE WAR

Bernard Baruch

Bernard M. Baruch was a political phenomenon for half a century. A brilliant Wall Street loner, he was asked to head the War Industries Board at a time when the system of procurement and supply, as Koistinen has shown, was in deep trouble. His intimate involvement with the war effort made him a prime source of example and advice for the rest of his long and active life. Although he did not always get his way, his role as "elder statesman" dictated that he had always to be consulted, and either followed or somehow gotten around.

In this selection, Baruch places the wartime experience firmly in the context of a developing corporate liberalism in the United States, and pleads for the continuance of that movement after the war.

The statement is frequently heard that a bill of requirements and specifications covering the military needs of the Government should have been prepared during the early spring of 1917 before war was declared. Had this been possible, it would unquestionably have saved millions of dollars and a vast amount of confusion. The impossibility of such a performance, however, is only too evident to one who will stop to consider the ramifications involved in the production of a war element so simple and direct as a shell. Even direct military needs change

Source: Bernard Baruch, *American Industry in the War: A Report of the War Industries Board* (Washington, D.C., 1921), pp. 30-37, 96-100.

from month to month with the changing fortunes of war, and always these changes are accompanied by adjustments reaching deep into the industrial life.

A shell is made principally of steel, brass, and copper. It is filled with an explosive and is fired by either a fixed or separate charge of proplellent powder. The production of such a shell involves first the preparation of a plant or plants to forge, machine, and measure it, equip it with a firing mechanism and with a band to take the rifling of the gun. It requires another plant for loading, packing, and shipping. Each of these processes involves, directly or indirectly, a vast group of industries turned to a new field. But the steel and copper used in the shell involve another set of forces as they are developed from the ore through the processes of extraction and refinement to the forges. The blast furnaces have to be supplied with coke, with lime, and with manganese. They have to be lined with refractory brick. Coke involves mining bituminous coal and passing it through coke ovens. They all involve a large amount of railroad transportation, for the most favored spot on earth does not contain all the elements for a piece of steel.

Turning to the explosive and propellant for loading and firing the shell, the nitric acid is made from nitrate of soda which has to be mined and refined in a desert part of Chile, carried to the coast on railroads whose rails, rolling stock, ties, and fuel have to be taken there from distant parts, and then it is carried 5,000 miles in vessels to our shores; the sulphuric acid required in great quantities is made from pyrites ore coming from Spain or brimstone from Texas, platinum from Russia being needed for the equipment of the acid-producing plants. From some cotton field of the South has to be collected a little of the fine lint sticking to the seed as it comes from the gin to form the basis of the propellent powder. And after all this preparation a shell on the front is fired in a few moments. One day its use is necessary, another day it is not, but its preparation has to go on and on until the conflict is over.

Shells are but one small feature of the equipment of an army. There must be guns and rifles, hand grenades and gas equipment, airplanes and motor cars, food supplies and uniforms, medicines and surgical dressings, sound ranging apparatus, telephone supplies, and optical instruments. Ships were required to carry the troops and supplies. When one realizes the extent to which an individual direct requirement of the Army involves the whole ramification of industry, it is not difficult to see how a large number of direct requirements projected on a vast scale will bring in their train an overlapping and confusion in indirect requirements. The program of supply had to grow with the growth of the military program on the one hand and the growing knowledge of the materials obtainable on the other.

For the purposes of supply our Army was organized to make purchases according to the use to which the commodity would be put. The Ordnance Department bought guns and ammunition; the Quartermaster, clothing, blankets, food, and trucks; the Signal Corps, telephone apparatus, field glasses, etc.; the Engineers, building materials, railroad supplies, and implements; and so on. Each service had subunits charged with responsibility for particular groups of supplies. More than one service frequently bought quantities of the same commodity. It will be seen that the Army method of classifying supplies did not correspond to any extent with the classifications of ordinary business. Particularly did requirements by services, when translated into terms once removed from direct requirements, fit awkwardly into the classifications of business usage. From the beginning the Board felt that it was advisable to develop its organization according to the classification of commodities used in business. Before the war was over, the Army found it necessary to reorganize its purchasing system, gradually drawing it together under one control and revising its classifications. Outside of the War Department; the Navy, and later the Emergency Fleet and the Railroad Administration were making Government purchases. In addition to all, the principal Allies had purchasing missions in this country.

All of these factors contributed to the difficulty of laying down a program of requirements. The separate units of the Army supply bureaus could not compute their requirements until they knew the size of the particular part of the Army for which it was their legal duty to provide. The size of the Army to be here and abroad at any given time could not easily be computed without a definite knowledge of the amount of shipping that would be available both for men and for supplies. Frequently the kind of equipment could not be determined until it was known what materials could be found available. Sometimes types, designs, and specifications were delayed in an effort to develop a more perfect product. It soon became clear that the comprehensive supply organization would have to be mobile enough to respond promptly to an ever-changing demand.

When the General Munitions Board was formed, the activities of all Government purchasing agencies consisted in energetically placing orders without any certainty of their being filled. The board received statements of immediate requirements only as they were brought before it, when it joined in the effort to supply them in the shortest possible time. When a request for assistance came, the board would consider whether the proposed order involved a conflict with other necessary orders and whether it required emergency action to provide material or determine prices, and then it attempted to assist in discovering the best available source of supply. At first there was no system forcing all orders to be brought before the board even in lines where there was a known shortage.

Action on such orders as were brought was advisory only, and there was no report back showing whether the advice had been followed. Many Government bureaus placed the bulk of their orders without reference to the board. Each sought those plants whose manufacturing facilities promised the best results as judged from experience in normal times. This procedure had a tendency to localize orders in the northeastern manufacturing district of the country and congestion soon began to appear, with inevitable slowing up of deliveries.

By the fall of 1917 many plants had orders far beyond their available capacity. Fuel and raw materials could not be transported in sufficient quantities to supply the plants. Each Government purchaser wanted his order filled first and each manufacturer wanted his coal and railroad service given preference on the ground that he was filling a Government order. There was competition in buying even between different Government agencies, and the competition between Government contractors was increasing in intensity. Prices rose not only because of actual shortages, but because of options and inquiries made to cover bids on Government orders.

Competition in buying among the Allies and between the Allies and the agencies of our own Government and our Government contractors was becoming more and more a source of confusion and hindrance to the common purposes of the war. That the Allies should be assisted rather than hindered in obtaining supplies here as a result of our going into the war was a policy announced by the President as early as April, 1917. Questions involving competition among the different Allies and conflicts between their purchasing programmes and ours began to arise in great numbers. A scheme of control for our own purposes alone would have been much more simple than with this added complication. The Allies were extremely anxious (a) to borrow money from our Treasury to make purchases here, and (b) to get priority in manufacture and delivery. Hence they readily agreed to place no orders and make no purchases except through or with the approval of our Government.

To handle the set of delicate and complicated problems involved, on August 27, 1917, the United States, acting through the Treasury Department, arranged with the Governments of England, France, Italy, Belgium, Russia, and Serbia, that all purchases made by these Governments in the United States should be handled through or with the consent of a commission to be called the Allied Purchasing Commission. Bernard M. Baruch, Robert S. Lovett and Robert S. Brookings were appointed to constitute the commission. Alex Legge was made business manager of it, being succeeded on May 1, 1918, by James A. Carr. The war missions of the several Governments would present to the Allied Purchasing Commission not only proposed orders, but also statements of future require-ments. It was the purpose of the commission to assist the missions in obtaining the best prices, terms of delivery, priority preference, etc., that was practicable. But the commission did not prepare and sign contracts, supervise their execution, determine technical details, nor inspect materials. The effort was to coordinate allied buying with our own Government buying with a view to obtaining the same prices and terms for all.

The business manager held frequent meetings attended by representatives of the allied missions, the priorities committee, the United States Treasury, the War Trade Board, such commodity sections as were interested in the problem of the day, and others. Conflicts of interest betweeen different Allies, or between an Ally and the United States were discussed and composed. Minutes of these meetings are preserved. Orders which the allied missions proposed to place were submitted by the Allied Purchasing Commission to the clearance committee in the same manner as other proposed orders and they took the same course. The expenses of the commission were shared by the allied missions in proportion to the purchases of each in this country. During the life of the Allied Purchasing Commission, all purchases, made in the United States by the Allies with money borrowed from our Treasury, were approved through the commission. The total of all purchases, made with such funds, during the entire war period aggregated upward of $12,000,000,000.

The first effort directed specifically to bringing system into the confusion of Government orders was the formation of the "clearance committee" as an administrative unit of the General Munitions Board, which became later the War Industries Board. The clearance committee was composed of a chairman, a secretary, and a representative from the Army General Staff, the Navy, several bureaus of the Army, the Marine Corps, the more important sections of the Board, and later the Allied Purchasing Commission. This committee prepared what is called a "Clearance List" setting forth those materials in which a shortage was believed to exist. Government agencies were requested not to place orders for any materials on this list without first having those orders cleared by the committee. The committee considered requests for the clearance of orders with a view to preventing their being placed where there was congestion and where they would interfere with the fulfillment of other orders of equal importance, with a view to adjusting the relative importance of deliveries and to preventing abnormal rises in price. The method was by discussion and agreement between the respective interests, each being represented. Each buying department read its proposed orders before the committee, and, if no objection developed, the orders were cleared. If objection was made by another department because of conflict with its program or by an agency of the Board because curtailment, substitution, or other plan of conservation was being hindered, the order was re-formed or clearance delayed until the matter could be adjusted.

It was not many weeks before the clearance committee began to be overwhelmed with duties. Shortages showed themselves in one commodity after another and the clearance list increased week by week. The function of deciding on the relative merits of two or more conflicting agencies who wanted delivery of the same thing and of ruling on which should be preferred in cases where all could not be served, in other words, the priority function, presented increasing difficulties and appeared as increasingly important. In the summer of 1917 a new agency, the priorities committee, was formed to take over this function, which later, as we shall see, became such an important feature of the work of the Board. It was found also, that the clearance process had little effect in the control of prices. This function also was early isolated and placed in the province of a price-fixing committee created to handle it. But the clearance function proper had not been developed in vain. It was evident by the spring of 1918 that one committee could not handle the volume of work which the administration of this function implied. Furthermore its performance by a single body was not necessary.

By July, 1918, the commodity sections, following the reorganization put into effect by the new Chairman, had developed such strength, containing as they then did representatives from each of the supply bureaus interested in their respective commodities; that these sections could take over the clearance function, and they did, the clearance committee being reorganized into a Clearance Office whose function it was merely to receive requests for clearance, record them, and transmit them to the proper commodity sections, the sections in turn reporting back through the Clearance Office. The first chairman of the clearance committee was Frank A. Scott. He was succeeded by Lieut. Col. C. C. Bolton, who in May, 1918, was succeeded by Rear Admiral F. F. Fletcher.

During the winter of 1917 and 1918 the clearance schedule not only increased by reason of the addition of many new groups of commodities, but the ruling was issued that all orders to be placed in the so-called congested district (outlined in the ruling) would have to be cleared, and that all orders involving the creation of new or additional facilities should be cleared. The clearance function, as developed through the commodity sections, was the means by which the record was maintained, commodity by commodity, of standing orders, and it was the means used for so distributing the Government orders that their benefit or their burden might be equitably shared by all the interests of the respective trades. Clearance, however, was never effective as a means for developing a program of requirements. Requests for clearance were statements of immediate requirements only.

When, in the spring of 1918, it had become evident that an enlarged control of industry would be necessary, the need for a systematic statement of requirements, projected far enough into the future to allow time to provide for their production, was keenly felt. In order "to anticipate the prospective needs of the several supply departments of the Government and their feasible adjustment to the industries of the country," a Requirements Division was organized in June, with Alex Legge as chairman, and embracing in its membership authorized representatives of each of the Government purchasing agencies (Army and Navy), the priorities commissioner, the commissioner of finished products, chiefs of divisions, section chiefs, manager of Allied Purchasing Commission, representatives of the Food, Fuel, and Railroad Administrations, the Capital Issues Committee, the Department of Commerce, the Red Cross, the Shipping Board, and other departments and bureaus.

Each of the several Government departments was requested to submit a statement of its requirements projected as far in advance as practicable. These statements were received by the Requirements Division where they were discussed from the point of view of their general relations to other requirements and then handed on to the appropriate commodity sections where detailed studies were made and reports sent back to the source of the statements concerning the possibility and means for meeting such requirements.

The division held a meeting every morning at 9 o'clock, at which the various requirements were discussed at length, modification of schedules being debated between the conflicting bureaus of the Government. The scope involved made this procedure very difficult of application, but the principle was sound. For the first time during the war, and perhaps for the first time in Government operations generally, this organization provided systematic machinery by which the various department buyers had the opportunity of learning one another's needs, and of knowing at what points their respective efforts conflicted or overlapped. It gave Government bureaus and section chiefs alike a more comprehensive vision of the whole course of the undertaking.

The procedure of the Board, as it developed with respect to these two functions was about as follows: The various Government purchasing units and the Allied Purchasing Commission were sending to the Requirements Division their best estimates of future requirements projected for six months or a year in advance. The commodity sections of the Board used these statements in their studies of curtailment and conservation programs, increased production programs, and other plans necessary in looking forward to meeting the needs. They also used them for the instruction of the trade through the war-service committees, and in the consideration of problems arising in connection with priorities and price-fixing. These statements were in the nature of estimates and did not necessarily imply that orders would actually be placed. They meant at least that orders were contemplated. The changing nature of military plans will make obvious the fact that full and accurate statements of all requirements for a year or even a half year in advance are quite impossible, however desirable they might be from the point of view of the officials responsible for mobilizing industry.

But in addition to the general estimates of future requirements, on which the broader lines of regulation and control were based; before the end of the period the rule was established that all orders ready to be placed should first be sent to the Board for "clearance." The commodity sections, on whom the burden of clearing rested, would act on these requests in one of six ways. (1) Clear without comment, in which case the purchaser was permitted to go into the market and order as he saw fit; (2) clear with restriction as to the area in which the order might be placed; (3) clear with restriction as to the electric power system on which the order would draw; (4) clear subject to restrictions as to certain named plants or with restrictions inhibiting the creation of new facilities for the execution of the order; (5) clear with an actual allocation of the order to a particular named source of supply; (6) clear with advice as to suitable source of supply. The application of this system varied with the peculiar problems incident to different lines of trade. There was no attempt to make it rigid. A licensing system for civilian as well as Government purchases was used in several industries. . . .

That much of the confusion experienced in collecting the supplies for this war could have been avoided by a more painstaking, thorough, and comprehensive effort on the part of the Government supply bureaus to work out a program of requirements, even a program tentative in many of its details, there is little doubt. That such a program would have been exceedingly difficult to frame is quite certain.

The experience of the Board in this respect suggests the thought that there should be established a large unit of specially qualified officers of the War Department devoted in time of peace to studies of supply programs for supposititious military undertakings. As these programs would always have to be based upon the obtainability of the supplies outlined, the bureau should be required to go deeply into a study of the industrial resources and possibilities of the country as they relate to war needs. These studies are a military function, but they might have also, as a by-product, a healthy effect upon business. . . .

This report is a record not alone of new methods of Government control over business; it is also a record of many new practices on the part of business itself. With purpose always defined, but method to be discovered by a process of trial and error, through months of unparalleled effort and devotion, at first by applying varying degrees of the principle of "advice and encouragement," the Board finally developed a scheme of positive "control" over the major portion of the industrial fabric, which, by the summer of 1918, was showing results of an extraordinarily satisfactory character. Success bred courage for more success, and trade after trade was taken under control with an increasing willingness on the part of the interests affected.

The thoughtful reader will find here and there stories which carry with them suggestions of problems relating to the industrial practices of peace, and the same stories will also, perhaps, point toward peace-time solutions of some of these problems. Reference has already been several times made to the evident value, as a measure of preparedness, of a comprehensive Government bureau devoted to industrial research and statistical information.

Recommendations which would follow as the fruit of the experience of the Board might be classified in two groups: (1) Those relating to peace-time preparation for a possible war emergency, and (2) those relating to the business practices of normal times.

Three lines of industrial preparedness will be briefly suggested here as the most important direct war lessons to be derived from the work:

First. There should be established a peace-time skeleton organization following the lines of the War Industries Board. It should be headed by a chairman who should have associated with him the chiefs of the centralized purchasing bureaus of the Army, of the Navy, and of any other Government department which might be called upon to make large purchases in case of war. Other members of the board should be selected to take charge of (1) raw materials, (2) finished products, (3) facilities, (4) price control, (5) labor, (6) priority, (7) conservation, and (8) planning and statistics. There should be a vice chairman, a general counsel, and a secretary. To function under the several principal divisions there should be selected about 50 chiefs of commodity sections. Each chief of a commodity section would name a committee to represent the industry under his charge. The committees of the different industries could meet separately as occasion required for the purpose of keeping acquainted with the general growth of the industry and the demands which a war would make upon it. The main organization should meet in general conference at least once a year to discuss and outline plans, to keep in touch with the general nature of war needs and to keep acquainted with one another. The office of secretary should be permanent and salaried, and the division of planning and statistics ought to be a moderately large permanent organization—a reservoir of information for all departments of the Government and the Congress. All other members and subordinates of the board should serve without compensation.

Second. During the war the country was constantly threatened with a shortage in available supply of nitrogen, manganese, chrome, tungsten, dyestuffs, coal-tar derivatives, and several other essential materials. These materials had always been imported into the United States and their production never developed, although sources for most of them exist here. The Government should devise some system for protecting and stimulating their internal production. Among these, nitrogen is of outstanding importance, not only because it is indispensable for war, but also because it is almost indispensable for agricultural purposes. There is only one natural source in the world, and the fixation process, having been proven to be practicable, should be developed to commercial proportions.

Third. Under the supervision of the proper departments of the Government, certain war industries should be encouraged to maintain skeleton organizations through which they could develop the rapid manufacture of guns, munitions, airplanes, and other direct military equipment. This might be done in some cases through Government purchases of factories, in others through the placing of sufficient orders to permit the owners to keep the plants in existence. It is extremely important that our recent development of machine tools, in nature of dies, jigs, etc., for the manufacture of munitions, should not be allowed to dissipate. At an expense bearing very little relation to the cost of building anew in time of emergency, present stocks could be carried forward and supplemented as new designs replace the old in the development of war devices.

These measures are suggested as direct methods of insuring against some of the heavy losses and unfortunate delays which the country experienced in the process of converting its industries from a peace to a war basis. They involve very small current expenditures, but are capable of being instruments for saving many millions of dollars in an emergency.

The experience of the Board in exercising control over American industry leads it to make a further suggestion, which has less to do with war than with the normal practices of business.

During the past few decades, while the American business man, uniting his talents with those of the technical expert, has, through the control of great masses of capital, made such extraordinary strides in converting the natural wealth of this country into means for human comfort and satisfaction; the processes of trade have so changed their nature that the older and simpler relations of Government to business have been gradually forced to give way before certain new principles of supervision. We have been gradually compelled to drift away from the old doctrine of Anglo-American law, that the sphere of Government should be limited to preventing breach of contract, fraud, physical injury and injury to property, and that the Government should exercise protection only over non-competent persons. The modern industrial processes have been rendering it increasingly necessary for the Government to reach out its arm to protect competent individuals against the discriminating practices of mass industrial power. We have already evolved a system of Government control of no mean significance over our railroads and over our merchant fleet, but we continue to argue, and in a measure believe, that the principles of competition can be preserved in sufficient power in respect to all other industries to protect the interests of the public and insure efficiency and wholesome growth in the development of natural wealth. With this in view, the Sherman and Clayton Acts have forbidden combinations in restraint of trade, monopolies, and many other vices attendant upon group action by individuals controlling great masses of capital. This legislation, while valuable for immediate purposes, represents little more than a moderately ambitious effort to reduce by Government interference the processes of business so as to make them conform to the simpler principles sufficient for the conditions of a bygone day.

The war has introduced a new element into this situation. The individual units of corporations which had been dissolved under the Sherman Act have, in many cases, grown during the war into corporations many fold larger than the parent organization which before the war the law construed as a menace. The conditions of war made this sort of thing necessary and in all respects desirable. The war gave rise to a kind of demand unknown in time of peace—an absolute demand, which was halted neither by prices nor difficulty of procurement. There followed an absolute shortage in some trades, and a time shortage in most of them. Group action, industry by industry, accompanied by Government control of prices and distribution, was the natural and, so far as we know, the only solution which could be devised.

In line with the principle of united action and cooperation, hundreds of trades were organized for the first time into national associations, each responsible in a real sense for its multitude of component companies, and they were organized on the suggestion and under the supervision of the Government. Practices looking to efficiency in production, price control, conservation, control in quantity of production, etc., were inaugurated everywhere. Many business men have experienced during the war, for the first time in their careers, the tremendous advantages, both to themselves and to the general public, of combination, of cooperation and common action, with their natural competitors. To drive them back through new legislation, or through the more rigid and rapid enforcement of present legislation, to the situation which immediately preceded the war will be very difficult in many cases, though in a few it is already occurring spontaneously. To leave these combinations without further supervision and attention by the Government than can be given by the Attorney

General's Department, or by the Federal Trade Commission in its present form, will subject business men to such temptations as many of them will be unable to resist—temptations to conduct their businesses for private gain with little reference to general public welfare.

These associations, as they stand, are capable of carrying out purposes of greatest public benefit. They can increase the amount of wealth available for the comfort of the people by inaugurating rules designed to eliminate wasteful practices attendant upon multiplicity of styles and types of articles in the various trades; they can assist in cultivating the public taste for rational types of commodities; by exchange of trade information, extravagant methods of production and distribution can be avoided through them, and production will tend to be localized in places best suited economically for it. By acting as centers of information, furnishing lists of sources to purchasers and lists of sources to purchasers and lists of purchasers to producers, supply and demand can be more economically balanced. From the point of vantage which competent men have at the central bureau of an association, not only can new demands be cultivated, but new sources of unexploited wealth can be indicated. In case of a national emergency, the existence of these associations at the beginning would be of incalculable aid to the supply organizations. Many of these considerations apply to large individual companies as well as to associations.

These combinations are capable also—and very easily capable—of carrying out purposes of greatest public disadvantage. They can so subtly influence production as to keep it always just short of current demand and thus keep prices ever high and going higher. They can encourage a common understanding on prices, and, without great difficulty, can hold price levels at abnormal positions. They can influence the favoring of one type of buyer over another. Nearly every business man in the country has learned by the war that a shortage in his product, if it be not too great, is distinctly to his advantage. Trade associations with real power can, in respect to most of the staples, so influence production as to keep the margin of shortage at a point most favorable to high prices and rapid turnovers.

The question, then, is what kind of Government organization can be devised to safeguard the public interest while these associations are preserved to carry on the good work of which they are capable. The country will quite properly demand the vigorous enforcement of all proper measures for the suppression of unfair competition and unreasonable restraint of trade. But this essentially negative policy of curbing vicious practices should, in the public interest, be supplemented by a positive program, and to this end the experience of the War Industries Board points to the desirability of investing some Government agency, perhaps the Department of Commerce or the Federal Trade Commission, with constructive as well as inquisitorial powers—an agency whose duty it should be to encourage, under strict Government supervision, such cooperation and coordination in industry as should tend to increase production, eliminate waste, conserve natural resources, improve the quality of products, promote efficiency in operation, and thus reduce costs to the ultimate consumer.

Such a plan should provide a way of approaching industry, or rather of inviting industry to approach the Government, in a friendly spirit, with a view to help and not to hinder. The purpose contemplated is not that the Government should undertake any such far-reaching control over industry as was practiced during the war emergency by the War Industries Board; but that the experiences of the war should be capitalized; its heritage of dangerous practices should be fully realized that they might be avoided; and its heritage of wholesome and useful practices should be accepted and studied with a view to adapting them to the problems of peace. It is recommended that such practices of cooperation and coordination in industry as have been found to be clearly of public benefit should be stimulated and encouraged by a Government agency, which at the same time would be clothed with the power and charged with the responsibility of standing watch against and preventing abuses.

6. TENTH ANNUAL REPORT

National Advisory Committee for Aeronautics

From its inception in 1915 until its absorption into the National Aeronautics and Space Administration (NASA) after Sputnik, the National Advisory Committee for Aeronautics (NACA) acted as a self-conscious agency for the deliberate coordination of the needs and efforts of the military with industrial aviation interests. Here mingled all the types which later were to become so familiar — the dollar-a-year bureaucrats, the college professors with their research grants, the air force generals and industrial executives. The lessons of cooperation and accommodation learned in NACA were directly applied to the war effort in 1940 when Vannevar Bush, NACA chairman and former vice president of the Massachusetts Institute of Technology, set up the National Defense Research Committee.

The National Advisory Committee for Aeronautics was created by act of Congress in 1915 as an independent establishment. It is composed of 12 members appointed by the President, all of whom serve without compensation. Its membership is drawn from official and private life as follows:

From the Government service:

Two from the War Department (the Chief of Air Service and the chief of the engineering division of the Air Service.)

Source: *Tenth Annual Report of the National Advisory Committee for Aeronautics, 1924* (Washington, D.C., 1925), pp. 56-57, 60-64.

Two from the Navy Department (the Chief of the Bureau of Aeronautics and the chief of the material division).

One from the Weather Bureau (the chief).

One from the Bureau of Standards (the director).

One from the Smithsonian Institution (the secretary).

From private life:

Five who are acquainted with the needs of aeronautical science or skilled in aeronautical engineering or its allied sciences.

The organic act creating the National Advisory Committee for Aeronautics provides: "That it shall be the duty of the Advisory Committee for Aeronautics to supervise and direct the scientific study of the problems of flight, with a view to their practical solution, and to determine the problems which should be experimentally attacked, and to discuss their solution and their application to practical questions. In the event of a laboratory or laboratories, either in whole or in part, being placed under the direction of the committee, the committee may direct and conduct research and experiment in aeronautics in such laboratory or laboratories."

The committee's laboratories for the direct conduct of fundamental research in aeronautics are located at Langley Field, Va., where the facilities of a large Army flying field are added to those of a well-equipped research laboratory.

The committee operates under rules and regulations approved by the President. It elects annually its chairman and its secretary from among its members and also an executive committee, which in turn elects its chairman and its secretary. The executive committee has immediate and entire charge of the activities of the committee during the interim between the stated meetings of the entire committee.

The executive committee has established three standing technical subcommittees, namely, the committee on aerodynamics, the committee on power plants for aircraft, and the committee on materials for aircraft. The organization of these subcommittees is patterned after that of the entire committee, each having specially appointed representatives from the Army and Navy Air Services, the Langley Memorial Aeronautical Laboratory, the Bureau of Standards, and private life, all of whom serve without compensation.

It is mainly through the instrumentality of the technical subcommittees that coordination of aeronautic research and experiment and cooperation among the agencies interested are made effective. The subcommittees originate the programs for aeronautical research in their respective fields, and after such programs are approved by the executive committee the subcommittees receive progress reports periodically and keep in touch with the active workers in their respective fields and with the progress of the investigations coming under their cognizance. Through these subcommittees, and largely by virtue of the opportunity afforded by regular and official contact and personal acquaintance that result from regular attendance at meetings, complete cooperation on the part of all responsible governmental officers concerned with the investigation of technical problems in aeronautics is assured.

With the subcommittees functioning efficiently, and with their activities coordinated by the director of aeronautical research, the executive committee is enabled to devote a portion of every meeting to the informal discussion of general problems regarding the development of military and civil aviation, and these informal discussions are often of greater advantage in promoting understanding and cooperative effort than are formal or official communications.

The committee's activities in the field of aeronautical development may be stated under four headings as follows:

1. The coordination of research and experimental work in aeronautics by the preparation of research programs and the allocation of particular problems to the various laboratories.

2. The conduct of scientific research on the more fundamental problems of flight, under the immediate direction of the committee in its own laboratory known as the Langley Memorial Aeronautical Laboratory, at Langley Field, Va.

3. The collection, analysis, and classification of scientific and technical data in aeronautics, including the results of research and experimental work conducted in all parts of the world.

4. The diffusion of technical knowledge on the subject of aeronautics to the military, naval, and postal air services, aircraft manufacturers, universities engaged in the teaching of aeronautics, and the public generally.

In addition, the committee holds itself at the service of the President, the Congress, and the executive departments of the Government for the consideration of special problems in aeronautics which may be referred to it.

The success of the National Advisory Committee for Aeronautics in performing its important functions depends fundamentally upon the following facts:

1. Its members and the members of its standing subcommittees serve without compensation, the Government thus receiving the services of men who would not otherwise be available.

2. The reason why these men are willing to serve is because the committee is an independent Government establishment, reporting directly to the President, receiving its own appropriation from Congress.

3. By virtue of such status, the committee is able to initiate and to conduct any investigation which, after full discussion by the subcommittee concerned is, is considered fundamental or desirable.

All these advantages would be lost were the committee to be made part of any Government department. . . .

THE INCREASING IMPORTANCE OF AIRCRAFT IN WARFARE

The Limitation of Armaments Conference held in Washington in 1921-1922 on invitation of President Harding examined into the possibility of limiting aviation development for war purposes and limiting the use of aircraft in warfare. A special committee of aviation experts representing the United States, Great

Britain, France, Italy, and Japan was appointed. That committee submitted a report which reviewed the situation at length. The "final conclusions" of the report follow:

> The committee is of the opinion that it is not practicable to impose any effective limitations upon the numbers or characteristics of aircraft, either commercial or military, except in the single case of lighter-than-air craft. The committee is of the opinion that the use of aircraft in warfare should be governed by the rules of warfare as adapted to aircraft by a further conference which should be held at a later date.

The fact that the Limitation of Armaments Conference placed no restriction on the development and application of aircraft for war purposes assures the greater relative importance of aircraft in future warfare. It is a maxim of military science that an army and a nation must be adaptable to changes in time of war. The best laid plans, whether for offensive or defensive warfare, are usually upset either by the success of the enemy or by changes and developments in the art of warfare. No one can foretell at this time what the use of aircraft will be in future wars, nor even in the next war. It is safe to say that there will be individual and group fighting in the air; there will be aircraft attacking troops on the ground, both with bombs dropped from great heights and with machine guns mounted on low-flying aircraft protected by armor from ordinary rifle bullets; there will be bombing of large cities, military and manufacturing centers, and routes of communication and transportation. And it has been proposed that aircraft be used to drop poisonous gases not only on the enemy's troops but also behind the lines and in the centers of population, to the same extent that long-distance bombing will be carried on. The bombs carried may not be limited to explosives and poisonous gases but may possibly be loaded with germs to spread disease and pestilence. Without limitations on the uses of aircraft in warfare a nation fighting with its back to the wall can not be expected to omit to use desperate means to stave off defeat. The uses of aircraft in warfare would then be limited only by the inability of human ingenuity to conceive further uses for this new agency of destruction.

A conference was held at The Hague in 1923, attended by delegates of the United States, which drafted rules and regulations covering the use of aircraft in war. There was evident a tendency to minimize as much as possible aircraft attack upon centers of population with the resulting consequences to noncombatants and to restrict such attacks to what are military objectives. In spite of the rules thus formulated, and even if they should be universally adopted, it is still inevitable that aircraft attacks would greatly terrify and undoubtedly seriously injure and damage many who have heretofore been classed as noncombatants.

It is believed quite probable that if the nations of the world do maintain adequate air forces, this may tend to the adjustment of international disagreements by conference, as the delegates to such conferences will have the strong backing of their national air forces capable of such destructive effect as that indicated above. When wars were fought within a limited territory by ground troops, the national patriotism of noncombatants strongly supported their armed forces, but in future wars when air power becomes a most vital factor in national defense, theaters of operation will no longer be limited to restricted territories, and noncombatants will probably and unavoidably be subjected to far greater personal danger and injury than in the past. It is not inconceivable that such pressure will be brought to bear upon the Governments concerned by their noncombatants, following a series of aircraft raids, that an early cessation of hostilities will be more earnestly desired by the people on both sides and will be forced by popular demand upon the nation least efficient in air power.

Aviation has made itself indispensable to military and naval operations. Under our present organization, where the function of national defense is vested principally in the War and Navy Departments, we must look to those departments to develop the possibilities of aviation in warfare, whether to be used in conjunction with military and naval operations, or to be used independently for attacking distant points behind the enemy's lines, or elsewhere. The problem of the air defense of this country is worthy of most careful study.

RELATION OF AERONAUTIC RESEARCH TO NATIONAL DEFENSE

So long as the development of aviation continues from year to year, the military and naval policies and programs for our national security and defense are necessarily subject to change, as they are largely dependent upon the probable use of aviation in future wars. So long as other nations are seriously engaged in the development of aviation, America must at least keep abreast of the progress of aviation abroad and never permit itself again to fall behind as it did before the World War. Substantial progress in aviation, whether in America or elsewhere, is in the last analysis dependent upon aeronautical research. It is necessary that accurate information, which is the result of scientific research on the fundamental problems of flight, should be made continuously available to the Army and Navy; and those agencies desire from the National Advisory Committee for Aeronautics the fundamental aerodynamic information on which the design of new types of military and naval aircraft is based. It is the function of the Army and Navy then to check this information and apply it in an engineering manner to the design of aircraft.

While national defense is the greatest use to which aircraft is applied in America to-day, the committee believes that the time will come when its military uses will be second in importance to its civil value in promoting our national welfare and increasing our national prosperity. But to-day, while the uses of aircraft are primarily military and the Air Services of the Army and Navy are not as large as those of other world powers, America is gradually forging ahead of other nations in the acquisition of knowledge of the scientific principles underlying the design and construction of aircraft. To this important but limited extent we are providing well against unpreparedness in the air.

THE AIRCRAFT INDUSTRY AND ITS RELATION TO NATIONAL DEFENSE

The present American aircraft industry is but a shadow of that which existed at the time of the armistice. With the great stimulus in aircraft development and performance during the war, the aircraft manufacturers were hopeful that civil aviation would rapidly come into being with a resulting great demand for their product. Civil aviation has not developed as it was hoped it would, and this makes the present situation more difficult.

These aircraft manufacturers have had to rely for orders upon Government agencies, and the limited amount of governmental purchases has forced a number of manufacturers to go out of the aircraft business. It is a matter of grave Government concern lest the productive capacity of the industry may become so far diminished that there may not remain a satisfactory nucleus. By a "satisfactory nucleus" is meant a number of aircraft manufacturers, distributed over the country, operating on a sound financial basis, and capable of rapid expansion to meet the Government's needs in an emergency.

After the very costly lessons of the war, it would be folly to say that the Government is not concerned with the state of the aircraft industry. It is concerned that there should be in existence, and in a healthy condition, at least an adequate nucleus of an industry. An aircraft industry is absolutely essential to national defense. One lesson of the war that will not be forgotten is that it takes a great deal of money to develop hastily an aircraft industry from almost nothing. The American people can ill afford to pay such a price a second time. To maintain a nucleus of an industry it has been proposed either that the Government substantially increase the volume of its orders for aircraft or devise a policy for the apportionment of orders at fair negotiated prices without regard to competition.

Neither of these propositions, however, in the judgment of the National Advisory Committee for Aeronautics, goes to the root of the trouble. To substantially increase orders will require substantially increased appropriations. To increase appropriations for the Army and Navy Air Services because they need more aircraft is one thing, but to increase appropriations primarily to maintain an aircraft industry is something else. Furthermore, the maintenance of an industry in a healthy condition does not involve the maintenance of any manufacturer who has failed to liquidate or reduce his plant and overhead expenses to an appropriate peacetime basis.

In the judgment of the committee, the existing bad situation in the industry should be substantially remedied. In an effort to help the situation, the committee suggests the following steps on the part of the industry and of the Government:

Steps to be taken by the industry:

First. Every manufacturer intending to remain in the aircraft business and who has not readjusted his war-time plant and overhead expenses to a peace-time basis should do so without further delay.

Second. The firms comprising the aircraft industry should specialize in the production of various types of aircraft with a view to the more continuous development of types by the same plants and the gradual recognition of proprietary rights in new designs.

Steps to be taken by the Government:

First. The Army, Navy, and Postal Air Services should agree upon a balanced program setting forth from time to time the probable requirements of the Government for each type of aircraft for at least one year in advance, and should announce the same to the industry for its information and guidance.

Second. Orders for the different types should be placed with the different manufacturers at such intervals as to insure continuity of production and the gradual development of special facilities and skill by each manufacturer in the production of a given type of aircraft.

The committee does not attempt to say that the method proposed is the ideal solution, but it submits that if followed it would produce the following beneficial results:

1. It would insure the continuous development of types by the same firms which is the most rational method of improving the quality and performance of aircraft to meet special needs.

2. It would reduce the cost of aircraft.

3. It would provide all manufacturers with an adequate market to enable them to continue in the airplane business without the periodical menace of dissolution or bankruptcy heretofore caused by long gaps, between orders.

COMMERCIAL AVIATION AND ITS RELATION TO THE GOVERNMENT

The stimulus of war forced the development of aviation for military purposes, and while the progress thus made was beneficial to all aviation, nevertheless there has been but little application of aviation to commercial purposes. In England, France, Italy, Germany, Holland, Belgium, Poland, and other European countries there are air lines for the transportation of passengers and goods on regular schedules across international boundaries and intervening seas. It is quite a customary thing for tourists and business men to travel by air, for example, between London and Paris. There is a great rivalry for business between French and English companies, all of which are subsidized by their Governments.

There is at the present time in the United States no large regular air transportation business, although enterprising firms from time to time have undertaken to establish more or less regular routes between points deemed peculiarly attractive for the development of an air transportation business. The Air Mail Service operated by the Post Office Department has given the best and most practical demonstration of the reliability and adaptability of aircraft to the useful purposes of commerce. The present experiment by the Air Mail Service to determine the practicability of night flying is the most important development in aviation to-day and should prove to be of substantial assistance in the development of commercial aviation in America.

The reason for the greater development of commercial aviation in European countries to date lies in the fact that they realize more keenly than we in America do the vital necessity of aviation to national defense. They are either adjoining neighbors or within a few hours of each other by air, and unless military aviation in those countries is to bear the entire cost of the maintenance of aircraft industries and of aviation development generally, those countries must in sheer self-defense encourage commercial aviation. This they have done in every practicable way, principally by subsidizing common carriers by air, especially those engaged in international aerial transport.

In the United States direct subsidy appears to be out of the question because of our adherence to a traditional policy. In our country aviation must make its own way. Civil aviation has not progressed very far because it has not yet reached that stage of development that justifies its use generally from an economic point of view, unless an inordinate value is to be placed upon speed. Speed and maneuverability may be prime factors in military aircraft, especially in time of war, but for commercial purposes aircraft must be made safer, more controllable at low speeds incident to taking off and landing, and less expensive in initial cost as well as in maintenance and operation.

Commercial aviation will have to be regulated, just as are other means of transportation. The initial legislation in this respect should be very carefully prepared, so that, while affording that degree of regulation considered necessary in the public interest and that degree of practical assistance that would be helpful, it will nevertheless leave the new art of aviation ample freedom to develop normally without unnecessary or unwise restrictions and without attempting to set up by legislation an artificial basis for the maintenance of the activity to be regulated.

7. REPORT ON GOVERNMENT MANUFACTURE OF MUNITIONS

Nye Committee

At the insistence of Senators like William E. Borah, and in response to wide-spread public interest, the Senate established The Special Committee on Investigation of the Munitions Industry, under the chairmanship of Senator Gerald Nye. Although the committee never developed a cogent theoretical framework to explain the relationship between the military and civilian agencies of the government and the nation's munitions makers, the data from which such a theory could be constructed were scattered over many volumes of testimony and committee reports. The operations of a complex were clearly revealed, but subsequent events proved that despite Progressive hopes, disclosure and public censure are insufficient defense against the machinations of a profitable and powerful alliance of public and private interests.

Much of the committee's interest centered on the building of naval vessels, not only because they were the largest and most expensive weapons systems of their time, but also because it was specifically in this area that several disarmament conferences had failed to reach meaningful agreement after World War I. Since the nineteenth century, when most Army ordnance was procured from federal arsenals, the shipbuilding industry had been probably the most important single element in the private munitions trade. Backed by such organizations as the Navy League, the industry had recently convinced President Roosevelt to divert some funds from unemployment relief to a program for building naval vessels.

Source: *Munitions Industry*. Report on Government Manufacture of Munitions, U.S. Senate, Special Committee on Investigation of the Munition Industry, 74th Cong., 2d sess. (1936), pp. 1-13.

The Special Committee on Investigation of the Munitions Industry was authorized by Senate Resolution 206 of the Seventy-third Congress, which began—

> Whereas the influence of the commercial motive is an inevitable factor in consideration involving the maintenance of the national defense; and
> Whereas the influence of the commercial motive is one of the inevitable factors often believed to stimulate and sustain wars . . .

and which directed the committee—

> (d) To inquire into the desirability of creating a Government monopoly in respect to the manufacture of armaments and munitions and other implements of war, and to submit recommendations thereon.

Under the authority the committee considered not only the cost of purchase and construction of certain munitions facilities, but also many other factors bearing on the problem, such as the general social desirability of munitions sales abroad, the activities of the munitions companies abroad, their relations with governmental departments, the price and profit experience of the Nation with these companies during the World War, the need for adequate national defense in peacetime as well as in wartime and the influence of the commercial motive "in considerations involving the maintenance of national defense. . . ."

I. THE RELATION BETWEEN PEACETIME AND WARTIME PROFITS

The committee did not have sufficient staff to check the peacetime profits of the munitions companies, on individual contracts, because this procedure would have involved years of work by a very large body of accountants. Several of the companies testified to large profits on peacetime munitions work for the Government, using their own figures, unchecked by the committee. Examples are: Bethlehem Ship Building Co., cruiser *Portland,* $2,058,796, 21.8 percent profit; cruiser *Northampton,* $2,200,000, 25.4 percent profit. Newport News Shipbuilding & Dry Dock Co., cruiser *Augusta,* $2,800,945, and *Houston* $2,800,945, 35 percent profit; aircraft carrier *Ranger,* $3,050,000, 23.1 percent profit. New York Shipbuilding Co., cruiser *Chester,* $2,946,706, 36.9 percent profit; cruiser *Indianapolis,* $3,007,049, 33.4 percent profit. Carnegie Steel Co., armor plate, *NOD-272,* profit 57.9 percent; *NOD-331,* profit 43.4 percent; *NOD-432,* profit 42.7 percent. Bethlehem Steel Co., certain gun-forging contracts showed 28.27, 18.47, and 18.09 percent. Sperry Gyroscope Co. (Army auditor's figures, exhibit 4917), 108 flight indicators for Army Air Corps, 54.6 percent profit; 114 turn indicators, 40.4 percent profit. Douglas Aircraft Co. (exhibit 4889), showed estimated costs and profits, before commissions, of 30 percent on fighters and attack planes for China.

The significance of these high prices and profits in war preparation during peacetime is the probability that such prices and profits will be used as the base of wartime profits and prices, and that the courts will insist upon their use to justify high wartime profits.

This was indicated clearly in the report of the special master and referee, District Court of United States, Eastern District of Pennsylvania (*U.S. Complainant* v. *Bethlehem Steel Corporation, etc.*) in 1933. The master used the following chain of reasoning (exhibit 4872):

> The Government aimed to win the war. Bethlehem was deemed essential to doing so. A failure to induce Bethlehem to undertake the ship-building program covered by these contracts, followed by the taking possession by the Fleet Corporation of the Bethlehem plants, could not have accomplished the desired result. It was Bethlehem's organization that was necessary to insure success to the shipbuilding program of the Fleet Corporation and, as the Government did not have power to compel performance by an unwilling organization, if Bethlehem demanded its price on the basis of substantial commercial profits rather than contribute such services on a patriotic basis, the Government was obliged to take the contracts on such basis or not at all.
>
> The evidence shows, and the master finds, that the Fleet Corporation made the contracts with open eyes, although resenting the commercial attitude of Bethlehem and condemning Bethlehem for demanding its "pound of flesh", and did so because of a realization of the necessity of attaining an objective with the ship-building program which, without Bethlehem, might not be possible.

The master then quotes the position of the Government from 823 of the bill of complaint in equity:

> Complainant avers that said representations were knowingly false in that the Bethlehem Shipbuilding Corporation, Ltd., as hereinbefore set forth, was in a position to know what would be the approximate cost of constructing said vessels, and the said amounts stated in said contracts were known by the said representatives of said corporation to be greatly in excess of any costs which could reasonably be anticipated, based upon the wage scale then in effect, and the existing costs of material. Complainant avers that said estimates and representations were made for the purpose of enabling the Bethlehem Shipbuilding Corporation, Ltd., to derive excessive, unreasonable, and unconscionable profits from said contracts.

The master also quotes the major brief for the Government (pp. 321-322):

> Having perpetrated a gross fraud upon the Government in connection with such contracts, it would be unconscionable to hold that notwithstanding such fraud, Bethlehem should receive as compensation the same amount which would afford just compensation to an honest shipbuilder for doing the same work done by it. Any such decision would mean that Bethlehem

had everything to gain and nothing to lose, finally, in attempting to defraud the Government and would encourage dishonest contractors to take advantage of the Government under like circumstances.

No one can say that this country is done with war or how soon a national emergency will again exist calling for the maximum production of every shipyard throughout the United States. At such time plant requisition will again prove impracticable. There will again be no time for haggling, and the Government will again be obliged to depend upon the integrity and patriotism of the manufacturers with whom it is forced to deal. At such time there will undoubtedly again be those who will look upon the national emergency as an opportunity to make enormous profits for their respective companies and themselves at the expense of the Government, and whose patriotism and sense of propriety will not, in themselves, be sufficient to restrain them from taking full advantage of such opportunity—in its influence upon such dealings—the decision in these proceedings will be of far more importance than the millions now involved.

In reply to this concern on the part of the Government, the master gave judicial notice to the findings and testimony of the Senate Munitions Committee, especially the increase of prices which followed the big naval-construction program and the admission of the shipbuilders that they were putting up prices because of the great amount of work available at the time. He cited the profits of 36.7 percent on the *Chester,* built by New York Shipbuilding Co., and of 25.4 percent on the *Northampton* built by the Bethlehem Shipbuilding Co. He found the average wartime profits to Bethlehem upon the contracts with the Emergency Fleet Corporation to be 22.245 percent of actual cost, and less than the peacetime profits and found no fraud on Bethlehem's part, as charged by the United States.

The case will presumably be appealed by the Government. Meanwhile, however, the committee is impressed with the fact that the master used figures of high profits during peacetime which were put on record for the first time by this committee, as a means of justifying wartime profits of over 22 percent. This sets a precedent and makes all the high profits earned in peacetime a base which can and doubtless will be used by the companies in wartime.

The committee is also impressed with the master's simple statement that the Government had no means to force Bethlehem to produce ships, and that if Bethlehem chose, as it did, to demand "its price on the basis of substantial commercial profits rather than contribute such services on a patriotic basis, the Government was obliged to take the contracts on such basis or not at all." The committee, in its report on wartime taxation and price control (S. Rept. 944, pt. 2, 74th Cong., 1st sess.) found numerous other such cases, and found that "the apparent alternative of commandeering industry is in fact not an available alternative."

The committee is also impressed with the Government's fear, expressed above, that a decision allowing high wartime profits, obtained under duress, will influence the attitude of the manufacturers with whom the Government is forced to deal, and that "at such time there will undoubtedly again be those who will look upon the national emergency as an opportunity to make enormous profits for their respective companies and themselves at the expense of the Government, and whose patriotism and sense of propriety will not, in themselves, be sufficient to restrain them from taking full advantage of such opportunity."

The committee feels that the way is now wide open for the munitions companies to claim the right to make profits in wartime as high as they did in peacetime, and that therefore strict profit control in peacetime is essential if the Government is not to pay through its nose in wartime. Failure to hold down munitions profits during peacetime will be paid for many million times over in wartime.

The committee notes also from the master's report the situation confronting the Government in wartime: It needs the manufacturing plants of the Nation for its program of munitions production and has no means of imposing that production upon them. They will, in fact, take it at their own price or leave it. The Government cannot afford to have them leave it, so they get it at their own price. Patriotism and sacrifice is something to talk about to the public, as the president of Bethlehem Steel did fully, early in 1917. To the War Department in private they talk prices and profits, and say, in effect, "take it or leave it", knowing that they have the Government at their mercy. When, as in the case cited above, the Government claims that it was forced to make contracts under duress, the master of a United States district court points out that the Government knew at the time that the prices in the contracts were too high, and, having its eyes open at the time, later has no redress.

This legalized use of a national emergency to obtain high profits must be considered in any discussion of the desirability of a governmental monopoly of the manufacture of munitions.

II. DIFFICULTIES OF REGULATION IN PEACETIME AND WARTIME

In considering the question of the desirability of producing all the naval ships (except auxiliaries) in Government navy yards, the committee recurs to the testimony developed in several months of hearings on the naval shipbuilding companies, and especially the committee's findings in its report on naval shipbuilding (S. Rept. 944, 74th Cong.):

A. Agreements on Naval Bidding. Specifically, the committee finds, under the head of Agreements on Naval Bidding:

The Navy has become a big business. It is one of the largest governmental contractors in the world.

During the years 1933 and 1934 it gave out to private companies contracts totaling over $180,000,000.

The committee heard 9 companies, 67 witnesses, largely on the subject of these contracts. It spent 38 days, and took 4,036 pages of testimony.

The committee finds that the evidence indicates clearly that:

1. In most cases the Navy wishes work to begin as soon as possible. The result of this is that there is often not time to prepare designs, let alone examine figures or to analyze the bids put before it by private companies.

2. The rush has made it impossible for the Navy to use its own navy yards as current up-to-date yardsticks of private bids. The navy yards do not even know such essentials of the bids of private yards as the speed guaranties or oil guaranties until after the private bids are opened.

3. The Navy has never examined the underlying costs or profits of the private builders. It makes no pretense of doing this. It has no staff for it. The figures studied by the Munitions Committee were all news to it.

The Navy makes no attempt to examine the costs of the private companies to determine whether the profit limitation of 11.1 percent in the Vinson-Trammell Act is enforced or evaded. That is left to the Treasury to do after 3 years, after a job is done.

4. This rush, this lack of staff, this lack of acquaintanceship with the strange ups and downs of bidding by the private companies on the part of the Navy, leaves the Navy at the mercy of the shipbuilders. A series of bids are put before the Navy, and the Navy has to take the low one, and the taxpayers have to hope and pray that the low one is somewhere within a few million dollars of being reasonable and proper.

5. The evidence presented to the committee showed that in 1933 on contracts worth $130,000,000 to the private shipbuilders, there was no hard-hitting competition among equally desirous bidders able to take on the work: On the aircraft carriers, worth $38,000,000; on the two light cruisers, worth $24,000,000; on the heavy cruiser, worth $12,000,000. There was no competition of that character on the heavy destroyer leaders, worth $30,000,000, nor on the light destroyers, worth $18,000,000. On the submarines there may have been honest competition, but one competitor possessed all the patents and would not tell the other company how much those patents would cost them. That is the way $130,000,000 worth of work was given out in 1933.

6. From 1927 on when the cruiser program started, the record is the same. If there was no collusion, there was a sympathetic understanding among the big companies of each other's desires.

If there were no conversations about bidding among them, there was telepathy.

In 1927 the shipbuilders made profits of 35 and 25.4 and 36.9 percent on the cruisers. That was too good to spoil by hard competition. In 1929 the Navy asked for bids on two cruisers. Not one of the "Big Three" yards obliged. They bid on 1 each, and got 1 each. Their profits on these were around 22 percent.

The record is the same in 1931.

7. In 1933 two shipbuilders knew and wrote down lists of the low bidders weeks in advance of the time the bids were opened. Mr. Bardo was one of them. Mr. Wilder was another. Mr. Bardo admitted discussing his desires for certain ships only with his two main competitors.

8. The fact that many bids are submitted by shipbuilders does not mean that there is real competition. It does not mean lower prices. In fact, quite the contrary is true. When there is lots of work to go around the charges go up. The shipbuilders know that the Navy feels it has to have the ships, and they raise the prices. They admitted this frankly.

B. Excessive Profits. The committee finds, under the head of Excessive Profits, that the profit figures on the only naval vessels on which such figures are available were 35 percent (Newport News, 2 cruisers); 36.9 and 33.4 percent (New York Ship, 2 cruisers); 25.4 and 21.8 percent (Bethlehem Shipbuilding, 2 cruisers); 23.1 percent (Aircraft Carrier *Ranger,* Newport News).

C. Prices Increased with Big Navy. The committee finds, under the head Prices Increased with Big Navy, that the need of the Navy for many ships in 1933 was the main cause for the increase in prices charged by the private shipbuilders, and that they frankly admitted this, and that the Navy recognized the fact.

> Q. They (the shipbuilders) were frank enough to say they were putting up prices because of the great amount of work at the time?—A. (Admiral Robinson) There is no question about that.

D. Navy Yards as Yardsticks. The committee finds, under the head of Navy Yards as Yardsticks, that preliminary studies show the cost of building cruisers in navy yards to have been $2,116,304 lower than in private yards in 1927 and $1,843,693 lower in 1929. It also finds that in 1933 the low navy-yard estimate was $1,122,000 below the lowest private-yard fixed-price bid and $5,351,000 below the highest fixed-price bid. It also finds that the navy-yard estimates on the cost of building light destroyers averaged $1,240,459 lower than the average bids of the private yards and $943,460 below the lowest private-yard bid on a fixed-price basis.

The committee finds, further, that Navy officials have been transmitting to congressional committees figures on comparative costs of private and navy yards showing the profits on a privately built ship, the cruiser *Chester,* as $983,000, whereas the New York Shipbuilding Corporation informed the Munitions Committee that its profit on this cruiser was $2,946,706.

The committee finds, further, that the opposition of the private shipbuilders to navy-yard construction has been intense, reaching the point where the vice president of Newport News thought it better "to kill the Navy bill entirely" than to spend part of it in navy yards.

The committee notes the language used concerning a naval appropriation in 1931 by the Washington representative of Bath Iron Works:

I understand the morning after the (appropriation) bill went through every East-coast yard had its representatives in Washington with their tongues hanging out and all teeth showing ready to fight for their share of the plunder, and the only thing that stopped the West-coast yards from being here was the fact that they couldn't come bodily by telegraph.

E. The Navy's Dependence on Private Yards. The committee finds, under the head of the Navy's Dependence on Private Yards, that at present light cruisers, aircraft carriers, light destroyers, destroyer leaders, and submarines are being built largely or entirely from the plans drawn by private companies, and that there are very definite disadvantages to a system in which the Navy has to depend on private companies for such an important part of the national defense.

The committee notes the awareness of several of the shipbuilding companies of the fact that the Navy is completely dependent on them for this work.

The committee notes the statement by Commander E. L. Cochrane:

The Navy's developments of 15 years were—handed to the Electric Boat Co. on a silver platter, so to speak, on the conviction that it was desirable to keep at least one commercial company in the submarine game . . .

and also notes the statements of Sun Shipbuilding officials who wanted to build submarines that they could not find out what the Electric Boat patents would cost them prior to entering a bid. The committee finds this apparent monopoly an unwholesome and unsatisfactory situation, especially in view of Electric Boat Co.'s foreign connections.

The committee finds further that a very considerable delay followed the allocation of $238,000,000 of Public Works Administration money to the Navy in 1933, and that a large amount of this was due to delay in the planning work by these shipbuilding companies which had contracted to do this part of the work for the others and for the navy yards. The committee notes that this delay took place in spite of pledges by all shipbuilders to begin work as soon as possible for the benefit of the unemployed.

The committee finds, further, that while the Navy is dependent on the private shipbuilders for ways and plans, the private shipbuilders are dependent on the Navy for special favors, and have received a considerable number of them. Most notable among these are the adjusted price contracts of 1933 and 1934, the failure to use the navy yards as yardsticks, the failure to make itself independent of the private yards in planning work, and the Navy's opposition to profit limitation in 1934.

The committee finds indications of the use by the Navy of the shipbuilders as a lobby for its interests.

F. Influence and Lobbying of Shipbuilders. The committee finds, under the head of Influence and Lobbying of Shipbuilders, that the Navy contractors, subcontractors, and suppliers constitute a very large and influential financial group

The committee finds that three big shipbuilding companies had $53,744,000 of work at stake in the Geneva Disarmament Conference which the Navy had given to them a few months before the opening of the conference in 1927. It notes the admitted interest of the companies in the unfavorable outcome of that conference. It notes Mr. Shearer's testimony that he was urged to go to the conference by Admiral Pratt, and was supplied with secret Navy information. It notes the secrecy of his employment by the shipbuilders, and the explanation for that secrecy. It notes his activities in the promotion of a war scare with England in 1928 and 1929, while being paid by the shipbuilders. It notes certain discrepancies between testimony given by the shipbuilders at the Shortridge hearings and the hearings of the Munitions Committee. It notes Mr. Shearer's claim that "as a result of my activities, eight 10,000-ton cruisers are under construction." Further, that owing to the failure of the tripower naval conference at Geneva, there is now before the Seventieth Congress a 71-ship building program costing $740,000,000. It notes Mr. Shearer's further testimony of his activities at the request of various Naval officials. It notes his description of his Geneva campaign as "fast and vicious." It notes his report at the "delight" of the shipbuilders at the result. It notes the payment by the shipbuilders of the costs of a pamphlet he wrote attacking certain private citizens, including Newton D. Baker and Franklin D. Roosevelt. It notes the payments he received from Mr. Hearst of $5,000 in 1929. It notes the spreading through a friendly newspaper syndicate of an alarmist story concerning alleged Japanese intentions by the president of the Bath Iron Works, with the intent and result of activity by a Senator and Representatives from Maine in connection with an appropriation bill in 1932.

The committee finds, on the basis of this and other testimony, that there is a clear and definite danger in allowing self-interested groups, such as the shipbuilders and their allied interests, to be in the close position of influence, as they are at present, to such an important instrument of national policy as the Navy is, and the danger in allowing them to remain in a position where it is to their financial interest to confuse public opinion between the needs of the country for a purely defensive Navy and their own continued needs for profits.

The committee finds, further, that there has been a large amount of bipartisan political activity on the part of the shipbuilders locally, in Congress, and also at the national headquarters of the two parties. It makes no claim to have gone into this field thoroughly. The committee notes the claims of the Washington representative of United Drydocks in 1934 that he could get a bill through Congress for $50,000, and that "there is no virtue in being quixotic at this state." It notes the placing of Congressmen on certain committees at the request of the shipbuilders. It notes their claim to have helped the Navy on certain bills and to have elected Members to the House Rules Committee. It notes the reference to United Drydock Co. securing through Dave Hogan, secretary to Mr. McCooey, prominent Brooklyn Democrat, the award of $6,800,000 in destroyers in 1933.

The committee finds that the matter of national defense should be above and separated from lobbying and the use of political influence by self-interested groups and that it has not been above or separated from either of them.

The committee finds, further, under this head, that the main lobby for the Merchant Marine Act of 1928 was conducted by the shipbuilders under the leadership of Mr. Laurence R. Wilder, then president of American Brown Boveri (New York Shipbuilding Co.), and that a sum of over $140,000 was spent in putting that bill over.

The committee finds further that New York Shipbuilding Co. was acquired as a speculative investment by the Bragg-Smith-Cord interests just prior to the 1933 naval awards; that the present owners are not experienced shipbuilders and have since tried to divest themselves of the ownership, and that it is not a satisfactory situation to have such an important part of our potentially necessary national defense in the hands of people who are willing to sell it to the first bidder. Speculators and speculation should have no place in our national defense.

The success of the shipbuilders in securing an allocation of $238,000,000 for shipbuilding from Public Works Administration funds has been their most recent demonstration of power. In this their purpose was aided by labor groups who later, when the expected employment failed to materialize, spoke of the matter as a "double cross" to the Navy officials who had solicited their support for the measure.

G. Attempts to Limit Profits. The committee finds, under the head of Attempts to Limit Profits, that the failure of the Navy Department to turn the navy yards into effective yardsticks by which the charges of private shipyards could be measured and kept down, has resulted in leaving the profits of the shipbuilders practically uncontrolled.

The committee finds that the Vinson-Trammell bill of 1934 limiting profits to 11.1 percent of cost cannot be enforced without a huge police force of accountants and that disputes concerning its interpretation, similar to those which delayed the payment of wartime taxes by the companies for 12 years may confidently be expected.

The committee finds that the Navy's grant of adjusted price contracts in 1933 with limitations on the amount of risk the Government assumed for the benefit of the shipbuilders and in 1934 without any limitation on the Government burden for increased costs has resulted, in effect, in clost-plus contracts. It finds these cost-plus contracts more profitable than the wartime contracts when only a 10-percent profit over cost was allowed.

The committee finds that in the case of the 1934 adjusted-price contracts on light cruisers, destroyer leaders, light destroyers, and submarines, the Government has assumed all the risk of increasing prices, and has lowered the risk for which the companies received 11.1-percent profit by an enormous amount.

The committee finds that the Navy, which has no responsibility for enforcing the act, and which has no reliable figures about private costs, is in a position to allow—and according to one company has actually allowed—increased overhead charges, which can invalidate the whole attempt by Congress to limit profits. The committee notes that it was by the allowance of such theoretical overheads during the war years above actual overheads that New York Shipbuilding Corporation was paid $2,152,976 more by the Government than it actually paid out itself.

The committee finds that the shipbuilding industry and its subcontractors and suppliers have united in efforts to find ways to avoid the incidence of this law, and that Mr. Gillmor, president of Sperry Gyroscope, Navy suppliers, told them, "If the shipbuilders, boiler manufacturers, and electrical manufacturers act in accordance with uniform rules, it will be so strong I think the Income Tax Bureau will have a hard time resisting it." The committee notes the unreliability of the shipbuilders' figures as indicated by the wide differences between their wartime reports and the audits of those reports by the Treasury (sec. VIII). It notes also in this matter of reliability the recent discrepancy of almost $2,000,000 out of a profit of $2,900,000 in the reports furnished by the New York Shipbuilding Co., passed on by the National Council of Shipbuilders and circulated recently among congressional committees by Navy officials. It also notes in this matter the evidence tending to show that the Bath Iron Works transferrred an item of $60,000 incurred on a lighthouse tender to the costs of the destroyer *Dewey.*

The committee finds that there is no enforcement of the profit limitation law in effect until 4 years after the beginning of a cruiser. It finds, from wartime experience (sec. VIII) enough evidence of the difficulty of auditing thousands of old vouchers and of properly allocating overhead which the companies may have improperly saddled onto Navy vessels, to declare that there is no effective profit-limitation law today.

It finds the price of real enforcement of the attempts of Congress to limit profits to be a costly policing force of accountants and auditors who would be in the yard for at least 3 years, and a series of costly lawsuits after those audits have been completed. It finds that the only way to prove that a company had not improperly allocated overheads from commercial jobs onto Navy jobs would be to audit all the commercial jobs being done by a private yard as well as the Navy work; in short, to audit all the work done by the yard and to establish uniform accounting.

The committee questions whether this additional cost for auditing and policing, plus the cost of lawsuits after such audits, on top of the 1 to 2 million dollars extra cost of private construction, and the $300,000 spent by the Navy for inspection of the privately built cruisers, justify the continuance of private yards as naval contractors. They have the appearance of being expensive luxuries.

The committee reserves decision on this phase of the matter until the completion of its investigation of the costs of governmental construction.

H. Wartime Attitude of Shipbuilders. The committee finds, under the head of Wartime Attitude of Shipbuilders, that the record of the present ship building companies during the war, wherever examined, was close to being disgraceful.

They made very considerable profits. On Treasury audits they showed up to 90 percent. They secured cost-plus contracts and added questionable charges to the costs. They took their profits on these ships after the wartime taxes had been repealed. They secured changes in contract dates to avoid war taxes. They bought from the Government, very cheaply, yards which had been built expensively at Government costs. In one case this was prearranged before the yard was built. One yard did not build necessary additions until it was threatened with being commandeered. Knowingly exorbitant claims were filed against the Government for cancelation. Huge bonuses were paid to officers. Profits were concealed as rentals.

After the war was over keels for $181,247,000 worth of destroyers were laid, which was probably the largest post-war favor done by any Government to any munitions group.

The committee finds no assurance in the wartime history of these companies to lead it to believe that they would suddenly change their spots in the case of another war.

After the committee's hearings on shipbuilding had closed, Gen. Hugh Johnson, at one time connected with the War Industries Board, later with B. M. Baruch, and later Director of the National Recovery Administration, explained that the N.R.A. had grown out of the plans developed by the War Department for the conduct of a future war. It was, he stated, developed directly from the war plans and was not shown to the industrialists for their approval until practically completed. In view of this statement, the committee finds significance in the testimony of a Department of Labor official concerning the unwillingness of the New York Shipbuilding Co. to observe the N.R.A. rules, with the result of a serious labor dispute in 1934. The company did not raise the question of constitutionality, and all that was involved was the question of observance or evasion of the law.

The committee finds in this evidence, taken together with the actual wartime experience of the Government with these companies, little hope for obedience by them of more stringent wartime provisions in the case of another emergency.

III. THE CRITICAL YEARS

Despite the tendency to overemphasize the 1940s at the expense of the developments of the previous two decades, the years of World War II were critical for the development of the military-industrial complex. The sheer scale of the effort, and the length of time it claimed the nation's primary attention, would be enough to insure its importance. But perhaps more important even than the war effort itself was the fact that it was not completely dismantled after V-J Day. The old paradox of perpetual war for perpetual peace came to have a kind of grim logic.

Historians are still unraveling the events that led up to the Cold War, and no doubt there will always be room for some difference of opinion about the roles of the United States and the Soviet Union, and disagreements over their respective intentions. It is already clear, however, that powerful forces within the United States saw a *Pax Americana* backed up by armed force as the most desirable state for the postwar world. Both world wars had lifted the nation from depression, and informed opinion feared a return of hard times with the end of fighting in Europe. The United States did not act in disregard of Soviet intentions and actions, but neither did it merely react to foreign threats.

The decision was made that this country should become the policeman of the world. Whether one merely feared another war, this time with the Soviets, or whether one boldly claimed that that war was already under way, a strong military, backed up by a strong munitions industry, became a cornerstone of public policy.

8. INVESTIGATION OF THE NATIONAL DEFENSE PROGRAM

Truman Committee

Those who attempted to organize the war effort after 1940 discovered that they faced many of the same problems, and tried to solve them with many of the same tools, encountered and used a quarter century before. This was, of course, only to be expected because the government, the economy, and the nature of war in 1940 were all logical extensions of institutions and conditions dominant twenty-five years before.

The successful and respected Special Committee to Investigate the National Defense Program, under the chairmanship of Senator Harry S. Truman of Missouri, operated throughout the war to keep Congress informed of and involved in the war effort. The committee recognized the need for primary responsibility to be lodged in the civilian administration, but it vigorously exposed and denounced programs or agencies it thought were not acting in the nation's best interest.

A defense and war program by its very nature requires a tremendous dislocation in the business economy of the Nation and in the relations between business and government. The fundamental theory of a democracy is that every individual determines the business in which he will engage, the type of articles he will

Source: *Investigation of the National Defense Program. Additional Report.* U.S. Senate, Special Committee to Investigate the National Defense Program, 77th Cong., 2d sess., Report 480, Part 5 (January 15, 1942), pp. 5-14.

manufacture, the materials he will use, the persons from whom he will buy, and to whom he will sell. The function of government in peacetime is simply to state the rules under which business will be conducted and to insure that there is fair play between businessmen and a fair deal to the public.

In a defense or war program the situation is very different. The Government, at least as to articles needed for the prosecution of the war, must determine what is to be produced, the quantities thereof, the materials to be used in connection therewith, and even the exact methods by which the articles are to be produced. In order to insure adequate supplies of war materials, it is necessary for the Government to go even further and determine the quantities and kinds of raw materials which should be produced and the extent to which such materials can be used for civilian economy.

The civilian economy cannot be treated as a separate problem, for a sound healthy civilian economy is an absolute essential for the successful prosecution of a modern war, especially if it is a protracted war. There are certain minimum and basic needs of the civilian population which must be met in order to keep up morale and the ability to continue producing war materials in the quantities needed. In a very real sense war materials are nothing more than the surplus which can be spared from civilian production without impairing the ability of the economy to continue producing. To use a homely example, you cannot get milk from a cow or eggs from a fowl unless you provide sufficient food to keep the animal sound and healthy.

Moreover, Government cannot neglect the fact that fundamentally the whole defense and war program was embarked upon for the purpose of preserving from Fascist aggressors the American way of living and that little will be gained if in winning the war we destroy the ability of the country to readjust itself and resume the American way of living.

To do this we must preserve to as great an extent as possible a sound civilian economy.

Under a war program the Government also has the responsibility for making long-range plans to cope with the emergencies which may arise so that the shifts that are made necessary by the defense and war program take place gradually to the end that plants and labor can be transferred from civilian work to defense work with a minimum of dislocation and unemployment.

These responsibilities of Government are so vast and so complicated in their nature that it is impossible and unfair to expect a perfect job. They cannot be met by legislation or by Executive orders. General principles of direction can be specified that way but the success or failure of the program in the last analysis depends upon the thousands of individuals who attempt to administer the program. Their success or failure in turn depends largely upon whether these individuals meet head-on the problems that are involved and see to it that some sensible solutions are found as soon as possible.

ORGANIZATION AND POWERS OF THE
OFFICE OF PRODUCTION MANAGEMENT

The task of correlating and administering most of the defense and war production program has been entrusted to the Office of Production Management, which was especially created for that purpose. Its record has not been impressive; its mistakes of commission have been legion; and its mistakes of omission have been even greater. It has all too often done nothing when it should have realized that problems cannot be avoided by refusing to admit that they exist. In an emergency of this kind where Government leadership and planning is an absolute essential, the Office of Production Management should have adopted the old Army maxim that "in an emergency it is better to do any intelligent act than to do nothing at all."

Apologists for the Office of Production Management have stressed the lack of authority on its part to require the other agencies of government with whom it must deal to follow its decisions. These apologists have contended furthermore that it is sufficient for the Office of Production Management to note the existence of problems and to refer them elsewhere for solution. It may well be that additional powers should be conferred on the Office of Production Management by Executive order or by legislation, and it may even be that ultimately we should have a so-called czar of business. Those are very important questions of high policy to which early attention should be given.

But, fundamentally, the disappointing record of the Office of Production Management is not so much due to its lack of power as to its failure to perform the functions for which it was created. Everyone knew that the Office of Production Management would require a considerable amount of time and would have to use skill and effort to obtain proper personnel and to determine the interrelationships which would best enable that personnel to operate. Any attempt at that time to have predetermined the exact structure of the Office of Production Management and to have specified the exact authority which should be given to each division thereof would have been most difficult and perhaps impossible. There had been studies of problems encountered in World War No. 1, which were useful, but the problems involved in the present defense program differed in many important respects from those involved in World War No. 1.

The Office of Production Management was properly given a very great amount of freedom to determine its own organization and the interrelations between the various departments and divisions of that organization. This freedom from arbitrary restrictions carried with it a corresponding duty on the part of the responsible heads of the Office of Production Management to see to it that an efficient, workable organization was created. If the powers given to them were not sufficient to accomplish that end, they had a plain duty not only to call attention to the lack of power but themselves to present a carefully prepared request for the Executive orders or legislation which they needed and the reasons why they needed them. This duty has been recognized by both the

War and Navy Departments, which have on numerous occasions presented requests for additional powers required by them. Neither the President nor the Congress has hesitated to grant such powers where a real need therefor has been disclosed.

The committee has found, however, that the public has not contested the authority of the Office of Production Management but, instead, has accepted its rulings. There has been a very real effort to cooperate, even though such cooperation has required tremendous sacrifices on the part of tens of thousands of small business men. The public has wholeheartedly supported the defense program, and has considered no sacrifice to be too great, where it has been convinced that the sacrifice was necessary and that all were being treated alike. The Office of Production Management, therefore, has had at its disposal at all times the most effective weapon which could be given to it, namely, the weapon of public opinion.

In those instances where it has failed, the failure has not been due so much to the lack of power as to the ineptness of the officials of the Office of Production Management and their unwillingness to use the weapon which they had. Where difficulties were incurred, the Office of Production Management should have thoroughly studied the problems involved and should have publicly made specific recommendations based on accurate, concise statements of facts. If the recommendations were sound and the facts correct, few persons would have dared to refuse to follow any reasonable program laid down for them. Those who did so, could have been summoned before this committee and asked to justify their recalcitrance. If and when that failed, the Congress could have been asked to pass appropriate legislation.

Instead of doing this, the usual procedure was to refrain from raising the issue and to avoid responsibility by claiming lack of authority and, if possible, by referring the matter to some other agency of Government.

DOLLAR-A-YEAR MEN

The principal positions of the Office of Production Management were assigned to persons holding important positions with large companies who were willing and anxious to serve on a dollar per year, or without compensation (w. o. c.) basis. They usually did not sever their business connections, but instead obtained leave of absence. In many instances they continued to act for their companies, publicly announcing that their Government work was part-time work only. Their companies continued to pay their salaries. In some cases their compensation was even increased.

As of January 5, 1942, there were 255 dollar-a-year men and 631 w. o. c. men employed in the Office of Production Management.

The Office of Production Management has had a rule that such men cannot pass upon contracts to their own companies, and the committee believes that the rule has been strictly observed. To have done otherwise would have been to violate principles of agency law which have been settled for centuries. This exclusion from working on matters in which their companies were interested does mean, however, that the dollar-a-year and w. o. c. men were generally assigned to tasks materially different from those in which they had engaged in private life and raises a question as to whether we can even say that in utilizing such men we gained the experience of big business. This generality is, however, subject to the qualification that many of the dollar-a-year and w. o. c. men are professional men who unquestionably had experience in the same fields in which they are now working for the Office of Production Management. They, however, are dealing with matters involving the welfare of the class of clients by whom they were formerly employed and by whom they naturally expect to be employed in the future.

Although the contracts obtained by the companies loaning the services of dollar-a-year and w. o. c. men are not passed upon by the men so loaned, such companies do obtain very substantial benefits from the practice. The dollar-a-year and w. o. c. men so loaned spend a considerable portion of their time during office hours in familiarizing themselves with the defense program. They are, therefore, in a much better position than the ordinary man in the street to know what type of contracts the Government is about to let and how their companies may best proceed to obtain consideration. They also are in an excellent position to know what shortages are imminent and to advise their companies on how best to proceed, either to build up inventories against future shortages, or to apply for early consideration for priorities. They can even advise them as to how to phrase their requests for priorities. In addition, such men are frequently close personal friends and social intimates of the dollar-a-year and w. o. c. men who do pass upon the contracts in which their companies are interested.

These are only a few of the advantages which large companies have obtained from the practice, and it should be especially noted that they are the very same ones which the small and intermediate businessmen attempt to obtain by hiring people who they believe have "inside information," and "friends on the inside" who could assist them in obtaining favorable consideration for contracts. Therefore, in a very real sense the dollar-a-year and w. o. c. men can be termed "lobbyists." This does not mean that either they or their companies are engaged in any illegal conduct, for lobbying as such is not illegal, but it does mean that human nature being what it is, there is a very real opportunity for the favoritism and other abuses which has led the public to condemn lobbying and the Congress to consider corrective legislation.

In addition to the above benefits, the companies loaning the services of dollar-a-year and w. o. c. men obtain other and less tangible, but perhaps even more important benefits. All important procurement contracts must be approved by these dollar-a-year and w. o. c. men, which means that contracts must conform to their theories of business. Since they represent the largest companies, this means that the defense program in all its ramifications must obtain the approval of the large companies. This does not mean that the boards of directors of the large companies are requested to determine the defense program, nor does it even mean that the dollar-a-year and w. o. c. men consciously favor their companies or their companies' methods of doing business. On the contrary, the committee believes that most dollar-a-year and w. o. c. men are honest and conscientious, and that they would not intentionally favor big business. However, it is not their intentional acts that the committee fears, but their subconscious tendency, without which they would hardly be human, to judge all matters before them in the light of their past experiences and convictions.

It is only natural that such men should believe that only companies of the size and type with which they were associated have the ability to perform defense contracts; that small and intermediate companies ought not to be given prime contracts; that the urgencies of the defense program are such that they have no time to consider small companies for defense contracts; that the large companies ought not to be required to subcontract items which they could profitably manufacture and as to which they express lack of confidence in the productive facilities of smaller concerns; that the producers of strategic materials should not be expected or required to increase their capacities, even at Government expense, where that might result in excess capacity after the war and adversely affect their post-war profits; and that large companies should not be expected or required to convert their existing facilities into defense plants, where they prefer to use their plants to make the profits from their civilian business and, at the same time, to have additional plants directly or indirectly paid for by the Government, which they can operate profitably on terms dictated by themselves. The dollar-a-year and w. o. c. men subconsciously reflect the opinions and conclusions which they formerly reached as managers of large interests with respect to Government competition, with respect to taxation and amortization, with respect to the financing of new plant expansion, and with respect to the margin of profit which should be allowed on war contracts. For a more detailed discussion of some of the effects of such subconscious thinking, the committee refers to its previous report on "Priorities and the Utilization of Existing Manufacturing Facilities. . . ."

The committee has been trying for months to force a greater use of our existing facilities, of both large and small plants, and believes that a belated but serious effort has been made to make progress in this direction. The past cannot be undone, but it is vitally important that the same mistakes should not be repeated in the future.

The committee is opposed to a policy of taking free services from persons with axes to grind, and the committee believes that the Government should not continue to accept the loan of dollar-a-year and w. o. c. men by companies with so large a stake in the defense program. The committee, therefore, suggests that steps should be taken by the Office of Production Management to offer Government salaries to the dollar-a-year and w. o. c. men within the range which the Government has paid for positions of similar responsibility in other departments, and that such persons should be required during the duration of their employment by the Government to disassociate themselves from any employment by or payment from companies which have obtained large defense contracts. This does not mean that they should not have an expectancy of returning to their companies after the Government has no further need for their services, but the committee does believe that they should have no commitments for reemployment, and that they should not receive compensation for services which they cannot properly render to their companies during their employment. No man can honestly serve two masters.

The propriety of such a recommendation was recognized by John Lord O'Brian, General Counsel of the Office of Production Management, when he required lawyers who were being appointed to his staff to sever connection with the firms with which they were associated. If such action was desirable with respect to lawyers, whose firms were not obtaining any defense contracts, it is all the more proper and desirable with respect to those dollar-a-year and w. o. c. men whose companies are directly obtaining the great bulk of the defense contracts.

METHODS OF PROCEDURE

The Office of Production Management has made a practice of holding conferences attended by scores and sometimes hundreds of persons. Usually the most important of these conferences have been secret. Some have even been conducted under a pledge of secrecy by the Office of Production Management.

Furthermore, the Office of Production Management has been in the habit of announcing to the press that such conferences have been held and of outlining the purpose for which held, and even the substance of what is supposed to have occurred at the conference. Under such circumstances, the conferences are secret only to the extent that the public cannot judge the effectiveness or ineffectiveness with which the problems were discussed.

Large conferences of this character are of use only at the beginning of the consideration of an important problem, for they cannot represent any more than an interchange of general views. To be effective they must be followed by detailed discussion of specific problems with each of the participants in the conference.

These large conferences are usually followed by a series of smaller conferences of which no formal record is made. In fact, in most instances, there is not even an informal record made in the Office of Production Management, so that the parties are reduced to relying upon their memories, which judging by answers to committee inquiries, have been very faulty.

These smaller conferences usually extended over a period of weeks and even months without producing tangible results. The lack of businesslike records makes it quite impossible to determine exactly why a practical solution of the problems involved was not reached.

The committee is of the opinion that the only justification for secrecy in these conferences is that possibly valuable information might be furnished to the enemy. It is hardly likely, however, that such information, disclosed as it is to large groups, and the essence of which is made available to the press, will long remain a secret to the enemy. In any event a record of the proceedings at such conferences should be kept, so that it will be possible when the need for secrecy no longer exists, or after the matter has been publicly disclosed, to ascertain exactly what took place at the meeting and how effectively the problems involved were considered.

The committee believes that the results of the smaller private conferences held with representatives of specific companies that take place after the large general conferences, should be recorded, and that the Office of Production Management should require its personnel to dictate and file brief summaries, in accordance with the regular practice of business and professional men. Matters of such importance should not be left to the fallible memory of men, who in their own business affairs do not neglect to keep accurate conference records.

The committee also recommends that there be a minimum of discussion and a maximum of action. By this is meant that where the Office of Production Management has concrete information, it should be able to present to the initial conference specific suggestions and a detailed request for further information. For example, before holding the conference of large copper producers on July 17, 1941, the Office of Production Management should have gathered information as to the major problems faced by producers and should have asked them to furnish information on those specified problems relating to individual mines operated by them. The returns should then have been immediately examined to ascertain whether they were factual or conclusory, and where they were conclusory, an immediate request should have been made for specific facts to support the conclusions. Responsibility for increasing the production of each mine should have been placed upon a single individual. The several persons having such responsibilities for similar mines would thus have been placed in competition and would have known that their records in increasing or failing to increase production would be checked one against the other.

Factual information furnished by the producers should have been checked or at least test-checked by examining into the actual files of the company. And more particularly the conclusions to be drawn from the facts should have been checked and cross-checked by consulting those persons having other interests, who were in a position to have knowledge or opinions of value. For example, contentions as to the efficiency of mining machinery, the possibility of using additional hoists, etc., should have been verified with the manufacturers of such machinery, who might very possibly have different views, from the mine operators, and who certainly would have some knowledge of such matters. Also, the possibility of using additional shifts or working longer hours should have been taken up with the miners who actually work in the mine. Only by obtaining the individual and collective views of all parties representing widely divergent interests could the Office of Production Management expect to learn the full facts or to be in a position to properly evaluate them.

Copper mining is used in the above example, but the same procedure could and should have been adopted generally. This, however, is not intended as a criticism of business. On the contrary, the committee believes that most businessmen, including the producers of copper, were desirous of assisting the defense program. They are more sinned against than sinning. They have many and very legitimate complaints to the general effect that it is impossible for them to ascertain exactly what they are expected to do for the defense program. Businessmen necessarily, and properly, have been deprived of the power to plan their own affairs because the exigencies of the defense program are such that the defense program must be considered paramount to private interests. No businessman can know exactly what he is going to be called upon to do until the Government has made its position known. For these reasons businessmen are entitled to a complete and detailed outline of what the Government proposes to do, and if they are asked to increase or decrease production they have the right to expect the Government to assure leadership and be specific in making requests to say nothing of making demands upon them. . . .

Instead of assuming the responsibility of presenting a clear-cut program to the businessmen, the Office of Production Management in almost every important instance (as for example automobiles, aluminum, steel, copper, lead, zinc, and numerous others) either has failed to foresee the nature and extent of problems or has tended to minimize the difficulty and to take half-hearted measures in the vain hope that the problem would solve itself. This has not only created uncertainty for businessmen, but has meant also that nothing much is done about problems until businessmen evolve solutions of their own. Naturally, each such program is limited to the particular company suggesting it, and is especially designed to protect the interest of the company. The committee has been critical of the extent to which such companies have protected their own interests, as for example the Aluminum Co. of America. But, the committee nevertheless believes that without the practical suggestions of such companies the program to increase production would be almost a complete failure, because the committee has seen little evidence of concrete proposals by the Office of Production Management.

In addition to the delay incident to such a method of proceeding, and to the heavy price which the Government must pay to obtain production thereby, it has the added weakness that only the largest companies can obtain any real attention from the Office of Production Management. After weeks and months of conferences the proposals of each company are referred for solution to some other agency of the Government. In cases where Government financing is expected, this agency is usually the Defense Plant Corporation, which is then placed in the very unsatisfactory bargaining position of being told that the Office of Production Management is of the opinion that the defense program requires that a specified large company should be given many tens of millions of dollars of Government funds to build a plant when only the general provisions of the proposed contract have been worked out. This is tantamount to issuing instructions to the Defense Plant Corporation to accept whatever terms are proposed by the large company under penalty of being criticized for holding up defense production. This is the worst conceivable bargaining position and is the equivalent of walking into a clothing shop which has no set prices for its merchandise and announcing that you must buy immediately a specified article adding that you have already concluded that you cannot possibly get it elsewhere. Thereupon you ask the shopkeeper how much he wants for it.

In addition, the practice has the vice that it is humanly impossible for any staff, even one as large as that of the Office of Production Management, to take up individually the thousands of situations that would necessarily have to be considered in order to assure fair treatment to all the small and intermediate producers. This is not only admitted by the Office of Production Management, but has been privately advanced as the reason why little or no consideration has been given to small producers. It is a situation especially aggravated by the fact that in the case of most of the strategic materials the Office of Production Management not only failed to foresee shortages, but stubbornly refused to admit the existence of shortages until long after they had occurred. Finally, when attention was focused on the problem, there was very little time to conduct individual negotiations to increase production.

In order to obviate this difficulty the committee suggests that the Office of Production Management determine generally the terms under which production can be increased, so as to give a maximum of information to small producers as to the treatment which they would receive if they should attempt to create new production or to increase existing production. A pound of lead or zinc, which would otherwise not be produced, is just as valuable to the defense program whether it is produced from the largest mine as part of a 5,000-ton increase, or from a newly opened mine with only a 50-ton annual capacity. Certainly, in this respect it is even more important to the small producer than it is to the big producer, because generally speaking the former operates on a very small capital and must interest others in any new venture or expansion of an old venture.

That portion of the dollar saving which can be realized from the change in the overhead provisions is itself many times greater than the cost of conducting a committee of this kind. The savings upon which no dollar value can be assigned are in the committee's opinion even greater. More important than any of these, in the committee's opinion, is the realization by business interests seeking contracts of this kind that their acts may be subjected to investigation and that they may be called upon to explain why they drive such hard bargains with the Government at a time when most people are making substantial sacrifices for the prosecution of the war.

9. WAR LORDS OF WASHINGTON

Bruce Catton

The Truman Committee, like the Nye Committee before it, criticized many facets of the developing military-industrial complex, but made no fundamental criticism of the system itself. Working in the War Production Board, however, was a young man who had not yet made a reputation as a historian but was already a shrewd observer of the American scene. Bruce Catton realized, as the phrase had it, that Dr. New Deal had been dismissed and Dr. Win-the-War had been called in to prescribe for the dangerously ailing nation.

As Catton pointed out, the two fundamental decisions made by the Roosevelt Administration were first, to win the war, and second to do so with as little disruption of existing institutions as possible. These simple, and apparently straightforward decisions, made inevitable much of what followed. The problem was that they were based in part on an erroneous notion of what the war was all about, and in part upon the very natural desire of the rich to get richer. Catton's account is an angry but accurate picture of these decisions and their consequences.

The luck of the committee which was planning the Adam Gimbel Centennial Banquet was both good and bad. Good, because the committee had succeeded in signing up Donald Nelson to be the speaker of the evening; bad, because as

Source: From *The War Lords of Washington,* copyright, 1948, by Bruce Catton. Reprinted by permission of Harcourt Brace Jovanovich. Pp. 111-122.

events worked out Nelson wasn't able to be present. In the end, good luck and bad were neatly blended. Nelson wasn't there but his speech was—certified as official, and duly read to the assembled guests by a proxy—and a freak of chance decreed that this speech should be the first public statement of the views and policies of the new boss of American war production.

Plans for the banquet had, of course, been laid well in advance. It was to be held in Vincennes, Indiana, on January 14, 1942. It honored the centennial of a pioneer American merchant, and as one of America's leading merchandisers Nelson had been happy to accept the committee's invitation. He had worked on his speech with a good deal of care, trying to spell out for his audience just what the war was going to mean to the nation's economy, fully aware that in the present chaotic state of affairs in Washington a strong pronouncement by someone was badly needed. And then, twenty-four hours before the speech was to be delivered, Nelson was called to the White House and told that he was to be chairman of a brand new War Production Board, which would be in charge of everything Nelson thought necessary and would be armed with all of the authority he might see fit to ask for.

Among the many matters that Nelson had to think about, therefore, on the morning of January 14, this speaking engagement in far-off Indiana was one of the least important but most pressing. The one thing he could not do, on that particular evening, was go to Indiana. He could not even spare the time and energy to deliver his speech from Washington via leased wire or electrical transcription. Someone else would have to read it for him, if it were to be given at all; that was clear, and it was so arranged.

Then there was the speech itself. When he wrote it, Nelson had been just one of a number of impatient officials who were watching the galvanic twitchings of the dying OPM and hoping that something could be done to bring real direction to the job of war production. In writing the speech he had tried to express his own idea of what the situation called for; not the organizational changes that were needed, but the fact that industrial America needed to take a deep breath and prepare to transcend all of its own limitations. He had designed his speech as a plea for the discarding of all preconceived notions, all prejudices or concepts or habits of mind that might in any degree stand in the way of victory. But now he was not just the critic; he was the boss. This speech would go out as an official pronouncement—the *first* official pronouncement—by the man who had just been put in charge of the whole works. He himself was the man who would have to live up to the fine sentiments which he had put on paper. Could he, as boss of the job, still say the things he had written when he had not been boss?

He could and he did. He called for the completed manuscript of his speech the first thing that morning—his first morning as chairman of the War Production Board—and read it carefully. Finally he said, "Well, it all stands up. I think it needs to be said. Let's say it." So his proxy made the speech as it was originally written.

It was an important speech. It not only showed the mental attitude of the man who had been put in complete charge of the nonmilitary side of the war effort; it reflected, unconsciously but very accurately, what turned out to be the key decision of the administration in regard to the waging of the war.

"We are going to have to rely on our great mass production industries for the bulk of our increase under this war program," Nelson said. "Wherever we can we must convert them to war production, and convert them quickly. The only gauge we can apply to this process is: What method will most quickly give us the greatest volume of war production in this particular industry?

"The answer to that question may be hard to swallow, at times; it may call for a pooling of tools, for a redistribution of skilled workers, for a concentration of civilian production in one set of plants and 100 per cent war production in others; it may, in fact, and probably very often will, call for utterly revolutionary changes in the method of operating that industry and the whole network of relationships as between government, management, suppliers, and workers. But what of it? The one thing that counts is to get the stuff out and get it out quickly. We cannot waste three months—or three weeks, for that matter—in wrangling and discussion; we cannot compromise this demand for all-out production, or accept a formula which gives us anything less than the absolute maximum of production, just because someone's toes are going to be stepped on."

Brave words, Captain Fluellen. Exactly what did they mean?

Two things. First, that the day of holding back was definitely over. What Nelson was saying was that he was ready—and the country must be ready—to try absolutely anything if it would help to win the war. Nelson was prepared to be ruthless, and he was not going to worry about labels like "radical" or "reactionary"; he could swallow, for instance, the Reuther plan, or any other conceivable plan, if he could be shown that the quickest road to victory lay that way. This bland, comfortable, hail-fellow-well-met from the mail order business was not going to boggle at formulas.

So far so good. But the second point, which grows out of the first and which went more or less unnoticed at the time, is that this declaration was in effect a statute of limitations. We would do, the war production chief was saying, anything under the shining sun that might be necessary for victory; but, by the same token, everything we did do would have to justify itself by that yardstick. The only consideration was the defeat of the Axis—the Axis, defined as a tangible, three-dimensional power to be conquered by armies and air fleets and warships and sheer weight of metal. Winning the war was all that counted. If we were fighting *for* something as well as against something, and if we would have to show what it was we were fighting for by the way in which we fought—well, all of that could be left to the great god of battles. We were getting a vision of a strange new world, maybe, in which all men worked together toward a common goal, and self-interest was gone with the mists of the morning, but the baseless fabric of that vision would dissolve and leave not a rack behind the moment the enemy laid down his arms.

Nelson wasn't trying to say all of that, to be sure. He was just trying to express his conviction that we were in a no-holds-barred fight, and that the crippling fear of change was not going to be allowed to handicap us any longer. He was not trying to set high administration policy, except as it applied to the business of making munitions. The trouble was that it was precisely in that field, more than in any other, that our underlying policy in respect to the war had to be made manifest, and our underlying policy had never been defined. If the word was to become flesh it had to become so in the way in which the flesh was put to work, and the word had not been uttered. Facing a problem in the production of war goods, Nelson took a leaf from Nathan Bedford Forrest's book and announced that our aim was to git thar fust with the most stuff. That was an excellent decision as far as it went, but it was framed and adopted in a vacuum. It was all the decision there was, and it became the controlling decision of the war, the point of departure for everything that was to be done.

Lacking any other prophet, we had gone back to Bill Knudsen's after-dinner speech three nights before Pearl Harbor. The Axis was a monstrous neighbor-hood nuisance and we were going to suppress it. The war was as simple as that and as limited. If, in the end, it refused to *be* simple, and if it turned out that it had no limits—well, that was not going to affect the way we fought it.

At the moment, however, there were other matters to think about. Before he could get his teeth into his new job, Nelson had to decide how he was going to handle two pressing issues: his relationship with the War Department, and the use that should be made of that useful, baffling, contradictory institution, the dollar-a-year man.

War Department first. Should it continue to sign the contracts for war goods, or should that job be taken over by a civilian ministry of supply—by Nelson's new War Production Board, to be specific?

Backward as OPM had been in getting a broad and speedy production program established, it had been no more backward than the War Department itself. Indeed, one of the chief criticisms of OPM had been centered on its inability to find any way to direct and to speed up the military procurement processes. Speed and volume of production depend, when all is said and done, on the contracts that are issued; the agency that issues the contracts, consequently, is apt to be the agency that ultimately calls the pitch on the production program. The War Department had given no faintest sign, up to the beginning of 1942, that it comprehended the size of the job that was to be done. Could it safely be left in charge of military procurement? Was military procurement, for that matter, actually a job for the Army at all? When the President announced that Nelson was to write his own ticket for the new War Production Board, and that he would be given any authority he asked for, it was pretty generally taken for granted that the first thing Nelson would demand would be the removal of the contracting power from the War Department.

He didn't do it, and while his decision not to disappointed his most ardent supporters, Nelson himself never doubted that it was the only decision he could have made. He estimated that to set up a new procurement agency would take many months; during those months, the all-out production job would inevitably be delayed. And there were no months to spare: not when the Axis was visibly winning the war on every front, and the turning of the tide so obviously waited on American war production. As Nelson himself said, there were not three months to spare—or, for that matter, three weeks, either. Furthermore, Nelson had a sneaking suspicion that to take over military procurement—to make himself the man who signed the contracts and actually placed the initial orders with industry—would be to cut himself in on the making of purely military decisions, for which he had no stomach. The man who signs the contracts for military goods can be, in the long run, the man who determines that weapon A gets made ahead of weapon B, that weapon C does not get made at all, and that weapon D is more to be desired than weapon E. For better or for worse, Nelson voted to leave procurement in military hands and to exert control through co-ordination and policy-setting rather than through outright expropriation.

Probably it was the only decision he could have made, under the circumstances. After the war ended he remarked that if he had it all to do over again he would do it exactly the same way. But it was a decision that was to fly up and hit him in the face, just the same, and in the end it had a profound effect on the shape of events. It was the enacting clause to the generalized decision that military victory was the only thing to worry about. Military victory is our one goal; and it is the military, in the end, that will tell us what we must do to reach it.

Hand in hand with this went the decision on dollar-a-year men.

The dollar-a-year man was in bad odor when Nelson took charge of war production. If the Roosevelt administration wanted to discredit business leadership and rob it of power and influence, as its more spirited opponents liked to believe, it certainly stood right on the edge of final victory in January of 1942. Business leadership had had eighteen months to show what it could do with a defense program, and the result had been bad both for the defense program and for business leadership. Maybe the choice of men had been bad, maybe the setup under which the chosen men had gone to work had been impossible; whatever the reason, the old idea that the only possible operators for an industrialized war were the industrialists themselves had suffered a sharp decline, and some sort of change was expected. If it was taken for granted that the new boss of war production would have to clip the wings of the War Department in order to get his job done, it was also assumed that he would have to get rid of the dollar-a-year men.

By no one was this conviction more deeply felt than by the Truman Committee of the Senate, which enjoyed more prestige than all other congressional committees put together, and which had earned it by being eminently fair, intelligent, and aggressive. The Truman Committee had come to the conclusion that the institution of dollar-a-year men ought to be abolished, root and branch, and it suggested as much to Nelson shortly after he took over his new office.

To the committee's pained surprise, Nelson flatly disagreed. He did announce that there would be some changes in the selection and use of dollar-a-year men, the principal change being an order that "no person shall be employed in any position in which he will make decisions directly affecting the affairs of his own company"—which, being interpreted, meant in substance that the president of the XYZ Refrigerator Corporation would not be allowed to fill a job which might require him, and no one else, to determine whether the XYZ Corporation could continue to make refrigerators in a limited and highly profitable market. But with minor modifications Nelson continued the dollar-a-year system in effect, and presently he went before the Truman Committee to defend this decision vigorously.

His reasoning was simple and direct, a logical extension of his pronouncement for the merchandisers at Vincennes. He told the committee that he had just one standard for passing on all such questions: What will contribute most toward winning the war in the shortest possible time? Following that standard, he could see no alternative to the continued use of industrialists, loaned to government by industry and kept on the payroll of their own corporations, and he told the committee exactly why he felt that way.

"On this job we must get the maximum results from American industry," he said. "To do that we must have down here men who understand and can deal with industry's intricate structure and operation. In other words, we must have men with expert business and technical knowledge. For the most part we have to get them from industry itself. But no matter where we get them or how we get them we simply must have them in the places where they are needed, when they are needed."

In which case, why not put them on the government payroll and be done with it? Why let them retain their corporate ties and financial interests? The Truman Committee was deeply curious on that point, and Nelson had the answer:

"All things being equal, these men ought to be brought in to serve on a regular government salary. I wish that were possible. It isn't. You can't get all the help you need, of the kind you need, on that basis. The reason is simple: most of these men, many of them specialists, have been getting salaries much higher than those which can be paid government employees. Since they have been getting such salaries, they naturally have incurred extensive financial obligations over the years—mortgages, life insurance, income taxes which they have to pay this year, and so on—so that it is extremely hard for them to adjust themselves abruptly to a much lower income. In many cases it is literally true that the man in question simply can't make the change to a government payroll without extreme hardship to his family.

"Furthermore, when we bring these men in for this war effort we are not offering permanent careers to them. In the very nature of things we are offering them temporary jobs. So if we did not have any provision for dollar-a-year men, we should in every case be forced to ask these men to sever their old connections entirely to take temporary jobs at salaries which might not enable them to meet their fixed obligations. In practice, then, we would usually get from industry only older men who were independently wealthy and who could therefore afford to make the break, or those who have already retired. I do not think the Congress could approve the principle of such an arrangement, and I do not think the Congress would like to limit the War Production Board to the ranks of the very wealthy in the selection of personnel."

It must be admitted that this reasoning did not impress the Truman Committee greatly. Senator Truman bluntly told Nelson as much.

"I don't think there should be any special class," Senator Truman said. "I just received a letter this morning from a young man who is getting $25,000 a year. He is a Reserve officer. He is going to get $140 a month, and he can't draw his $25,000 while he is gone. He is satisfied to do that because he wants to win the war, just as you do and just as I do, by every means possible, no matter what it costs him, because if he doesn't win it his $25,000 a year won't be worth a cent.

"I am laboring, and have been, under the delusion, maybe, that if the government has the power to take these young men away from their jobs and their outlook on life for the purpose of this emergency, the dollar-a-year men could face the same situation and face it adequately, and would be glad to do it. However, if that is not the case, and their morale won't stand it—and you say it won't—we want to win the war. Therefore we are not going to hamper you in that effort and in your way of handling it."

A few days later Senator Truman spelled it out in detail in a letter to Nelson, making it clear that the committee—which for months had been demanding unified, coherent direction for the war production program—was going to support Nelson, now that he had been given the job, and was willing to go along with him even on his dollar-a-year policy, but that it still thought that he was wrong.

"The committee believed," Senator Truman wrote, "that the problem of substituting the right men for the wrong men was so great that the practice of retaining dollar-a-year men should be abandoned, so that those who were more interested in their remuneration than in their public service would automatically be eliminated, and those public-spirited individuals, like yourself, would be retained. You have informed the committee that you desire to retain some dollar-a-year men who, by reason of the standard of living to which they have accustomed themselves, cannot afford even temporarily to work for the government for $10,000 a year, or less. The committee does not like to have procurement matters entrusted to men who have given such hostages to fortune. Those who cannot forego large incomes temporarily cannot reasonably be expected to take a chance of foregoing them permanently by taking positions on behalf of the government with which the controlling officials of their corporations are not in sympathy. In the committee's opinion, this was one of the principal reasons for the now generally admitted failures of the Office of Production Management.

"However, the committee believes that the best interests of the procurement program require that it be administered by a single head who will be able to do things in his own way and who will be judged by his accomplishments as a whole and not by his position on individual matters. The committee will, therefore, support you even on matters in which it disagrees with you, and believes that all other agencies of the government should afford you a similar unquestioning support until you have had a full opportunity to achieve the success which we all hope that you will achieve."

With this highly qualified and reluctant clearance, then, Nelson's decision on the dollar-a-year men remained in effect for the duration of the war. Like his decision on the place of the War Department in respect to procurement, this decision may well have been the only one Nelson could have made under the circumstances; for the circumstances included, first and foremost, the binding imperative of the original decision—winning the war is all that counts, and right now winning the war involves getting the biggest possible volume of production in the shortest possible time.

Experts from industry *were* necessary; if they served no other purpose—and they served many others—they constituted, at the very least, an indispensable two-way channel of communication between government, which framed and issued orders, and industry, which had to carry the orders out. These experts were needed at once—not next April, but now, in mid-January. Was there time to stop for a reshuffle? Nelson thought not, and the Truman Committee refused to quarrel with him even though it clearly felt that he was mistaken.

So we kept the institution of the dollar-a-year man, for good or for ill; for good *and* for ill, since it was like most human institutions, a blend of the excellent and the deplorable. The decision, as noted, grew logically out of the fundamental decision that while we were fighting an all-out war we were going to fight it for limited objectives—which is to say, for purely military objectives—and it was a decision of the most far-reaching importance. In effect, even if not by conscious intent, it was a decision to cling to the status quo.

For the decision to keep on using dollar-a-year men did nothing less than preserve the existing corporate control of American industry; not just because the dollar-a-year man did things on purpose to safeguard that control, but because the possible alternatives to the dollar-a-year man system were all so far-reaching.

The great feature of the dollar-a-year-man system was that it insured a high degree of understanding and co-operation between industry and government. It meant that when the rulers of industry were told by government what they could or could not do, or were called in by government for exhortation and exposition, they received their orders and their exhortations from men whom they were willing to recognize as big shots. Philip Reed, for instance, was in charge of consumer goods divisions for WPB in the early months of the war. What he said to the industrialists affected by the orders of his divisions carried weight, not just because he had a high position in WPB, but because everybody knew that in private life he was chairman of the board of the great General Electric Corporation. In or out of government, he was a leader of industry.

Reed was one of hundreds of dollar-a-year men, and the same thing was true of all of them in a greater or a lesser degree. Some of them were very big big shots indeed, and some of them were minor big shots, but all of them came from the businessman's own team. They were officials from whom the industrialist was willing to take orders.

Now contrast that with the position of such a man as Leon Henderson. He had nothing to stand on but the force of his own personality, the power of his own intelligence, and the authority vested in him by law and by executive order. Industry did not listen to him gladly; it listened because it had to. He did get more co-operation than might have been expected, but his official career in OPM and OPA was one long dog-fight.

The whole basis of the nation's war production program was—in spite of the innumerable orders and controls—willing co-operation by industry. When Nelson was made chairman of WPB he was commonly spoken of as the "czar" of war production. Actually, neither he nor his organization, nor anyone else in government, really did very much czaring as far as the actual production process was concerned. America's enormous volume of war production grew out of a very few basic actions. WPB put progressive restrictions on the goods industry might make and the materials it might use—it said "no more automobiles," for instance, and it kept aluminum out of the hands of producers who weren't in war work—and the armed services flooded industry with enormous orders for munitions. WPB, in turn, then set up the machinery to distribute materials and component parts, and did various things to make sure that there would be enough of them to meet essential needs. All the rest was up to industry. And while it is true, of course, that government's part in all of this was almost incomprehensibly intricate, difficult, and important, the fact remains that the production job itself remained in industry's hands. Even at the height of the war, government did not—except, perhaps, by the standards of a few Neanderthal diehards—go in for "telling the businessman how to run his business." The most striking thing about the whole war production program was not that there were so many controls but that all of them fell within the established patterns of industry.

It all worked, and the quantity of munitions obtained startled everybody. But suppose, now, that the countless WPB officials who put this process in motion and kept it running had been Leon Hendersons instead of Philip Reeds;

bureaucrats (by the industrialists' definition) instead of captains of industry; New Deal careerists, instead of dollar-a-year men. Beyond any question there would have been much less co-operation by industry, much less willing understanding, much less feeling that government talked the industrialist's lingo and relied on his brains and ingenuity. That would almost certainly have meant more compulsion. A New Deal government simply could not have let itself get into the position of being about to lose the war because it had refused to "use the best brains of industry."

So what? So the alternative to the dollar-a-year men was an entirely different kind of war effort. Almost inevitably, it would have turned out to be deeply and permanently revolutionary. Something along the lines of the Murray plan, for instance—some use of the industry council idea all up and down the line, with authority and responsibility directly vested in workers, technicians, and managers—would have been almost inescapable. There would not only have been more controls; they would have been controls of a different kind, controls which more explicitly asserted the right and duty of the central government to disregard the last vestige of property rights in time of crisis. To decide against using dollar-a-year men would have meant working out an entirely new kind of setup; and such a setup, created in the incandescent heat of war, would not have passed away quickly with the war's end.

The decision Nelson made was, fundamentally, a decision to bank on the existing order—and, banking on it, to preserve it. It was not without reason that Kiplinger's *Washington Letter,* on January 24, 1942, quoted "business-minded men within government" as saying that the WPB program constituted "the last stand of private enterprise." Kiplinger had it dead to rights. And as things turned out, this last stand was to be a honey.

10. ECONOMIC CONCENTRATION AND WORLD WAR II

Smaller War Plants Corporation

Two of the major consequences of the decisions described by Catton were that (1) we won the war, and (2) we entered the postwar period with an economy (and with a society) in which many of the least desirable aspects had been strengthened. The Smaller War Plants Corporation was a small island of dissent in the wartime government of President Roosevelt. Charged with the responsibility of seeing to it that war work was shared with small business (for the good of both), it was dismayed and disgusted with the economic concentration it saw as the inevitable and predictable result of wartime economic policies. In cold statistics it documented much of the story Catton described in hot rhetoric.

Employment Changes by Size of Firm, 1939-44. The relative importance of big business, particularly the giant corporations, increased sharply during the war, while the position of small business declined. Although small business increased its actual production and employment during the war, the gains made by big business were much greater. . . .

Source: *Economic Concentration and World War II.* Report of the Smaller War Plants Corporation to Special Committee to Study Problems of American Small Business. U.S. Senate, Special Committee to Study Problems of American Small Business, 79th Cong., 2d sess., Senate Doc. 206 (1946), pp. 21, 24-33, 37, 39, 46-61.

The growth of the war industries, and more particularly, of big business within these industries, is indeed striking. Employment in the iron and steel industry rose by 500,000 persons between 1939 and 1944, almost all of which took place in firms with more than 500 employees. Employment in the nonferrous metals industry rose by 200,000, and again it was the larger firms which accounted for most of the increase.

The ordnance industry was virtually nonexistent in 1939, but by 1944 employed 700,000 people. All but a minor fraction of this employment was in the larger firms. In the transportation equipment industry there occurred the most dramatic expansion of all, a jump from 725,000 employees to more than 3,200,000. The part played by small firms in this expansion was insignificant. In machinery (both electrical and nonelectrical), chemicals and allied products, rubber, and in petroleum and coal products, changes during the war were of roughly the same nature, sharp increases in employment occurring mainly in the larger firms.

In a few of the nonwar industries, such as food, lumber and timber, and paper, there were minor increases in employment between 1939 and 1944. In a few others, such as tobacco, printing, leather, and textiles, there were minor declines. In no case did there occur sharp changes in employment. . . .

As a result of these great employment increases in the large firms of the war industries, small business was shoved into the background. Small firms (those with less than 500 employees) accounted for 52 percent of total manufacturing employment in 1939. In 1944 this figure had fallen to only 38 percent.

The percentage of the total number of firms and of the total employment accounted for by small business in 1939 and 1944 is shown in Table 10.1.

Particularly sharp declines in the relative importance of small business, as measured by employment, occurred in the machinery (except electrical) industry, from 60 to 41 percent; and in chemicals, from 51 to 36 percent. In all the war industries the relative importance of small business declined substantially.

Changes were smaller and more diverse in the nonwar industries. In some of these industries—for example, stone, clay and glass, furniture, lumber and timber, and food—there were fairly small declines in the relative importance of small business. In some others—printing, leather, and textiles—there were minor increases. Only in the tobacco industry was there a substantial increase in the share accounted for by small business.

While the importance of small firms in manufacturing declined, the relative number of these firms remained preponderantly large. In 1939, as Table 10.1 shows, 99 percent of all manufacturing firms had less than 500 employees; in 1944 the figure was 98 percent. Moreover, in every industry small firms were in the overwhelming majority, even accounting for 74 percent in the typically big-business ordnance industry. Only in the ordnance, transportation equipment, and rubber products industries did small firms in 1944 account for less than 90 percent of the number of firms.

Table 10.1 SMALL BUSINESS IN MANUFACTURING, 1939-1944

	Firms with Less than 500 Employees			
	Percent of Employment		Percent of Firms	
	1939	1944	1939	1944
Total manufacturing	51.7	38.1	98.9	97.8
War industries:				
Iron and steel and their products	43.2	35.6	97.6	94.6
Nonferrous metals and their products	41.2	35.7	98.7	97.8
Ordnance	–	9.5	–	74.1
Machinery (except electrical)	59.9	41.8	98.4	97.1
Electrical machinery	27.4	15.2	95.3	90.8
Transportation equipment	15.9	7.3	95.3	87.8
Chemicals and allied products	51.0	36.0	98.4	97.7
Petroleum and coal products	31.8	23.1	95.2	90.7
Rubber products	30.5	15.4	96.8	89.0
Nonwar industries:				
Tobacco manufactures	21.7	36.6	95.4	97.6
Printing and publishing	71.3	73.9	99.6	99.5
Leather and leather products	56.5	61.5	96.8	97.7
Textile mill products	33.8	40.9	91.7	92.5
Food and kindred products (and beverages)	48.5	52.2	99.3	98.7
Stone, clay, and glass products	62.7	50.2	98.4	98.0
Furniture and finished lumber products	75.6	69.3	99.2	98.8
Apparel and products from fabrics	78.7	83.7	99.6	99.3
Lumber and timber basic products	81.6	78.2	99.7	99.5
Paper and allied products	54.6	53.9	97.9	95.2
Miscellaneous	83.8	58.8	99.7	98.7

The reverse side of this picture, the position of big business, is, of course, one of tremendous growth. Big firms, those with 500 employees or more, remain a tiny minority in the business population, but their size and power has grown more dominating than ever. In 1944 these large firms represented only 2 percent of all manufacturing firms in the United States and yet they accounted for 62 percent of total employment.

   . . . It was the industrial giants, the biggest of the big firms, which made the greatest gains during the war. In each of the war industries, with but one exception, firms with 10,000 or more employees grew in relative importance. In manufacturing as a whole, these few giants accounted for 13 percent of total employment in 1939, and for fully 31 percent of the total in 1944.

   In manufacturing as a whole, the rise in the relative importance of the industrial giants was accompanied by a decrease in the relative position of the small firms, those with less than 500 employees. This general pattern of change was closely followed in the nonferrous metals industry, in machinery, electrical machinery, transportation equipment, chemicals, petroleum and coal products, and rubber products.

   The most important exception to the general rule occurred in the iron and steel industry. Here, the industrial giants, firms with 10,000 employees or more, as well as the small and very small firms, declined in relative importance from

1939 to 1944, while the large firms (500 to 10,000 employees) increased sharply. This change, however, reflects the growth of many medium-sized fabricators of steel products during the war, and does not denote a change in the structure of the basic iron and steel industry, which is still dominated by the giants.

In the machinery (except electrical) industry there occurred substantial increases not only for the industrial giants, but also for the large firms (with from 500 to 10,000 employees.)

In summary, the relative importance of small business dropped sharply in all manufacturing and in the industries which expanded most during the war. In the nonwar industries, which made few gains during the war, small business, generally speaking, held its own. Taking manufacturing as a whole, the giants expanded greatly, while all other firms, especially small business, suffered a substantial decline.

The figures above relate to manufacturing only. Small firms, however, operate in great numbers in trade, services, construction, and also in some branches of the mining industry.

Taking the nonagricultural economy as a whole, what has happened to small business during the war?

The record of the war years shows a constant increase in the importance of big business and a constant decline in that of the little concerns. This was due, in part, to the complete disappearance of half a million small retail, service, and construction firms. . . .

In 1939 firms with less than 50 employees accounted for 34 percent of all the employees of American trade and industry, and for 30 percent of the dollar value of the total pay roll. By 1943 the share of these small firms had shrunk to 25 percent of all employees and 19 percent of the total pay roll.

. . . There were also declines, though more moderate, in the relative importance of firms with from 50 to 99 employees and of firms with from 500 to 999. The only group to improve its relative position in the economy as a whole consisted of the largest firms, those with 1,000 or more employees.

The position of these big firms increased in each successive year. In 1939 firms with over 1,000 employees accounted for 30 percent of the total employment of all American trade and industry, and 36 percent of the total pay roll. By 1943 these figures had risen to 44 and 53 percent, respectively.

It is clear that during the war these large companies have come to dominate not only American manufacturing but the entire economy as a whole.

Prime Contracts. The increases in concentration which took place during the war were due largely to the distribution of the great bulk of the war contracts to a small number of great firms. It was the distribution of the nearly 200 billion dollars of prime supply contracts which was the key to the control of productive resources during the war. Those "prime" contracts were made between the Army, Navy, and other Government procurement agencies and the suppliers of end products. They contained no stipulation as to who should participate in the production of these items as subcontractors or suppliers.

Companies obtaining prime contracts secured thereby the instruments of economic power. They received money in the form of substantial profits for the production of goods, the sale of which was assured. They obtained materials and supplies, since naturally, they were granted priorities and allotments for needed materials, parts, components, etc. And, further than this, they were granted the power of determining how much of these priorities and allotments should be passed down to subcontractors, who and how many the subcontractors should be, and how much of the allocations each should receive.

In addition, the receipt of a substantial prime contract generally gave to a company the right, if it desired to use it, of expanding its own facilities under the extremely favorable amortization and carryback provisions provided by the tax laws. Companies holding large prime contracts experienced little difficulty in obtaining "certificates of necessity" which allowed them to take advantage of the special amortization tax provisions.

Also, it was the companies that were the principal recipients of prime contracts which operated most of the Government-owned facilities built during the war, and these companies generally obtained options to buy the plants after the war.

These are but a few of the instruments of power which were inherent in prime contracts. There were many others, including the scientific and technical research conducted at Government expense in the laboratories and plants of these companies.

How concentrated, then, was the distribution of these prime contracts? Did the bulk of them go to a few large companies or were they widely dispersed to small as well as to large firms? The answers to these questions are to be found in data compiled by the War Production Board. From June 1940 through September 1944 prime contract awards amounting to $175,000,000,000 were made to 18,539 corporations. No less than two-thirds of this vast amount ($117,000,000,000) went to the top 100 corporations. Fully 30 percent of the value of the contracts awarded during this 4-year period went to the first 10 corporations, 12 percent to the next 10, and 7 percent to the next 10, or nearly one-half of the total (49 percent) to the top 30 corporations. As can be seen in the following table, over one-half (51 percent) went to only 33 corporations, each of which received awards totaling $1,000,000,000 or more.

The extent of concentration was even higher when it is measured in terms of the active contracts outstanding at a given date, instead of in terms of the total amount issued over an extended period of time. Thus the top 100 corporations held 75 percent of the prime contracts outstanding on September 30, 1944, as compared to 67 percent of the awards issued during the period, June 1940 to September 1944.

This concentration of prime contracts remained fairly stable through the war period. According to the WPB there was no apparent decrease in the participation in the war program by the larger corporations. "The measure of that participation is more accurately portrayed by the holding of active contracts. . . . Similarity of the 100 leading corporations' percentages for active

Table 10.2 CORPORATIONS, PLANTS, AND VALUE OF PRIME SUPPLY CONTRACTS,
BY AGGREGATE. VALUE OF PRIME SUPPLY CONTRACTS AWARDED
BETWEEN JUNE 1940 AND SEPTEMBER 1944

Value awarded per corporation (millions)	Corporations		Plants		Contracts	
	Number	Percent	Number	Percent	Value (billions)	Percent
Total	18,539	100	22,956	100	$175.1	100
$1,000 and over	33	[1]	621	3	89.5	51
$100 to $999	148	1	878	4	40.8	24
$10 to $99	944	5	2,075	9	26.7	15
$1 to $9	4,223	23	5,474	24	14.4	8
Under $1	13,191	71	13,908	60	3.7	2

Source: War Production Board, op. cit.
[1] Less than 0.5 percent.
Note—The above table is compiled on a parent-corporation, or consolidated, basis. An undetermined number of unincorporated enterprises are included.

contracts as of September 1944, and cumulative contracts through December 1941—the majority of which may be considered to have been active on that date—*suggests that there has been no significant change in concentration between 1941 and 1944 with respect to active contracts."* [Italics added.]

Who are these 100 corporations? And how much of the war contracts did they receive? The answers are to be found in the following table, which lists the 100 largest corporations and presents in terms of dollar and percentage figures the prime contracts which each of these corporations received.

At the top of the table is the General Motors Corp., which received $13,813,000,000 in prime contracts, or nearly 8 percent of the total. The top five corporations, which received 20.3 percent of the prime contracts, consist of three aircraft companies—Curtiss-Wright Corp., Consolidated Vultee Aircraft Corp., and Douglas Aircraft Co., Inc.; and two automobile companies—General Motors and Ford Motor Co. In the second five are two aircraft companies— United Aircraft Corp. and Lockheed Corp.—as well as Bethlehem Steel Co., Chrysler Corp., and General Electric Co. In the third five, there are three aircraft companies—North American Aviation, Inc.; Boeing Airplane Co., and Glenn L. Martin Co.—together with American Telephone & Telegraph Co., and E. I. du Pont de Nemours Co.

From that point on, the corporations become much more diversified, with the aircraft companies no longer dominating the awards. Thus, in the fourth group of five companies there is only one wartime aviation parts company— Bendix Aviation Corp.; a steel company—United States Steel Corp.; an automobile company—Packard Motor Car Co.; an instrument company—Sperry Corp.; and a shipbuilding company—Henry J. Kaiser Co. Among the 100 corporations are to be found companies which before the war were engaged primarily in the fields of textiles, petroleum, food, machinery, rubber products, chemicals, railway equipment, etc.

This enormous centralization of prime contracts in corporations engaged in such a variety of industries clearly meant an increase in the concentration of the American economy. That the American economy had indeed become highly concentrated before the war has been shown in a previous part of this report. But the economy has never been concentrated to the extent which is implicit in the distribution of these prime contracts. On this matter the WPB states that:

> The 100 leading corporations, ranked by value of product shipped in 1935, accounted for *almost one-third* of the total value of products, while the 100 highest in terms of active supply contracts held *three-fourths* of all the value. The former group of figures includes all manufacturing industries, whereas the supply contracts data are limited to war industries and exclude subcontracts as well as prime awards under $50,000. *However, available evidence indicates that adjustment for these differences would not significantly affect the percentages.* [Italics added.]

Subcontracts. In addition to prime contracts, war production is also based upon another type of agreement, namely subcontracts. Under the system of procurement adopted at the very beginning of the war effort, prime contractors were given complete responsibility to obtain the materials, components, and parts needed to produce the end-item for which they had been awarded the prime contract. This meant, of course, that the figures on prime contracts overstate the concentration of war production, since a portion of the prime contract awards was passed down to other firms in the form of subcontracts.

An analysis of the available data on subcontracting, however, indicates, first, that it was never carried on as extensively as has been commonly assumed, and, second, that most of the value of the subcontracts placed by big prime contractors went, not to small firms, but rather to other large concerns. The Smaller War Plants Corporation in 1943 conducted a survey of the prime and subcontracting records of 252 of the Nation's largest corporations, which received the great bulk of the prime contract awards. In this survey it was found that these companies subcontracted 34 percent of the value of their prime contracts, but that three-fourths of the value of these subcontracts went to other large companies (firms with over 500 workers). The large company subcontractors, in turn, passed along 13 percent of their subcontract business to further subcontractors, with other large companies receiving 56 percent of this lower tier of subcontracts and small companies receiving the balance of 44 percent. Large companies (with more than 500 workers), according to reports submitted to the SWPC by the procurement agencies, were receiving some 78 percent of the prime contracts. Thus, it can be estimated that small companies accounted for some 30 percent of total war production consisting of (1) 22 percent of the prime contracts, (2) 7 percent of subcontracting at the first tier of subcontracts, and (3) 1 percent of subcontracting at lower levels. . . .

This figure of 30 percent is at best only a rough approximation. However, it corresponds fairly closely with the results provided by the BOASI data on employment as presented above.

Table 10.3 PRIME WAR-SUPPLY CONTRACTS: 100 CORPORATIONS RANKED
BY VOLUME OF PRIME WAR SUPPLY CONTRACTS CUMULATIVE
JUNE 1940 THROUGH SEPTEMBER 1944

Corporation	Millions of dollars[1]	Percent of total	Cumulative percent of total
All companies—Total	175,062.9	100.0	100.0
100 specified corporations—Total	117,634.4	67.2	67.2
1. General Motors Corp	13,812.7	7.9	7.9
2. Curtiss-Wright Corp	7,091.0	4.1	11.9
3. Ford Motor Co	5,269.6	3.0	15.0
4. Consolidated Vultee Aircraft Corp	4,875.4	2.8	17.7
5. Douglas Aircraft Co., Inc	4,431.3	2.5	20.3
6. United Aircraft Corp	3,923.0	2.2	22.5
7. Bethlehem Steel Co	3,789.3	2.2	24.7
8. Chrysler Corp	3,394.8	1.9	26.6
9. General Electric Co	3,300.1	1.9	28.5
10. Lockheed Aircraft Corp	3,246.2	1.9	30.4
11. North American Aviation, Inc	2,768.5	1.6	32.0
12. Boeing Airplane Co	2,700.2	1.5	33.5
13. American Telephone & Telegraph Co	2,562.7	1.5	34.9
14. Martin, Glenn L., Co	2,344.8	1.3	36.3
15. du Pont, E. I., de Nemours Co., Inc	2,186.2	1.2	37.5
16. United States Steel Corp	1,974.0	1.1	38.7
17. Bendix Aviation Corp	1,869.2	1.1	39.7
18. Packard Motor Car Co	1,783.8	1.0	40.7
19. Sperry Corp	1,531.5	.9	41.6
20. Kaiser, Henry J., Co	1,384.4	.8	42.4
21. Westinghouse Electric & Manufacturing Co	1,375.7	.8	43.2
22. Grumman Aircraft Engineering Corp	1,330.4	.8	44.0
23. Newport News Shipbuilding & Drydock Co	1,245.8	.7	44.7
24. Republic Aviation Corp	1,231.5	.7	45.4
25. Bell Aircraft Corp	1,228.3	.7	46.1
26. Todd Shipyards Corp	1,191.9	.7	46.8
27. Nash-Kelvinator Corp	1,162.6	.7	47.4
28. Studebaker Corp	1,143.8	.7	48.1
29. Consolidated Steel Corp., Ltd	1,097.4	.6	48.7
30. Goodyear Tire & Rubber Co	1,091.2	.6	49.3
31. Standard Oil Co. of New Jersey	1,053.1	.6	49.9
32. Aviation Corp	1,045.6	.6	50.5
33. International Harvester Co	1,035.8	.6	51.1
34. American Locomotive Co	889.2	.5	51.6
35. Western Cartridge Co	880.5	.5	52.1
36. American Car & Foundry Co	854.9	.5	52.6
37. United States Rubber Co	798.0	.5	53.1
38. Continental Motors Corp	782.9	.4	53.5
39. Sun Oil Co	712.5	.4	53.9
40. Baldwin Locomotive Works	712.3	.4	54.3
41. Pressed Steel Car Co., Inc	664.3	.4	54.7
42. Permanente Metals Corp	635.4	.4	55.1
43. Radio Corp. of America	610.0	.3	55.4
44. Caterpillar Tractor Co	602.7	.3	55.8
45. Allis-Chalmers Manufacturing Co	585.7	.3	56.1
46. Norden, Carl L., Inc	555.2	.3	56.4
47. Diamond T. Motor Car Co	535.7	.3	56.7
48. Willys-Overland Motors, Inc	522.2	.3	57.0
49. California Shipbuilding Corp	503.5	.3	57.3
50. Bath Iron Works	498.6	.3	57.6

Table 10.3 Continued

Corporation	Millions of dollars[1]	Percent of total	Cumulative percent of total
51. American Woolen Co., Inc	493.9	0.3	57.9
52. Emerson Electric Manufacturing Co	487.1	.3	58.1
53. Consolidated Builders, Inc	478.1	.3	58.4
54. White Motor Co	471.6	.3	58.7
55. Firestone Tire & Rubber Co	455.2	.3	59.0
56. Pullman, Inc	455.0	.3	59.2
57. Philco Corp	452.8	.3	59.5
58. Anaconda Copper Mining Co	446.8	.3	59.7
59. Federal Cartridge Corp	439.1	.3	60.0
60. Fairbanks, Morse Co	414.1	.2	60.2
61. Northern Pump Co	411.1	.2	60.4
62. Eastman Kodak Co	407.6	.2	60.7
63. Mack Trucks, Inc	396.1	.2	60.9
64. Food Machinery Corp	392.2	.2	61.1
65. Hercules Powder Co	366.6	.2	61.3
66. Remington Rand, Inc	359.8	.2	61.5
67. Goodrich, B. F., Co	359.6	.2	61.8
68. Brown Shipbuilding Co	357.1	.2	62.0
69. Beech Aircraft Corp	351.3	.2	62.2
70. Higgins Industries, Inc	349.6	.2	62.4
71. Raytheon Manufacturing Co	348.8	.2	62.6
72. Dravo Corp	343.7	.2	62.8
73. Fairchild Engine & Airplane Corp	334.1	.2	62.9
74. Smith, A. O., Corp	329.6	.2	63.1
75. Standard Oil Co. of California	327.6	.2	63.3
76. General Cable Corp	325.6	.2	63.5
77. Electric Boat Co	324.1	.2	63.7
78. Jack & Heintz, Inc	312.2	.2	63.9
79. Royal Dutch Co	308.1	.2	64.0
80. Crucible Steel Co. of America	300.5	.2	64.2
81. American Shipbuilding Co	294.0	.2	64.4
82. Moore Drydock Co	292.2	.2	64.5
83. Hudson Motor Car Co	290.0	.2	64.7
84. Brewster Aeronautical Corp	281.8	.2	64.9
85. Autocar Co	279.5	.2	65.0
86. Socony-Vacuum Oil Co., Inc	276.5	.2	65.2
87. Jacobs Aircraft Engine Co	269.4	.2	65.3
88. Ingalls Iron Works	265.6	.2	65.5
89. Western Pipe Steel Co. of California	264.3	.2	65.6
90. American Can Co	261.8	.1	65.8
91. General Machinery Corp	261.7	.1	65.9
92. Chicago Bridge & Iron Co	260.2	.1	66.1
93. Texas Co	260.1	.1	66.2
94. Galvin Manufacturing Corp	243.8	.1	66.4
95. Stewart-Warner Corp	242.6	.1	66.5
96. Revere Copper & Brass, Inc	241.6	.1	66.7
97. New England Shipbuilding Corp	235.5	.1	66.8
98. Missouri Valley Bridge & Iron Co	233.8	.1	66.9
99. Colt's Patent Fire Arms Manufacturing Co	233.8	.1	67.1
100. Northrop Aircraft, Inc	232.3	.1	67.2

Omitting industries not covered by the SWPC 1943 survey on subcontracting—specifically tobacco, printing and publishing, leather, food, stone, clay and glass, furniture, apparel, lumber, and paper—the BOASI data show that in 1944 small firms (with less than 500 workers) in the remaining industries employed 26 percent of the manufacturing workers. Although there are a number of differences between the two sets of data, including the difference in years (1943 as against 1944), nonetheless the close similarity of the two figures strongly points to the conclusion that large firms produced somewhere in the neighborhood of 70 percent of the total war output.

The fact that subcontracting to small firms was so limited obviously meant that a large number of small firms never obtained any subcontracts whatsoever. Yet success in obtaining subcontracts also had its disadvantages. By becoming subcontractors, many small firms lost their status as independent enterprises. For example, since their market was the prime contractor, they had little need for sales forces. Similarly, since they usually obtained their materials and supplies from the prime contractor, they frequently were able to get along without their purchasing staffs. Yet, sales and purchasing forces are generally requisites to survival in a competitive economy. It remains to be seen whether or not small firms which disbanded these vital forces during the war can quickly rebuild them and thus regain their independent status.

Materials. With big business receiving the great bulk of the prime contracts and doing comparatively little subcontracting to small firms, it was almost inevitable that big business would obtain the major share of the Nation's resources in the war effort. One of the most vital of these resources was materials, particularly metals. Materials were allocated by the War Production Board during most of the war period, but the flow of these materials had to follow the pattern of production which was set by the contract awards. The WPB obviously had to supply materials to companies which had received contracts from the war agencies. . . .

Facilities. The way in which the war-built production facilities are distributed will, probably more than anything else, determine the extent of concentration in manufacturing during the postwar years.

The Nation's manufacturing facilities in existence in 1939 had cost about 40 billion dollars to build. To this capacity there was added by June 1945 about 26 billion dollars of new plant and equipment. Roughly two-thirds of this 26-billion-dollar plant expansion was provided directly from Federal funds, and the other third from private funds.

Of the total 26-billion-dollar outlay, 14 billion dollars was for new plants, 4.2 billion dollars was for expansion of prewar plants, and 7.8 billion dollars for conversion of prewar plants to war production and for replacement of old equipment. Of the 26 billion dollars, 10.5 billion dollars was for construction and 15.5 billion dollars for equipment.

Not only was the expansion program of tremendous proportions, but, in addition, the quality of the new plants and equipment was generally very high. Most of the expanded plant was authorized in the early part of the war. More than half of the 5-year total had been completed by the end of 1942 and more than four-fifths by the end of 1943. Most of the plants contain the best materials, since the restrictions of WPB order L-41 generally were not applicable or in effect when the projects were authorized. The new plants usually have the most modern factory layouts, lighting, power installations, etc. Very few of them are temporary structures.

In general, it may be said that most of this plant expansion took the form of what is commonly regarded as high-quality and high-cost construction. In this respect, it was similar to much of the prewar plant, a major portion of which dates from the high-cost decade of the twenties. . . .

Facilities Usable for Peacetime Production. The above figures give some idea of the magnitude of the wartime expansion. In analyzing the effects of these facilities upon the postwar economy, there is the further question of the extent to which these new facilities are usable for peacetime production. In other words, how much of the vast productive plant created during the past 5 years can readily and feasibly be turned to the production of peacetime goods, irrespective of what the demand for these goods may be?

This report offers the estimate that *about $20,000,000,000 of the $26,000,000,000 wartime plant is usable for the production of peacetime products,* either immediately or after only minor conversion. This estimate does not involve any prediction that this portion of the new plant will actually be used in the years ahead, nor does it involve any estimate of the general business level that would be required for the actual use of these facilities. It is simply an estimate of the portion of the new facilities which are readily adaptable from a physical point of view to the production of peacetime products in the postwar economy. . . .

Facilities—Private. Of the 26 billion dollars of new plant added during the war, 8.6 billion dollars, or 33 percent, was privately financed. More than half, 4.8 billion dollars, represented war facilities. Nearly all of the privately financed facilities are designed for peacetime production, since the Government undertook to build those facilities which would require conversion to be useful for peacetime production.

In order to stimulate industry into building and financing its own facilities for war production, Congress made two important changes in the Nation's tax laws. The more significant of these relates to amortization. In the Second Revenue Act of 1940 industry was granted the privilege of amortizing "certified" facilities over a 5-year period. Under these amortization provisions, which became effective in 1940 and prevailed throughout the war, private concerns had the right, upon being issued a certificate of necessity, to amortize the cost of specific new war facilities at the extremely favorable rate of 20 percent a year. The certificates of necessity were issued for the most part by the War and Navy Departments and also to some extent by the War Production Board.

The greater allowance for depreciation lowered the total tax liability since it reduced the amount of the tax payable under the high wartime rates. Without this accelerated amortization, the rate of depreciation would have been constant over an extended period of years, thus affording small relief since high wartime tax rates would have been assessed against much more of the corporation's income.

The carry-back provisions, which constituted the second change in the tax laws, were designed specifically to lessen the financial risk of concerns in expanding their facilities for war production. They became effective in 1942, and were adopted in order to permit the charging of war-induced costs and losses in the postwar period against wartime income, thereby reducing the amount of income subject to high wartime rates. Under the carry-back of unused excess-profits credits, if a corporation's income during or following the war, and not later than December 31, 1946, drops below its excess profits credits (regardless of whether the credits were based upon invested capital or average earnings) it may carry-back the difference between its earnings and its excess-profits credits. It may then add this difference to its excess-profits credits of one of the last two prior years. The tax for the prior year is then recomputed on the basis of this larger credit, in many cases reducing the tax and resulting in refunds. In effect, this results in a partial averaging of the income of the postwar years with the income of the corporation during the war years, in the final determination of war profits and taxes thereon.

The same is true of corporations which incur an actual loss after the war, except that in this case a firm's taxes in the two prior years are lowered by a recalculation which deducts the loss of the current year from the income of the prior year and recomputes the tax in the prior year on the basis of the reduced income. This may result in refunds in addition to the refunds which may be obtained under the unused excess-profits credit.

As a result of these two wartime features of the tax laws, private industry was granted permission to write off the cost of facilities in 5 years or less which, under normal circumstances, could not have been written off in less than 20 to 30 years or more, and at the same time, through the carry-backs, it was not only protected against losses but assured of income resulting from the expansion of its facilities for war production.

Since it was big business which received most of the prime contracts, it was also big business which was responsible for most of the privately financed expansions of facilities for war production.

Of the 4.8 billion dollars of privately financed war facilities, 2.9 billion dollars, or 60 percent, were built by the Nation's 250 largest corporations. The hundred largest corporations were responsible for 51 percent of these privately financed facilities. . . .

Facilities—Public. The most massive economic resource created during the war consists of the plants and facilities which were built by the Government, financed with public funds. Some idea of the enormous value of these Government-owned plants can be gained from the fact that they exceeded, in value, the entire industrial economies of most other industrial nations. The immense production capacity represented by these plants and facilities makes of them the most powerful instrument of economic control which ever existed in this country. Their disposal will do more than anything else to determine the future economic destiny of this country.

During the war the Government built some 17.2 billion dollars of industrial facilities. Of this, 2.2 billion dollars represents facilities operated directly by the Government and 3.4 billion dollars represents management-fee operated facilities which produced small arms ammunition and explosives and loaded bombs and artillery shells; such plants are considered as extensions of the arsenal system with the operator having relatively no control over their activities. Eliminating the Government-operated and the management-fee operated facilities, the Government constructed 11.6 billion dollars of industrial facilities which were operated by private concerns. These facilities were financed by the following agencies:

	Millions of dollars
Agency:	
Defense Plant Corporation	7,388
War	1,658
Navy	1,443
Maritime	494
Reconstruction Finance Corporation	327
British	107
Other[1]	152
Total	11,569

[1] Includes Department of Agriculture and Defense Supplies Corporation.

The tendency of the various types of productive resources to be distributed in accordance with the pattern of prime contracts prevailed also in the operation of these Government-owned facilities. Big business, having received the great bulk of the prime contracts, also operated nearly all of these facilities. The concentration that existed in the operation of these facilities actually exceeded the concentration of prime contract awards.

This was due in part to the fact that the Government agencies relied especially heavily upon the industrial ability and know-how of the giant concerns for the operation of the new public facilities. In many Government quarters it was felt that the big firms were best equipped to operate the new Government-owned facilities, since they were experienced in operating their own big plants. It was believed that volume production could be obtained most quickly from the facilities by having them operated by the big corporations which were in a position to provide patents, engineers, production men, and general technical ability.

This report is not concerned with the question of whether or not these were correct assumptions. The important fact is that they prevailed. As a result, the concentration in the operation of Government-owned facilities was higher than in any other phase of the war economy.

No less than 83.4 percent of the value of the privately operated, publicly financed industrial facilities (excluding management-fee and Government-operated facilities) were operated by 168 corporations, each of which operated facilities totaling 10 million dollars or over. The hundred largest corporations operated exactly 75 percent of the value of the Government-owned facilities. Nearly half (49.3 percent) were operated by the top 25 corporations.

The top five corporations consisted of two automobile companies (General Motors and Ford), two metal-producing companies (Aluminum Co. and United States Steel) and one aviation company (Curtiss-Wright).

In the next 10 are to be found 2 aircraft companies (United Aircraft and Douglas Aircraft), 3 metal-producing companies (Bethlehem Steel, Republic Steel, and Anaconda Copper Mining Co.), 2 chemical companies (Dow Chemical Co. and Union Carbide and Carbon Corporation), 1 electric machinery firm (General Electric), 1 automobile company (Chrysler) and 1 shipbuilding firm (Henry J. Kaiser Co.).

Table 10.4 shows, in terms of dollar value and percentages, the amount of the public facilities operated by each of the hundred largest corporations.

Scientific Research. During the war scientific research was conducted on a scale never before contemplated. Before the war the Nation spent between $300,000,000 and $400,000,000 a year on scientific research, of which approximately one-fifth was provided by the Government. During the war the total shot up to more than $800,000,000 a year, more than three-fourths of which consisted of Government expenditures. Private expenditures on research declined about one-half, while Government expenditures increased by nearly 10 times.

During the period of the 5 fiscal years, 1940 through 1944, the Federal Government spent nearly $2,000,000,000 in research and development. Nearly half of this took the form of contracts to private industrial laboratories. The way in which the various Government agencies distributed their expenditures for research development between their own agency laboratories, private industrial laboratories, educational institutions and foundations, and State and other governments, etc., is shown in Table 10.5.

The heavy reliance by the Government on private industrial laboratories—which consisted mainly of the laboratories of large private corporations—is also shown by the fact that in the fiscal year 1944 about half of the total Federal expenditures for research, or approximately $350,000,000 went for work in industrial laboratories.

It was almost inevitable that research in wartime would be conducted by a relatively small number of corporations. This was due largely to the fact that the private industrial research facilities before the war were owned almost exclusively by the big corporations—which, of course, received the great bulk of the war contracts and produced most of the war output. Prior to the war nearly all industrial research was carried on by a handful of large firms. The National Research Project, in a report on the subject issued in 1940, stated that—

> According to the evidence presented, 13 companies employed one-third of the industrial research personnel reported for 1938: 140 companies, representing less than 10 percent of the number reporting, employed two-thirds of the workers. The remaining third was employed by 1,582 concerns. About 150,000 industrial corporations were without research laboratories. In 9 leading industries one-fourth of those companies which operated laboratories employed between 55 and 90 percent of the research workers in the respective industries.

In a report issued September 1945 the Subcommittee on War Mobilization of the Senate Committee on Military Affairs called attention to the prewar concentration in industrial research and stated that during the war the Federal Government had tended to follow that pattern. The report stated:

> A major problem in the economic development of this country before the war was the increasing concentration of industrial research resources in a few large industrial corporations and a lack of the overwhelming majority of American businesses of adequate access to the benefits of scientific research and advancement. . . . *The prewar pattern was accepted by the Federal Government during the war years in the allocation of funds to commercial laboratories for military research.* [Italics added.]

The report went on to state that:

> This great store of research presents the Nation with its greatest technological potential in its history. It presents, also, important questions as to the role of smaller businesses and of educational institutions in the maintenance of the high level of research development in the postwar years.

The great bulk of the war contracts to private industrial laboratories for scientific research went to a very small number of large firms. Nearly 2,000 industrial organizations received, as shown in Table 10.5, a total of almost $1,000,000,000 of research contracts from the Government. The high degree of concentration in these awards is made clear from data compiled by the Senate Military Affairs Committee. These data include all funds spent by Government agencies for scientific research conducted by private industrial laboratories except the funds spent on atomic research and those spent by the Signal Corps of the War Department, for which data by company are not available.

From Table 10.6 it can be seen that only 68 top corporations received two-thirds of the value of Federal research and development contracts and the top 10 corporations received nearly two-fifths of the total. Certainly, if 68

Table 10.4 PRIVATELY OPERATED GOVERNMENT-OWNED FACILITIES—LISTING OF TOP 100 CORPORATIONS AND INDEPENDENT COMPANIES OPERATING PUBLICLY FINANCED INDUSTRIAL FACILITIES AS OF JUNE 30, 1944[1] [thousands of dollars]

Corporation or company	Total value	Cumulative Value	Cumulative Percent
Total industrial facilities (excluding management fee and Government operated)	11,185,412	11,185,412	100.0
Total for 168 companies	9,325,723	9,325,723	83.4
1. General Motors Corp	794,721	794,721	7.1
2. Aluminum Co. of America	491,905	1,286,626	11.5
3. Curtiss-Wright Corp	475,884	1,762,510	15.8
4. United States Steel Corp	429,908	2,192,418	19.6
5. Ford Motor Co	361,483	2,553,901	22.8
6. Bethlehem Steel Corp	265,144	2,819,045	25.2
7. Chrysler Corp	209,658	3,028,703	27.1
8. United Aircraft Corp	206,232	3,234,935	28.9
9. Kaiser, Henry J., Co	199,769	3,434,704	30.7
10. General Electric Co	198,863	3,633,567	32.5
11. Douglas Aircraft Co., Inc	196,893	3,830,460	34.2
12. Republic Steel Corp	189,563	4,020,023	35.9
13. Dow Chemical Co	177,314	4,197,337	37.5
14. Anaconda Copper Mining Co	156,244	4,353,581	38.9
15. Union Carbide & Carbon Corp	146,071	4,499,652	40.2
16. Consolidated Vultee Aircraft Corp	142,712	4,642,364	41.5
17. Standard Oil Co. of N. J.	123,426	4,765,790	42.6
18. Bendix Aviation Corp	108,939	4,874,729	43.6
19. Packard Motor Car Co	102,810	4,977,539	44.5
20. Continental Motors Corp	101,719	5,079,258	45.4
21. Studebaker Corp	93,288	5,172,546	46.2
22. Bell Aircraft Corp	92,855	5,265,401	47.1
23. Goodyear Tire & Rubber Co	86,727	5,352,128	47.8
24. Todd Shipyards Corp	83,186	5,435,314	48.6
25. Koppers United Co	81,350	5,516,664	49.3
26. North American Aviation, Inc	78,425	5,595,089	50.0
27. United Engineering & Foundry Co	76,162	5,671,251	50.7
28. Cities Service Co	74,292	5,745,543	51.4
29. Sperry Corp	73,713	5,819,256	52.0
30. Nash-Kelvinator Corp	73,385	5,892,641	52.7
31. Boeing Airplane Co	71,089	5,963,730	53.3
32. Permanente Metals Corp	70,479	6,034,209	53.9
33. Martin, Glenn L., Co	67,424	6,101,633	54.5
34. Sinclair Oil Co	67,273	6,168,906	55.2
35. du Pont, E. I. de Nemours Co	66,958	6,235,864	55.7
36. United States Foil Co	66,206	6,302,070	56.3
37. Mathieson Alkali Works, Inc	63,922	6,365,992	56.9
38. Smith, A. O., Corp	63,362	6,429,354	57.5
39. Neches Butane Products Co	60,000	6,489,354	58.0
40. Goodrich, B. F., Co	57,513	6,546,867	58.5
41. American Rolling Mill Co	54,007	6,600,874	59.0
42. Aviation Corp	47,794	6,648,668	59.4
43. United States Rubber Co	47,358	6,696,026	59.9
44. Pullman, Inc	47,112	6,743,138	60.3
45. Newport News Shipbuilding & Drydock Co	45,470	6,788,608	60.7
46. Standard Steel Spring Co	45,228	6,833,836	61.1
47. Republic Aviation Corp	45,135	6,878,971	61.5
48. Westinghouse Electric & Manufacturing Co	45,050	6,924,021	61.9
49. Tennessee Gas & Transmission Co	44,000	6,968,021	62.3

Table 10.4 Continued

Corporation or company	Total value	Cumulative	
		Value	Percent
50. Phillips Petroleum Co	43,998	7,012,019	62.7
51. Sun Oil Co	42,156	7,054,175	63.1
52. Allis-Chalmers Manufacturing Co	41,442	7,095,617	63.4
53. Phelps Dodge Corp	40,538	7,136,155	63.8
54. Fairchild Engine & Airplane Corp	40,374	7,176,529	64.2
55. Royal Dutch Co	39,661	7,216,190	64.5
56. Inland Steel Co	35,111	7,251,301	64.8
57. Remington Rand, Inc	34,151	7,285,452	65.1
58. Revere Copper & Brass, Inc	32,692	7,318,144	65.4
59. Baldwin Locomotive Works	32,107	7,350,251	65.7
60. Higgins Industries, Inc	30,572	7,380,823	66.0
61. Thompson Products, Inc	30,553	7,411,376	66.3
62. International Harvester Co	30,319	7,441,695	66.5
63. Otis Elevator Co	30,310	7,472,005	66.8
64. Firestone Tire & Rubber Co	30,255	7,502,260	67.1
65. Crucible Steel Co. of America	29,791	7,532,051	67.3
66. Texas Co	29,103	7,561,154	67.6
67. Budd, Edward G., Manufacturing Co	28,628	7,589,782	67.9
68. Lukens Steel Co	28,248	7,618,030	68.1
69. Abercrombie, J. S., & Harrison Oil Co	28,077	7,646,107	68.4
70. Grumman Aircraft Engineering Corp	27,888	7,673,995	68.6
71. Dravo Corp	27,483	7,701,478	68.9
72. Monsanto Chemical Co	27,283	7,728,761	69.1
73. California Shipbuilding Co	27,011	7,755,772	69.3
74. Lockheed Aircraft Corp	26,853	7,782,625	69.6
75. Eaton Manufacturing Co	26,819	7,809,444	69.8
76. Standard Oil Co. of Indiana	26,600	7,836,044	70.1
77. Consolidated Steel Corp., Ltd	26,227	7,862,271	70.3
78. Blaw Knox Co	26,179	7,888,450	70.5
79. American Steel Foundries	26,045	7,914,495	70.8
80. Walsh-Kaiser Co., Inc	25,950	7,940,445	71.0
81. Alabama Drydock & Shipbuilding Co	25,876	7,966,321	71.2
82. Houdaille-Hershey Corp	25,751	7,992,072	71.5
83. Jones, J. A., Shipbuilding Co	25,695	8,017,767	71.7
84. Bohn Aluminum & Brass Corp	25,673	8,043,440	71.9
85. Savage Arms Corp	25,546	8,068,986	72.1
86. Standard Oil Co. of California	24,472	8,093,458	72.4
87. Lone Star Steel Co	23,789	8,117,247	72.6
88. Bridgeport Brass Co	23,255	8,140,502	72.8
89. Kennecott Copper Corp	22,710	8,163,212	73.0
90. Consolidated Builders, Inc	22,409	8,185,621	73.2
91. Cleveland Pneumatic Aerol, Inc	22,377	8,207,998	73.4
92. Jacobs Aircraft Engine Co	21,918	8,229,916	73.6
93. Cramp Shipbuilding Co	21,606	8,251,522	73.8
94. New Jersey Powder Co	20,945	8,272,467	74.0
95. American Locomotive Co	20,843	8,293,310	74.1
96. Northern Pump Co	19,809	8,313,119	74.3
97. Caterpillar Tractor Co	19,757	8,332,876	74.5
98. Diamond Alkali Co	19,683	8,352,559	74.7
99. Copperweld Steel Co	19,107	8,371,666	74.8
100. Worthington Pump & Machinery Corp	19,088	8,390,754	75.0
68 other corporations operating facilities valued at $10 millions or more	934,969	9,325,723	83.4

corporations received 66 percent of these contracts, it is probable that the 100 top corporations received more than 70 percent of the total.

In the long run the concentration of economic power may be greatly strengthened as a result of this centralization of research. The peacetime

Table 10.5   FUNDS SPENT BY MAJOR GOVERNMENT AGENCIES ENGAGED IN RESEARCH AND DEVELOPMENT, BY FACILITIES USED: TOTALS FOR THE 5 FISCAL YEARS, 1940 TO 1944 [in thousands of dollars]

	Agency laboratories	Private industrial laboratories	Educational institutions and foundations	Others (State and government, etc.)	Net total expended[1]
Departments:					
Agriculture	113,880	—	—	34,565	148,445
Commerce	33,986	490	304	—	34,781
Interior	88,431	—	1	—	88,432
Navy	97,853	248,834	1,939	—	348,626
War	227,129	523,669	3,520	328	754,647
Independent offices:					
Public Health Service	15,259	199	463	77	15,998
National Advisory Committee for Aeronautics	93,429	75	958	—	94,462
Tennessee Valley Authority	10,049	—	2,873	7	12,929
Others	1,578	2,891	364	45	4,878
Emergency war agencies:					
Office of Scientific Research and Development	5,956	110,047	220,817	—	336,820
Reconstruction Finance Corporation; Defense Plant Corporation	—	19,030	40	—	19,070
War Production Board; Office of Production Research and Development	—	2,630	2,756	311	5,697
Others	176	6,873	1,221	138	8,408
Semigovernmental: National Academy of Sciences and National Research Council[2]	1,083	—	—	—	5,991
Total funds spent	688,810	914,738	235,257	35,470	1,879,183

Source: U.S. Senate, Subcommittee on War Mobilization, Military Affairs Committee, the Government's Wartime Research and Development, 1940-44, pt. 1, pp. 277-326.
[1]Omits interagency transfers.
[2]Net total includes $4,908,000 of National Academy of Sciences and National Research Council expenditures for which no break-down into facilities is available.

applications and uses of this scientific knowledge will be enormous. The nature of most scientific research is such that it has a wide variety of practical applications—military as well as peacetime. Obviously the companies in whose laboratories this research work has been carried on will be its chief beneficiaries not only because of their direct acquaintanceship and knowledge of the research but also because of patents. The investigations of the Subcommittee on War Mobilization of the Senate Military Affairs Committee show that over 90

Table 10.6   VALUE OF FEDERAL RESEARCH AND DEVELOPMENT CONTRACTS
HELD BY MAJOR INDUSTRIAL ORGANIZATIONS, 1940-1944

Number of corporations (cumulative)	Amount	Percent (cumulative)	Number of corporations (cumulative)	Amount	Percent (cumulative)
First 10	$280,460,000	37.1	First 60	$489,970,000	64.8
First 20	374,608,000	49.5	First 68	499,187,000	66.0
First 30	422,639,000	55.9	Grand total	756,329,000	100.0
First 40	454,687,000	60.1			
First 50	475,044,000	62.8			

percent of the contracts made between Government agencies and private
industrial laboratories for scientific research and development placed the
ownership of patents with the contractor, the Government receiving a
royalty-free license for its own use. The research contracts of the War
Department, Navy Department, Reconstruction Finance Corporation, and Office
of Scientific Research and Development—which accounted for 98 percent of the
Federal funds spent for research in private industrial laboratories—were generally
of this nature. The only exception were patents on military items which were
considered by the War and Navy Departments to be of a highly strategic
character.

This means, in effect, that the large corporations which carried on the great
bulk of the federally financed wartime industrial research will have control,
through patents, of the commercial applications of that research.

Atomic Power. The above figures on scientific research do not include the
funds spent by the Federal Government in developing the atomic bomb. Of the
$2,000,000,000 cost of the entire bomb project, some $1,300,000,000 was
spent on facilities. Of this, $1,167,000,000 represented funds spent on three
major facilities, each of which was operated by one of the Nation's largest
private industrial concerns. These were the diffusion plant, costing
$500,000,000, which was operated by the Union Carbide & Carbon Corp.; the
electromagnetic plant, costing $317,000,000, which was operated by Eastman
Kodak; and the Hanford plant, costing $350,000,000, which was operated by
E. I. du Pont de Nemours Co.

Furthermore, most of the equipment used in creating this amazing new
development was built specifically for the plants by large machinery corporations. For example, in the electromagnetic plant, Westinghouse supplied the
mechanical equipment, General Electric the electrical equipment, and Allis-
Chalmers the magnetic equipment.

It is generally conceded among scientists that atomic power will be adapted
to certain peacetime uses in the near future. Dr. Smythe, in his official report,
states that peacetime uses may well be a reality in 10 years. Other authorities are
even more optimistic. But regardless of when the peacetime applications are
developed, the fact remains that the concerns which made the equipment for the

manufacture of fissionable materials and the firms which operated the plants in which they were produced will inevitably have a tremendous head start over all other firms in terms of scientific and technical knowledge, production "know-how", and general familiarity with the subject.

Wartime Role of Top 100 Corporations. The economic concentration which characterized war production is summarized in the following list, which shows the extent of concentration by the 100 top corporations in the value of prime contracts, materials, facilities, and scientific research. In the table, the 100 top corporations are ranked in accordance with each of the items involved. Thus, the 100 top prime contractors are a somewhat different group of firms than the 100 top carbon steel-consuming corporations, etc.

	Top 100 corporations (percent of total)
Prime contracts:	
Cumulative (June 1940-September 1944)	67
Active (September 1944)	75
Materials (third quarter, 1942 consumption):	
Carbon steel	45
Alloy steel	70
Aluminum	81
Copper	79
Copper-base alloy	66
War facilities:	
Private 1940-1945	51
Public 1940-1945	75
Scientific research (1940-1944): 68 corporations	66

OUTLOOK FOR THE FUTURE

What will be the effect of this wartime concentration upon the peacetime economy? That is the heart of the problem. Will the wartime gains in concentration be retained or increased, or will the economy return to its prewar state?—which, it should not be forgotten, was already highly concentrated. Some idea of this prewar concentration in the economy as a whole, and in manufacturing in particular, can be gained from the following summary:

1. The 45 largest transportation corporations owned 92 percent of all the transportation facilities of the country.

2. The 40 largest public-utility corporations owned more than 80 percent of the public-utility facilities.

3. The country's 20 largest banks held 27 percent of the total loans and investments of all the banks.

4. The 17 largest life-insurance companies accounted for over 81.5 percent of all the assets of all life-insurance companies.

5. The 200 largest nonfinancial corporations owned about 55 percent of all the assets of all the nonfinancial corporations in the country.

6. One-tenth of 1 percent of all the corporations owned 52 percent of the total corporate assets.

7. One-tenth of 1 percent of all the corporations earned 50 percent of the total corporate net income.

8. Less than 4 percent of all the manufacturing corporations earned 84 percent of all the net profits of all manufacturing corporations.

9. No less than 33 percent of the total value of all manufactured products was produced under conditions where the four largest producers of each individual product accounted for over 75 percent of the total United States output.

10. More than 57 percent of the total value of manufactured products was produced under conditions where the four largest producers of each product turned out over 50 percent of the total United States output.

11. One-tenth of 1 percent of all the firms in the country in 1939 employed 500 or more workers and accounted for 40 percent of all the nonagricultural employment in the country.

12. In manufacturing 1.1 percent of all the firms employed 500 or more workers and accounted for 48 percent of all the manufacturing employment in the country.

13. One-third of the industrial-research personnel were employed by 13 companies. Two-thirds of the research workers were employed by 140 companies and the remaining third were employed by 1,582 concerns. About 150,000 industrial corporations were without research laboratories.

These facts make it quite evident that a return to prewar conditions would mean a return to an economy which had already become highly concentrated. But will such a return take place or will the wartime gains in concentration be retained? In other words, did the way in which the Nation's resources were mobilized for war put into the hands of big business instruments of power which it can, to improve its position, use in the years to come?

Some insight into this question might be gained by examining what happened after the last war. One of the outstanding characteristics of production in wartime is an increase in the relative importance of large plants. Small plants become larger, large plants become giants, new big plants are added, and the average size of plants tends to increase all along the line. This means, of course, that a greater proportion of workers are employed in larger plants.

With the return to peace, this trend will undoubtedly be reversed, and the average size of plants will drop below the wartime heights. In relation to total output, the peacetime demand for products which are produced in big plants will undoubtedly be less than in wartime.

But will the relative importance of large plants drop all the way back to the prewar level? This is of great importance to the whole subject of concentration, because large plant operations are generally associated with big concerns. The available information, as presented below, strongly suggests that in postwar years the importance of the big plants declines somewhat from the wartime heights, but does not fall all the way back to the prewar levels.

During World War I the percentage of employment in large establishments mounted greatly in both manufacturing and metal products and a large part of

PERCENTAGE OF WAGE EARNERS IN ESTABLISHMENTS
EMPLOYING MORE THAN 1,000 WAGE EARNERS

	Manufacturing	Metal products		Manufacturing	Metal products
1909	15.1	21.3	1939	22.4	33.4
1919	26.0	40.4	1945	–	64.7
1929	24.2	37.4			

these wartime gains was retained. In other words, the historical pattern is that of a retention of much of the war-induced, increased importance of large plants.

It is interesting to note that in the metal products industries—the only group for which such data are available—the percentage of employment in large establishments nearly doubled in World War II.

Quite apart from this historical pattern, however, the evidence is compelling that big business will be able to use a number of other wartime developments to increase its relative importance in the postwar economy. These include such factors as production improvements, scientific research, wartime advertising, increased working capital, and new facilities.

Production Improvements. Most of the wartime technological improvements were developed in the plants of big business, and the major part of these can readily be adapted for peacetime output. Of a sample of 1,471 wartime technological developments culled during 1942 and 1943 from 167 technical periodicals, it has been estimated that 77 percent "clearly can be used in the postwar period."

In addition to these technological developments, big business has gained invaluable know-how from producing a vast variety of munitions items under the pressure of war schedules. These developments and know-how, when applied to peacetime production, will inevitably cut costs and improve the efficiency and competitive advantage of big business.

Scientific Research. The few big corporations which received during the war years more money from the Federal Government for scientific research and development than the entire Nation spent on such research in prewar years can certainly be expected to apply many of the findings of this scientific research to peacetime production. There is only the narrowest of gaps between scientific knowledge developed in wartime and the application of that knowledge to peacetime production. Wartime scientific developments which have no peacetime uses are few and far between.

Big business, in whose laboratories and plants this Government-financed research was conducted, will have not only the "first crack" at putting into effect the peacetime applications of most of the wartime industrial research but also the patent rights on the commercial applications of that research.

Advertising. During the war many large firms were able to keep their company names, their trade-marks, or their brand names before the public eye by means of expensive advertising campaigns. Much of this was of the so-called institutional type in which the firm identified itself with the war effort. Further more, much of it was ultimately paid for by the Federal Government, the advertising campaigns being charged as an expense before taxes, thereby reducing the corporation's tax payments.

Certain aspects of wartime advertising were criticized by President (then Senator) Truman in a speech delivered on November 11, 1943, before the annual meeting of the central council of the American Association of Advertising Agencies. He stated:

> There has been too much of what advertising agencies refer to as "blue sky" advertising. It is virtually impossible today to pick up a magazine or newspaper without finding page after page of glowing tribute to American industry. To read the dramatically written pages, and to see the highly colored photographs and drawings, one would almost think that our battles were not won by our fighting men at all, but by our war industries.

He went on to point out some of the extremes to which this type of advertising had been carried:

> Some of these companies have even used advertising, the cost of which is borne by the taxpayer, to create false impressions or to counteract criticism which has legitimately been directed at them. For example, one corporation advertised an airplane as the best dive bomber in the world at a time when it had spent over $100,000,000 of Government money in a plant, built at Government expense, without producing a single dive bomber which could be used in combat. Another airplane company inserted a number of advertisements, the plain import of which was that its planes were blasting the Axis and making a large contribution to victory abroad, when the fact was that none of the planes in question were in use, or are ever expected to be placed in use, at any fighting front.
>
> Other corporations inserted numerous advertisements to the effect that the Navy was using helicopters against submarines, when the fact was that the Army and not the Navy was developing helicopters, and that the Navy deserved criticism, rather than praise for its action with respect to helicopters.
>
> In other cases, corporations have inserted advertisements, indirectly paid for by the taxpayer, in which they try to justify corporate action under investigation. These advertisements frequently contain half-truths and innuendoes and even false statements. Certainly the taxpayers should not be asked to pay for them.

Working Capital. Since it was operating at a high rate of output during the war, producing for an assured market, big business greatly improved its working capital position. In the immediate postwar years, big business will have billions of dollars in cash that can be used in a variety of ways to improve its position. According to the Securities and Exchange Commission, the 802 listed corporations in manufacturing—which are all large firms—increased their net working capital from 8.6 billion dollars in 1939 to 14.1 billion dollars as of June 1945—a rise of 64 percent.

Their net working capital should increase by more than 2 billion dollars because of excess-profits-tax refunds and tax credits such as those arising from final amortization of war plants, raising the total to over 16 billion dollars. Furthermore, the current assets of these corporations are extremely liquid—including cash and Government receivable notes and securities totaling nearly 15 billion dollars, which will be augmented by termination settlements of approximately 2 billion dollars.

By the middle of 1945, the 63 largest listed manufacturing corporations with assets of over $100,000,000 had increased their net working capital to 8.4 billion dollars, more than that of all listed manufacturing corporations in 1939, and, for the reasons indicated above, at the end of 1945 they will hold nearly 10 billion dollars of highly liquid net working capital. (See Table 10.7.)

With this 10 billion dollars, these 63 giants could increase their power in a multitude of ways. They could launch sales and advertising campaigns on a scale never before contemplated. They could expand forward by obtaining sales outlets, backward by obtaining sources of materials, and horizontally by entering into the production of a wide variety of auxiliary or different products. With this capital they could purchase all of the usable Government-owned facilities at their option price, or they could purchase the assets of 71,700 smaller

Table 10.7   CURRENT ASSETS AND LIABILITIES OF 63 MANUFACTURING CORPORATIONS WITH ASSETS OF $100,000,000 AND OVER DECEMBER 1939-JUNE 1945 [Millions of dollars]

	1939	1941	1943	1944	June 1945
Current assets:					
Cash on hand and in banks	1,843	2,206	2,934	2,713	2,855
United States tax and savings notes	—	873	1,186	1,078	1,127
Other U. S. Government securities	369	341	1,822	2,606	2,873
Other marketable securities	169	148	69	69	67
Receivables from U. S. Government	4	232	2,106	2,090	1,770
Other notes and accounts receivable	1,259	1,811	1,422	1,450	1,354
Inventories	3,085	4,275	5,062	4,835	4,733
Other current assets	7	18	21	21	31
Total current assets	6,736	9,904	14,622	14,862	14,810
Current liabilities:					
Notes payable to banks	39	148	242	359	401
Advances and prepayments, U. S. Government	3	271	874	755	692
Other trade notes and accounts payable	613	981	1,697	1,805	1,546
Federal income taxes accrued	225	1,630	2,617	2,424	2,367
Other taxes accrued	224	327	422	441	465
Renegotiation provisions	—	—	583	277	189
Other current liabilities	409	637	693	733	748
Total current liabilities	1,513	3,994	7,128	6,794	6,408
Net working capital	5,223	5,910	7,494	8,068	8,402

manufacturing corporations with assets of less than $3,000,000 each, which represent 94 percent of the total number of manufacturing corporations in the United States. Large firms are, in fact, now using their wartime financial gains to buy up small firms, as is indicated by the current sharp increase in mergers and acquisitions.

Facilities. The effect of the war on economic concentration will probably hinge more on the disposition and use of the war-built facilities than on anything else. Insofar as the privately financed facilities are concerned, concentration will undoubtedly be increased, since the bulk of these facilities were acquired by big business. Furthermore, a considerable portion of the Government-owned facilities will inevitably be acquired by big business, since they are scrambled in with their existing plant and equipment and cannot possibly be operated by any other firms. In many cases these scrambled facilities nicely round out their capacity for peacetime production.

It is in regard to the remaining Government-owned facilities which are capable of independent operation that the question of "who is going to get them" really applies.

Before the question of whether it will be large or small business that will acquire these facilities can be discussed, another question presents itself. Will these new facilities be sold at all? Will they actually be used in the postwar world, or will they be permitted to lie idle?

The answer to these questions will depend greatly upon the general rate of business activity. If it is low, then only a comparatively small amount of facilities will be sold. In most cases, the facilities disposed of will probably be acquired not so much to increase a firm's total production but more to reduce its production costs.

Under depressed conditions big business will undoubtedly acquire a greater percentage of the facilities which it operated than will small business. The reason for this is that small business traditionally experiences the greatest difficulty in obtaining finances during depressed times. And this difficulty is most pronounced in obtaining finances for the acquisition of capital equipment. On the other hand, big business will experience little difficulty in obtaining whatever finances it wants.

If, on the other hand, the rate of business activity is high, it may be expected that both big and small business will seek to purchase a considerable proportion of these facilities, particularly since most of the Government-owned plants and equipment are highly efficient and of excellent quality.

If an active demand does develop for these facilities, there are a number of reasons for believing that they will be sold largely to big business; that, specifically, big business will acquire a greater proportion of the amount of usable publicly owned facilities which it operated than will small business.

In the first place, big business has options to purchase most of the Government-owned plants that it operated during the war—which, of course, comprise the great bulk of these facilities.

Big business also holds a somewhat similar superpriority on much of the readily movable equipment; that is, Government-owned equipment which can readily be moved out of the plants in which it was located during the war and installed in other plants. Under Surplus Property Administration Regulation 6, the private firms that operated Government-owned machine tools during the war in their own plants are granted the first chance to purchase such tools. More than 40 percent (232,000) of the Government-owned machine tools are located in contractors' plants, and, consequently, are subject to disposal first to the contractors which operated them.

Furthermore, big business certainly has the money to buy the Government-owned facilities. As was pointed out above, the 63 giant manufacturing corporations hold some $10,000,000,000 of liquid assets with which they could purchase all the usable Government-owned facilities at their option price.

If, for these or other reasons, big business does acquire the usable facilities which it operated during the war, it will dominate the manufacturing economy through the sheer weight of its productive capacity. . . . The usable facilities which would be held by the 250 giant corporations would nearly equal those of all manufacturing corporations in 1939. And the facilities of corporations controlled by five great financial interest groups—Morgan, Rockefeller, Mellon, du Pont, and the Cleveland group—would be equal to nearly half that of all manufacturing corporations in 1939.

Of course, this is an oversimplification of the situation, since the particular facilities held by these large corporations are not sufficiently diversified to produce all the different types of goods at a 1939 level of output. But the exaggeration is not as great as might be supposed, because of the tremendous degree of interchangeability of modern facilities particularly in the metal fabricating and chemical fields.

This reasoning may be projected still further into the future. Suppose that the end of the war is followed by a few years of prosperity, in which both big and small business acquire the great bulk of the usable facilities which they operated during the war. Suppose, then—as is more than possible—that this period of prosperity is followed by a depression. In such circumstances, would it be the facilities of big or of small business that would tend to be retired?

The answer lies in the fact that big business, as is generally assumed, has more staying power than small business and could better withstand the vicissitudes of a depression. Besides its production facilities, big business has the liquid capital, the sales forces, distributive organizations, established trade-marks, brand names, patents, production know-how, and the general, all-around economic strength required for survival. Small business, particularly in the war-expanded industries, would be put to the severest test of survival. This would call for all the ingenuity and resourcefulness for which small business has traditionally been famous. It would also call for the financial, technical, and management assistance which it has traditionally lacked.

In short, if the war is followed by a prolonged depression, small business can be expected to obtain only a very small amount of the Government-owned facilities, because of the extreme difficulties which it experiences during hard times in raising funds, especially when those funds are to be used for the purchase of capital equipment.

If, however, the war is followed by a long period of prosperity, small business will probably also lose out as compared to big business, but for other reasons. Under prosperous conditions, it may be expected that both big and small business will seek to acquire much of the usable publicly owned facilities. In such a contest, big business, with its options, with the favorable regulations of the Surplus Property Administration, with its immense amounts of liquid funds, will hardly encounter a serious rival in small business. Small business generally does not even know where the surplus plants and equipment are located. Furthermore, many small firms—even in prosperous times—would have diifficulty in obtaining the funds with which to purchase them. Once having obtained the usable facilities which it operated, big business would clearly dominate the economy through the tremendous magnitude of its production capacity.

Finally, if the war is followed by prosperity—in which both big and small business would acquire most of the facilities they operated—which, in turn, would be followed by a depression, it would be largely the facilities of small business that would be retired, because of the greater staying power of big business.

To summarize, economic concentration will probably be higher in the postwar years than before the war as a result of: The production improvements and scientific research which big business gained during the war; the increase in the liquid funds and general financial strength of big business; the ability of big business to keep its name and trade-marks before the public eye during the war; and finally the fact that big business will probably acquire a greater share of the war-built facilities which it operated than will small business, regardless of whether economic conditions are prosperous or depressed.

11. SURVIVAL IN THE AIR AGE

Finletter Commission

After the second great crusade to make the world safe for democracy, most Americans thought they could look forward to a well-deserved rest. If in fact Hitler had merely been a neighborhood bully disrupting an otherwise quiet scene, his death marked the return to normalcy. The issues of world history, which the war effort had ignored, however, now rose up to haunt the nation. Economists were determined that the prewar depression should not return with the soldiers from Europe and the Pacific. Businessmen were concerned that American capital should have ready access to all areas of the world so that trade and profits might flourish. The military determined never again to be caught unprepared by a war emergency. In short, those who made national policy were convinced that a strenuously pursued *Pax Americana*, backed up by an imperial army, was necessary for the formation and maintenance of the kind of world in which Americans could wax prosperous and proud.

The needs of a demobilized and demoralized aircraft industry and a triumphant, ambitious Air Force, came together in the Finletter Report, which called for a large air force and a healthy industry — both of which could be served by an arms race with the Soviet Union. The Finletter Commission was made up of the same breed of corporate liberals that had dominated war planning since 1915, and its report articulated a rationale for the military-industrial complex.

Source: *Survival in the Air Age*. A Report to the President's Air Policy Commission (Washington, D.C., January 1, 1948), pp. 7-10, 19, 26-27, 45-66, 133-134.

THE APPROACH OF THE COMMISSION
TO A PROGRAM OF NATIONAL DEFENSE

Our report discusses in considerable detail the preparedness program which we believe is now required if we are to have the relative security to which we have referred. But before we deal with this program we will state our general approach to this matter of preparation in time of peace for the possibility of war.

1. The Commission does not subscribe to the proposition that armaments are a guarantee of peace. History does not assure us that a strong armament policy by a peacefully inclined nation is certain to frighten off aggressor governments. An authoritarian government bent on aggression may calculate that it can arm better and faster than the nations it has chosen as its victims, and that if it hits hard enough and with no warning, it can conquer. Indeed, an authoritarian government may seek war for war's sake or to divert attention from its internal troubles, even though it may not be certain that it will win.

Nevertheless, the Commission believes that a strong United States will be a force for peace. Our armaments will not guarantee that peace absolutely. But the chances of avoiding a war will be greatly increased if this country has the available force to strike back and to defeat anyone who breaks the peace. A strong United States will be welcomed by all peace-loving nations. The countries who want to live under regimes of freedom will see in our armaments not a threat but an assurance.

2. It is difficult for a representative democracy to keep up with an authoritarian state in an armament race in peacetime. It can, however, be done. We gained supremacy of the seas by the weight of our naval armament. We can be supreme in the air by the weight of our air power. The United States can build a Military Establishment which will keep up with any nation and be a powerful force for peace.

In our opinion this Military Establishment must be built around the air arm. Of course an adequate Navy and Ground Force must be maintained. But it is the Air Force and naval aviation on which we must mainly rely. Our military security must be based on air power.

3. Maintenance of a proper air establishment will require heavy appropriations. Not only must the equipment be of the finest quality that science can devise and money provide, but there must be enough of it, in being and ready for immediate use. Research and development must be increased. For a second-best air force, when war takes place, is almost as bad as none.

Already the payments which have to be made every year on account of past wars and current preparations for possible future wars are draining away a large part of the money and energy of the country that should be applied to better things—things that could add to the wealth of the country and the intellectual and physical well-being of its people. The taxpayer's money goes mainly for war. The Bureau of the Budget has informed us that about 80 percent of the budget for the current fiscal year ending June 30, 1948, is for payments for past wars or for our present Military Establishment. Indeed, the figures show that since 1915 about 85 percent of our total Federal budgets have been spent for war or preparation or payment for war.

And yet, as will be seen, this Commission has been compelled to report that the evidence is overwhelming that even this amount is not enough and that (1) the Federal Government should increase substantially its expenditures for the Air Force and naval aviation in the years 1948 and 1949, and (2) that expenditures may be needed in later fiscal years up to the end of 1952 substantially in excess of the 1948 and 1949 figures. The expenditures which we recommend, however, would be small in comparison with the cost of another war.

The Commission has reached its recommendations for increased military expenditures with the utmost reluctance. Every dollar spent for military establishments is a dollar to be grudged. Large military expenditures will help to keep taxes high and will drain away from the people a large part of the product of their labor. For these reasons we have not accepted military estimates without submitting them to critical analysis and we have required that all estimates meet the test of strict necessity under the broad principles as to the strategic needs of the country which are set out in this report.

On the other hand we believe that self-preservation comes ahead of economy. No concession should be made from the principle that our Military Establishment must be adequate for the defense of the country. Substantial savings within the Military Establishment are possible, and later in this report we make recommendations on this subject. But in making these savings the adequacy of our forces must not be impaired. Economies, desirable as they are, must not be made if making them would jeopardize our safety.

4. We believe that the recent unification of the services under the Secretary of Defense will result in greater efficiency in the spending of the security dollar.

The National Security Act of 1947 puts the duty squarely on the Joint Chiefs of Staff, subject to the President and the Secretary of Defense, (1) to prepare the over-all strategic and logistic plans to support the foreign policy of the United States and to protect the country, and (2) to review the major material and personnel requirements of the Services in accordance with these strategic and logistic plans.

By establishing constantly revised strategic and logistic plans and by relating expenditures strictly to these plans it should be possible to eliminate many expenses not sufficiently directly related to our strategic purposes, and consequently to have a force capable of carrying out those purposes without expenditures which would seriously strain the economy.

THE NEW STRATEGIC CONCEPT OF THE DEFENSE OF THE UNITED STATES

We have said that we believe that the defense of the United States must be based on air power. We have reached this conclusion as a result of prolonged discussions with the Armed Services and with many private citizens who have appeared before us. We believe that it is the overwhelming view of those most qualified to know that the country must have a new strategic concept for its defense and that the core of this concept is air power.

We need a much stronger air establishment than we now have. The reason for this is that we can no longer follow our traditional procedure of relying entirely on the Navy as our force in being in peacetime. Heretofore the United States has been able to make most of its preparations for war after war began. In World Wars I and II the oceans lay between us and the enemy. Protected by the Navy, and by the land, sea, and air forces of our Allies, we were able to convert our great industrial machine and our manpower for war after war had begun. No enemy action interfered with us as we got our factories going. Our army was trained in peaceful areas. Our cities were untouched. In World Wars I and II not a single enemy weapon except a few Japanese balloons and a few shells from submarines touched the United States mainland, and sabotage was but a minor nuisance.

This will not be the case in a future war. . . .

The conclusions which the Commission has reached as to the development by other nations of the means of delivering a direct attack on the United States by transpolar or transoceanic aircraft or missiles are these: (1) It is probable that other nations will develop atomic weapons before they develop supersonic bombers in quantity with a striking range of 5,000 miles, or supersonic, accurate, guided missiles with a 5,000-mile range. (2) Nevertheless, it would be unwise to assume, in the planning of our defense establishment, that other nations will not have the planes and missiles capable of delivering a sustained attack on the United States mainland by the same date we have assumed they may have atomic weapons in quantity—namely, by the end of 1952. If they want them enough they can surely have them at some date; just when will be determined by the amount of effort they put into getting them. (3) It is not certain that the United States will be the first to develop such aircraft or missiles. On the contrary, the Germans were ahead of us in these matters at the war's end and other nations may well be even with or ahead of us now. (4) The United States must press most energetically and immediately its basic and applied research and development programs in aerodynamics, power plants, electronics, and related fields with a view toward the development at the earliest possible date of the most effective piloted aircraft and guided missiles and the defenses against them.

The conclusions of the Commission thus fix as the target date by which we should have an air arm in being capable of dealing with a possible atomic attack on this country at January 1, 1953. For convenience we will refer to this date as A-day. . . .

Once committed to combat, losses of planes and personnel are very high. From experience in the European and Pacific theaters, we know that many operating groups lose 25 percent of their equipment every month of actual combat. Losses must be replaced immediately. At the outbreak of a war, industry cannot expand in time to make up combat losses in the first year. Unless, therefore, there are planes in reserve, combat forces would diminish rapidly after the beginning of hostilities and we would be left without a fighting Air Force after a few months of war.

The solution of this problem is one of the most serious tasks faced by the Air Force and the aircraft industry. Plans for the rapid expansion of industry will help, but no evidence presented to us indicates that any plan can be devised which will insure the production of planes by industry in time to replace combat losses in the first year of a war. Moreover there is the grave danger that enemy attack may so disrupt our industrial production that all forecasts of plane manufacture after war begins will prove to be unrealistic. Therefore, a reserve of aircraft in storage must always be maintained. This reserve is expensive to procure and costly to keep modernized. Planes in storage become obsolescent and must be replaced.

At the present time, we are reasonably well off because World War II surplus planes are still usable. Fortunately the Air Force retained a substantial number of planes as a reserve and sold or otherwise disposed of only those planes considered unusable. This reserve is gradually being used up. It must be replenished before the end of 1952. Estimates by the Air Force show that 8,100 new planes must be procured for this reserve between January 1, 1950, and January 1, 1953. The 8,100 figure for reserve planes is reached by establishing the deficiency between losses, computed on the basis of past experience, and replacement forecast under a theoretical mobilization plan. Since both losses and replacements are estimates, later studies may cause a revision in the recommended 8,100 plane reserve.

In summary, the problems of the Air Force are threefold: (1) The force in being must be increased from its present level to a minimum regular establishment of 70 groups (6,869 front line aircraft), an Air National Guard of 27 groups (3,212 front line aircraft) and an adequately equipped 34 group Air Reserve. (2) The level of procurement of new aircraft must be high enough to keep this force modern at all times. And (3) an adequate reserve, now estimated at 8,100 aircraft, must be created and maintained in a proper state of modernization.

We must start now on such a program and complete it before the end of 1952. . . .

BASIC CONSIDERATIONS FOR NATIONAL SECURITY

A strong aircraft industry is an essential element in the Nation's air power. Our air establishment would be useless unless backed by a manufacturing industry skillful in technological application, efficient in production, capable of rapid expansion, and strong in basic financial structure.

On the basis of the evidence, the over-all aircraft industry of the United States now meets only the first of these specifications. A parade of witnesses has testified as to its current productive weakness as an industry, its general lack of preparation for rapid expansion, and its general financial instability. How to remedy those deficiencies is a matter that has engaged the Commission's close attention.

As a point of departure, it is necessary to calculate the minimum level at which the industry must be held to provide a safe base for expansion in an emergency. Our own studies, together with figures supplied by the industry and the military services, tend to confirm the general range of requirements set by the Air Coordinating Committee in its report of October 22, 1945.

Two levels were set by the Air Coordinating Committee. The lower level was an estimate that the aircraft industry required military purchases in the amount of 30,000,000 pounds of airframe weight annually. This was considered "as a minimum which could be reached only after maintenance of world peace is well assured and a substantial degree of disarmament has taken place." The Air Coordinating Committee also proposed an alternate level of about 60,000,000 pounds of airframe for the event that world conditions were such that "we have . . . need for a substantial striking force ready at all times to cooperate in the maintenance of world peace." The military requirements listed in section I would lead to a steady build-up throughout this range over the next few years.

This Commission believes that military requirements for 30,000,000 to 40,000,000 pounds annually, in addition to demands for commercial and private planes, would provide a sound basis for expansion in an emergency.

No artificial stimulation to achieve this result appears to be necessary. If the program outlined in section I is carried out, the necessary base for expansion of the aircraft industry will exist. The rate of procurement recommended in section I would increase the present military procurement (which is now at the rate of about 21,000,000 pounds annually) by contracts for an additional 13,000,000 pounds during the calendar year 1948, and for 22,000,000 pounds in 1949 more than in 1948.

This, of course, is not a permanent solution. It satisfies only the demands of the immediately foreseeable future. If the threat of war diminishes, or if war becomes imminent, new levels of military demand (lower or higher) must be calculated and maintained. As is recommended throughout this report, periodic reviews of the military needs must be made, and plans and programs adjusted to fit conditions as they change.

It was widely predicted before the end of World War II that rising demand for commercial aircraft, both transport and personal, would tide a number of companies over the postwar adjustments of 1946 and 1947. For various reasons, some of which are dealt with elsewhere in this report, these hopes have not been justified. Although conditions may change in the future, it is certain that current commercial demands alone will not carry us through the present crisis. Whether we like it or not, the health of the aircraft industry, for the next few years, at least, is dependent largely upon financial support from Government in the form of orders for military aircraft.

To justify that support, the aircraft industry of the United States must be capable of turning out superior war weapons. The importance of adequate aeronautical research programs cannot be overemphasized. This phase of the problem is discussed in section III of this report.

At the time the Morrow Board convened (1925) the design of a successful military aircraft depended largely upon the efforts of a single man—the final product was almost wholly a reflection of one individual's ideas. Today, every design is the end point of many contributions by many individuals. The concept of the engineering team is almost universally accepted. Group engineering know-how is one of the most valuable assets carried forward by aircraft manufacturers out of the World War II period. If, for any reason, too many of the war-trained teams are dispersed, we are in danger of losing this hard-won knowledge and experience.

But the aircraft industry must do more than design aircraft of top performance. It must also design them for efficient production in quantities to meet the needs of the armed services. Since World War II, military aircraft have become much more complicated. The net result has been to increase the number of their component parts and to complicate their final assembly. The most efficient aircraft in the world, no matter how brilliant its performance, is of little value to the national defense unless it can be manufactured quickly in large quantities.

The team concept is not limited to research and design. Production planning and production control groups are equally necessary, but it is more difficult to keep such teams together in peacetime. When production drops off to mere jobbing levels, their functions simply disappear. Means must be found to keep alive the special skills that have been evolved in these particular fields during the war years. If they are allowed to be dissipated, time and effort will be needed to replace them in a future emergency.

The techniques of aircraft manufacture vary widely with changes in the volume of orders. It is uneconomical to do extensive special tooling, either for manufacture or assembly, to turn out a few units. If, on the other hand, thousands of similar airplanes are required, the expenditure of relatively large sums for special jigs, fixtures, and tools is justified. Between the two extremes are wide areas in which the exercise of good judgment is the only controlling factor. The only way such judgment can be generated is through actual production experience. How to provide the aircraft manufacturer with orders in sufficient quantity in peacetime to develop that kind of experience and to justify planning and tooling to a reasonable level for emergency expansion is one of the most important questions facing the services.

In a freely competitive economy the number of companies manufacturing a particular product levels off at a point determined by the ordinary laws of economics. In the case of the aircraft industry, however, it would be dangerous to rely only on the operation of these laws. The demand factor fluctuates too violently from peace to war. If a reasonable degree of expansibility is to be maintained for periods of emergency, it is necessary to exercise some industry-wide control in the interests of national security. It may even be desirable to keep a few marginal manufacturers in business who might be forced out if the normal laws of supply and demand were allowed to operate.

Based on considerations of maximum security, it is essential to maintain at least two sources of supply for similar products. It has long been the practice for the procurement agencies of the Army and Navy to keep alive at least two separate producers of each type of aircraft, as well as two or more separate sources for each of the major components. We believe that this policy is sound and should be continued. It develops automatically a degree of manufacturing dispersal which might otherwise not exist. In a field in which the technology is changing rapidly, competition between design and development groups results in continuously improved products, and price competition between suppliers results in lower unit costs.

The financial difficulties which harass the aircraft industry today stem from many causes. Uncertain Government policies account for many of them. Some reflect faulty judgment by management. Others have come about from particular circumstances which have surrounded this peculiar industry in the postwar period of readjustment. Some of them are:

1. A product that is, almost indivisibly, a weapon of war and a carrier of commerce;

2. A market with but one major customer, the Government, which purchases 80 to 90 percent of its entire output;

3. A violently fluctuating demand, due to uncertainty of requirements of its major customer;

4. A lack of the production continuity which is vitally important in sustaining a trained work force and in keeping production costs to a minimum;

5. A rapidly changing technology which causes a high rate of design obsolescence and abnormally high engineering costs;

6. An extremely long design-manufacturing cycle;

7. An organization in excess of present requirements.

The financial strength of any individual company or of the industry cannot be measured by the amount of sales, the extent of working capital, or the total floor space of its plants. It depends upon profitable operation. A profitable organization will attract capital and credit. It will be able to employ and retain the most capable engineers and craftsmen. The concern which consistently loses money will deteriorate, its financial position will weaken, and the quality of its product will suffer as its best employees drift away in search of better opportunities.

The Government cannot guarantee profits. Government can and should, however, create an atmosphere as conducive as possible to profitable operations in the aircraft manufacturing business. This can be done by longer-range planning, adequate volume, and the abandonment of uneconomic procurement practices. Under these circumstances, it will be the task of each manufacturing company to work out its own salvation.

THE STATE OF THE AIRCRAFT MANUFACTURING INDUSTRY

The aircraft manufacturing industry covers all those manufacturers whose products are included in finished aircraft, military or civil. The normal airplane consists of the airframe (fuselage, wings, tail surfaces, landing gear); the propulsion system (engines, turbo-jet units, rocket motors, propellers); instruments (control, navigational, recording); communication equipment; accessories (pumps, generators, landing lights); and furnishings (seats, fire-extinguishers, and miscellaneous fixtures).

The airframe manufacturer is responsible for the final product. He designs and builds the basic structure and installs the numerous components. He also test-flies the airplane before delivery to the customer and is responsible for its satisfactory performance.

The price of the airplane to the commercial customer usually includes the cost of all components. The aircraft manufacturer purchases them from their producers just as he does his raw materials. In aircraft for the military services, however, the airframe manufacturer bases his price on the cost of the airframe and of installing in it the various components. The Government usually buys the engines, propellers, instruments, and accessories separately. These are delivered to the airframe manufacturer as Government furnished equipment (GFE).

About half of the cost of the finished military aircraft is represented by the cost of the airframe and its assembly plus the cost of installing the GFE. The other half is the cost of the GFE. Thus, of a billion-dollar aircraft procurement program, about $500,000,000 goes to the airframe companies and the balance is spread among the hundreds of companies that build engines, propellers, radios, instruments, lights, heaters, and other gear.

Patent Cross Licensing. All the principal manufacturers of aircraft are members of the Manufacturers Aircraft Association, through which they license each other and the Government on all their aircraft patents. Over 90 percent of such patents are licensed without fee. On others, small royalties per airplane are paid. There is, accordingly, complete freedom among the MAA membership to adopt, and incorporate in new aircraft, features developed by other companies. Design patents are offered for license on a percentage royalty basis.

Composition of the Industry. The aircraft manufacturing industry may be roughly divided into (a) the 15 major companies or groups which produce the majority of the airframes, engines, and propellers for the military services and for the airlines and other users of transport aircraft; (b) the nine major manufacturers of personal and small commercial aircraft; (c) and numerous additional small companies making personal and other aircraft. The divisions are not sharply defined as some personal airplanes and helicopters are made by certain of the 15 major companies, while some of the personal plane manufacturers also make transports and military liaison airplanes.

The 15 major airframe companies are:

1. Bell Aircraft Corp.
2. Boeing Airplane Co.
3. Consolidated Vultee Aircraft Corp.[1]
4. Curtiss-Wright Corp.[2]
5. Douglas Aircraft Co., Inc.
6. Fairchild Engine & Airplane Corp.
7. Grumman Aircraft Engineering Corp.
8. Lockheed Aircraft Corp.
9. The Glenn L. Martin Co.
10. McDonnell Aircraft Corp.
11. North American Aviation, Inc.
12. Northrop Aircraft, Inc.
13. Republic Aviation Corp.
14. Ryan Aeronautical Co.
15. United Aircraft Corp.[3]

The nine major makers of personal and small commercial planes, most of whom were important producers of small military aircraft and aircraft components during the war, are:

1. Aeronca Aircraft Corp.
2. Beech Aircraft Corp.
3. Bellanca Aircraft Corp.
4. Cessna Aircraft Co.
5. Engineering & Research Corp.
6. Luscombe Airplane Corp.
7. Piper Aircraft Corp.
8. Taylorcraft, Inc.
9. Texas Engineering & Manufacturing Co.

Facilities and Output. The accompanying table shows the floor areas, number of employees, and airframe production of the major companies for 1939, at the war peak, for 1946 and for the first 10 months of 1947. Included in the figures for airframe weight of large civil airplanes are aircraft of 4-place and over, some of which are the products of the personal plane manufacturers.

Financial Condition. Pertinent financial data on the 15 major companies are presented in the table below. Total sales are shown for the calendar years 1939, 1944, and 1946, and for the first 6 months of 1947. Net profit or loss and the ratio of profit or loss to sales are shown for the years 1939, 1944, and 1946. Net worth, working capital, investment in plant and equipment, and the ratio of sales to each of these, is shown for the years ending on December 31, 1939, 1944, and 1946.

The $13,000,000 net loss in 1946 was after application of nearly $72,000,000 in tax-refund credits. A substantial portion of the loss was attributable to development costs of commercial aircraft and other nonmilitary

Floor area (covered) (in millions of sq. ft.)	1939	War peak	1946	1947
Total for all manufacturers of military and large civil airframes, engines and propellers.	13 (Jan. '40)	175	54 (Dec.)[4]	53 (June).[4]
Airframe prime contractors	10 (Jan. '40)	111	41 (Dec.)[4]	40 (June).[4]
Engine prime contractors	3 (Jan."40)	55	11 (Dec.)[4]	11 (June).[4]
Propeller prime contractors	[1]	9	2 (Dec.)[4]	2 (June).[4]
Employees[2] (in thousands)				
Industry total for both military and civil airframes and engines.	76 (Dec.)	1,708	221 (Dec.)	200 (Oct.).
Industry total for military and civil airframes.	63 (Dec.)	1,257	184 (Dec.)	164 (Oct.).
Production—Yearly[3] (in millions of airframe pounds)				1947 (1st 10 mos.)
Total military and large civil[5]	13	1,101	24	23
Total military	11	1,101	15	10
Total large civil[5]	*2	0	9	13

*Estimated.
[1]Less than 0.5 million sq. ft. (492,000 sq. ft.).
[2]Includes prime contractors and sub-contractors.
[3]Includes spares.
[4]In the 1946 and 1947 year columns, the floor areas shown are for those companies contracting with the military services during these periods, although some of these companies also make commercial aircraft.
[5]Four-place and over.

activities. Other losses resulted from difficulties in curtailing expenses as rapidly as sales declined, expense of rearranging plants for decreased postwar volume and for new models, delays in obtaining raw materials due to postwar shortages, acceleration of production schedules to meet airline demands for new transports in some companies, and heavy development costs and losses on nonaeronautical commercial ventures by other companies.

Not shown in the table, but worthy of comment, is the decrease in working capital of nearly $83,000,000 in 1946. Of this amount, $45,000,000 was used to purchase plant and equipment.

		1939	1944	1946	1947 (1st 6 mos.)
Sales	millions of $	244	8,204	711	375
Net profit (or loss)	do	30	133	(13)	
Net worth	do	138	596	640	
Working capital	do	64	424	541	
Plant and equipment	do	62	105	89	
Ratio—net profit (or loss) to sales	percent	12.4	1.6	(1.9)	
Ratio—sales to net worth	do	1.8	13.8	1.1	
Ratio—sales to working capital	do	3.8	19.4	1.3	
Ratio—sales to plant and equipment	do	3.9	77.8	8.0	

Note. Value figures are rounded to nearest million; ratios were computed on actual figures.

Backlogs. In compiling the backlog figures submitted to us by the 15 major aircraft manufacturing companies, it was apparent that a statement of any composite figure, even with the explanations given, would be confusing and might be misleading. This is largely due to the lack of a uniform basis of accounting methods within the industry, particularly in this respect. While we have recognized and given weight in our recommendations to the backlog figures, it was deemed advisable to omit the publication of the exact total amount of contracts reported to be on the books of the aircraft industry.

Capacity. The peak capacity of the present aircraft manufacturing industry may be estimated. At the peak of war production, "on-site" air frame output was 9 pounds per square foot per year. The present covered floor area of the major air-frame manufacturers now contracting with the military measures 41,000,000 square feet. At 9 pounds per square foot per year, this area should support a peak output (under full wartime conditions) of 369,000,000 air frame pounds per year.

Plants now held in reserve have a total area of 21,200,000 square feet. Applying the same ratio, they should support an additional 191,000,000 air frame pounds per year at peak utilization. The potential industry peak capacity under the best conditions attained in 1944, and without allowance for the possible contribution of the companies specializing in personal plane production, is approximately 560,000,000 pounds of air frame (including spares) per year. Available space, even under normal peacetime rates of output is thus more than adequate for the production of the aircraft for which procurement is recommended in section I. Testimony has indicated that plants now producing airplanes are readily convertible to the production of guided missiles. Their capacity to produce poundage of such missiles should be equal to or greater than their capacity in terms of air frame pounds.

Civil Aircraft Production. The relative importance of civil aircraft manufacture is illustrated graphically in the accompanying chart.

This shows (1) the 1946 output, in air frame pounds, of military airplanes and of

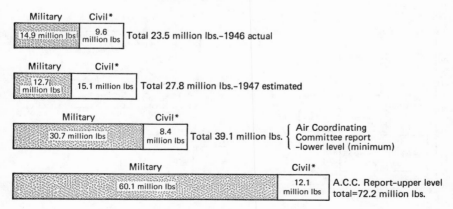

AIRFRAME PRODUCTION
(*Excluding small private planes)

Military   Civil*
| 14.9 million lbs | 9.6 million lbs | Total 23.5 million lbs.–1946 actual

Military   Civil*
| 12.7 million lbs | 15.1 million lbs | Total 27.8 million lbs.–1947 estimated

Military   Civil*
| 30.7 million lbs | 8.4 million lbs | Total 39.1 million lbs. { Air Coordinating Committee report –lower level (minimum)

Military   Civil*
| 60.1 million lbs | 12.1 million lbs | A.C.C. Report–upper level total=72.2 million lbs.

large (4-place and over) civil airplanes, (2) the estimated 1947 output figures, (3) the corresponding figures for the lower level of the Air Coordinating Committee report of October 22, 1945, and (4) the upper level figures of the ACC report. All weights include spares (estimated for 1946-1947) and excluding experimental production. Although the production of small personal aircraft has fallen off sharply, the output of larger civil aircraft continues in substantial volume.

An additional chart has been included to show the total military and civil (4 place and large) airframe weight produced monthly from 1938 to late 1947. For the postwar period, the inset shows the total production divided between the military and the large civil aircraft.

Helicopters. Two of the major military aircraft manufacturers (Bell and the Sikorsky Division of United Aircraft) produce helicopters for both military and civil users. A number of smaller companies are developing helicopters and one, Piaseki Helicopter Corporation, is producing transport helicopters for the Navy.

Lighter-Than-Air. Little or no production of lighter-than-air craft has taken place since the war, although one company, the Goodyear Tire & Rubber Co., remains a source of supply for blimps for the United States Navy and is also fostering new designs of large dirigible types for both military and commercial uses.

Power Plants. Prior to the war, only conventional reciprocating engines were manufactured in the United States. Two large companies, Pratt and Whitney and Wright Aeronautical, supplied the greatest number of large engines for the military and for the larger civil aircraft. Near the end of the war, Allison (which

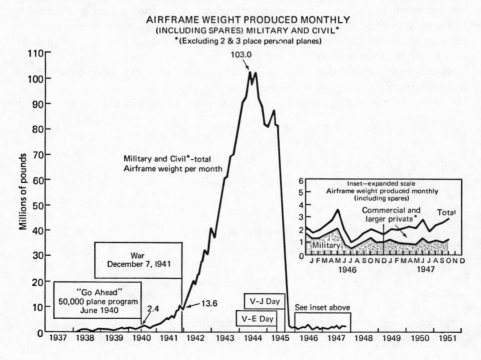

AIRFRAME WEIGHT PRODUCED MONTHLY
(INCLUDING SPARES) MILITARY AND CIVIL*
*(Excluding 2 & 3 place personal planes)

also made reciprocating engines), General Electric, and Westinghouse developed new type turbo-jet engines and are currently supplying them in quantity for military aircraft. Pratt and Whitney and Wright Aeronautical are in the process of developing turbo-jet engines while continuing to produce conventional engines for use in current commercial and civil type aircraft.

Instruments and Other Aircraft Equipment. The aircraft industry also includes numerous companies (or divisions of companies) which develop and manufacture instruments, radio and communication equipment, accessories, and other items required in the modern airplane. This group generally produces for both the military and commercial markets. Their combined importance is indicated by the fact that over 17 percent of the cost of an average military aircraft is represented by Government furnished equipment procured from these companies.

Exports of Aircraft, Engines, and Equipment. In the year 1946, the United States exported 2,243 civil aircraft valued at $64,206,000 and 59 military aircraft valued at $1,057,000. In numbers, the markets for the civil aircraft were: South America 827, the rest of North America (chiefly Canada and Mexico) 791, Central America and the Caribbean Area 169, Europe 195, and the rest of the world, 261. By value, the markets for these civil aircraft were: South America, $15,200,000, the rest of North America, $7,200,000; Central America and the Caribbean area $3,100,000, Europe $29,300,000, and to the rest of the world, $9,400,000.

The value of the 2,490 aircraft engines exported in 1946 reached $11,900,000, while exported propellers accounted for $1,000,000. The markets for the exported engines were: South America 718, valued at $2,200,000; Central America and the Caribbean area 217, valued at $1,000,000; the rest of North America 602, valued at $1,900,000; Europe 780, valued at $5,800,000; and to the rest of the world 173, valued at $1,100,000.

RECOMMENDATIONS

Most of the problems which beset the aircraft-manufacturing industry in 1946 and 1947 resulted from (a) over optimistic development and production of commercial aircraft; (b) low-level military procurement and (c) the absence of long-range military planning. As we have said, military procurement in accordance with our recommendations in section I of this report will provide sufficient business to maintain the industry in a sound condition—but such business must be wisely distributed.

The services must undertake more extensive planning and control of procurement. We recommend that they be given the legislative authority to do so.

We have pointed out that the industry comprises a number of separate companies. Although competition between these units should be utilized to provide incentive to low costs and low prices, the aircraft-manufacturing industry, being essential to the national defense, cannot be freely competitive to such an extent that vital design teams or production organizations are liquidated. Means must be devised to avoid undue concentration of business in a few companies. This, it is recognized, implies a greater degree of planning and control than the services have heretofore undertaken, or is, in fact, permitted by the peacetime procurement legislation which will again become effective on the expiration of the War Powers Act. Some continuation of those special powers must be allowed if we are to achieve a balanced aircraft industry.

Such planning must be directed toward avoidance of discontinuities in production. As has been stated repeatedly in testimony, such breaks in production result in high costs. Not only do many expenses continue while production is interrupted, but the training of a new labor force on resumption of operations involves a great increase in unit costs.

Long-range Planning. Year-to-year planning of aircraft production, which has been forced upon the services by current budgeting practice, must give way to long-term planning. Evidence submitted to us indicates that the savings on the uninterrupted production of airplanes over a 5-year period, as compared to five annual procurements of the same total number of planes, could run as high as 20 to 25 percent. Such savings result in part from the ordering of materials and parts in larger quantities and to the more extensive tooling warranted by the larger number of airplanes on the single order, but even more from the more effective use of tools and manpower.

Long-range planning does not imply a single frozen procurement program for a period of years, but rather the integration of several concurrent plans, the duration of each of which will depend on its particular character. While many projects can be planned for 5 years, others are of such a nature that they cannot be planned for more than 2, 3, or 4 years ahead. The aggregate of such 2-, 3-, 4-, and 5-year plans will constitute the "plan" for which a budget must be prepared. All of these plans should be reviewed at least annually.

Forward Contract Authorization. We recommend that the services plan their aircraft procurement as far in advance as possible and that the Congress provide the legislative base for such planning. We recommend the placing of orders for planes for delivery over a 5-year period whenever possible. We propose that the budget be charged each year with the necessary progress payments and the funds needed to pay for the airplanes accepted in that year. Congress might provide funds for such planned procurement by appropriating funds disbursable in the current year and for 5 or more years ahead. To do so, however, would commit current funds needlessly. We propose, instead, that the Congress make appropriations only of the moneys to be disbursed in the current fiscal year, and provide for the additional years of the procurement program by forward contract authorization, permitting the services to contract for deliveries over the following 5 fiscal years. We recommend that the Congress retain complete control over such procurement through its subsequent annual appropriation of funds to liquidate the forward contract authorizations.

Industrial Mobilization Planning. The ability of the aircraft manufacturing industry to expand will control, to a large extent, the magnitude of our strength in a future war. In section I of this report we have concluded that the Air Force will need a storage reserve of 8,100 airplanes to replace combat losses in the early months of war, because industry will not be able to supply the needed planes in time. This reserve would cost, at present standards and prices, from $6 billion to $7 billion and, in addition, would require about $2 billion a year to keep modern. An industrial mobilization plan which can be depended upon to speed production after war starts may reduce the size of the reserve which will be required.

According to the National Security Act of 1947, the coordination of military, industrial and civilian mobilization is the responsibility of the National Security Resources Board. Based on the advice of the Board, the President may direct the Secretary of Defense and the heads of the appropriate civil departments to undertake the planning of military and industrial mobilization. On the military side the Secretary of Defense holds the Secretaries of the Army, the Navy and the Air Force responsible for military and industrial mobilization planning within their respective services. On the civilian side, it is our recommendation outlined in section V of this report that the Secretary of Commerce and the Secretary of Civil Aviation take an active part in mobilization planning.

We urge that the Under Secretaries of the Army, the Navy, and the Air Force give special attention to effecting such planning. We recommend that, at the administrative level, industrial mobilization planning receive attention comparable with that given to research, development, and procurement.

It was urged on the Commission that all procurement and mobilization planning functions of the Air Force should be carried out by civilian personnel rather than by pilot officers whose tours of duty in such activities are likely to be interspersed with other assignments. We believe that it would be extremely difficult, because of Government pay levels and civil service restrictions, to recruit and hold the quality of civilians necessary for this type of work in numbers sufficient to do the job adequately. We recommend, however, that the practice of passing combat officers through such assignments on the assumption that a well-trained officer must have had experience in all branches of the Air Force should be discarded. With its maturity as a full-fledged service under the National Security Act, the Air Force should accept the fact that procurement and mobilization planning call for officers with specialized industrial training who wish to make a lifelong career in those fields. Such officers should have the same opportunity for advancement in rank as those in other commands.

We recommend that, in the industrial mobilization planning program, studies be made for all planning necessary to place one model of each basic type of aircraft in production in a reserve plant in an emergency, such planning to include the preparation of shop drawings, operation sheets, bills of material, work orders, and the design of all jigs, fixtures, and special tooling. This planning must also include continual revisions to keep all material up to date.

We believe that top level attention should be given in each aircraft manufacturing organization to industrial mobilization planning in peacetime. Subcontract arrangements should be worked out in advance outside the aircraft industry. Licenses or other agreements for the production of aircraft, power plants, propellers, instruments and accessories by nonaeronautical firms should be entered into, ready for activation in an emergency. The peacetime integration of such companies within the air industrial mobilization plan should expedite any expansion greatly.

We have heard a great deal of criticism of the current condition of industrial mobilization planning. We believe, however, that with the establishment of the responsibilities and procedures above outlined this important work should go forward satisfactorily.

Mobilization Authority. Industrial mobilization planning is futile if the mobilization cannot be carried out according to plan when the emergency comes. To give value to such planning it is essential (a) that the National Military Establishment reflect such plans annually in a mobilization budget showing the appropriations and forward contract authorization necessary to put this budget into effect should mobilization be initiated in the then current fiscal year; (b) that the Congress authorize (but not appropriate for) such mobilization budget annually; (c) that the National Security Resources Board set up an Office of War Mobilization, with the necessary subsidiary offices for the control of materials, production facilities, machine tools, and other capital goods, to be held ready for activation upon declaration of a national emergency and mobilization by the President; and (d) that in the event of such mobilization the Congress immediately vote the necessary forward contract authorization and appropriation to support the authorized mobilization budget. These first three actions, taken by the National Military Establishment and by the Congress in peacetime, when they can be considered calmly and carefully, will avoid the necessity for a repetition of the hasty and costly improvisations of World War II. We emphasize the importance of this preparation. It is essential, in any future emergency, that all controls and all planned procurement be initiated immediately upon the declaration of an emergency by the President.

Strategic Materials. No mobilization planning can be carried out in the absence of the materials from which the aircraft and other aeronautical equipment are to be constructed. The Strategic and Critical Materials Stock Piling Act (Public Law 520, 79th Cong.) and the National Security Act of 1947 establish the authority and responsibilities of the National Security Resources Board, the Munitions Board, and of the Secretaries of Defense and of the Treasury, in respect to the stock piling of strategic and critical materials. Attention is directed to the importance of maintaining domestic sources of critical and strategic materials as an effective and advantageous alternative to the stock piling of certain imported items and materials.

Procurement Policies. We point out that the procurement policies of the services must be directed to the provision of incentives to (a) the design and development of aircraft which are both technically superior and readily producible, (b) the production of such aircraft at the lowest possible cost, and (c) maintenance of expansibility.

Design and Development. Aircraft are initially designed and developed on contracts which provide for the reimbursement of cost, plus a fixed fee for administration. We believe this type of contract is desirable for such initial procurement because the cost of developing a new airplane cannot be ascertained in advance, and because the contractor should have the greatest possible freedom in making changes both to increase performance and, by improving producibility, to develop an airplane which will be cheaper to build in quantity production.

Under present contracts, all rights for reproduction of a new design become Government property although the success of the airplane may be due largely to the contractor's particular knowledge and special skills. The retention of some rights by the developing contractor would provide an incentive to superior effort. We recommend that some consideration be given to this point in drafting future legislation.

Producibility. The importance of superior performance is so obvious that the attention given it has, in the past, tended to obscure the equally important factor of producibility. An airplane must be superior both in performance and in producibility if it is to be an effective military weapon. Of only slightly less importance is the ease of maintenance which, in general, is related to producibility. An aircraft easy to produce is also usually easy to maintain. We recommend that the services put heavy emphasis on producibility in all future aircraft-development contracts.

Low Cost Production. The aircraft procurement program we have recommended will cost the American taxpayer a great deal of money. Every effort must be made by the procurement agencies to see that the most effective use is made of that money. All possible incentives must be provided for production at low unit costs and at low prices.

Expansibility. Lowest cost production will sometimes be incompatible with expansibility, which would be increased by a greater degree of tooling than is economical for the number of articles being produced. Such additional tooling should be regarded as a part of industrial mobilization planning and its added cost should not be a charge against the production contract.

Design, Development, and Production Continuity. To be able to plan for reasonable continuity of production, each company should, at any given time, have at least one type in production, one in development, and one in the design-study stage. The type or type of planes to be developed and produced by each company should be determined (a) by the needs of the service, and (b) by the interest and special skills of the manufacturer. Companies which fail to develop successful aircraft or which fail to produce at competitive cost levels will, of course, eliminate themselves from military business. Conversely, a new group submitting a promising design should be encouraged and given the opportunity to become a producer upon demonstration of its capabilities.

In as far as possible aircraft should be produced by the developing company. More often than not the production airplane differs materially in detail from the original design. Engineering changes resulting from the changing requirements of the services are frequent during all stages of production. They may be complicated, and may exert an important influence on the ultimate performance and the final cost of the aircraft. It is considered essential, therefore, that the company which initiated the design should be responsible for all design changes during the course of production. It is accordingly recommended that as a normal procedure, production contracts be given to the organization which made the original design.

Where such a production order would overload that manufacturer's facilities however, the contracting service should require him to subcontract a certain percentage of the new contract (or the equivalent man-hours on a prior contract) elsewhere in the industry. Such a subcontract could involve complete aircraft, or any parts or subassemblies thereof. If the placing of such an order with the developing company would concentrate too much production in a single area, the service should place it elsewhere, arranging with the developing company for any necessary engineering assistance to enable the producing company to build the aircraft economically, and to keep up with any design changes.

Accessory Development. In the procurement of equipment from companies which do not operate exclusively in the aircraft field, it is important to provide incentives for military development. The Attorney General has recently proposed that all rights to patentable inventions made in the course of performing a Government-financed contract be assigned to the Government. The adoption of such a policy would turn research and development brains from Government developments to commercial and industrial developments. Unless instrument and accessory companies are permitted to retain design rights commensurate with the risks taken, they will tend to avoid Government development contracts. . . .

Never before in our history have we maintained a large military organization in peacetime. After each war, we have demobilized most of our ground and air forces, keeping as our only force in being the Navy. In the immediate years to come, however, we will face a new situation. We must also keep a strong air force in being, and our ground Army, because of occupation duties and the need for a skeleton force capable of rapid expansion, must be larger and more mobile than in the past. This degree of preparedness—new in American life—calls for a new concept for the organization of the civilian branches of the Government whose activities directly relate to military plans.

The creation of a Military Establishment capable of defending the country will put a disproportionate share of the power of Government in the hands of the military, and at the same time will place new and heavy burdens on the civilian agencies of Government in matters contributing to the national security. This will require the strengthening of the civilian departments in those areas which are of common concern to the Military Establishment and the civilian agencies of the Government.

As we are not an aggressor nation, and as attack upon us may be delayed for years, our will to continue to carry the financial burden, which will increase from year to year for several years, may weaken, especially if we should have a period of depression combined with calculated changes for the better in the public attitude of a possible enemy.

That is our gravest danger.

For a potential enemy is apt to be contentious and threatening when getting ready and reverse his attitude when preparing to strike.

While we believe that a planned war will not start until other countries have the atomic bomb or other comparable weapons in quantities, the possibility that constant friction may cause war will compel us to continue in a state of partial mobilization of our productive resources to be adequately prepared for war.

Our people will look to the military agencies to formulate the programs for their requirements and to civilian agencies to organize industry and foreign and domestic commerce to be prepared to furnish those requirements.

During this entire period commerce and industry must be maintained on the highest possible productive level to yield earnings which will enable business, and the public sharing the profits distributed, to meet the mobilization costs without unbearable taxes.

We accordingly have been influenced in our recommendations for changes in the organization and procedures of the Government dealing with aviation by the need to make the civilian agencies having to do with aviation more efficient in themselves and to strengthen them in relation to the growing military establishment. . . .

FOOTNOTES

[1] Includes the Stinson Division (personal airplanes).
[2] The Curtiss-Wright group includes the Curtiss Airplane Division, Curtiss Propeller Division, and the Wright Aeronautical Corp. (engines).
[3] The United Aircraft Corp. group includes the Chance Vought (aircraft), Sikorsky (helicopters), Hamilton Standard (propellers), and Pratt & Whitney (engines) divisions.

12. PROBLEM OF NATIONAL SECURITY

Committee for Economic Development

The Eisenhower years were frustrating ones for many people, especially those liberals who worried about the "stagnation" of the economy at home and our lack of vigorous activism abroad. Especially after the Soviet Union orbited the world's first artificial satellite, Sputnik I, in October 1957, there was a great deal of concern that the Russians had a larger missile-booster capability than did the United States. During the presidential campaign of 1960 John F. Kennedy would turn this concern into the charge that economies at home had led the United States, during the Eisenhower years, into a "missile gap." Although no such gap existed, the allegation helped build up pressure for increased defense spending.

One of the influential groups seeking increased defense spending was the liberal Committee for Economic Development (CED). In 1958 this group consisted of "150 leading businessmen and educators." According to the CED, its trustees were "generally . . . Presidents or Board Chairmen of corporations and Presidents of universities," and the group was "supported by voluntary contributions from business and industry. It is non-profit, non-partisan and non-political."

On the CED's Subcommittee on Economic Policies for National Security were ten prominent businessmen. The subcommittee was served by six advisors, including Richard M. Bissell, Jr., of the Central Intelligence Agency, and Charles Hitch, who would later follow Robert McNamara to the Pentagon and have

Source: The Committee for Economic Development, *The Problem of National Security: Some Economic and Administrative Aspects.* A Statement on National Policy by the Research and Policy Committee of the Committee for Economic Development (New York, July 1958), pp. 50-55. Reprinted by permission.

major responsibility for the revolutions of programming and cost-effectiveness analysis. Viewing the world in harsh, Cold War ideological terms, the CED recommended not only an increase in spending for defense (in part to help boost the entire economy) but also many of the specific reforms in management McNamara was to carry through a few years later.

We may now recapitulate the major points that we have made. We again stress that this statement is not directed to all aspects of the problem of providing for national security, but deals only with selected questions of an economic and, to some extent, administrative character.

1. The United States faces a peacetime security problem more demanding of thought, treasure, and toughness than ever before because:

The rulers of more than one-third of the world's population with huge and increasing military power, have declared themselves our implacable enemies, and have shown that they will not flinch from military action whenever and wherever it promises to be profitable and reasonably safe.

We must assume that the Communist threat will continue into the distant future, and that its removal is not within our control.

Atomic and hydrogen bombs and ballistic missiles have placed us under the continuing threat of instantaneous and immeasurable destruction.

To deter or meet such an attack, only capabilities in being for retaliation and for restoring a stricken society count; a huge industrial war potential, our greatest asset in the past, is no longer a protection.

The Soviet bloc possesses a great capacity to conduct limited war around its periphery without resort to nuclear power. It has adherents throughout the world, and in various countries they are numerous enough to threaten the stability of governments. It uses economic blandishment on an increasing scale and capitalizes on the attraction of the Soviet model for rapid economic development. In short, the potential for Communist expansion without all-out war is great.

Since the United States will not resort to armed aggression, we must accept the circumstance that any "hot" war would come at a time and place chosen by our adversaries. This necessarily adds greatly to the difficulty of defense and is inevitably costly and wasteful in the sense that it requires frequent changes of plans and preparations for contingencies that never arise.

Provision for national security is expensive. From 1955 to 1957 national security expenditures averaged 11 percent of our gross national product, as compared with a little over 1 percent in the thirties. It now appears that even this huge amount may have been inadequate. The Soviet Union has developed a series of operational modern weapons systems with great speed and appears capable of continuing to do so. The rapid growth of Soviet science and industry and the ability of Soviet leaders to allocate the best of Russia's human and material resources to the increase of military power betokens Communist ability to further increase the pressure upon us.

2. Since the Soviet bloc is engaging us in a conflict that takes many forms, of which the field of arms is only one, our counter-effort must be equally varied. With the total effort we are willing and able to make limited, we are ever confronted with the necessity to determine allocations among the military budget, economic development assistance, and various other non-military programs, and within the military budget among many kinds of forces and weapons. The choices as to how to divide our national security dollars are numerous and difficult in the extreme. Opportunities for errors in selection are likely to be frequent and, if errors occur, they are likely to be disastrous and irrecoverable.

3. With any given degree of intelligence in making decisions, the less we spend on defense the harder become our choices, the more we must rely on our frail capacity to foresee the future, and the fewer are the contingencies against which we can protect ourselves.

4. In determining the size of our defense effort, we must distinguish sharply between the limitation imposed by the amount of our total production that we are *willing* to devote to this purpose, at the sacrifice of other desirable uses of output, and the limitation imposed by the consideration that too heavy a defense burden may weaken our economy, and hence our long-term ability to maintain our security.

The amount we are willing to devote to defense is for the public to decide. There is, however, the problem of placing before the citizenry the facts that are necessary for informed decisions to be reached. Frankness and clarity by high government officials is a requisite. Congressional and private investigations can be invaluable. Improvement in budgetary procedures and presentation, and strengthening of Congressional staffs, are necessary parts of this process. But a full and certain solution is not in sight.

Fear that a high defense burden will weaken the economy has been exaggerated and should not be decisive in the determination of the size of a defense budget representing 10 to 15 percent of the gross national product, or even more. There is no factual basis for the notion that we are within reach of or exceeding some "breaking point" beyond which tax-financed expenditures will critically impair economic growth. *We can afford what we have to afford.*

The retarding effect of taxes on growth comes less from the total size of the tax load on the economy as a whole than from an irrational structure of taxes that bears heavily on some categories of taxpayers that are important to growth, is burdensome to saving, and impairs incentives.

While we believe possible restraints on the size of the defense program have been overstated, this does not in itself mean that the defense program should be stepped up beyond present plans. It is possible that the costs of adequate defense have also been exaggerated.

5. Swift technological advance in weapons is crucial to our security, and an important ingredient of "getting the most for each defense dollar."

The present close tie-up between research and development and the selection of major weapons—intended to avoid delays, duplication, and projects with uncertain pay-offs—should be reconsidered in the light of actual experience and the charge that in practice it retards research and technological advance, forces major commitments for entire weapons systems to be made upon the basis of wholly inadequate information, and is inherently wasteful. Whether a change in this approach is the solution or not, ways must be found to explore a much wider variety of technological possibilities and to provide more freedom for experimentation in research. We also need to make choices among major weapons systems on the basis of more information than is now brought to bear, and after more systematic, quantitative analyses of the prospective cost and effectiveness of competing strategies and weapons.

R&D procurement practices should be revamped to give contracting firms more technical discretion about materials, components, and techniques; to provide contractors more incentives to cut costs; and to provide adequate awards for research and development contracts, as such, and thus break the trend toward limitation of research and development by private firms to companies with production facilities. Simplification of administrative procedures and longer-term commitments are needed in contracts with the universities.

This Committee associates itself strongly with the proposals for a substantial division of labor in R&D among the United States and its allies.

6. Efficiency in the management of the defense effort is indispensable in a period when the burden of defense necessarily is heavy. We must strive to maximize the amount of security that each defense dollar will buy.

Efficiency in defense management must not be confused with the amount that we spend for our security. To assume that merely squeezing the defense budget will eliminate waste while retaining the fighting efficiency of the services is wholly unwarranted. Imposition of arbitrary cuts in expenditures followed by crash programs is not conducive to improvement of military management.

The search for greater efficiency must deal with specific improvements and take account of deep seated causes of inefficiency. Among the obstacles to improvement are ingrained distrust among military men of civilian economizers; interservice rivalry; political realities outside the armed services; the difficulty outsiders have in recognizing disadvantages, as well as advantages, of proposed reforms; the extent to which defense management depends upon military personnel trained as soldiers rather than managers and accountants, an impediment compounded by the traditional rotation of duties; and the difficulty of adapting concepts of efficiency appropriate for business management to the more difficult, and in important respects different, problem of maximizing national security.

7. Although the problems of defense management are not open to easy or uninformed solutions, substantial improvement by a series of selective innovations is both promising and imperative. Proper approaches toward reform appear to us to include the following:

Military service and civilian participation in defense should be made more attractive as a career, in order to make it possible to attract and retain persons possessing outstanding ability or scarce skills, and to reduce the costs imposed by exorbitant labor turnover.

There is urgent need to eliminate from our national security programs the waste imposed by pressure from special interest groups, and to absolve the Defense Department of statutory responsibility for advancing numerous political, social and economic objectives unrelated to defense. There should also be a review of other statutory requirements imposed on the armed forces to see whether they are still necessary, or are obsolete or too costly compared with the benefits they achieve.

There should be a search for excessive specifications in equipment that add greatly to cost and slow down programs but add relatively little to dependability and versatility in combat use.

There should be a continuous search for functions now performed by military personnel that can be both transferred to and performed better by civilian personnel, for jobs that can be done more efficiently by private contractors, and for basic innovations in management—that is, the discovery and introduction of improved practices.

Improvement in the top administrative structure of the Defense Department is an outstanding requirement for greater efficiency in defense management. An experienced group of former civilian and military defense officials have made recommendations in this field embodied in the President's recent message to the Congress on reorganization of the Defense Department. These recommendations appear to have been competently arrived at and should be adopted promptly.

There is an evident need to make Congressional participation in defense planning more effective. Reforms in budget presentation and adequate professional staffs for the congressional committees dealing with defense would be helpful.

13. FAREWELL ADDRESS

Dwight D. Eisenhower

President Eisenhower during his eight years in office, experienced firsthand the awesome pressures that could be brought to bear upon policy makers by munitions makers, in concert with the bomber generals and carrier admirals. His own Secretary of Defense once said that what was good for General Motors was good for the country. In his Farewell Address to the nation, the General-President gave a warning as solemn and necessary as that of Washington against entangling foreign alliances.

My fellow Americans:

Three days from now, after half a century in the service of our country, I shall lay down the responsibilities of office as, in traditional and solemn ceremony, the authority of the Presidency is vested in my successor.

This evening I come to you with a message of leave-taking and farewell, and to share a few final thoughts with you, my countrymen.

Like every other citizen, I wish the new President, and all who will labor with him, Godspeed. I pray that the coming years will be blessed with peace and prosperity for all.

Source: Dwight D. Eisenhower, "Farewell Radio and Television Address to the American People, January 17, 1961," *Public Papers of the President of the United States, Dwight D. Eisenhower, 1960-61* (Washington, D.C., 1961), pp. 1035-1040.

Our people expect their President and the Congress to find essential agreement on issues of great moment, the wise resolution of which will better shape the future of the Nation.

My own relations with the Congress, which began on a remote and tenuous basis when, long ago, a member of the Senate appointed me to West Point, have since ranged to the intimate during the war and immediate post-war period, and, finally, to the mutually interdependent during these past eight years.

In this final relationship, the Congress and the Administration have, on most vital issues, cooperated well, to serve the national good rather than mere partisanship, and so have assured that the business of the Nation should go forward. So, my official relationship with the Congress ends in a feeling, on my part, of gratitude that we have been able to do so much together.

II

We now stand ten years past the midpoint of a century that has witnessed four major wars among great nations. Three of these involved our own country. Despite these holocausts America is today the strongest, the most influential and most productive nation in the world. Understandably proud of this pre-eminence, we yet realize that America's leadership and prestige depend, not merely upon our unmatched material progress, riches and military strength, but on how we use our power in the interests of world peace and human betterment.

III

Throughout America's adventure in free government, our basic purposes have been to keep the peace; to foster progress in human achievement, and to enhance liberty, dignity and integrity among people and among nations. To strive for less would be unworthy of a free and religious people. Any failure traceable to arrogance, or our lack of comprehension or readiness to sacrifice would inflict upon us grievous hurt both at home and abroad.

Progress toward these noble goals is persistently threatened by the conflict now engulfing the world. It commands our whole attention, absorbs our very beings. We face a hostile ideology—global in scope, atheistic in character, ruthless in purpose, and insidious in method. Unhappily the danger it poses promises to be of indefinite duration. To meet it successfully, there is called for, not so much the emotional and transitory sacrifices of crisis, but rather those which enable us to carry forward steadily, surely, and without complaint the burdens of a prolonged and complex struggle—with liberty the stake. Only thus shall we remain, despite every provocation, on our charted course toward permanent peace and human betterment.

Crises there will continue to be. In meeting them, whether foreign or domestic, great or small, there is a recurring temptation to feel that some spectacular and costly action could become the miraculous solution to all current difficulties. A huge increase in newer elements of our defense;

development of unrealistic programs to cure every ill in agriculture; a dramatic expansion in basic and applied research—these and many other possibilities, each possibly promising in itself, may be suggested as the only way to the road we wish to travel.

But each proposal must be weighed in the light of a broader consideration: the need to maintain balance in and among national programs—balance between the private and the public economy, balance between cost and hoped for advantage—balance between the clearly necessary and the comfortably desirable; balance between our essential requirements as a nation and the duties imposed by the nation upon the individual; balance between actions of the moment and the national welfare of the future. Good judgment seeks balance and progress; lack of it eventually finds imbalance and frustration.

The record of many decades stands as proof that our people and their government have, in the main, understood these truths and have responded to them well, in the face of stress and threat. But threats, new in kind or degree, constantly arise. I mention two only.

IV

A vital element in keeping the peace is our military establishment. Our arms must be mighty, ready for instant action, so that no potential aggressor may be tempted to risk his own destruction.

Our military organization today bears little relation to that known by any of my predecessors in peacetime, or indeed by the fighting men of World War II or Korea.

Until the latest of our world conflicts, the United States had no armaments industry. American makers of plowshares could, with time and as required, make swords as well. But now we can no longer risk emergency improvisation of national defense; we have been compelled to create a permanent armaments industry of vast proportions. Added to this, three and a half million men and women are directly engaged in the defense establishment. We annually spend on military security more than the net income of all United States corporations.

This conjunction of an immense military establishment and a large arms industry is new in the American experience. The total influence—economic, political, even spiritual—is felt in every city, every State house, every office of the Federal government. We recognize the imperative need for this development. Yet we must not fail to comprehend its grave implications. Our toil, resources and livelihood are all involved; so is the very structure of our society.

In the councils of government, we must guard against the acquisition of unwarranted influence, whether sought or unsought, by the military-industrial complex. The potential for the disastrous rise of misplaced power exists and will persist.

We must never let the weight of this combination endanger our liberties or democratic processes. We should take nothing for granted. Only an alert and knowledgeable citizenry can compel the proper meshing of the huge industrial and military machinery of defense with our peaceful methods and goals, so that security and liberty may prosper together.

Akin to, and largely responsible for the sweeping changes in our industrial-military posture, has been the technological revolution during recent decades.

In this revolution, research has become central; it also becomes more formalized, complex, and costly. A steadily increasing share is conducted for, by, or at the direction of, the Federal government.

Today, the solitary inventor, tinkering in his shop, has been overshadowed by task forces of scientists in laboratories and testing fields. In the same fashion, the free university, historically the fountainhead of free ideas and scientific discovery, has experienced a revolution in the conduct of research. Partly because of the huge costs involved, a government contract becomes virtually a substitute for intellectual curiosity. For every old blackboard there are now hundreds of new electronic computers.

The prospect of domination of the nation's scholars by Federal employment, project allocations, and the power of money is ever present--and is gravely to be regarded.

Yet, in holding scientific research and discovery in respect, as we should, we must also be alert to the equal and opposite danger that public policy could itself become the captive of a scientific-technological elite.

It is the task of statesmanship to mold, to balance, and to integrate these and other forces, new and old, within the principles of our democratic system—ever aiming toward the supreme goals of our free society.

V

Another factor in maintaining balance involves the element of time. As we peer into society's future, we—you and I, and our government—must avoid the impulse to live only for today, plundering, for our own ease and convenience, the precious resources of tomorrow. We cannot mortgage the material assets of our grandchildren without risking the loss also of their political and spiritual heritage. We want democracy to survive for all generations to come, not to become the insolvent phantom of tomorrow.

VI

Down the long lane of the history yet to be written America knows that this world of ours, ever growing smaller, must avoid becoming a community of dreadful fear and hate, and be, instead, a proud confederation of mutual trust and respect.

Such a confederation must be one of equals. The weakest must come to the conference table with the same confidence as do we, protected as we are by our moral, economic, and military strength. That table, though scarred by many past frustrations, cannot be abandoned for the certain agony of the battlefield.

Disarmament, with mutual honor and confidence, is a continuing imperative. Together we must learn how to compose differences, not with arms, but with intellect and decent purpose. Because this need is so sharp and apparent I confess that I lay down my official responsibilities in this field with a definite sense of disappointment. As one who has witnessed the horror and the lingering sadness of war—as one who knows that another war could utterly destroy this civilization which has been so slowly and painfully built over thousands of years— I wish I could say tonight that a lasting peace is in sight.

Happily, I can say that war has been avoided. Steady progress toward our ultimate goal has been made. But, so much remains to be done. As a private citizen, I shall never cease to do what little I can to help the world advance along that road.

VII

So—in this my last good night to you as your President—I thank you for the many opportunities you have given me for public service in war and peace. I trust that in that service you find some things worthy; as for the rest of it, I know you will find ways to improve performance in the future.

You and I—my fellow citizens—need to be strong in our faith that all nations, under God, will reach the goal of peace with justice. May we be ever unswerving in devotion to principle, confident but humble with power, diligent in pursuit of the Nation's great goals.

To all the peoples of the world, I once more give expression to America's prayerful and continuing aspiration:

We pray that peoples of all faiths, all races, all nations, may have their great human needs satisfied; that those now denied opportunity shall come to enjoy it to the full; that all who yearn for freedom may experience its spiritual blessings; that those who have freedom will understand, also, its heavy responsibilities; that all who are insensitive to the needs of others will learn charity; that the scourges of poverty, disease and ignorance will be made to disappear from the earth, and that, in the goodness of time, all peoples will come to live together in a peace guaranteed by the binding force of mutual respect and love.

IV. DIMENSIONS OF THE SYSTEM

It took five years and the festering war in Indochina to bring people to the realization that President Eisenhower's farewell warning was anything more than the swansong of an old and naive man who had spent eight years in a situation he neither understood nor controlled. Defenders of the complex are fond of charging that except for Vietnam, no one would have thought of attacking the military ascendency in the country, and by implication, that once the Vietnam war is over we shall wish that we had not been so prodigal of our criticism. But other symptoms are coming to light, and it is unlikely that the disease will be forgotten before it is either cured or fatal.

The attacks on the complex continue to grow. Senators William Proxmire and J. William Fulbright are among the most prominent congressmen who are demanding an end to what they call the "blank check" issued to the military. In March 1969 a bipartisan group from the Senate and the House held a Congressional Conference on the Military Budget and National Priorities. "We initiated the Conference," wrote its backers, "in the conviction that Congressional control of military policy must be reasserted and that the level of Congressional analysis of these critical issues can be raised through a greater intimacy between the legislative branch and the intellectual community." The controversies over the TFX (F-111), the ABM, the corporate employment of high-ranking military officers, as well as other revelations concerning the C-5A transport and similar weapons, have been critical in focusing attention on the power of the Pentagon.

14. ESSENCE OF SECURITY

Robert S. McNamara

Robert S. McNamara has sometimes been called the "first" Secretary of Defense in recognition of the fact that he came closest to exercising control and leadership over the Pentagon's farflung and stoutly defended military satraps. The reforms he brought to the Department of Defense sought to rationalize decision making, discipline it to the national welfare, and make efficient the procurement of weapons systems. Unlike many of his detractors, he did not deny the existence of a military-industrial complex. He persisted in his belief, however, that a forceful Secretary of Defense, aided by modern management techniques, could keep it under control and reap its benefits while avoiding its dangers. The fact that he came to the Pentagon on the tail of President Kennedy's missile-gap campaign, and that shortly before he left office he authorized the building of an antiballistic missile (ABM) system, which he admitted would tend to undermine rather than enhance the national security, cast some doubt on whether his reforms were sufficient.

MANAGING FOR DEFENSE

The challenge of the Department of Defense is compelling. It is the greatest single management complex in history; it supervises the greatest aggregation of

Source: 'Managing for Defense" from *The Essence of Security* by Robert S. McNamara. Copyright © 1968 by Robert S. McNamara. Reprinted by permission of Harper & Row, Publishers. Pp. 87-104.

raw power ever assembled by man. Yet my instructions from both President Kennedy and President Johnson were simple: to determine and provide what we needed to safeguard our security without arbitrary budget limits, but to do so as economically as possible.

In many respects the role of a public manager is similar to that of a private manager. In each case he may follow one of two alternative courses. He can act either as a judge or as a leader. As the former he waits until subordinates bring him problems for solution, or alternatives for choice. In the latter case, he immerses himself in his operation, leads and stimulates an examination of the objectives, the problems and the alternatives. In my own case, and specifically with regard to the Department of Defense, the responsible choice seemed clear.

From the beginning in January, 1961, it seemed to me that the principal problem in efficient management of the Department's resources was not the lack of management authority. The National Security Act provides the Secretary of Defense a full measure of power. The problem was rather the absence of the essential management tools needed to make sound decisions on the really crucial issues of national security.

Two points seem to me axiomatic. The first is that the United States is well able to spend whatever it needs to spend on national security. The second point is that this ability does not excuse us from applying strict standards of effectiveness and efficiency to the way we spend our Defense dollars.

Within that framework, our early studies led us into three major efforts: improvement of our strategic retaliatory forces, increased emphasis on our non-nuclear forces, and a general upgrading of effectiveness and efficiency in the Defense Establishment. For that matter, the first two of our major objectives commanded wide support by the time I took office, as I mentioned earlier.

The third caused considerable controversy. Not that there was much disagreement about the need; for years everyone who thought seriously about the Department of Defense felt that major improvements were needed. The solutions offered ranged from drastic proposals for complete unification of the armed forces to vague suggestions about "cutting the fat out of the military budget." But there was no consensus on just what should be done.

Moreover, there was an additional and inevitable human problem. These reforms would necessarily change traditional ways of doing things, and limit the customary ways of spending Defense money. It is inevitable that people will take more easily to suggestions that they should have more money to spend, as in the improvement of our nuclear and non-nuclear capabilities, than to suggestions that they must spend less or that they must abandon established ways of doing things. Yet the very substantial increases in the budget which we felt necessary added a further strong incentive, if any were needed, to move ahead on these problems of increasing efficiency and effectiveness.

What we set out to do can be divided into two parts: the first essentially a series of management reforms of the kind to be found in any well-run organization, an effort which is in large part covered by the formal Five-Year Cost Reduction Program we set up in July, 1962. The common characteristic of such reforms is that they have very little to do with military effectiveness, one way or the other. They merely save money by introducing more efficient methods of doing things.

The second and more important part of the effort did bear directly on military effectiveness. Although dollar savings are sometimes an important by-product, here the essential point was to increase military effectiveness. We found that the three military departments had been establishing their requirements independently of each other. The results could be described fairly as chaotic: Army planning, for example, was based primarily on a long war of attrition; Air Force planning was based, largely, on a short war of nuclear bombardment. Consequently the Army was stating a requirement for stocking months, if not years, of combat supplies against the event of a sizable conventional conflict. The Air Force stock requirements for such a war had to be measured in days, and not very many days at that. Either approach, consistently followed, might make some sense. The two combined could not possibly make sense. What we needed was a coordinated strategy seeking objectives actually attainable with the military resources available. The fact was that, in the past, so-called requirements bore almost no relation to the real world: enormous requirements existed on paper, often almost entirely disembodied from the actual size and nature of the procurement program.

Our new form of budget for the first time grouped together for planning purposes units which must fight together in the event of war. The Navy strategic forces, the Polaris submarines, are now considered together with the Air Force Strategic Air Command; Navy general-purpose forces are considered together with the Army and Marine divisions and the Air Force Tactical Air Command. This kind of reform provides substantial improvement in the effectiveness of our military establishment. Even where it does not lead directly to lower expenditures, it is economical in the true sense of the word; that is, it gives us the maximum national security obtainable from the dollars we do spend. We can imagine many different kinds of wars the United States must be prepared to fight, but a war in which the Army fights independently of the Navy, or the Navy independently of the Air Force, is not one of them. Quite obviously, the coordination of the planning of the four services makes eminently good sense on the narrowest military grounds.

The situation becomes more complicated when decisions must be made on requested force-level increases or the development or procurement of new weapons. Adding a weapon to our inventory is not necessarily synonymous with adding to our national security. Moreover, even if we were to draft every scientist and engineer in the country into weapons-development work, we could still develop only a fraction of the systems that are proposed. This process of choice must begin with solid indications that a proposed system would really add something to our national security. The United States cannot even seriously consider going ahead with a full-scale weapons-system development until that basic requirement has been met.

Development costs alone on typical major weapons systems today are enormous. Over a billion dollars were spent on the atomic airplane, which was little closer to being a useful weapon when we canceled it, shortly after I took office, than it had been half a dozen years earlier.

The B-70 bomber also was an example of a weapon which, it seemed to me, failed to meet the basic requirement for a major systems development. It happened to be a particularly expensive weapon, since to develop, procure and operate a modest force of these planes would have cost us at least $10 billion. Yet considering the weapons we already would have by the time the B-70 could be operational, it was very hard to see how this weapon would add to our national security.

In fact, the whole debate on the B-70 tended toward terms which had very little to do with the facts of the situation. There was a lot of talk about missiles versus bombers. I have no feeling about missiles versus bombers as such. If bombers serve our national interest, then we should be interested in bombers; if missiles, then we should be interested in missiles; if a mix, then we should be interested in the mix. But the B-70 would have carried no bombs. It would have attacked its target with a very complex air-launched missile system from distances of hundreds of miles. The question was not bombs versus missiles. We were all agreed that it must be missiles. The debate was about alternative launching platforms and alternative missile systems. And the particular launching platform and missile system proposed in the B-70 program just was not an effective means to accomplish the missions proposed for it. Despite the enormous controversy and criticism when development was canceled, I think there now is general agreement that the decision was sound.

Obviously one reason for restraint in choosing new weapons systems is their growing complexity. We need to keep the number of new systems as low as possible consistent with security, in the interest of maximum reliability. The efficiency demonstrated by a weapon on a test range may drop sharply under the chaotic conditions of combat. We must avoid putting ourselves in the position of the camera bug who weighs himself down with so much specialized equipment that he actually gets poorer results than a more lightly equipped competitor. And let me add that not only do the proliferation and complication of weapons reduce dependability, but they are major factors contributing to enormous excess inventories of parts and equipment.

What becomes clear, then, is that the question of how to spend Defense dollars and how much to spend is more complicated than is often assumed. A new weapon cannot be viewed in isolation. Anyone who has been exposed to so-called brochuremanship knows that even the most outlandish notions can be dressed up to look superficially attractive. Instead, each new weapon must be considered against a wide range of issues: its place in the complex of missions to be performed; its effects on the stability of the military situation in the world; other alternatives available.

These decisions must be made ultimately with a high degree of judgment, but there is an important difference between the way we went about them and the way they used to be made. Formerly an arbitrary budget ceiling was fixed for national defense and funds were then apportioned among the services. Today we examine all our military needs, in the context of our national security in the broadest sense, and fill them accordingly.

Up to this point I have emphasized the general considerations we applied in the Defense Department after January, 1961; the goals we sought and how we set about making the decisions to reach them. As I mentioned earlier, there was no lack of management authority, but we felt sharply the need for more efficient machinery with which to exercise it.

The problem may be considered this way: in order to make crucial decisions on force levels and weapons, the President, the Secretary of Defense and Congress must have complete information focused on those questions and their place in the over-all military system. They need to know, for example, the military effectiveness and the cost of a B-52 squadron as it relates to a Minuteman missile squadron and a Polaris submarine. The data must include not only the cost of equipping these units but also the cost of manning and operating them for various periods. Only under these circumstances can the alternatives be made fully clear.

One of the first things we did in 1961 was to design a new mechanism which would provide this information and integrate it into a single, coherent management system. The product of this effort was the Planning-Programing-Budgeting System, which is now being widely applied throughout the U.S. Government and which is being introduced in foreign governments as well.

For the Defense Department, this system serves several very important purposes:

1. It provides the mechanism through which financial budgets, weapons programs, force requirements, military strategy and foreign policy objectives are all brought into balance with one another.

2. It produces the annual Five-Year Defense Program, which is perhaps the most important single management tool for the Secretary of Defense and the basis for the annual proposal to Congress.

3. It permits the top management of the Defense Department, the President and the Congress to focus their attention on the tasks and missions related to our national objectives, rather than on the tasks and missions of a particular service.

4. It provides for the entire Defense Establishment a single approved plan, projected far enough into the future to ensure that all the programs are both physically and financially feasible.

In short, the new planning system allowed us to achieve a true unification of effort within the Department without having to undergo a drastic upheaval of the entire organizational structure. It would be a shell without substance, however, were it not backed by the full range of analytic support which operations research and other modern management techniques can bring to bear on national security problems. To this end we developed highly capable systems-analysis staffs within the Office of the Secretary of Defense, the Joint Chiefs of Staff organizations and the military departments. These staffs provided the civilian and military decision-makers of the Department with an order of analytical support far higher than had ever been the case in the past. I am convinced that this approach not only leads to far sounder and more objective decisions over the long run but yields as well the maximum amount of effective defense we can buy with each Defense dollar expended.

The creation of the Defense Department stemmed directly from one of the great lessons learned in World War II: that separate land, sea and air operations were gone forever, and that in future wars the combat forces would have to be employed as teams under unified strategic direction. The National Security Act of 1947 and its subsequent amendments established the Department and shaped its basic mode of operation. Three separate military departments reporting to the Secretary of Defense were retained to train, supply, administer and support the respective land, sea and air forces. However, operational direction of the combat forces in the field was made the responsibility of the unified and specified commanders, reporting to the Secretary through the Joint Chiefs of Staff. Thus, from a functional viewpoint, the Department of Defense has been given a bilineal organizational structure. The operational control and direction of the combat forces extend down through one chain of command, and the direction and control of the supporting activities down through another. While this basic structure proved to be entirely sound and workable, we have found it necessary over the past seven years to make a number of changes in both parts of the organization.

With respect to the first chain of command, it seemed to me that two major deficiencies still remained to be corrected. Some of the combat-ready forces had not yet been placed under the unified and specified command structure. Also, the Joint Chiefs of Staff had not yet been provided the organizational and management tools they needed in order to give the most effective day-to-day operational direction to the combat forces.

To correct the first deficiency, we created in 1961 the U.S. Strike Command, putting under a single joint command the combat-ready forces of the Tactical Air Command and the Strategic Army Corps. They previously had been controlled directly by their respective military departments. With that organizational change, all combat-ready forces are now assigned within the unified and specified command structure. The Strike Command provided us with an integrated, mobile, highly combat-ready force, available to augment the unified commands overseas or to be employed as the primary force in remote areas. Moreover, as a result of the improved operational concepts developed under Strike Command and the joint training received, the entire Army-Air Force team is now better integrated and works together more efficiently and effectively than at any other time in our history.

To meet the need for better managerial tools, we carefully reviewed both the internal organization of the Joint Chiefs of Staff and the various support functions. We found that two of the most important services to field commanders—communications and intelligence—were being performed separately by the three military departments with virtually no regard for the role of the JCS in the operational direction of combat forces in the field. It was clear that both of these functions should be brought under the direct supervision of the JCS. But they were too large and diverse to be placed within the Organization of the Joint Chiefs of Staff and too important to be fragmented among the individual unified and specified commands. Accordingly, we decided to consolidate them in two new Defense agencies which report to the Secretary of Defense directly through the Joint Chiefs.

Actions were already under way in 1961 to form the Defense Communications Agency. We expanded its functions to include not only the long-haul communications facilities of the Defense Establishment, but also those required for command and control functions, intelligence, weather services, logistics and administration for all components of the Department. The intelligence functions formerly performed by the three services moved under the new Defense Intelligence Agency.

Several measures were taken to improve the organization surrounding the Joint Chiefs of Staff. A new National Military Command System was created to ensure that the JCS can continue to direct the armed forces under all foreseeable circumstances. Several new offices were added, including special assistants in such diverse areas as strategic mobility and counterinsurgency.

When we looked into the support functions, we found that organization had lagged far behind technological advance. The logistics structures of the military departments simply had not kept pace with the demands of rapidly changing technology. The inefficiencies drew repeated attention and criticism from the Congress, which continually prodded the Department in the direction of a fully unified logistics management. The Defense Establishment, however, had moved very haltingly toward that objective with various improvisations. Our solution was to create in 1961 the Defense Supply Agency. We consolidated into it the eight existing separate managers for common supplies, the manager for traffic management, the Armed Forces Supply Support Center and the surplus property sales offices. Later we assigned additional responsibilities to DSA, including the management of common electrical and electronics items, chemical supplies and industrial production equipment. All this resulted in substantial reductions in inventories and operating costs, plus wide improvements in supply services.

Before we organized the Defense Supply Agency, the various elements of the Department—to cite a typical example—were using slightly different forms for requisitions, no less than sixteen in all. As a result, nearly every time a piece of property was transferred from one part of the Department to another, a new requisition form had to be typed. By the simple expedient of establishing a common requisition form and system, we eliminated literally tens of thousands of man-hours of labor formerly wasted in having clerks retype the forms. Other minor but colorful instances of improvement were the consolidation of eighteen different types and sizes of butcher smocks, four kinds of belt buckles and six kinds of women's exercise bloomers.

In addition to these changes in the support field, many more were found necessary in the three military departments, particularly in the broad area of logistics management. In the Army the logistics functions of the old "technical services" were merged into a new Army Matériel Command. In the Navy the logistics functions performed by its bureaus were replaced by a Naval Matériel Command. In the Air Force a realignment between the Research and Development Command and the Air Matériel Command resulted in two new commands: the Air Force Systems Command and the Air Force Logistics Command. We made each of these organizational changes to meet the need for increased efficiency in the procurement and support of new weapons systems, as well as to keep pace with rapidly changing technology.

All these organizational changes were important in the improvement of Defense Department management. But in the end, economy and efficiency in the day-to-day execution of the Defense program rests largely in the hands of tens of thousands of military and civilian managers in the field. How to motivate them to do their job more efficiently, and how to determine whether or not they do so, have always been among the most difficult and elusive problems facing the top management of the Defense Department. Even where poor performance is found, the practical remedies are more limited than one would imagine. The competition for competent management personnel is extremely keen. We had no absolute assurance that the people we could hire would be any better than those we might fire. My task was to devise a management system through which I could mobilize the capabilities of the managers at the lower levels, involve them more intimately in the entire management process, and motivate them to seek out and develop more efficient ways of doing their jobs. And that in essence is the purpose of the Defense Department's Cost Reduction Program.

Since almost three-quarters of the total Defense budget is spent for logistics in the broadest sense of that term, we concentrated our efforts first on that entire process. From various studies, we were able to identify the key areas in which improvements were urgently needed and where the potential for significant savings was the greatest.

The problem was how to organize the effort on a broad continuing basis. We knew that "one-shot" efforts soon played out, leaving behind no real long-term benefits. Finally, we realized that unless the top management itself placed a high priority on the effort, managers at lower levels would soon lose interest in the program.

Initially we laid out a five-year program. Some twenty-eight distinct areas of logistics management were carefully delineated and grouped under the three major over-all objectives of the program: to buy only what we needed, to buy at the lowest sound price, and to reduce operating costs. We fixed specific annual cost-reduction goals, and designed a quarterly reporting system to measure progress against these goals. Each service Secretary and agency head was directed to review personally the progress achieved and to report the results to my office. I then carefully reviewed these results myself, and reported on them to the President and the Congress each year.

We consistently tried to apply one basic test: that a reportable savings must result from a clearly identifiable, new or improved management action which actually reduced costs while fully satisfying the military requirement. I believe that by and large the savings we reported over the years have met that basic test.

Beyond those savings—more than $14 billion during the five-year period—the program has raised significantly the effectiveness of our world-wide logistics system. We have developed new procurement techniques to broaden competition for Defense work and reduce the use of cost-plus-fixed-fee contracts. More realistic standards determine requirements. New procedures ensure maximum use of excess inventories throughout the Department. Special staffs were organized to eliminate unneeded frills from specifications.

With the completion of the five-year program in fiscal 1966, I established the program on an annual basis the following year. We set a goal of $1.5 billion in savings to be realized in three years from decisions to be made in fiscal year 1967. The results have already exceeded our objectives. The current estimate for the three-year period stands now at $2.059 billion.

The management task is never finished, of course, and this is particularly true of cost reduction. Even while old deficiencies are being corrected, entirely new ones appear. The very large savings achieved during the first five years are not likely to be duplicated during the succeeding five years, but there are a number of logistics areas where the opportunities for improvement are virtually unlimited. One in which activity will no doubt continue is the program through which we closed installations we no longer needed. In many cases they simply were surplus; in others consolidation was dictated by sound managment. Altogether, we took 967 actions in the seven years, releasing 1,818,000 acres (over 3,000 square miles) of real estate and eliminating 207,047 jobs.

We recognized, of course, that this program could have serious impact on local communities and on our own employees. From the beginning, the Department worked closely with the communities affected, seeking to find other uses for the facilities we no longer needed. We guaranteed every displaced employee an offer of a new job, and guaranteed as well his former salary level for two years when he took a lower-paying job.

These, then, are the sorts of problems, large and relatively small, which fall to the Secretary of Defense. Sharp differences arise as to how much we should spend on defense and where we should spend our marginal Defense dollars. And here is where the responsibility most clearly falls upon the Secretary. At the end, these problems come down always to the same question: what is really in our national interest? Every hour of every day the Secretary is confronted by a conflict between the national interest and the parochial interests of particular industries, individual services or local areas. He cannot avoid controversy in the whole range of issues which dominate the headlines if he is to place the interest of the many above the interest of the few. And yet it is the national interest, above all, which he has sworn to serve.

15. NIXON AND THE ARMS RACE

I. F. Stone

One of Robert McNamara's proudest achievements was the conception and procurement of the TFX, or F-111, fighter-bomber. This complex and expensive weapons system was the result of his effort to save money through the more efficient design and contracting of weapons. When the contract for the F-111 was awarded, two controversial questions were raised: Could the air force and the navy use the same airplane? Had improper influence affected the decision to award the contract to General Dynamics rather than to Boeing. Hardly discussed was the question of whether any such plane was needed in the first place, and virtually unforeseen was the bleak picture of cost-overruns and the craft's underperformance. It appears, in retrospect, to be one of McNamara's greatest failures and one, as Stone points out, President Nixon was quick to embrace.

I

The No. 1 question for the new Nixon Administration is what it will do about the arms race. If it opts for higher military spending, the consequence will be intensified social conflict. If the new President's policies in office follow his campaign pledges, the decision has already been made. Nixon has begun by promising to perpetuate one of McNamara's greatest errors and to undo his

Source: I. F. Stone, "Nixon and the Arms Race: The Bomber Boondoggle," *The New York Review of Books,* XI (January 1, 1969), 5-10. Reprinted with permission from *The New York Review of Books.* Copyright © 1969 The New York Review.

greatest accomplishment. The error is that miscarriage of an airplane, the TFX, now known as the F-111, which has already cost the country several billion dollars. His accomplishment was to make the country realize that at a certain point in the awful arithmetic of nuclear power, superiority in weapons became meaningless.

In his Security Gap speech over CBS on October 25, Nixon said one of his major aims would be to "correct its [the Pentagon's] over-centralization" in order to give greater weight in decision-making to the military as against the top civilians. "I intend to root out the 'whiz kid' approach which for years," Nixon said, "has led our policies and programs down the wrong roads." But he is following McNamara down his most costly wrong road, just when the military have been proven right and the top civilians wrong, and indeed—as we shall see—on the one issue where the "whiz kids" sided with the military against McNamara. On the other hand, Nixon has set out, in the search for nuclear superiority, to follow the military down a dead-end path where the military are demonstrably wrong and the "whiz kids" are demonstrably right. To examine these two divergent courses is to see the trouble which lies ahead, on many different levels, for the new Administration and the country.

Let us begin with the TFX and with the speech Nixon made November 2 at Fort Worth, Texas. Fort Worth is where General Dynamics builds the TFX or F-111, the plane that was the focus of the longest and bitterest controversy of McNamara's years in the Pentagon. "The F-111 in a Nixon Administration," the candidate said at Forth Worth that day, "will be made into one of the foundations of our air supremacy." This pledge, which received too little attention, may prove to be the biggest blooper of the campaign, and the beginning—if Nixon tries to keep that pledge—of the biggest fight between the Nixon Administration and the very forces he might have counted on for a honeymoon, the Senate conservatives who specialize in military policy and who were most critical of McNamara in the TFX affair.

This Nixon pledge at Fort Worth will repay patient examination. It is startling that a man as cautious as Nixon should have made so unqualified a pledge to a plane which has become a tragic joke.

Last May, when the Senate Appropriations subcommittee on the Department of Defense was holding hearings on the budget for the fiscal year 1969, the Chairman, Senator Russell of Georgia, booby-trapped the Air Force Chief of Staff, General McConnell, with what appeared to be an innocent question on this plane, the F-111:

> *Senator Russell:* Would it be a very serious matter if one of these planes were recovered by any potential enemy in a reasonably good condition?
> *General McConnell:* Yes, we have quite a few things in it that we would not want the enemy to get.
> *Senator Russell:* That is mainly electronic devices.
> *General McConnell:* That is true of practically all the aircraft we have.

Senator Russell: Of course the Russians got a B-29 when they were one of our allies. They fabricated a great many of them as nearly comparable to the B-29's as they could. I was hoping if they got a F-111 they would fabricate some of them as near ours as they could and see if they had as much trouble as we did. It would put their Air Force out of business.[1]

Neither General McConnell nor his civilian superior Air Force Secretary Harold Brown dared say one word in reply to Senator Russell's cruel jibe.

Russell's sardonic view of the F-111 is shared on both sides of the aisle in the Senate. On October 3, Senator Curtis of Kansas, a senior Republican, a member of the Aeronautical and Space Sciences Committee, delivered a devastating attack on the F-111 in the Senate, in which he said McNamara's "obstinacy" in producing the F-111, "will be a major problem that the new Administration must face." Just one month later Nixon began to face it by pledging himself at Fort Worth to make this plane "one of the foundations of our air supremacy."

Either Nixon and his staff do not read the newspapers, much less the *Congressional Record* and the hearings, or Nixon like McNamara is determined to override military judgment and keep the billions flowing into General Dynamics for this jinxed plane. The difference is that when McNamara overrode the military, it was difficult for outsiders to judge so complex a technological controversy; especially when so many of the facts were still classified. Newspapermen like myself, who start with a strong bias against the military, assumed that McNamara was probably right. But 1968 is the year when the F-111 finally went into combat; the results have led many people inside and outside Congress to look at the old controversy with a fresh eye.

Nixon's reckless pledge was the only bright spot for the F-111 in the year 1968. The latest, 1969, edition of *Jane's Aircraft*[2] says succinctly,

> The 474th Tactical Fighter Wing at Nellis [Air Force Base, Nevada] was the first to be equipped with the F-111As [the Air Force version of the F-111]. Six aircraft from Nellis arrived at the Takhli base in Thailand on 17 March 1968 and made their first operational sorties over Vietnam on 25 March. Two were lost in the next five days.

The Foreword, which went to press later, says "Three of the first 8 F-111A's dispatched to Vietnam were lost in a matter of weeks and the type was grounded shortly afterwards." No mention was made of these losses by Secretary of the Air Force Brown when he read his prepared statement to the Senate appropriations defense subcommittee in executive session last May 6. On the contrary he said the F-111 "is proving, in its tests and operational units, to be an outstanding aircraft." By then three of the original six had been lost, as may be seen from the following colloquy, where the reader will notice Secretary Brown's squeamish reluctance to use the word "lost."

> *Secretary Russell:* How many of these have we sent over to Southeast Asia?

Secretary Brown: We sent six and have sent two replacements.

Senator Russell: You have lost three, so you have five?

Secretary Brown: There are five there now.

Senator Russell: Do you have any information on these three that were lost? Do you know whether any of them fell into the hands of the North Vietnamese to be sent to Moscow along with all the secret equipment of the Pueblo?

General McConnell [Air Force Chief of Staff] : No, sir.[3]

In his Senate speech of October 3, Senator Curtis disclosed, "Thus far, 11 F-111 aircraft have crashed with a number of fatalities." He revealed that the wings were broken off one plane during a "static ground test" just six weeks before the first six planes were deployed to Southeast Asia, and that the week before his Senate speech another F-111A had crashed during a training flight owing to "a fatigue failure in the wing carrythrough structure."

If rightists treated Nixon and the Defense Department the way he treated the State Department in the days when he was a practicing witchhunter, a proposal to make such a plane, with such a record, a foundation stone of American air supremacy would have been adduced as proof positive that the Pentagon had been infiltrated with Red and pinko saboteurs.

Last January the British Royal Air Force cancelled its order for fifty F-111K's. In March Congress ordered work stopped on the F-111B's, the version for the US Navy. On October 7, Senator Symington followed Senator Curtis with a speech suggesting that production of the F-111's for the Air Force also be stopped: He said "the series of crashes in the past five months" makes it doubtful that it will ever prove to be "a truly reliable airplane" and declared that its future should "receive highest priority upon convening of the new Congress."

The strangest discovery which turns up in studying Nixon's pledge at Fort Worth is that he and his staff were either unaware of, or ignored, his own famous "position papers." The one on "Research and Development: Our Neglected Weapon,"[4] which was made public in May, 1968, says of the F-111:

> The effort to transform the TFX (F-111) into an all-purpose all-service aircraft has created serious problems. Against military advice, the F-111 was selected as a superior, yet economical, weapons system. . . . The aircraft were to cost approximately $2.4 million each. Now they are priced at more than $6 million each. . . . In view of the recent decision that the F111B, the Navy version, is unacceptable, and a substitute aircraft be initiated, the final cost of the program will increase enormously coupled with years of delay. The program has resulted in the Air Force having a new aircraft that does not meet the original requirements. . . . The F111B has been found unacceptable and the F111 Bomber version does not meet Air Force requirements for an advanced bomber in the 1970 time frame.

Nixon devoted one of his main campaign speeches to "the research gap." The

Fort Worth speech showed his own research gap. Did he and his staff fail to read their position papers? Another of these papers, "Decisions on National Security: Patchwork or Policy?" is also in conflict with his Fort Worth speech. That paper says "a notable example" of how the top civilians overrode military judgment in the McNamara years was the original award of the contract for the F-111. "The contractor unanimously recommended by both the military analysts and Weapons Evaluation Systems Group," it says, "was rejected." The rejected bidder was Boeing. The contractor McNamara chose was General Dynamics. Nixon at Fort Worth affirmed the same choice.

II

We are not dealing here with a minor item. General Dynamics is the country's biggest weapons producer. A Defense Department press release of November 18 on the nation's top ten defense contractors showed General Dynamics as No. 1. In the fiscal year ending last June 30, it received $2.2 billion in arms contracts, or 5.8 percent of the total awarded in those twelve months. More than 80 percent of the firm's business comes from the government. The TFX represented the biggest single plum in military procurement. The original contract was for 1,700 planes at a total cost of $5.8 billion, or about $3 million per plane. These figures have since skyrocketed. This year, before the Navy contract was cancelled, the Pentagon admitted the cost of the Navy version would be $8 million apiece and of the Air Force version $6.5 million. As usual these, too, were understatements. Senator Curtis disclosed that the contractor's cost information reports put the average cost of the Navy plane at $9.5 million and that internal budgeting projections at the Pentagon put the Air Force plane at $9.1 million each. The original contract would have run up in the neighborhood of $15 billion.

Even with the cutbacks, more than $6 billion has already been spent and at least between $3 and $4 billion more "will be added in succeeding years," Senator Curtis said, "if present Defense Department plans are carried to completion." If Nixon keeps his word, they *will* be completed, perhaps expanded. But if he tries to do so, he will almost certainly find himself embattled with the Air Force buffs in Congress. For Curtis, Symington, Russell, and McClellan speak for a group of Senators who feel that the Air Force has been starved and stunted while all this money has been wasted on the TFX. We are in the presence of a wide-open split not only between the proponents of General Dynamics and Boeing respectively but within the Air Force and the whole military-industrial complex.

History is repeating itself, and it is the history of subordinating military efficiency to moneyed and political pressures. The only difference is that Nixon will find it harder than did McNamara to hide the realities, now that the F-111 has finally begun to fly—and fall. When the Kennedy Administration took over, General Dynamics was drifting close to receivership. It lost $27 million in 1960 and $143 million in 1961. *Fortune* Magazine in January and February of 1962 published a fascinating two-part study of its misjudgments and its business losses by Richard Austin Smith. Smith said its losses on its civilian plane business had been so disastrous that its working capital had dropped below the minimum required by its agreement with its bankers and if the bankers had not reduced the minimum this "technically could have started the company down the road to receivership." Smith wrote that the output of the General Dynamics plant at Fort Worth in 1962 would be half what it was in 1961. *Fortune* said in its strangulated prose that General Dynamics would have to shut down its facilities "unless it gets contract for joint Navy-Air Force fighter." This was the TFX.

The TFX contract saved General Dynamics in 1962. The cancellation of the F-111 could ruin it in 1969. The effect of cancelling the Navy version of the plan was already reflected in a third quarter deficit, as of September 30, 1968, amounting to $1.51 a share compared with a net profit of $1.13 a share in the third quarter of 1967. *Moody's News* showed General Dynamics had to write off $39.6 million in contracts in 1968 as against only $12 million in 1967. Its net after taxes for the first nine months of 1968, after allowing for sales of assets which made the accounts look better than they otherwise would have, was only $9 million as compared with $36 million for the same period the previous year.

Standard & Poor's Outlook, October 7, 1968, said the stock of General Dynamics was "a speculation in the success of this F-111 program" and that "the most important price determinant over the near term will be developments in this trouble-plagued F-111 program." *The Value Line* October 18 said, "Since our July review the ever sensitive stock market has sold these shares down to a two-year low." It said that if the problems of the F-111 were not soon resolved, it was "vulnerable to further procurement cutbacks." This was the bleak outlook two weeks before Nixon's speech at Fort Worth. McNamara saved General Dynamics in 1962. Nixon promised on November 2 to save it again.

III

McNamara's error on the TFX, which Nixon is now taking over, is worth close study because it shows the diminishing relationship between military procurement and genuine considerations of defense. It demonstrates the growing extent to which procurement is determined by military-bureaucratic and industrial considerations. The prime determinants were to save the largest company in the military-industrial complex financially and to appease the bomber generals, who simply will not admit that their expensive toys have grown obsolete. Billions which could do so much for poverty are squandered to maintain these favorite Pentagon clients on the military relief rolls in the lush style to which they have become accustomed.

General Dynamics, behind its glamorous front, is almost as much a creature of the government as the Air Force. In 1967 some 83 percent of its sales were to the government. *Moody's* observes of the huge Fort Worth establishment, where Nixon gave so much solace to this peculiar form of free and private enterprise, that the "plant, including most machinery and equipment, is leased from the US government." The chief asset of General Dynamics seems to be its ability to wangle contracts out of the Pentagon.

The error in the TFX affair occurred on three levels, which have had varying degrees of attention, in inverse ratio to their importance. McNamara was wrong—so events seem to have proven—(1) in giving the TFX contract to General Dynamics instead of Boeing, (2) in insisting that the same basic plane be adopted for the diverse needs of the Air Force and Navy, and (3) in surrendering to the pressure of the Air Force for a new bomber and the Navy for a new missile weapons system to meet a non-existent Soviet bomber threat just so they could go on with their expensive bomber game.

The first, the least important, got the most attention in earlier years since it promised Republican and conservative Democratic critics of the Kennedy and Johnson Administrations a scandal. But the shock of the Kennedy assassination cut short the McClellan committee investigation. A key figure was Roswell Gilpatric, a corporation lawyer who has done two tours of duty at the Pentagon, the first as Under Secretary of the Air Force in 1951-1953 and again as Deputy Secretary of Defense in 1961-1964, returning on each occasion to the famous Wall Street law firm of Cravath, Swaine and Moore with which he has been associated since 1931. Through Gilpatric's efforts the firm became counsel for General Dynamics in the late Fifties and Gilpatric has combined his law work with activity in foreign and military policy in the Council on Foreign Relations and as member of the Rockefeller Brothers Special Study project, which called for a sharp increase in military expenditures in January, 1958. In 1960 he was named as adviser on national security affairs by Kennedy during his campaign for the Presidency and after the election became Deputy Secretary of Defense, No. 2 man to McNamara at the Pentagon. There he played a major role in awarding the TFX contract.

General Dynamics has always been adept at having friends at court. It chose for its president in the fifties a former Secretary of the Army, Frank Pace. The $400-million losses of its Convair division during his incumbency make one wonder whether his chief qualification for the job was that he knew his way around Washington. Similarly it did not hurt General Dynamics to have its ex-counsel as No. 2 man in the Pentagon while it was fighting for the contract which could alone save it from receivership. Nor was General Dynamics hurt by the fact that Fred Korth, whom the Kennedy Administration had for some unfathomable reason made Secretary of the Navy, was a Fort Worth, Texas, banker, a past president of the Continental Bank which had loaned money to General Dynamics, "and that Korth had kept an active, though not a financial, interest in the activities of this bank"[5] while in public office.

Korth told the McClellan committee "that because of his peculiar position he had deliberately refrained from taking a directing hand in this decision [within the Navy] until the last possible moment."[6] But it was "the last possible moment" which counted. Three times the Pentagon's Source Selection Board found that Boeing's bid was better and cheaper than that of General Dynamics and three times the bids were sent back for fresh submissions by the two bidders and fresh reviews. On the fourth round, the military still held that Boeing was better but found at last that the General Dynamics bid was also acceptable.

It was at this last moment that the award was made to General Dynamics. The only document the McClellan committee investigators were able to find in the Pentagon in favor of that award, according to their testimony, was a five-page memorandum signed by McNamara, Korth, and Eugene Zuckert, then Secretary of the Air Force, but not—interestingly enough—by Gilpatric. Senator Curtis charged in his Senate speech, October 3, that some months after the contract was announced in November, 1962, "a team of experts was assembled in the Pentagon to review the designs. . . . The experts were directed to find strong points for General Dynamics and weak points for Boeing so the decision could be defended in Senate hearings."

During the McClellan committee hearings in 1963, Senator Ervin of North Carolina focused on another angle to this contract when he said to McNamara, "I would like to ask you whether or not there was any connection whatever between your selection of General Dynamics, and the fact that the Vice President of the United States happens to be a resident of the state in which that company has one of its principal, if not its principal office." The reference of course was to Lyndon Johnson, to Texas, and to Fort Worth. McNamara answered, "Absolutely not."[7] In the dissolute atmosphere of Washington there were few to believe such political virginity possible. When General Accounting Office investigators asked McNamara how he came to override military judgment, "The Secretary said that, after finding the Air Force estimates inadequate for judging the cost implications of the two proposals [i.e., General Dynamics' and Boeing's], he had made rough judgments of the kind he had made for many years with the Ford Motor Company." The most charitable comment is that the TFX, then, proved to be the Edsel of his Pentagon years.

Under normal circumstances one would have expected all this to be aired in the 1968 campaign. But the military-industrial complex plays both sides of the political fence, and the defense contractors are an easy source of campaign funds. Nixon not only kept silent but pledged himself to the very same plane. The same cynical charges made behind the scenes about the original TFX contract will no doubt be made again about Nixon's reaffirmation of it. The first point in favor of General Dynamics was and is its financial weakness. Boeing, with a better record for engineering and on costs, is in good shape; half its business is commercial, a testimony to its reputation. Why let the weaker company go down the drain? The TFX affair illustrates the survival of the unfittest in the military corporate jungle.

The second point in favor of General Dynamics was and remains political. General Dynamics is in Texas, a swing State with twenty-four electoral votes, and its biggest subcontractor on the F-111, Grumman, is in New York with forty-five electoral votes. Boeing would have produced the plane in Kansas with eight votes, which go Republican anyway, and in the State of Washington with nine. Nixon's November 2 pledge shows that any major new plane must show it can fly successfully through the electoral college. Its aerodynamics must be designed for a maximum number of votes. Nixon's pre-election speech at Fort Worth recalls two other comparable appearances there, one *opera buffa,* one tragic. The former occurred on December 11, 1962, a month after General Dynamics won the TFX contract, when Johnson made a triumphant visit to the plant at Fort Worth and was greeted by union members waving banners which said "LBJ Saved The Day" and "We're Here to Say Thanks to LBJ."[8] The other was the morning of November 22, 1963, a few hours before he was assassinated, when President Kennedy addressed a rally in Fort Worth and paid tribute to the TFX as "the best fighter system in the world."[9] For Johnson and Kennedy, as for Nixon, in the TFX contract electioneering and defense were inextricably mingled.

A key word in the TFX controversy was "commonalty." McNamara wanted a plane which could be used by the Air Force and the Navy in common. With the cancellation of the contract for the Navy's version of the F-111, the battle for commonalty between the two services was lost. But Nixon's pledge on the F-111 shows that commonalty still exists in defense politics. For Republican as well as Democratic administrations, what is best for General Dynamics is best for the country.

IV

This mention of "commonalty" brings us to the other two misjudgments involved in the TFX decision. One was to try to build one plane for many diverse Air Force and Navy missions. The other was to counter a Soviet bomber threat which does not now exist and is unlikely ever to come into being. With these misjudgments[10] we come to technological details which must become part of public knowledge if we are to understand the expensive and nightmarish nonsense in which the arms race has engulfed us.

President-elect Nixon, as we have seen, pledged himself to "root out 'the whiz kid' approach" to national defense. As it happens the "whiz kids" were as opposed to the TFX as Generals and Admirals to the idea of trying to build a common plane for both services. "Pressure within the Defense Department for a single sophisticated multimission aircraft [using the new swing-wing design] came from the Office of Defense Research and Engineering which was headed in the early 1960s by Harold Brown, the present Secretary of the Air Force," *Congressional Quarterly* reported last February 16. "Although the concept was opposed by the young systems analysts that Defense Secretary McNamara had brought with him to the Pentagon, they were not then in a position to conduct a running battle with Brown. At the time the Office of Systems Analysis was subordinate to the Pentagon comptroller, which was one level below Brown."

Nixon to the contrary, this mistake might not have been made if the "whiz kids" had had more influence.

McNamara had been trying to cut down duplication in supplies among the three services, a source of enormous waste, and he accomplished substantial savings in this field. His critics in Congress say privately that to an automobile man, accustomed to mounting various kinds of cars on much the same chassis, the idea of using the same "chassis" in military planes must have seemed a natural. Indeed to an outsider there seems to be little reason why the same plane should not be used by the various services for the same type of mission. Why—for example—can't the Air Force and the Navy use the same dogfighter?

The trouble in the case of the TFX or F-111 is that the Air Force and the Navy had such diverse missions to be performed by the common plane on which McNamara insisted. It is being built for a tactical fighter, a long-range strategic bomber, a reconnaissance plane, and—until the Navy contract was cancelled—a new weapons system, a plane carrying a new type of missile.

The Navy wanted the plane to be light enough for a carrier but big enough to carry a special missile—the Phoenix—and a big load of radar equipment. Its Naval mission would be to loiter hour after hour over the fleet to protect it from a nuclear supersonic bomber attack; the radar would enable the plane to detect an incoming plane and hit it with the missile far enough away so that the fleet would be safe from nuclear blast and radiation. The Air Force wanted the plane to be able to fulfill a very different mission. It was to be able to fly at supersonic speed under the radar defenses around the Soviet Union and then, after unloading its nuclear bombs on target, make altitude swiftly enough to elude not only enemy ack-ack or fighter planes but the effects of the nuclear blast it had set off. To fit one plane to two such diverse purposes would seem to require the ingenuity of a Rube Goldberg. This particular mistake has been thoroughly debated, since it serves intra-service animosity. There's nothing the Navy hates worse than losing a battle to the Air Force.

A second level of misjudgment, the most basic of all, has hardly been discussed at all, at least in public. Here one is led to question the good sense of both the Air Force and the Navy. The Navy is still as full of bomber Admirals as the Air Force is of bomber Generals. They started the bomber gap nonsense in the fifties and still suffer from the obsessions which the arms lobby exploits so skillfully. "In the early 1950s we were told the Russians were going to build thousands of supersonic bombers," Senator Symington commented ruefully last May during the Senate hearings on the 1969 defense budget. "They did not build any long-range bombers of that type."[11] Symington was himself once the captive and spokesman of those inflated fears, as he was several years later of the "missile gap" campaign which he later helped to expose as fraudulent.

In the hearings last April on "The Status of US Strategic Power," which reflected the views and fears of those who favor a bigger arms budget, Chairman Stennis said of the present Soviet bomber fleet, "I have never looked upon these bombers as a serious threat to the US unless we just let our guard down completely. They are the same old bombers, the Bear and the Bison." These are the subsonic bombers whose appearance in Moscow in the fifties set off the bomber gap scare. The Russians just aren't spending money on long-range supersonic nuclear bombers when the same delivery job can be done so much more cheaply and quickly by missiles.

When Stennis's Preparedness Subcommittee of Senate Armed Services filed its report October 4 on the US Tactical Air Power Program, it said "The F-111B [i.e., the Navy version of the F-111 armed with the Phoenix missile—IFS] was designed primarily for fleet air defense against a Soviet supersonic bomber. But that threat is either limited or does not exist." Yet the Navy, having got rid of the F-111B, is planning its new VFX-1 to carry a Phoenix missile for use against the same non-existent supersonic Soviet bomber attack. The Navy insisted in the fiscal 1969 hearings that the Phoenix-armed plane "is the only system that provides the Navy with an acceptable level of Fleet Air Defense for the 1970-80 era, particularly for any missile threat against the fleet."[12]

This assumes that the Soviets will play the game our way and build the supersonic nuclear bombers the Phoenix is designed to counter. In chess, when one sees the other side concentrating his forces in one sector, one attacks in another. But our Joint Chiefs of Staff do not seem to play chess. *Congressional Quarterly,* which has good sources in the Pentagon, reported last May 3 that many Navy aviators were hostile to both the F-111B and its successor, the VFX-1 project, for a Phoenix-armed plane. It quoted a Pentagon source as saying the whole program was based on a false premise. It said Soviet doctrine envisioned the use of fighters, submarines, and missile-launching patrol boats instead of nuclear supersonic bombers for attacks on carriers and battleships. Obviously an attack would come where the other side can see we are least prepared. The Phoenix is likely to prove not only a waste of funds but an impediment to genuine defense by concentrating on a threat which does not exist now and is not likely to exist later.

V

The main Air Force mission for the F-111 is a reflection of the same bomber delusions, but on a larger scale. To see this in perspective one must step back and observe that we now have three major ways of destroying the Soviet Union. One is the ICBM, the intercontinental ballistic missile. The second is the submarine-launched nuclear missile, the Polaris. The third is the intercontinental bomber force of the Strategic Air Command. Any one of these three forces can itself deliver much more than the 400 megatons which McNamara estimates would destroy three-fourths of the Soviet Union's industrial capacity and 64 million people or one-third its population.

Of the three mega-murder machines, the only one which can be stopped is the bomber fleet. It's an expensive luxury, a toy on which the bomber Generals dote, and which the aircraft industry is only too happy to supply. High-flying bombers cannot get through the Soviet's radar and SAM (surface-to-air) missile defenses. So the F-111 is designed to duck low under Soviet radar defenses, drop nuclear bombs, and make a high fast getaway, all at supersonic speeds. The basic argument against the F-111 is that if we ever want to hit major targets in the Soviet Union, we would do so with missiles which can reach their targets in thirty minutes with fifteen-minute warning time instead of planes whose flight and warning time would be measured in hours. If we tried to use bombers first, they would only warn the enemy and provide plenty of time for retaliatory missile strikes against our cities. If these bombers were to be used for a second strike *after* a Russian attack on us, the bombers (if any were left) would arrive hours after the missiles, and there would be little if anything left to destroy anyway. The intercontinental bomber is a surplus and obsolete deterrent but 1\frac{1}{3}$ billions is allocated to the F-111 in the fiscal 1969 budget, much of it for these bombers.

But this is not the end of this expensive nonsense. The military always assumes that the enemy will do what we do, that anything *we* produce *they* will produce. This is sometimes but not always true. The geographical and strategic situation of the Soviet Union is not the same as that of the United States; this dictates differences in weapons systems. In addition—no small consideration—the country which is poorer and has fewer resources to waste will be more careful in its expenditures. But we always estimate that the enemy will spend as prodigally as we do. This is how the bomber and missile gap scares originated. So we are spending billions to "keep ahead" of Soviet bombers and bomber defenses. We are also assuming that the Soviets will be as silly as we are and also build a fleet of F-111's to "get under" our radar defenses. So Congress has already embarked on another multi-billion-dollar program of building new radar "fences" and new types of interceptor planes to deal with these hypothetical Soviet F-111's.

To make all this plausible, the Air Force does its best to hide from the Congress the true facts about the Soviet air force. Twice during the past year Senator Symington, who feels that the billions spent on this bomber are diverting funds which could more sensibly be spent on new fighter planes, has asked Pentagon witnesses for the numbers of the various Soviet bombers. "Do you believe," he asked Dr. John S. Foster, Jr., director of Defense Research and Development, "that the Soviet Union poses a serious bomber threat to the United States today?" The answer was "Yes, Senator Symington, I do." Symington replied incredulously, "The Soviets have not built a bomber for years, except the Blinder—and the latter's performance is not as good as the B-58 which we abandoned. In spite of that we now have to spend billions of dollars defending against bombers also."

He then asked Dr. Foster to supply the Appropriations Committee with the numbers of each type of Soviet bomber. The numbers were deleted by the censor.[13] But if one turns to McNamara's final statement in the same hearings[14] he gives the number of Soviet intercontinental bombers as 155 as compared with our 697. These Soviet bombers are mostly the old subsonic Bear and Bison bombers, neither of which could possibly duck under US radar defenses in the way the F-111 is supposed to duck under the Soviet Union's.

Even the report on *The Status of US Strategic Power* filed last September 27 by the Senate's Preparedness Subcommittee under Senator Stennis, which argues for larger arms expenditures, says, "There is no evidence that the Soviets are proceeding with the development of a new heavy bomber and, should they elect to develop one, it is probable we would see indications of the program 3 to 4 years before the aircraft becomes operational."

To counter this, the Air Force sophists have come up with a new argument. When Senator Symington asked Dr. Foster, as head of Pentagon research and development, why they were planning new types of bomber defense against non-existent types of Soviet planes, Dr. Foster replied, "discouragement of Soviet aspirations to develop a more advanced bomber."[15] But why spend billions to discourage the Soviets from building a bomber they show no signs of building anyway?

Another favorite reason often used by the Air Force may be found in Air Force Chief of Staff General McConnell's presentation to the Stennis hearings on strategic power last April. "A bomber force," the General said, "causes the Soviets to continue to develop bomber defenses rather than concentrating their expenditures just on missile defenses."[16] *So we waste money to make them waste money.* Though we are richer, this may be worse for us than them, because our planes are far more elaborate and expensive.

Since the Air Force thus admits that there is no sign as yet of a new supersonic Soviet bomber able to penetrate our existing defenses, why does it go on talking of a Soviet bomber "threat"? As usual, it turns out that this simple word has an unexpected meaning in the special language developed at the Pentagon. This prize item of military semantics may be found in the testimony of Air Force Secretary Brown to these same Stennis committee hearings. Dr. Brown was explaining to the committee that if Soviet anti-aircraft defenses were improved and we had to build in additional "penetration aids" to get past more efficient radar devices, we would have to build bigger bombs than we now have. "Otherwise," he said, "we will find ourselves carrying many penetration aids and comparatively few weapons." Dr. Brown went on to say there was "general agreement" at the Pentagon that such an advanced US bomber "probably will be needed at some time in the future" but just when would depend on "how fast and far the Soviet threat is likely to evolve." Then he explained, "By threat here we are principally talking about Soviet defenses against bombers."[17]

The threat, in other words, is not that they might be able successfully to attack us with their bombers but that they might build up their anti-bomber defenses to the point where we might not be able to attack them successfully with *our* bombers! It would be only a short step from this to defining aggression as the building of defenses to discourage an enemy attack.

The reductio ad absurdum is in a passage I found in the fiscal 1969 defense budget hearings before the House Appropriations Committee. Mahon of Texas, the able chairman of the defense subcommittee, was questioning Air Force officials about the Soviet bomber menace. Here is the colloquy which spills the whole and final truth about this costly nightmare:

> *Mr. Mahon:* Officials of the Department of Defense have not indicated to this committee that they think the Soviets will go very strong on the manned bomber. They will rely principally on the ICBM. Is that right?
> *General McConnell* [Air Force Chief of Staff] : That is the consensus.
> *Mr. Mahon:* The Air Force has a little different view?
> *General McConnell:* [Deleted by censor].
> *Mr. Mahon:* [Deleted by censor].
> *General McConnell:* [Deleted by censor].
> *Mr. Mahon:* How long have the Soviets had, Secretary [of the Air Force] Brown, to develop a follow-on[18] bomber?
> *Secretary Brown:* They have had ten years.
> *Mr. Mahon:* Have you seen any evidence?
> *Secretary Brown:* I see no evidence of it, Mr. Chairman. The Air Force view is at least as much a view that "they ought to have one" as it is "they will have one."[19]

Billions in contracts for new bombers and new bomber defense are threatened should the Russians stubbornly persist in not building a new bomber force. In extremity perhaps Congress might be persuaded to add the Soviet Union to our foreign aid clients and give them an advanced bomber force to keep the US aircraft business strong and prosperous. Or General Dynamics and the other big companies in the military-industrial complex might pass the hat among themselves and buy Moscow a new bomber. Should those old obsolete subsonic Bears and Bisons stop flying altogether, it would be a catastrophe for Fort Worth, a form of economic aggression in reverse. Ours—the rich man's strategy—is to make the Russians waste their resources by wasting ours. Theirs--the poor man's strategy—might be to strike a mortal blow at the arms business here by cutting their own expenditures to the minimum the balance of terror requires.

Nothing so terrifies the military-industrial complex as this notion of a *minimum* deterrent, as we shall see in our next installment, when we analyze Nixon's pledge to restore that crucial notion of "nuclear superiority," about which McNamara had finally succeeded in making the country see a little sense.

FOOTNOTES

[1]Senate Appropriations Committee Hearings on the 1969 Defense Department budget, Part I, Department of the Air Force, p. 103. Released September 19, 1968.
[2]*Jane's All the World's Aircraft, 1968-69,* edited by John W. R. Taylor, McGraw-Hill, p. 279.

[3]Senate 1969 Defense Appropriations Hearings, *op. cit.,* pp. 102-103.

[4]All these position papers have been reprinted in a one-volume compilation, *Choice for America: Republican Answers to the Challenge of Now,* published July, 1968, by the Republican National Committee, 1625 Eye St. N.W., Washington 20006.

[5]*The TFX Decision,* by Robert J. Art, Little, Brown, p. 4.

[6]*Ibid.,* p. 5.

[7]*Ibid.*

[8]Fort Worth *Star-Telegram,* December 12, 1962, quoted in McClellan Committee hearings on the TFX, p. 2658.

[9]*Public Papers of the Presidents, John F. Kennedy 1963,* p. 8.

[10]I venture to speak so dogmatically not only because of what has happened this year to the F-111, but because among men at the Pentagon devoted to McNamara I have found no one who does not feel the TFX was a mistake.

[11]1969 Senate Defense Appropriations Hearings, Part V, p. 2664.

[12]*Ibid.,* Part IV, p. 1426.

[13]See p. 2362, 1969 Defense Department Budget Hearings, Part IV.

[14]*Ibid.,* Part V, p. 2718.

[15]*Ibid.,* p. 2719.

[16]"Status of US Strategic Power," Preparedness Investigating Subcommittee of the Senate Committee on Armed Services, 90th Congress, 2nd Session, April 30, 1968, Part II, p. 169.

[17]*Ibid.,* p. 179.

[18]Air Force lingo for a new bomber.

[19]House Appropriations Committee Hearings on the Fiscal 1969 Defense budget, Executive Session, February 26, 1968, Part I, p. 751.

"The Missile May Not Be So Hot, But—Boy— What A Delivery System!"

16. AT&T AND THE ABM

Joseph Goulden and Marshall Singer

Although an aerospace firm such as General Dynamics — defense-oriented and
Texas-based — seems to be the most typical corporate component of the
military-industrial complex, the real giants of corporate America are also very
much involved. In 1967 General Electric, General Motors, and AT&T were all
among the top ten defense contractors. AT&T and its subsidiaries, Bell
Laboratories and Western Electric, have always been highly placed in the
nation's defense counsels. The emphasis of the defense establishment on
electronics since World War II has given much work to these companies. Reports
in the spring of 1970 that Bell Laboratories was withdrawing from defense work
(because of pressure from peace groups and technical difficulties with the ABM)
were promptly denied by the Chairman of AT&T. Bell Labs did not seek defense
work, he said, and consented to undertake it only when "our qualifications are
unique."

The American Telephone & Telegraph Company should receive a citation for
inadvertent candor on the basis of an advertisement it ran this spring in trade
journals of the military-industrial complex. The stark white page bore only a
small AT&T trademark and two brief lines of miniscule six-point type. The first

Source: Joseph Goulden and Marshall Singer, "Dial-A-Bomb: AT&T and the ABM,"
Ramparts, VIII (November 1969), 30-37. Copyright Ramparts Magazine, Inc. 1969. By
Permission of the Editors.

line, centered in mid-page, whispered: "Command/Control Systems use our network." The second, at the very bottom, observed: "We know how to keep a secret."

Indeed, our phone company is discreet about all its military engagements; the Bell System has managed to keep well-subdued, if not absolutely secret, the fact that it is the prime contractor and chief profit-maker for the highly controversial Anti-Ballistic Missile system, the ABM. Normally, an American corporation could be expected to boast just a bit about bagging a project with a potential price tag of anywhere from $6- to $400 billion, the speculation range of the ABM. The two low-keyed sentences devoted to the ABM in AT&T's annual report, however, give no indication of the financial avalanche that may soon fall into its lap. Southern militarist senators may shout themselves hoarse over it, but the phone company has yet to mention its own ABM aloud.

The present Nike-X Sentinel Safeguard ABM system is only the latest and most extravagant in a series of Nike defensive missiles which have brought the telephone company nearly $10 billion in prime contracts since 1945. AT&T is presently the nation's sixth largest defense contractor, doing work on anti-submarine projects as well as the ABM. Yet AT&T's image is worlds away from the paraphernalia of war and devastation: what could be more pacific and tame than the phone company? It seems no more likely a purveyor of nuclear missiles than does Macy's or the A&P. The story of demure Ma Bell's discreet but lucrative intimacy with the "defense establishment" tells much about the real nature of the military-industrial complex, which is so much discussed but still so little understood.

After all, what is the prevailing image of the military-industrial complex? On the industrial side: a pack of hustling upstart Texas yahoos and San Diego John Birch industrialists, inhabiting the new untamed wild west outlands of the American economy. On the military side: crackpot Strangelovean generals foisting their exorbitant arms-race war-games on an unwitting civilian society. But the reality is that the military-industrial complex is centered in the old respectable heartlands of corporate power, which have provided the basic impetus and thrust behind America's trillion-dollar postwar war machine. The power of the complex is clothed neither in brass and braid nor bermuda shorts and a ten-gallon hat, but sensibly in a dark suit and a sober tie. And the big money Washington boondoggle is far from a new game; it is a grand tradition, subject to the kind of reverence expressed in *Guys and Dolls* for "the oldest established, permanent floating crap game in New York."

The top 25 U.S. defense contractors include, besides AT&T, such other stalwarts of the corporate aristocracy as Ford, General Electric, General Motors and Standard Oil of New Jersey—the four largest industrial corporations in America. AT&T itself, the largest American corporation of any kind, is a giant among giants. Its incredible assets of $40 billion approach the combined assets of America's 50 largest transportation companies (including airlines, railroads, etc.), or those of the three greatest industrial giants. Its net income is a third larger than that of the 50 largest U.S. commercial banks or of the 50 largest retailing companies combined. Who better, then, to take the role of prime contractor for the system that has become the very symbol of military-industrial boondogglery in America? For, in accord with the ground rules of modern American corporate statism, the lush ABM fiefdom was granted to AT&T as a natural prerogative of its station.

It is clear that Bell did not get the Sentinel contract because of any unique proficiency in building missiles. This fact emerges obliquely from the AT&T annual report, which carries the following note on the Sentinel: "Fundamental responsibilities . . . rest on Western Electric [AT&T's wholly owned manufacturing subsidiary] and Bell Laboratories [another subsidiary] but most of the aggregate volume of business will be handled by subcontractors." For the phrase "the aggregate volume of business" one can read "the work." And as for the "fundamental responsibilities," they often seem to come down to raking in the profits. Five years ago, a similar arrangement with Bell on an earlier version of Nike was summed up by Senator John McClellan in this way: "For 18 years, from 1945 through 1963, the Army has been buying tens of thousands of missiles from Western Electric, which has yet to make its first missile."

As prime contractor, Western Electric takes whatever work it cannot do on a project and farms it out to subcontractors. On the contract which so angered Senator McClellan, Western itself produced only one of the four main elements: the radar and guidance system. The other three—the missile, the launcher apparatus, and the trailers and vans that housed the system—were subcontracted to Douglas Aircraft. Douglas produced the missile and sub-subcontracted the last two elements—the launcher to Consolidated Western Division of U.S. Steel; the trailers and vans to Fruehauf Trailer Corporation.

The Army paid Western Electric $1.6 billion on this contract, out of which the company took $113 million as profit, about 7.9 percent, which could be considered reasonable. Reasonable, that is, were it not for the fact that Western *did* only a fraction of the work. Out of the entire $1.6 billion contract, Western's own work accounted for only $359 million (and this includes a generous $82 million for general and administrative expenses). When Western's profit is figured against the work it actually did, it comes not to a 7.9 percent return, but to a patently unreasonable 31.3 percent.

This doesn't mean that Western grabbed everyone else's profits for itself; this is a game in which everybody wins. Douglas received $645 million from Western, out of which it took $46 million, 7.6 percent, as profit. But Douglas itself did an even smaller portion of the work than Western; it did $103 million—little more than a sixth—and sub-subcontracted the rest. Douglas's profit on its work was a hefty 44.3 percent.

The trick is that in military contracting a fair profit if figured as a reasonable percentage of a contractor's "costs," but the contractor includes in his costs not only the expenses of the work he did, but also all the payments he made to the next contractor down the line. Thus the government ends up paying profits on the work done on trailers by Fruehauf not just to Fruehauf, but also to Douglas for the "cost" of paying Fruehauf to do the work, and to Western for the "cost" of paying Douglas the money with which to pay Fruehauf. The government pays profits three times, once for the work and twice for the mere service of passing the government's money on down the line. Even stranger is the fact that Douglas's "cost" is larger than Fruehauf's because it also includes Fruehauf's profit; and since Douglas's cost is greater, its profit is larger, even though Fruehauf did the work. Western, the farthest removed, has the greatest basis for profit, since its costs include the profits of both subcontractors: Profits on profits on profits.

This profit-taking sometimes reaches unthought of levels of absurdity. On one contract for 1,032 additional launchers, Consolidated manufactured the launchers at a price of $13.5 million (including profit) and delivered them directly to the Army. Douglas made plastic rain covers for the launchers at a cost of $3 each, for a total of $3,361. Douglas then took a profit on that amount *plus* the Consolidated price, a profit of $1.2 million on $3,361 worth of work. The percentage: 36,531 percent. Western Electric, which gave each missile a quick $14 inspection at the base, proceeded to pyramid its return on top of Douglas's. Western did not do quite as well, coming out with a mere 6684 percent return on its effort.

Of course AT&T doesn't itemize its profits in this manner—any more than they itemize their profits on phone bills. A Bell merchandising man explained the point in a way that applies to both contexts, charges to consumers and to taxpayers: "People don't like to pay 'more' for something. Do you? People are not really interested in the rate and they don't particularly want to hear the word 'charge' associated with something in which they have expressed an interest."

It is reassuring to know that a decade of military generosity on this scale did not go unnoticed by the Army. Western Electric got the Nike production contract in 1951. It was not two years before the Army's sharp-eyed chief of ordnance noticed that millions could be saved if the Army could (in its own apt phrase) "break out" subcontracted elements of the system, that is, buy them directly from the manufacturer rather than through one or two middlemen. Even in military procurement this procedure is not entirely unheard of. But to "break out" is easier said than done. And when it was suggested to Western Electric, the company went straight to the Secretary of the Army, Robert T. Stevens, to complain. Secretary Stevens was naturally scandalized by the effrontery, and ordered that no break-out be initiated without Western's concurrence. After all, it was Western's profits that were being trifled with.

The Army spent the next eight years waiting for this concurrence, but Western just couldn't find it in its heart to be parted from its family of Nike subcontractors. Not until the McClellan committee began an investigation in

1961, did Western consent to the break-out of the missiles; in fact, sensing what was in store, they suggested it.

When the Army did succeed in obtaining some break-outs, the effect was startling. Spare parts vans, which had cost $20,000 apiece when obtained through the profit pyramid, dropped to $14,300—nearly a third less—on direct purchase even without competitive bidding. Highway missile transporters that had cost $12,000 came down to $10,300 on break-out, and a year later competitive bidding reduced them to $5304, less than half the Western Electric "retail" price.

Probably the greatest chutzpah shown by Western however, was in its scrupulous insistence on paying rent of $3 million to the government for the use of two surplus plants where much of the Nike production work was done. Ordinarily the government would have simply donated the use of the plants, but Western insisted on paying. Then again, Western has to make a buck too, so it added the $3 million to its "costs." The government had to turn around and give the rent money back as a reimbursement, plus $209,000 profit on it. Nothing excessive, just about 7 percent. A reasonable profit.

It is clear that, although items are being purchased and money dispensed, this is not quite what the academicians who still theorize about competition in the marketplace have in mind. Once the winner is picked, each roll of the dice just adds to the take. There are no merciless principles of competitive efficiency at work here. This is the marketplace of power. For it is power to which the Army obligingly deferred through eight years of particularly blatant profiteering, just as it is power that may bring on the actual deployment of an ABM missile defense which is widely recognized as an extravagant put-on from any military point of view.

In a sense, one could at least begin to answer the question of why a Sentinel or Nike X ABM is going to be built by saying: AT&T has always built Nikes; it's their thing. Or, to put it differently, it is a case of a traditional corporate sphere being respected and maintained. If voice communications has been AT&T's fiefdom since the nineteenth century, then since WW II defensive missilery has been added to AT&T's turf, staked out clearly over the years.

In June 1940, a man named C. N. Hickman was working for Bell Telephone Laboratories, which was then casting around for an entree into defense work. Hickman got permission from his old teacher, Dr. Robert H. Goddard, the father of modern rocketry, to present Goddard's ideas to the government. Goddard himself had attempted this without success, but Hickman had Bell behind him.

Hickman presented the rocket proposal to Dr. F. B. Jewett, a division chairman of the newly-formed National Defense Research Committee (NDRC). Dr. Jewett was also president of Bell Labs. He was "much impressed," and asked Hickman to write up a report, which resulted in the formation of a special NDRC section for rocket research and development—a section which drew heavily upon the personnel and scientific talents of the Bell System.

By summer 1941, work had progressed to the point where contracts were awarded for such rocket work as armor piercing and plane-to-plane weapons. An official history notes that the amounts "then seemed large and now seem small." Even at that, Western Electric's initial share was a mere $10,000. In historical perspective, Western's allotment of military research contracts throughout World War II now seems trifling. It totaled only $17 million, ranking fifth, although it was surpassed only by educational institutions (MIT led all with $117 million). What was *not* trifling for Western Electric, however, was the foothold that it gained.

Toward the end of the war Western devised a control system that vastly improved the Army's anti-aircraft gun batteries. Radar detection was linked to a computer which automatically aimed the gun at the incoming target. This system, known as the M-33, was in production at Western plants by the end of the war. When German scientists, with their advanced knowledge of rocketry, fell into U.S. hands, the Army decided to replace the anti-aircraft shell with a missile that could be guided from the ground. On February 8, 1945, the Army issued Western Electric its Letter Order W-30-069-ORD-3182 for "investigation and research and development work required to produce a suitable guided missile."

Naturally AT&T has insisted piously ever since that it would prefer to devote itself exclusively to adding new improvements to the art of communication: digit dialing, walking fingers, Princess phones. In a 1964 Senate report, for instance, AT&T claimed that in 1945 "there was . . . some reluctance on the part of Western Electric to undertake work in what then appeared to be a dying defense industry. It had wanted to concentrate all of its available plant and manpower in catching up and expanding as supliers of telephones and telephone equipment for its parent company, the American Telephone & Telegraph Company." But Ma Bell just couldn't say no.

The initial missile contract in 1945 was for only $181,450 but it set a significant precedent by which AT&T, through Western Electric, established defensive guided missiles as its own permanent cut of the defense spending loot. From that time AT&T has progressed through prime contracting for four generations of Nike ground-to-air defensive missiles—the current but not necessarily the last being the Sentinel "Safeguard" system.

The lineage was headed by the Nike-Ajax anti-aircraft missile, first fired successfully at a drone B-29 bomber at the White Sands, New Mexico proving grounds in 1949. Senator Stuart Symington recently told the Senate that the Nike-Ajax brought AT&T $2.25 billion in production contracts alone. But this system was soon superseded by the Nike-Hercules, also for use against planes but equipped with a nuclear warhead to give it the capability of "destroying entire fleets of incoming aircraft" (the Pentagon's words). The Nike-Hercules has been AT&T's biggest missile bonanza to date. Only the current unlimited potential of the ABM can overshadow it.

The money rolled in with ease well into the fifties. In a period of nuclear trauma, with dog tags and "Take Cover!" drills in the schools, when the mere roar of an airplane could often induce a sense of panic, it was not hard to sell the AT&T anti-aircraft missiles. By the late fifties, however, the market for the Nike-Hercules began to be saturated; there were only so many places for them to be deployed. More importantly, the nature of the offensive threat to the U.S. was changing from incoming bombers to incoming missiles, and thus defense requirements were shifting from the anti-aircraft missile to the anti-missile missile—the ABM.

For AT&T, the replacement of the bomber threat by the missile threat meant a whole new strategic ball game, and potentially a fresh new market for defensive missiles—a new bonanza. Potentially. But there were obstacles. And although in 1956 a go-ahead had been given for preliminary research and development on a new Nike-Zeus anti-ballistic missile, ABM, it was only a meager beginning.

The main problem with the Nike-Zeus was the one that remains with the Sentinel today: it probably wouldn't work, and if it did, it would be easier for an enemy to thwart it than for us to build it. As a result, when Congress added $137 million to Eisenhower's military budget for Nike-Zeus production in 1958, he said he wouldn't spend it.

This evoked a huge pressure campaign from AT&T and friends. *Army,* the magazine of the Association of the U.S. Army, devoted almost an entire issue to Nike-Zeus. Commanders on active duty contributed ghosted articles praising the anti-missile missile. Western Electric and eight subcontractors bought full-page advertisements with maps showing where the $410 million they wanted for Nike would be spent. Senator/Major General Strom Thurmond, a director of the Army Association, insisted, "We must start production now." So did Senator Frank Carlson of Kansas (scheduled to receive $8.5 million in ABM funds); Senator Everett Jordan of North Carolina ($36 million); Representative George Miller of California ($111 million); and Representative Daniel Flood of Pennsylvania ($10 million). Representative John McCormack, then the majority leader, urged that Congress "close the gap in our missile posture, muzzle the mad-dog missile threat of the Societ Union, [and] loose the Zeus through America's magnificent production line." Eisenhower finally gave in and restored the money to the budget, but only for further research and development—not for production.

Deployment of this unlikely weapon has been similarly deferred year after year until today; meanwhile research and development money kept flowing, bringing AT&T $3.5 billion in prime contracts by the end of last year. The ABM has been kept on the fire. But now it appears that it is finally going to be deployed. The timing is clearly significant, because as far as its substantial military value goes, the system could just as well have been deployed years ago—or never.

The Cold War strategic universe of Mega-death and Counterforce always seems mad and unreal, but it is linked to the real ambitions of national policy. Even with all the waste, giveaways, misallocations and blunders of military weapons planning and procurement, strategic imperatives have provided a basic thrust and direction for the war machine's juggernaut.

The deployment of the ABM, however, seems to lack even this kind of basis in reality. It seems as if the important weapons have been built, and overkill has been stockpiled beyond comprehension. But the structure that was built up to accomplish this—the military-industrial complex—has taken on a life of its own. If there is no military need for a new manned bomber or an ABM system to be built, there is still an industrial need to build them.

Military requirements may once have provided the opportunity for corporate power to run rampant at public expense, but now that power appears to have grown into an independent self-sustaining force, with its own need for the military-industrial complex to persist and expand. The ABM then is really the ideal product: having been wrought of the purest military fantasy, it can be stretched and shaped to meet industrial needs, thin or thick, $4 billion or $40-, whatever is called for at the time. The ABM is a kind of "ever normal granary" helping to maintain military industrial economic parity.

The ABM is a revealing case because, as the military basis for costly new weapons systems declines, the fact that they are designed to serve corporate needs becomes increasingly clear. The military-industrial complex can then be seen not as a distinct and unique phenomenon, but as part of an overall pattern of government subordination to corporate interests. The military-industrial relationships in this network tend to stand out from the larger pattern simply because over the last 25 years the military has so vastly increased its capacity and eagerness to provide this service.

The case of AT&T itself is particularly interesting here because it places the military element in proper perspective without minimizing its importance. For one thing, it illuminates the basic dynamic of government-corporate relationships which underlies the specifically "military-industrial" ones. In a perfect parallel to the progression of strategic weaponry through the ABM, AT&T's commercial monopoly (which may have been born of technological necessity in a dim and shady past) has in recent years been sustained and extended only as a result of active government solicitude for AT&T's corporate power. Moreover, the story of AT&T's successful maintenance of its monopoly shows how pervasive the use of the military has become, for assistance from the military has consistently been an integral part of the government's protection even of the company's primary commercial interests, which lie clearly in the civilian mainstream of the economy.

It was one of the rare moves any branch of government has made to seriously threaten AT&T's vital interests which brought out most clearly the extent of the company's influence. The government support it was able to muster in its time of need was overwhelming. The offending party was the anti-trust branch of the Justice Department under the Truman Administration, and its target was AT&T's peculiar relationship with its subsidiary, Western Electric.

AT&T has found numerous ways over the years to overcharge its customers, despite the fact that its earnings are regulated by government. One such overcharge, now running as high as $1 billion a year, is made possible by the way the Bell System, through Western Electric, in the words of the California Public Utilities Commission: "makes a profit by taking in its own washing." The consumer, of course, Bell takes to the cleaners.

The telephone company is considered an inevitable or natural monopoly: if there were competing companies, their customers' children couldn't call each other up for dates. But it is clear that the telephone monopoly does not have to include a monopoly on the manufacture of telephone equipment. Nevertheless, the Bell System manufactures its own phones, cables, switching equipment, etc., a business whose volume is a fourth as large as the telephone business itself, and which, being unregulated, provides a higher return on investment. The Bell System's manufacturing capacity is housed in Western Electric Inc., which is in its own right the twelfth largest industrial corporation in America. It is also through Western's manufacturing capacity that Bell is able to handle such lucrative military ventures as the ABM. Government contracts make up about a sixth of Western's $4 billion in annual sales, the remainder of its business going to the other companies in the AT&T family. There is, of course, a funny money aspect in this: buying from yourself. And the result is remarkably similar to the profit pyramiding in military contracting.

The rates the Bell System charges its customers for telephone service are regulated by the various state agencies and the FCC to assure the company a certain percentage of return on its investment in telephone plant and equipment (including the phones themselves, which they own and rent), the total value being called the Rate Base. Since the plant and equipment are purchased largely from Western Electric, their "value" (and therefore the amount of Bell's profits and its customers' rates) depends on the prices paid to Western by the Bell System companies. The prices they pay include an allowance for Western's profits, so once again we are paying profits on profits. And in this case it is compounded because each increase in the Rate Base permits a 7 percent return year after year. Clearly it is in Bell's interest that Western's prices be as high as possible so as to inflate the Rate Base.

In the late 1930's, the FCC made a study of Western's pricing policies to determine how much its prices exceeded its costs and whether this margin of profit was excessive. Although, as the FCC's telephone division chief commissioner Paul A. Walker reported, "All efforts to obtain manufacturing costs of Western materials . . . [had] been thwarted," the Walker Report was able to estimate that Western could cut its prices on sales to Bell by approximately *37 percent* and still earn a yield of 6 percent on its investment. The report was released in June 1939, but nothing came of it.

Ten years later, however, one of the investigators who had worked with Walker, having moved on to the Justice Department, was able to convince Attorney General (later Supreme Court Justice) Tom C. Clark to update the findings and bring suit against AT&T. The suit, filed on January 14, 1949, asked among other things that AT&T be divested of its ownership of Western (which would be broken up into three competing concerns) and that Bell System companies be required to buy their equipment on the basis of competitive bidding.

AT&T filed an answer conceding little more than its involvement in the telephone business. The Justice Department made no further moves for nearly two and a half years. When, in August of 1951, they asked AT&T to produce documents relating to more than 100 points raised by the suit, it began to look as if they might go ahead with the case after all.

Bell, however, was not about to have such sensitive, private matters as its relations with Western Electric come out in court. Significantly, they went straight to the Defense Department to get support for an indefinite postponement of the case. Dr. M. J. Kelly, president of Bell Laboratories, appealed directly to then Secretary of Defense Robert A. Lovett. His argument was a curious one: not that the loss of Western would be a disaster, but that the *mere trial* of the case would require key Bell officials to turn their attention away from military projects essential to the conduct of the Korean War, thus hampering the war effort. A bit far-fetched perhaps, but Lovett (who is a partner in the investment house of Brown Bros. Harriman, one of the largest AT&T stockholders) found it persuasive. He had his staff draft a letter to the Justice Department adopting the AT&T position. Acting Attorney General Philip Perlman rejected the appeal, noting that Bell did have lawyers who could go to court, leaving its key personnel free for war projects. Nevertheless, with AT&T working through the agreeable Secretary of Defense, the case was still pending by the time the Republicans took over after the 1952 elections. AT&T lobbyists wrote a memorandum on the case for Lovett, and he signed it (in the words of a Bell lawyer) in "substantially the same form" as it was submitted and passed it on to his successor.

The new Defense Secretary, former General Motors chief Charles Wilson, proved as accommodating as Lovett had been. Bell's president, Dr. Kelly, went to see him and later drafted a memorandum which, with two minor changes, was signed by Wilson and sent on to the Justice Department. As Representative Emmanuel Celler later commented, Dr. Kelly "became a sort of ghostwriter for the Department of Defense."

Wilson sent his letter on July 10, 1953, but by this time AT&T had already received some sympathetic encouragement from the Justice Department itself—in fact from the Attorney General, Herbert Brownell. To Brownell, it seems, the case was more an embarrassment than anything else.

He expressed this very clearly in a conversation with AT&T vice president and general counsel, T. Brooke Price, at the Greenbriar Hotel in White Sulphur Springs, West Virginia, where golf foursomes with combined assets of a billion dollars are not uncommon. Price gives a lucid account of his discussion with Brownell in a memorandum later obtained from AT&T files by congressional investigators.

> I had brought with me the memorandum we had recently filed . . . for dismissal of the case. . . He told me he had read it, was quite familiar with it, and considered it an excellent piece of work.
>
> I then made a number of statements about the injury the case threatened to our efficiency and progress as a communications company and to our contribution to the national defense. . . .
>
> He reflected for a moment and said in substance that a way ought to be found to get rid of the case. He asked me whether, if we reviewed our practices, we would be able to find things we are doing which were once considered entirely legal, but might now be in violation of the antitrust laws or questionable in that respect . . . he thought we could readily find practices that we might agree to have enjoined with no real injury to our business.
>
> As I got up to go he walked down the steps with me and repeated his statement that it was important to get this case disposed of. He said the President would understand this also and that if a settlement was worked out he could get the President's approval in five minutes.

The government literally pleaded with Bell to offer up some harmless business dealings which it could prohibit with Bell's agreement, but Bell was not going to let them off so easily. They demanded complete dismissal of the case.

Brownell's next move was to withdraw from the case the quixotic antitrust attorneys in his department who had been tactlessly pressing on with it. He replaced them with one Edwarde A. Foote, who had never tried an antitrust case before (this was of course one of the biggest on record).

Foote shared Brownell's dislike for such legal formalities as trying a case on its merits in court. Bell's Price reported that Foote "indicated to us he would like a more informal down to earth contact with this case and generally an opportunity to talk it out in an informal way." So Foote invited Price to dinner and there told him he thought the government's case weak and the idea of bringing it to trial "silly" (to his colleagues Foote indicated that it was "unwise, even evil"). He outlined the various debates and strategies brewing in his department over the case. He told Price these things, as he later explained, because "I thought he might be interested."

As final insurance, the FCC sent to the Justice Department a report which (after being carefully edited) implied that the regulatory agencies had sufficient powers, without court action, to deal with questions of Western's prices and profits and their effect on affiliated companies.

With this FCC opinion in hand, the Justice Department moved ahead on a consent decree. To make sure it was just right, seven of the nine points were written by Bell lawyers—at Foote's request. The three men in the department most intimately involved in preparing the case—Victor Kramer, Walter D. Murphy, and W. D. Kilgore Jr.—filed written memoranda of dissent.

And so, on January 12, 1956, AT&T and the surviving government lawyers trooped into the U.S. District Court in Newark and presented their decree to Judge Thomas F. Meany. After a short discussion in chambers, he mounted the bench and approved it.

Justice Department spokesmen called it "miraculous" and a "major victory" for the government.

An AT&T executive's note in the margin of one copy of the decree sums it up more accurately: "It's only window dressing." Fredrick R. Kappel, then president of Western Electric and later head of AT&T, in an outline for a talk to Western officials on the decree, had to admonish: "Use discretion in passing along. Don't brag about having won victory or getting everything we wanted. . . . Antitrust suit disposed of, but still have politicians, etc. to think of."

AT&T had good reason for smug satisfaction. The military and civilian branches of government had joined ranks behind it with inspiring solidarity to protect its monopoly. But within a few years the great corporation began to face an even more basic threat to its monopoly than the Western case—this one technological rather than legal. It is interesting, moreover, that the technological threat was primarily a military development, for if the military were really tied to its own special, independent realm of corporate power, AT&T would have been in very serious trouble indeed.

In 1961, an official of billionaire Howard Hughes' Hughes Aircraft Company announced that if a communications satellite system then on their drawing boards were authorized by the government, station-to-station telephone calls could be placed to any spot on earth for just a dime. It was a brash proposal by any measure, but it was a time of enthusiasm. In the preceding three years the Army and Air Force had successfully tested the precursors of Early-Bird (SCORE, ECHO, and COURIER), sending various wise words from President Eisenhower to the wondering listeners of Europe. It seemed as if the aerospace companies could do anything, even move into the phone business and take on the power of AT&T.

The Hughes proposal summed up the two dangers for Bell in the new technology of satellite communications. The technology was revolutionary, and Bell did not control it. It was a product of military research and development, and aerospace companies like Hughes and Lockheed, which were closely associated with the military-industrial complex, seemed to be in on the ground floor.

The satellite threat was fundamental to AT&T because the company's whole corporate position was based on its monopoly control of basic voice communications technology. The Western divestiture would have removed a portion of this control from Bell's domain, but the heartland would have remained secure. No one was about to come along and plunk down $40 billion to build a competing telephone network—a situation similar to that of the railroads, where the scale of resources necessary to lay down the networks of roadbeds and rails precludes a competing line from moving in alongside. But the railroads fell before competition from the air, and now a new airborne technology seemed about to make obsolete the terrestrial network of telephone lines as well.

When communications satellites got their real start in the early sixties, there were just a few hundred telephone circuits—cable and microwave—across the North Atlantic. Satellite capacity has already far surpassed that. An AT&T projection envisions a satellite system with 83,000 voice circuits by 1976, and Bell spokesmen speak of *ten million* circuits in the future. The unit cost of these circuits is almost indefinitely reducible, and it does not increase with distance. The circuits do not replace the local lines and switching apparatus that make up local phone systems, but they may well replace the "Long Lines" system that connects the local systems together and routes calls between them. It is this integrated long-distance network on a national and international scale that justifies the existence of one huge national phone company. Thus if the new technology were to fall into hostile competitive hands, the Bell System's very raison d'être would be threatened.

AT&T's situation was different in at least one basic respect from that which' the railroads faced with the advent of the airplane. Here the new technology was not up for grabs; it was in the hands of the government, to be dispensed at its discretion. And AT&T could hope that the government's criterion, like Alexander's, would be: "to the strongest."

AT&T's first tactic on satellites was to try to just walk in and pick up all the marbles. In December 1959, they made an offer to NASA administrator James E. Webb to take satellite communications off his hands, exclusively and permanently. He turned them down, and AT&T never has achieved that ultimate wish. To measure how much they have achieved, however, one must consider the range of disasters that were then in view. First there was the possibility that the government, having invested about $25 billion in the technology that put the satellites up, would operate them itself in the public interest—an idea the Wall Street *Journal* later denounced as "Socialism in the Sky." But Ike would have none of it, and in his farewell address he even took time out from warning against the military-industrial complex to call for private development of the satellites. Kennedy took the same line, though Harry Truman commented with a simple partisanship, "I don't think the President understands the bill. The damned Republicans and some Democrats are trying to give away public property. The public spent $25 or $30 billion developing satellites, and the communications system ought to be publicly owned. The Republicans will give away everything if you don't watch them." (As it developed, the giveaway was completely bipartisan.)

AT&T was inclined to forget the public billions spent to put the satellites up, as when they claimed to have achieved the 1962 Telstar experiment entirely on their own, saying in national advertisements, "Bell System microwave-in-the-sky satellite is the latest American triumph in communications arising from telephone research." This pitch was not only aimed at discouraging notions of public ownership, but also designed to deal with a more menacing possibility. For it promoted Bell's theme that communications satellites were a communications development rather than a satellite or space development. The aerospace firms, of course, worked hard to emphasize the other side of the matter. The fact is that once there were satellites, the communications part was relatively simple.

Meanwhile Bell was contending that the satellites were "just another variety of telephone pole" and should be deemed part of the telephone business, reserved to them by law—which was like saying that jetliners are another kind of Pullman coach and should be turned over to the railroads. But on this point turned the question of who would control this vast business and who would be secondary in it: would the aerospace companies merely sell their rockets and satellites to the communications industry, or would the communications people lease circuits from satellites operated by the aerospace industry? In the end, military-industrial complex or not, aerospace lost hands down.

First of all AT&T, its request to take over the whole project having been turned down by NASA, went to friendlier territory and got the FCC to license it to put up the first privately owned communications satellite. Meanwhile NASA, which had been awarding to aerospace firms contracts that encroached ever more deeply into communications, was itself brought into line. On February 28, 1961, NASA signed a "memorandum of understanding" restricting itself to the "technological phase" of space communications and leaving "implementation and utilization" policy to the FCC—thus defining the new field as a communications as opposed to an aerospace enterprise.

This still left a welter of communications industry interests (ITT, RCA etc.), other economic forces (like TV broadcasters who lease long-distance circuits), and political and public relations considerations, all of which precluded any straight giveaway to AT&T. The vehicle that was finally adopted to accommodate all these factors was the congressionally-created, private, profit-making Communications Satellite Corporation, COMSAT, which was designated as the sole owner and operator of communications satellites. The COMSAT bill passed the Senate over a filibuster by ten liberal senators—the first filibuster voted to a close in the Senate since 1927.

COMSAT was to be owned half by communications companies and half by publicly issued stock. AT&T promptly bought up 58 percent of the communication carriers stock, and holds three seats on the 15-member board. But its real influence is greater than mere arithmetic would indicate. On the one hand COMSAT remains under the jurisdiction of the FCC, which tends to be careful of AT&T's vital interests; on the other, there is the company's great corporate weight, both in general and as by far the largest stockholder. So, for example, COMSAT's first chairman, James McCormick, even when opposing AT&T on a certain question, noted, "As a practical matter, there is no way to get a domestic system going without the willing cooperation of AT&T."

Meanwhile Hughes Aircraft has seen the basic satellite conception which it had pushed all along, and which AT&T had fought against on "technical grounds," accepted by AT&T and COMSAT. But Hughes' vindication is mainly spiritual. As Senator Wayne Morse prophesied during the Senate COMSAT debate: "AT&T wants these vested legal rights now, through this bill. Then Howard Hughes can develop his high altitude satellite, but he will have to deal with the corporation by way of the legal instrument which is created by the bill."

Technologically, the potential of the communications satellite has surpassed all early expectations. Commercial development, however, has been stymied for several years by the FCC, which is searching for ways to establish the new technology with minimum damage to the established communications interests, AT&T foremost. Of course this is also likely to mean minimum benefit to the public from the full potential opened up by the satellites. *Fortune* magazine, for instance, in 1967 wrote of the satellite as the "Cinderalla in the Sky" with the sub-head: "Satellite to home broadcasting is technologically feasible now, but rich relatives would just as soon keep it from getting a fair test."

But, while AT&T continues to lay expensive new underwater cables which will soon be obsolete and which consumers will pay for anyway, they have no illusions of standing in the way of progress forever. The company simply means to get as big a piece of the action as possible. And they have already managed to take a technology that could have created chaos in their business, fragmenting and displacing it (a technology that they had little hand in developing, the property of the military-industrial aerospace companies), and by the grace of government they have its potential benefits divided largely between themselves and a corporate creation of which they are the principal owner. And thus the great hounds of the military-industrial complex were brought to heel.

Once again AT&T retained its position in the marketplace of goods and services by virtue of its preeminence in the marketplace of power. But AT&T is not unique in this respect, and focusing on it does not imply that such unofficial "plural monopolies" as exist in steel or autos or elsewhere throughout the economy are substantially more responsive to or constrained by the public interest. Indeed they can fix prices and determine quality with greater arrogance and impunity than AT&T, since not even the *forms* of regulation hem them in. An indictment of AT&T does not acquit them any more than the ABM makes hydrogen bombs and germ warfare sane and healthful. Rather, both AT&T and the ABM—and, in a sense, the whole military-industrial complex—are the extreme, limiting cases that can epitomize a larger reality. They are the pure idols of the marketplace of power which operates without any regard for human benefit or need.

17. RETIRED HIGH-RANKING MILITARY OFFICERS

William Proxmire

During the late 1960s, William Proxmire of Wisconsin came forward as one of the U. S. Senate's leading opponents of the military-industrial complex. Although accepting most of the rationale for a strong military and munitions industry, Proxmire used his position as chairman of the Joint Economic Committee's Subcommittee on Economy in Government to investigate and publicize some of the grosser manifestations of the complex's operations, such as cost-overrides, publicity campaigns on behalf of weapons systems, and inefficient or defective weapons. One of his most sensational revelations, in the spring of 1969, was that over 2,000 retired military officers were employed by the leading 100 defense contractors.

Mr. Proxmire. Mr. President, recently I asked the Department of Defense for a list of certain high-ranking retired military officers employed by the 100 companies who had the largest volume of military prime contracts. I did this in connection with the hearings of the Subcommittee on Economy in Government of the Joint Economic Committee.

Source: Speech by Senator William Proxmire, "Over 2,000 Retired High-Ranking Military Officers Now Employed by 100 Largest Military Contractors," *Congressional Record,* 91st Cong., 1st sess., March 24, 1969.

In fiscal year 1968 these 100 companies held 67.4 percent of the $38.8 billion of prime military contracts, or $26.2 billion.

The Defense Department has now supplied to me the list of high-ranking military officers who work for these 100 companies. They include the subsidiaries. In one case, that of the 35th ranking contractor, four firms were involved in a joint venture.

I asked only for the names of those retired military officers of the rank of Army, Air Force, Marine Corps colonel or Navy captain and above. Excluded are all officers below those ranks. I asked for only retired regular officers and not reserve officers, although in a very few cases the reserve officers may be included.

TOP 100 COMPANIES EMPLOY OVER 2,000 RETIRED OFFICERS

The facts are that as of February, 1969, some 2,072 retired military officers of the rank of colonel or Navy captain and above were employed by the 100 contractors who reported. This is an average of almost 22 per firm. I shall ask to have printed in the RECORD as exhibit A of my statement a list of the 100 companies, ranked according to the dollar volume of their prime military contracts, and the number of high ranking retired officers they employ.

TEN COMPANIES EMPLOY OVER 1,000

The 10 companies with the largest number on their payrolls employed 1,065 retired officers. This is an average of 106 per firm. These 10 companies employed over half the total number of high-ranking former officers employed by all the top 100 defense contractors. These companies, listed according to the number of retired officers employed by them are given in Table 17.1, as follows:

Table 17.1   TEN MILITARY PRIME CONTRACTORS EMPLOYING LARGEST NUMBER OF HIGH-RANKING RETIRED MILITARY OFFICERS, AND VALUE OF THEIR FISCAL YEAR 1968 CONTRACTS

Company and rank by number of high-ranking retired officers employed	Number employed, Feb. 1, 1969	Net dollar value of defense contracts, fiscal year 1958
1. Lockheed Aircraft Corp.	210	$1,870,000,000
2. Boeing Co.	169	762,000,000
3. McDonnell Douglas Corp.	141	1,101,000,000
4. General Dynamics	113	2,239,000,000
5. North American Rockwell Corp.	104	669,000,000
6. General Electric Co.	89	1,489,000,000
7. Ling Temco Vought, Inc.	69	758,000,000
8. Westinghouse Electric Corp.	59	251,000,000
9. TRW, Inc.	56	127,000,000
10. Hughes Aircraft Co.	55	286,000,000
	1,065	9,552,000,000

KEY ABM CONTRACTORS EMPLOY 22 PERCENT OF TOTAL

Among the major defense contractors involved in producing the key components of the anti-ballistic-missile system—ABM—nine of them employ 465 retired officers. This is an average of 51 each.

In 1968 they held contracts valued at $5.78 billion and, of course, will receive many billions more if the ABM system is deployed. These companies and the number of retired officers they employ are given in Table 17.2, as follows:

Table 17.2 MAJOR PRIME CONTRACTORS INVOLVED IN ABM
SYSTEM AND NUMBER OF HIGH-RANKING
RETIRED MILITARY OFFICERS EMPLOYED
BY THEM

1. McConnell Douglas	141
2. General Electric	89
3. Hughes Aircraft	55
4. Martin Marietta	40
5. Raytheon	37
6. Sperry Rand	36
7. RCA	35
8. AVCO	23
9. A.T. & T.	9
Total	465

COMPARISON OF 1969 WITH 1959

Mr. President, almost 10 years ago in connection with hearings before the Senate Finance Committee on the extension of the Renegotiation Act, former Senator Paul H. Douglas asked for and received a similar list from the Pentagon. We can, therefore, make comparisons over a decade as to what has happened with respect to the employment of high-ranking retired military officers by the top 100 defense contractors.

In 1959, the total number employed was only 721—88 of 100 companies reporting—or an average of slightly more than eight per company.

In 1969 the 100 largest defense contractors—95 of the 100 companies reporting—employed 2,072 former high military officers, or an average of almost 22 per company.

In 1959 the 10 companies with the highest number of former officers employed 372 of them.

In 1969 the top 10 had 1,065, or about three times as many.

Some 43 companies which reported were on both the 1959 and 1969 list of the top 100 largest contractors. There were several more who were on the list in both years but failed to report in one or the other year. But we can compare the 43 companies. These 43 companies employed 588 high ranking former officers in 1959. In 1969 these same companies employed 1,642 retired high-ranking officers.

In each case where a comparison can be made; namely, in the total number of former high-ranking officers employed by the top 100 contractors, the top 10 contractors employing the largest number, and the number employed by firms reporting in both 1959 and 1969, the number employed has tripled. It has increased threefold.

Roughly three times the number of retired high-ranking military officers are employed by the top 100 companies in 1969 as compared with 1959.

SIGNIFICANCE

What is the significance of this situation? What does it mean and what are some of its implications?

First of all, it bears out the statement I made on March 10 when I spoke on the "blank check for the military," that the warning by former President Eisenhower against the danger of "unwarranted influence, whether sought or unsought, by the military-industrial complex," is not just some future danger.

That danger is here. Whether sought or unsought there is today unwarranted influence by the military-industrial complex which results in excessive costs, burgeoning military budgets, and scandalous performances. The danger has long since materialized. The 2,072 retired high-ranking officers employed by the top 100 military contractors is one major facet of this influence.

NO CONSPIRACY OR WRONGDOING

Second, I do not claim nor even suggest that any conspiracy exists between the military and the 100 largest defense contractors. I do not believe in the conspiracy theory of history. I charge no general wrongdoing on the part of either group.

In the past many of the officers have performed valiant and even heroic service on behalf of the United States. The country is indeed grateful to them for their past service and for their patriotic endeavors.

We should eschew even the slightest suggestion of any conspiracy between the Pentagon, on the one hand, and the companies who hire former employees, on the other. There is not a scintilla of evidence that it exists.

COMMUNITY OF INTEREST

But what can be said, and should properly be said, is that there is a continuing community of interest between the military, on the one hand, and these industries on the other.

What we have here is almost a classic example of how the military-industrial complex works.

It is not a question of wrongdoing. It is a question of what can be called the "old boy network" or the "old school tie."

This is a most dangerous and shocking situation. It indicates the increasing influence of the big contractors with the military and the military with the big contractors. It shows an intensification of the problem and the growing community of interest which exists between the two. It makes it imperative that new weapon systems receive the most critical review and that defense contracts be examined in microscopic detail.

I am alarmed about this trend not because I question the integrity or the good will of the retired officers who have found employment with military contractors but because I believe that the trend itself represents a distinct threat to the public interest.

DANGERS WHEN COUPLED WITH NEGOTIATED CONTRACTS

Third, this matter is particularly dangerous in a situation where only 11.5 percent of military contracts are awarded on a formally advertised competitive bid basis. It lends itself to major abuse when almost 90 percent of all military contracts are negotiated, and where a very high proportion of them are negotiated with only one, or one or two, contractors.

Former high-ranking military officers have an entree to the Pentagon that others do not have. I am not charging that is necessarily wrong. I am saying that it is true.

Former high-ranking officers have personal friendships with those still at the Pentagon which most people do not have. Again, I charge no specific wrongdoing. But it is a fact.

In some cases former officers may even negotiate contracts with their former fellow officers. Or they may be involved in developing plans and specifications, making proposals, drawing up blueprints, or taking part in the planning process or proposing prospective weapon systems. And they may be doing this in cooperation with their former fellow officers with whom they served with and by whom, in some cases, even promoted.

With such a high proportion of negotiated contracts there is a great danger of abuse.

In addition, there is the subtle or unconscious temptation to the officer still on active duty. After all, he can see that over 2,000 of his fellow officers work for the big companies. How hard a bargain does he drive with them when he is 1 or 2 years away from retirement?

This danger does not come from corruption. Except in rare circumstances this is no more prevalent among military officers than among those with comparable civilian responsibilities.

MUTUAL INTERESTS—UNCRITICAL VIEWS

The danger to the public interest is that these firms and the former officers they employ have a community of interest with the military itself. They hold a narrow view of public priorities based on self-interest. They have a largely uncritical view of military spending.

As a group they have what has been termed "tunnelvision." But in this case their narrow training can be fortified by self-interest. In too many cases they may see only military answers to exceedingly complex diplomatic and political problems. A military response, or the ability to make one, may seem to them to be the most appropriate answer to every international threat.

SUMMARY

When the bulk of the budget goes for military purposes; when 100 companies get 67 percent of the defense contract dollars; when cost overruns are routine and prime military weapon system contracts normally exceed their estimates by 100 to 200 percent; when these contracts are let by negotiation and not by competitive bidding; and when the top contractors have over 2,000 retired high-ranking military officers on their payrolls; there are very real questions as to how critically these matters are reviewed and how well the public interest is served.

That, Mr. President, is the point. That is why I think it important that there be public disclosure of these facts so that the American public can know more about the community of interests involved in our huge defense contract spending.

I ask unanimous consent that a list of the 100 largest defense contractors and the number of high-ranking officers they employed in early 1969 be printed in the RECORD as exhibit A;

That a similar list of the 100 largest military contractors and the number of high-ranking former officers they employed in 1959 be printed in the *RECORD* as exhibit B;

That a list of the 100 largest military contractors for fiscal year 1968, and the dollar value and percent of military contracts each held, be printed as exhibit C; and

That a list of the names of the former high-ranking officers employed by the 100 largest defense contractors in February 1969 be printed as exhibit D.

There being no objection, the exhibits were ordered to be printed in the *RECORD* as follows:

Exhibit A. A LIST OF THE 100 LARGEST COMPANIES RANKED BY 1968 VALUE OF PRIME MILITARY CONTRACTS AND NUMBER OF RETIRED COLONELS OR NAVY CAPTAINS AND ABOVE EMPLOYED BY THEM, FEBRUARY 1969

1. General Dynamics Corp.	113
2. Lockheed Aircraft Corp.	210
3. General Electric Co.	89
4. United Aircraft Corp.	48
5. McDonnell Douglas Corp.	141
6. American Telephone & Telegraph	9
7. Boeing Corp.	169
8. Ling-Temco-Vought, Inc.	69
9. North American Rockwell Corp.	104
10. General Motors Corp.	17
11. Grumman Aircraft Engineering Corp.	31
12. AVCO Corp.	23
13. Textron, Inc.	28

14. Litton Industries, Inc.	49
15. Raytheon Co.	37
16. Sperry Rand Corp.	36
17. Martin Marietta Corp.	40
18. Kaiser Industries Corp.	11
19. Ford Motor Co.	43
20. Honeywell, Inc.	26
21. Olin Mathieson Chemical Corp.	3
22. Northrop Corp.	48
23. Ryan Aeronautical Co.	25
24. Hughes Aircraft Co.	55
25. Standard Oil of New Jersey	2
26. Radio Corp. of America	35
27. Westinghouse Electric Corp.	59
28. General Tire & Rubber Co.	32
29. Int'l Telephone & Telegraph Corp	
30. IBM	35
31. Bendix Corp	25
32. Pan American World Airways	24
33. FMC Corp	6
34. Newport News Shipbuilding	6
35. Raymond/Morrison, etc.[1]	6
36. Signal Companies, Inc. (The)	9
37. Hercules, Inc.	13
38. Du Pont, E. I. de Nemours & Co.	3
39. Texas Instruments, Inc.	7
40. Day & Zimmerman, Inc.	1
41. General Telephone & Electronics Corp.	35
42. Uniroyal, Inc.	6
43. Chrysler Corp.	11
44. Standard Oil of California	6
45. Norris Industries	2
46. Texaco, Inc.	4
47. Collins Radio Co.	3
48. Goodyear Tire & Rubber Co.	6
49. Asiatic Petroleum Corp.	0
50. Sanders Associates, Inc.	17
51. Mobil Oil Corp	
52. TRW, Inc.	56
53. Mason & Hanger Silas Mason	5
54. Massachusetts Institute of Technology	5
55. Magnavox Co.	3
56. Fairchild Hiller Corp	7
57. Pacific Architects & Engineering	16
58. Thiokol Chemical Corp.	3
59. Eastman Kodak Co.	15
60. United States Steel Corp.	
61. American Machine & Foundry	7
62. Chamberlain Corp.	3
63. General Precision Equipment	23
64. Lear Siegler Inc.	4
65. Harvey Aluminum, Inc.	4
66. National Presto Industrial Inc.	0
67. Teledyne, Inc.	8
68. City Investing Co.	4
69. Colt Industries, Inc.	4
70. Western Union Telegraph Co.	5
71. American Manufacturing Co. of Texas	0
72. Curtiss Wright Corp.	1
73. White Motor Co.	6
74. Aerospace Corp.	0

75. Cessna Aircraft Co.	0
76. Emerson Electric Co.	3
77. Seatrain Lines, Inc.	4
78. Gulf Oil Corp.	1
79. Condec Corp.	1
80. Motorola, Inc.	3
81. Continental Air Lines, Inc.	4
82. Federal Cartridge Corp.	1
83. Hughes Tool Co.	13
84. Vitro Corp. of America	25
85. Johns Hopkins Univ	
86. Control Data Corp.	14
87. Lykes Corp.	0
88. McLean Industries, Inc.	2
89. Aerodex, Inc.	5
90. Susquehanna Corp.	7
91. Sverdrup & Parcel Assoc., Inc.	9
92. States Marine Lines Inc	0
93. Hazeltine Corp.	7
94. Atlas Chemical Indus., Inc.	0
95. Vinnell Corp	0
96. Harris-Intertype Corp.	4
97. World Airways, Inc	4
98. International Harvester Co.	6
99. Automatic Sprinkler Corp.	3
100. Smith Investment Co.	0
Total	2,072

[1]Raymond Int'l. Inc.; Morrison-Knudsen Co., Inc.; Brown & Root, Inc.; and J A. Jones Construction Co.

Exhibit B. THE 100 LARGEST COMPANIES RANKED BY 1958 VALUE OF PRIME MILITARY CONTRACTS AND NUMBER OF RETIRED COLONELS OR NAVY CAPTAINS AND ABOVE EMPLOYED BY THEM, JUNE 1959

1. American Bosch Arma Corp.	None
2. American Telephone & Telegraph Co.	1
3. Asiatic Petroleum Corp.	None
4. Avco Corp.	4
5. Bath Iron Works Corp.	2
6. Beech Aircraft	Not available
7. Bell Aircraft Corp.	3
8. Bendix Aviation Corp.	14
9. Bethlehem Steel Co.	8
10. Blue Cross Association	None
11. Boeing Airplane Co.	30
12. Brown-Raymond-Walsh	None
13. California Institute of Technology	None
14. Cessna Aircraft Co.	1
15. Chance Vought Aircraft Inc.	6
16. Chrysler Corp.	11
17. Cities Service Co.	4
18. Collins Radio Co.	5
19. Continental Motors Corp.	2
20. Continental Oil Co.	2
21. Curtiss-Wright Corp.	4
22. Defoe Shipbuilding Co.	None
23. Douglas Aircraft Co. Inc.	15
24. E. I. du Pont de Nemours & Co.	1
25. Eastman Kodak Co.	12
26. Fairchild Engine & Airplane Corp.	7

27. Fairbanks Whitney Corp	4
28. Firestone Tire & Rubber Corp.	3
29. Food Machinery & Chemical Corp.	6
30. Ford Motor Co.	5
31. The Garrett Corp.	2
32. General Dynamics Corp.	54
33. General Electric Co.	35
34. General Motors	Survey being taken
35. General Precision Equipment Corp.	Not available
36. General Tire & Rubber Co.	28
37. Gilfillan Brothers, Inc.	None
38. B. F. Goodrich Co.	1
39. Goodyear Tire & Rubber Co.	2
40. Greenland Contractors	Not available
41. Grumman Aircraft Engineering Corp.	1
42. Hayes Aircraft Corp.	3
43. Joshua Hendy Corp.	None
44. Hercules Powder Co. Inc.	1
45. Hughes Aircraft Co.	7
46. International Business Machine Corp.	3
47. International Telephone & Telegraph Corp.	24
48. The Johns Hopkins University	16
49. The Kaman Aircraft Corp.	1
50. Peter Kiewit Sons Co.	1
51. Lear, Inc.	2
52. Lockheed Aircraft Corp.	60
53. Marine Transport Lines, Inc.	1
54. Marquardt Aircraft Co.	2
55. The Martin Co.	15
56. Massachusetts Institute of Technology	Not available
57. Mathiasen's Tanker Industries, Inc.	1
58. McDonnell Aircraft Corp.	4
59. Minneapolis Honeywell Regulator Co.	None
60. Motorola, Inc.	Not available
61. Newport News Shipbuilding and Dry Dock Co.	6
62. North American Aviation, Inc.	27
63. Northrop Aircraft, Inc.	16
64. Olin Mathieson Chemical Corp.	6
65. Oman-Farnsworth-Wright	None
66. Morrison-Knudsen Co., Inc.	1
67. Pan American World Airways, Inc.	Not available
68. Philco Corp.	17
69. Radio Corp. of America	39
70. The Rand Corp.	14
71. Raytheon Mfg. Co.	17
72. Republic Aviation Corp.	9
73. Richfield Oil Corp.	4
74. Ryan Aeronautics Co.	9
75. Shell Oil Corp.	None
76. Sinclair Oil Corp.	1
77. Socony Mobil Oil Co.	1
78. Sperry Rand Corp.	(Gen. Douglas MacArthur not included) 12
79. Standard Oil Company of California	Not available
80. Standard Oil Company of Indiana	Not available

81.	Standard Oil of New Jersey	1
82.	States Marine Corp.	None
83.	Sundstrand Machine Tool Co.	Not available
84.	Sunray Mid-Continent Oil Co.	None
85.	Sylvania Electric Products, Inc.	6
86.	Temco Aircraft Corp.	6
87.	Texaco, Inc.	None
88.	Thikol Chemical Corp.	8
89.	Thompson Ramo Wooldridge, Inc.	6
90.	Tidewater Oil Co.	3
91.	Tishman (Paul) Company, Inc.	None
92.	Todd Shipyards Co.	2
93.	Union Carbide Corp.	4
94.	Union Oil Company of California	None
95.	United States Lines Co.	None
96.	United Aircraft Corp.	15
97.	Westinghouse Air Brake Co.	42
98.	Westinghouse Electric Corp.	33
99.	The White Motor Co.	None
100.	System Development Corp.	2
	Total:	721

Source: *Congressional Record*, June 17, 1959, pp. 11044-11045. Statement by former Senator Paul H. Douglas.

"It's The Multiple Head Re-Entry Principle"

18. CIVILIAN COMPLEX

Barry Goldwater

Another Senator, Barry Goldwater of Arizona, was quick to answer Senator Proxmire and to comment on the whole question of whether there is a military-industrial complex in America and what its consequences might be. Goldwater, who is also a Reserve Air Force General and unsuccessful Republican Presidential candidate (1964), has remained one of the staunchest defenders of the military and their corporate suppliers.

Mr. President:

As a member of the Senate Armed Services Committee and as a member of the Senate Preparedness Subcommittee, I am greatly interested in the growing preoccupation of some groups and individuals these days with the so-called military-industrial complex in the United States. Indeed, if I were a psychologist, I might be tempted to the conclusion that the left wing in American politics has developed a "complex over a complex."

Judging from the view expressed by many of our public officials and commentators, the so-called military-industrial complex would seem to be responsible for almost all of the world's evils. Certainly a determined effort is under way to place at its doorstep almost full responsibility for the unfortunate war in Vietnam and the high cost of American defense.

Source: Senator Barry Goldwater, "Civilian Complex," Remarks by Senator Barry Goldwater of Arizona on the Senate Floor, April 15, 1969.

We further find great attention being paid to the number of former military officers who have gone to work for defense-related industry. It has been shown with considerable flourish and head-shaking that some 2,000 former members of the United States Armed Services now are employed by companies that do business with the Defense Department. This revelation seemed to imply some kind of an unholy but non-specific alliance on the part of industry and one-time military officers to cheat and defraud the American taxpayer.

In presenting information on former military men employed by defense industries to the Senate on March 24, the gentleman from Wisconsin, Senator Proxmire, was careful to say that he was not charging any general wrongdoing on anybody's part and that he had found no evidence that any conspiracy exists. He seemed most concerned about a condition he described as "the old school tie" and the fact that many former high-ranking officers working in defense industries still retain personal friendships with some men still in the services. He accurately observed that "there is a continuing community of interest between the military, on one hand, and these industries on the other."

Now, Mr. President, I don't see how anyone could deny either the fact that friendships continue or that a community of interest exists between the military and the people who supply them with the tools of their trade.

Consequently, I am quite mystified to understand why this situation strikes the gentleman from Wisconsin as—and I use his exact words—"most dangerous and shocking." I am sure that the gentleman would agree that former members of Congress now working for industries that do business with the United States Government still retain friendships with present members of the House and Senate. I am also sure that he would agree that former government officials now employed by companies doing business with the government retain "old school tie" relationships with friends they made while in the government and with friends still working in the government. This situation even exists, I believe, with some officials who once worked for government regulatory agencies and now are employed by industries which are being regulated. But apparently the critics of the military-industrial complex do not find situations like this shocking or dangerous.

Mr. President, perhaps the "old school tie" is more binding if it happens to be the Khaki-colored type worn by military men. Critics of the military seem to think so.

And in this connection I would like to point out that the figure of 2,000-plus retired military officers working for defense-related industries is impressive only when it is permitted to stand by itself and without the proper explanation. These 2,000 officers are employed by 100 of the largest corporations in the world. They are employed by industries which do many billions of dollars worth of business every year. And these 2,000 former military men are only a very small fraction of the tens of thousands of employees who work for these 100 industries. What's more, they represent only a small portion of the military officers who have been retired. I am informed by the Pentagon that the number of former military officers recieving retired pay as of June, 1968 totaled 232,892. I also discovered that since the end of World War II some 36,800 officers in the highest grades (colonels and above) have been retired. A total of 21,484 were retired between the years 1961-1968.

Mr. President, I believe these figures make it amply clear that high-ranking military officers are not rushing into retirement at the beckoning of defense contractors.

Be that as it may, I believe it is long past time when these questions relating fundamentally to the defense of this nation should be placed in their proper perspective. Let us take the military-industrial complex and examine it closely. What it amounts to is that we have a big military establishment, and we have a big industrial plant which helps to supply that establishment. This apparently constitutes a "complex." If so, I certainly can find nothing to criticize but much to be thankful for in its existence. Ask yourselves, for example, why we have a large, expensive military establishment and why we have a large and capable defense industry. The answer is simply this: We have huge worldwide responsibilities. We face tremendous worldwide challenges. In short, we urgently require both a big defense establishment and a big industrial capacity. Both are essential to our safety and to the preservation of freedom in a world fraught with totalitarian aggression.

Merely because our huge responsibilities necessitate the existence of a military-industrial complex does not automatically make that complex something we must fear or feel ashamed of. You might consider where we would be in any negotiations which might be entered into with the Soviet Union if we did not have a big military backed by a big industrial complex to support our arguments. You might wonder how we could possibly pretend to be interested in the freedom of smaller nations if the only military-industrial complex in the world was possessed by Communist Russia or Communist China.

Mr. President, in many respects I am reminded of the problem which confronted our nation in the early days of World War II. The madman Hitler was running rampant. Freedom was being trampled throughout all of Europe. Suddenly the United States found itself forced to fill the role of the "arsenal of democracy." This nation had to start from scratch and finally out-produce the combined efforts of the Axis powers. And we had to do it quickly. The very existence of freedom in the world as we knew it in the early 1940s depended on it. And how did we perform this miracle? Well, I'll tell you that we performed it with the help of an industrial giant called an integrated steel industry. Although this industry and others like it performed miracles of production at a time when the chips were down all over the world, it still was the subject of long and harassing investigation after the war because of its "bigness." Incredible as it seems, the very size of an industry which enabled us to defeat the Fascists' armies and remain free became the reason for investigation by liberals in the Congress during the immediate postwar period.

We never, Mr. President, seem to understand that size is not necessarily an evil. When the Russian Sputnik went up, this nation was deeply concerned. And that concern had to do with our inability at that time to duplicate the Soviet feat. Now that we have the industrial capacity to equal the Russians in space or in matters related to defense, there seems to be a nationwide effort to make us feel guilty.

What would the critics of the military-industrial complex have us do? Would they have us ignore the fact that progress occurs in the field of national defense as well as in the field of social sciences? Do they want us to turn back the clock, disband our military establishment and do away with our defense related industrial capacity? Mr. President, do these critics of what they term a military-industrial complex really want us to default on our worldwide responsibilities, turn our backs on aggression and slavery and develop a national policy of selfish isolation?

Rather than deploring the existence of a military-industrial complex, I say we should thank heavens for it. That complex gives us our protective shield. It is the bubble under which our nation thrives and prospers. It is the armor which is unfortunately required in a world divided.

For all those who rant and rave about the military-industrial complex, I ask this question: What would you replace it with?

What's more, I believe it is fair to inquire whether the name presently applied is inclusive enough. Consider the large number of scientists who contributed all of the fundamental research necessary to develop and build nuclear weapons and other products of today's defense industries. Viewing this, shouldn't we call it the "scientific-military-industrial complex." By the same token, don't forget the amount of research that has gone on in our colleges and universities in support of our defense-related projects. Maybe we should call it an "educational-scientific-military-industrial complex." Then, of course, the vast financing that goes into this effort certainly makes the economic community an integral part of any such complex. Now we have a name that runs like this: "An economic-educational-scientific-military-industrial complex."

What we are talking about, Mr. President, is an undertaking which grew up from necessity. It is the product of American initiative, incentive and genius responding to a huge global challenge. It is perhaps the most effective and efficient complex ever built to fill a worldwide function. Its ultimate aim is peace in our time regardless of the aggressive, militaristic image which the left wing is attempting to give it.

Mr. President, I don't find the employment of military officers by 100 of the largest companies in this nation alarming or menacing. Many of those officers were technically trained to provide special services, many of which are required by the companies involved. And I hasten to point out that these same companies employ other free Americans, some of them former Senators, some of them former Congressmen, some of them former civilian employees of the government. It is my contention that a retired military officer is a private citizen. He has a right to seek employment wherever he can. It is only natural that he should look to sources of employment which involve matters he was trained to work in. The fact that he once was an Army officer and the company he works for does business with the Army does not automatically insure an undesirable relationship from the public viewpoint. I would like to say that anyone who has evidence of wrongdoing, of deliberate and unlawful favoritism in the dealings which involve defense industries and former military officers should come forth and make the circumstances clear. I say that anyone who has evidence that a conspiracy exists between the Pentagon on one hand and former military officers on the other should say so and produce evidence to back it up. I say that anyone who charges that a "military elite" is at work trying to turn the United States into an aggressive nation should stop dealing in generalities and come forward with names, specific dates, meeting place locations, and all the rest of the kind of data it takes to back up such a charge.

So far, Mr. President, I have yet to hear of any specific case of wrongdoing involving former military officers working for companies that do business with the Pentagon. In fact, I believe the record will show that the largest single cloud ever to hang over the so-called military-industrial complex stemmed from decisions made by civilian officers in the Department of Defense. I am, of course, speaking about the incredible circumstances surrounding the awarding of the largest defense contract in the history of the world to a company whose bid had been rejected by nearly all the military specialists and evaluation boards in the Pentagon. The contract was the multi-billion dollar TFX contract which former Defense Secretary Robert McNamara, former Navy Secretary Fred Korth and former Undersecretary of Defense Roswell Gilpatrick jammed down the throats of the Navy and Air Force.

This was undoubtedly the costliest fumble in American history. It has never been properly dealt with and I suggest to those, especially those in this body, who are sincerely interested in the dangers of a military-industrial complex becoming too powerful in this nation that a full investigation be launched into all aspects of the TFX-F111 fiasco. I would recommend that the activities of all present and former military and civilian officials involved in the awarding of the TFX contract be examined. I find it highly interesting, by the way, that one of those most directly involved in this questionable decision—Mr. Gilpatrick—is now part of the panel of experts being consulted by a member of the United States Senate in connection with his campaign to defeat the deployment of a missile defense in this country.

Mr. President, I hope I shall be fully understood in this respect. If there is wrongdoing, whether of a conflict of interest nature or something else, in our defense establishment I want it investigated and stopped and the guilty parties punished. And this goes for wrongdoing by anyone concerned, whether he be a military man, a former military man, a defense industry executive or a civilian officer of the government. I feel that this is our true concern. Maybe the hugeness of the system which we are now compelled to maintain does lend itself to improprieties. If so, let us concern ourselves with such improprieties and find means to deal with them legislatively. This is the constructive way to proceed. It does no good for us to gaze with awe on the tremendous increase in defense expenditures with which the McNamara era saddled us and then pretend that denunciation of a military-industrial complex will somehow make it all right.

In the attacks on the military also you will find repeated reference to a speech once made by former President Eisenhower.

But I would remind you that when Dwight Eisenhower mentioned the possibility of unwarranted influence being acquired by such a complex, he had some other profound things to say. I want to quote one passage in particular. He said and I quote, "We face a hostile ideology—global in scope, atheistic in character, ruthless in purpose and insidious in method. Unhappily the danger it poses promises to be of indefinite duration. To meet it successfully, there is call for, not so much the emotional and transitory sacrifices of crisis, but rather those which enable us to carry forward steadily, surely, and without complaint the burdens of a prolonged and complex struggle—with liberty the stake. Only thus shall we remain, despite every provocation, on our charted course toward permanent peace and human betterment. . . .

A vital element in keeping the peace is our military establishment. Our arms must be mighty, ready for instant action, so that no potential aggressor may be tempted to risk his own destruction."

As I have pointed out, many of the problems that are being encountered in the area of national defense today stem not so much from a military-industrial complex as they do from the mistakes and miscalculations of a "civilian complex" or perhaps I should say a "civilian-computer complex." My reference here, of course, is to the Pentagon hierarchy of young civilians (often referred to as the "whiz kids") which was erected during the McNamara era in the questionable name of "cost effectiveness." And this complex, Mr. President, was built in some measure to shut out the military voice in a large area of defense policy decision-making.

I suggest that the military-industrial complex is not the all-powerful structure that our liberal friends would have us believe. Certainly nobody can deny that this combination took a drubbing at the hands of Mr. McNamara and his civilian cadres during the past eight years.

If the military-industrial complex had been as strong and as cohesive as its critics would have us believe, it is entirely possible this nation and its taxpayers would not today be facing the need for rebuilding the defenses of freedom. I have already mentioned one example. The TFX decision which has proven to be such a costly fiasco was made by the civilian complex against the advice of experienced military men.

If the military-industrial complex had been the irresistible giant its critics describe, we would certainly today be better equipped. We would undoubtedly have a nuclear-powered navy adequate to the challenge presented by Soviet naval might. We would certainly have in the air—and not just on a drawing board—a manned, carry-on bomber. We would never have encountered the kind of shortages which cropped up in every area of the military as a result of the demands from Vietnam. There would have been no shortage of military helicopters. There would have been no shortage of trained helicopter pilots. There would have been no need to use outdated and faulty equipment. No concern ever would have arisen over whether our supply of bombs was sufficient to the task in Southeast Asia.

In conclusion, Mr. President, I want to point out that a very strong case can be made for the need for *a more powerful* military-industrial complex than we have had during the past eight years. At the very least, I wish to say that the employment practices of industries doing business with the Pentagon—practices which lead them to hire the most knowledgeable men to do their work—are no cause for shock. Nor are these practices dangerous to the American people.

I have great faith in the civilian leaders of our government and of our military services. I have no desire to see the voice of the military become all-powerful or even dominant in our national affairs. But I do believe that the military viewpoint must always be heard in the highest councils of our government in all mattters directly affecting the protection and security of our nation.

V. THE COMPLEX ASSESSED

There are three basic positions one may take on the question of the
military-industrial complex. One may say, first, that it is a splendid example of
American ingenuity and has worked magnificently for a quarter of a century to
keep us out of a major war with the Soviet Union. Or, second, that while the
complex is necessary for the national defense, some abuses in its operations have
crept in through the negligence of the Congress. Repair of these abuses will free
several billion dollars a year, which may then be used to promote the general
welfare. Or, third, that the complex is, by its very nature, counterproductive—
that it undermines rather than adds to our national security. After spending over
one trillion dollars since the end of World War II, we are less secure today than
we were a quarter of a century ago—our position abroad is less tenable and our
society is more decayed.

    The positions are of fundamental importance. If the first is true, unwise
tinkering will undermine the chances for our survival in a hostile world. If the
second is true, reform stands to save us a very large annual sum of money which
we desperately need for social rebuilding. If the third is true, the destruction of
the complex will be necessary if we are not to lose all semblance of democracy
at home, and finally drag the entire world into a thermonuclear or
chemical/bacteriological holocaust.

19. THE MEN, THE MACHINES, THE MAKERS

Paul Thayer

Rarely are important figures within the military-industrial complex itself heard by the general public. Usually they speak only to each other, or to congressional committees in which their words are buried from public view. Paul Thayer, the author of the following speech, was president and chief executive officer of LTV Aerospace Corporation of Dallas, Texas, and, in the spring of 1970, he was elected president of the conglomerate Ling-Tempo-Vought, Inc. In 1967 LTV was the nation's tenth largest defense contractor with $535,000,000 worth of prime defense contracts.

I would like to say at the outset that it gives me great pleasure and pride to address this group this morning. Knowing as many aerospace writers as I do, I feel that we speak each other's language, and that's comforting for a change. I therefore feel secure that anything I have to say today will not be heavily diluted or blown out of proportion by "translation."

    I don't intend to be especially cautious in my remarks today because my topic has been so widely discussed and so poorly stated by so many people with

Source: Paul Thayer, "The Men, the Machines, the Makers," Keynote Address to the 1969 Annual News Conference and Meeting of the Aviation/Space Writers Association, Dayton, Ohio, May 12, 1969. Reprinted by permission.

divergent views that it's high time for some top people in our business to step up to the subject and "tell it like it is."

My subject is, "The Men, the Machines, the Makers." We all realize that I could have said, "The Military-Industrial Complex." As a matter of fact, the military-industrial complex is my topic, but I want to address it in the three parts identified in the title.

Many of us have become deeply concerned by certain political leaders, university professors, authors and even a segment of the news media who have made some very loose statements about a very complex subject.

They appear to have a "complex" about a complex. This would not bother me except that lately so many of the speakers that address themselves to the subject leave the implication that this so-called complex is too big. Being big, it is therefore dangerous, and a threat whose influence is detrimental to the best interests of our country—Nonsense!

Now with regard to that part of my talk devoted to the "Men," I find some self-appointed experts strongly suggesting that the military—especially those recently retired with the equivalent rank of colonel or above—have joined the industrial complex in some unholy alliance to perpetuate the arms race and foster conflict.

Let me assure you that I am not on this platform as a spokesman for the military establishment of the United States of America. The Eisenhowers, the Marshalls, the Halseys, the Arnolds, the Pattons, the MacArthurs, the Wheelers, and the millions of other uniformed men, past and present, neither ask for, nor need, such support. Their conduct, their records and their dedication speak with sufficient clarity.

I also know from serving under, and working with, and working for, many of our national military leaders that they are too dedicated, and have too much character, to mount the public platform in order to refute the malicious charges being leveled against them and their retired members; they refuse to lend such loose talk that much dignity.

I can only sympathize with these fine men as they suffer in silence the insinuation that they have compromised the integrity for which they are renowned for the sake of a few dollars. It is so preposterous to me that it's almost laughable—if it weren't so serious—that pseudo-experts in our universities write whole books on this subject. They organize a research team, which practically anyone can do in a week's time, and plot the course of retired military officers. From this antiseptic collection of facts—seldon balanced by any personal experience in either the top echelons of industry or the military—they then draw the conclusion that retired military men who are employed by industry constitute, and I quote, "a most dangerous and shocking situation."

I can speak from personal experience that I have never met a general who wanted to go to war. And I can also say that I have never met one who backed away from a war he was dealt, and further, I can also say that I have never met one who deliberately planned to procure equipment that would not enhance his chances of winning a war.

The military man is dedicated to defend his country if it is threatened, but to imply that this would lead him to create an international crisis for personal advancement is absolute rot. Today in Viet Nam, as in all recent conflicts, the military man is merely following instructions. He is not, by any stretch of the imagination, operating outside of a set of constricting instructions set down by his civilian superiors.

Day and night, year in and year out, some lonely military sentinel mans the "crow's nest"; another man stands the "midnight watch" and yet another flies the "dawn patrol." This they don't do because they enjoy the taste of salt, the risk of darkness or the peril of a new military day. No, they do it because it has become their tradition, drawn from the Constitution, *"to ensure domestic tranquillity and to provide for the common defense."* [Italics added.]

Now to slide into the second phase of my remarks—the "Machines." Public attacks are being leveled almost daily at our weapons systems. Some critics go back as far as the 1950s to disclose, with great fanfare, all the systems that were funded and found lacking. The costs of these systems are tabulated as proof of a tremendous and stupendous waste of funds on so-called military equipment blunders.

Reasonable men should be rational enough when examining complex weapons systems to understand that failures themselves in many cases serve the useful purpose of pointing the way to workable, efficient and economical systems later downstream.

If anyone would compare the total dollars spent on projects that have been cancelled before deployment against the total dollars expended in the procurement of weapons systems, they would find that the "blunders" represent a very small fraction of the total.

I certainly don't have to enumerate before this audience the staggering list of unprecedented first-class hardware we have built. It is worthwhile to mention that within the time span in question our magnificent come-from-behind space effort last Christmas orbited the first human beings around the moon. I might add, these human beings were the same so-called potentially corrupt military men and they piloted a vehicle produced by the "scandalous" American industrial complex.

I am not prepared to speculate on what might have happened had we not maintained a strong military posture to support our national objectives and policies during the 1950s and 1960s. I must assume though, that were we caught in a weakened state, our avowed enemies might well have seized the opportunity to hasten the demise of the democracy that Karl Marx was so certain would destroy itself without outside influence.

I wonder if those so critical of our military hardware would care to speculate whether Russia would have removed the missiles from Cuba were it not for the overwhelming military force President Kennedy was able to concentrate, on such short notice, in our southern states.

In my view, world opinion is that we have not always been consistent in our foreign or domestic policies or actions. But, make no mistake, this same world opinion will readily admit that the American military-industrial might has been sufficient to rectify or neutralize any inadequacy caused by the other weaknesses inherent in our democratic form of government.

Now let's consider that portion of the American free enterprise system that I call the "Weapons Makers." Please don't let this fresh, new term throw you. You have heard it described more often as "war monger," "merchants of death" or again, the "military-industrial complex."

It is rather difficult to define all that the United States military weapons makers are accused of except that we allegedly extract profits which are not earned from our defense budget and entice key military officers in retired and active status to assist us in this overall vicious scheme to dupe the public and work against the national interest.

We find strong indictments by normally responsible political figures such as "the Military-Industrial Complex of this country is preparing its greatest coup, one that will make all previous robberies of the public purse seem like petty thievery." The same individual who made that statement also said "a vast complex of defense-oriented firms have made a fortune from supplying armaments to the U.S. government."

The allegations are so numerous that it is pointless to attempt to comment upon all of them so I will confine my reply, and directly, to the issues concerning the use of retired military personnel in defense-oriented industries and the alleged excess profits being made in the past ten years by the so-called defense contractor "fat cats."

It has been cited, again and again, that in the past ten years over 2,000 retired officers in the equivalent rank of colonel and above have taken positions with the 100 largest defense contractors in the United States. One of our leading political figures often repeats this fact; but he then goes on to say that he does not claim, or even suggest, that any conspiracy exists between the military men and the contractors. He also charges no general wrongdoing on the part of either group. My only question then is, why was he so concerned that he had the statistics entered in the Congressional Record including:

1. Naming each of the contractors.
2. The number of high-ranking retired officers each employs.
3. A comparison of 1969 employment statistics with the 1958 employment statistics.
4. Listing the names of the officers with each of the 100 contractors by first, middle and last name.

Yet this same individual says, "we should eschew even the slightest suggestion of any conspiracy between the Pentagon, on the one hand, and the companies who hire former employees on the other. There is not a scintilla of evidence that it exists." May I ask then—what is his point?

Next he reports "that this is a most dangerous and shocking situation and the trend does represent a distinct threat to the public interest." He then switches around in his conclusion to say that he is not charging that this is necessarily wrong but merely that it is true. He states that former high-ranking officers have personal friendships—which most people do not have—with those still at the Pentagon. But again, he charges no specific wrong-doing.

I become so confused when I wade through this vascillating good guy, bad guy, good guy harangue that I can only assume that the author hopes that his readers and listeners will charge the retired military officer with disloyalty and lack of dedication. He would like someone else to draw a conclusion that for some reason he does not quite want to do himself.

Recently from a speech by a high-ranking national political figure at a midwestern university, we see such shocking allegations as "spawned by our global military involvements the Military-Industrial Complex has become a powerful force for the *perpetuation of these involvements.*" To this he added, "In armament as in other lines of work it is not the price received but the service rendered *that gives a profession its name.*" If that were not enough, he then informed the students that the universities have been drawn primarily into military research in the physical and social sciences, becoming in the process, *"card-carrying"* (his phrase) members of the military-industrial complex.

With respected public citizens, in high government positions, making public statements such as these on our campuses, it does not surprise me one iota that the existence of our Reserve Officer Training Corps is being threatened and that students rise up in militant protest against the efforts of American defense industries to recruit graduating students for employment.

I have not been ordained by the American industrial complex to act as a spokesman on their behalf. On my *own* behalf, since I am one of the Corporate Presidents whose company employs retired high-ranking military officers and is proud of it, and because we also deal in military hardware, I feel I am in a position to state my own case.

First, I wholeheartedly subscribe to the need of the freedom to use retired military talent in our defense industries today—and in the future. But, I do not consider this a one-way street. I also feel that competent civilians from defense industries, regardless of their company, should continue in the future as they have in the past, to fill responsible positions in the Department of Defense.

This exchange, in my opinion, has led to an increased ability by all categories of civilian and military personnel in arriving at sound conclusions in the complicated process of evaluating national-security threats, establishing defense requirements, assessing technical capabilities and maintaining a competitive environment in the procurement of military hardware.

Now, *if* we found that the 2000-plus officers who work for defense contractors were all working for *one* contractor or even if they worked for only the top ten contractors, we might have cause for concern. But, since they are in fact distributed among 100 competing firms, it would be naive not to recognize that this establishes a highly competitive intracontractor environment.

If it is considered unreasonable or dangerous to have retired military men employed by defense industries, we should then advance this argument to its logical conclusion. Let's prohibit any federally connected employee (hired, elected, or appointed) from holding a position with industry where he can put his demonstrated skill and dedication to work. Let's see that former Bureau of the Budget or Auditor General personnel cannot be employed by lending institutions or banks. Let's see that no member of the Federal Judiciary can serve as legal counsel for or against defense industries. Let's see that no member of the Department of Transportation can be employed by a rail, airplane or automobile company.

Obviously, this is ridiculous, but it is also equally ridiculous to give credence to the slander campaign currently being carried out against a selected number of individuals and a selected segment of American industry.

As to the charge that excess profits are being made by defense contractors, I would recommend that those who make this claim read the Defense Industry Profit Review for 1958-1967 (conducted by the Logistics Management Institute) and published last April 14.

This meticulous report concludes that commercial business is increasing at a ratio of 4 to 1 over defense business and is almost twice as profitable. Any comments?

In summary, I would like to go on record as stating unequivocally that I see absolutely no threat to the safety, the security, or the prosperity of this nation from the so-called military-industrial complex. As a matter of fact, we would be in a very sorry situation without it. I would like to enter a plea that objective and respected American public figures step forward and make a knowledgeable analysis of this so-called national dilemma.

It's quite possible that this is the most complex business in the world. For one thing, we have so many people involved in our business that are outside of either the military or industry. There are countless people who involve themselves in the decision-making process, but who are very hard to find when mistakes are uncovered.

We deal at all times on the feather edge of technology. When the threat is certain we sometimes have to schedule inventions to satisfy a need. And, as everyone knows, in that kind of environment, mistakes are inevitable. The mix of military and industrial talent is a huge asset in helping to minimize mistakes.

If the people in the leadership of the country want the military-industrial complex to assume a "fall-back" position in terms of meeting the potential threat with a low-technical risk, low-cost inventory of weapons, I can promise you we will make very few mistakes. But, I can also promise you that our defense posture will be less than satisfactory.

If the opponents of the military-industrial complex are seeking praise and applause for such a proposal they are quite likely to get it. I only hope they note from which corner of the globe the loudest applause originates.

20. HOW TO CONTROL
THE MILITARY

John Kenneth Galbraith

One of the most optimistic critics of the military-industrial complex has been
the economist John Kenneth Galbraith. As the title of his book indicates,
Galbraith believes that the military can be brought under control, and that the
key to that control lies in the nature of the conditions that brought about
military dominance in the first place.

Six things brought the military-industrial bureaucracy to its present position of
power. To see these forces is also to be encouraged by the chance for escape.

First, there has been, as noted, the increasing bureaucratization of our life. In
what Ralph E. Lapp has called the weapons culture, both economic and
technological complexity are raised to the highest power. So, accordingly, is the
scope and power of organization. So, accordingly, is the possibility of
self-serving belief.

It is a power, however, which brings into existence its own challenge. The
same technical and social complexity that requires organization requires that
there be large numbers of educated people. Neither these people nor the

Source: From *How to Control the Military* by John Kenneth Galbraith. Copyright 1969 by
John Kenneth Galbraith. Reprinted by permission of Doubleday & Company, Inc. Pp.
32-43.

educational establishment that produces them are docile in the face of organization. So with organization come people who resist it—who are schooled to assert their individual beliefs and convictions. No modern military establishment could expect the disciplined obedience which sent the young by the millions (in the main, lightly schooled lads from the farm) against the machine guns as late as World War I.

The reaction to organized belief may well be one of the most rapidly developing political moods of our time. Clearly it accounted for much of the McCarthy strength in the last year—for if Dean Rusk or General Westmoreland were the epitome of the organization man, Eugene McCarthy was the antithesis. Currently one sees it sweeping ROTC off the campuses—or out of the university curricula. It is causing recruiting problems for big business—and not alone the defense firms. One senses, if the draft survives, that it will cause great trouble for the peacetime armed forces.

But so far the impressive thing is the power that massive organization has given to the military-industrial complex and not the resistance it is arousing. The latter is for the future.

Second in importance in bringing the military-industrial complex to power were the circumstances and images of foreign policy in the late forties, fifties and early sixties. The Communist world, as noted, was viewed as a unified imperium mounting its claim to every part of the globe. The postwar pressure on eastern Europe and on Berlin, the Chinese Revolution and the Korean War, seemed powerful evidence in the case. And, after the surprisingly early explosion of the first Soviet atomic bomb, followed within a decade by the even more astonishing flight of the first Sputnik, it was easy to believe that the Communist world was not only politically more unified than the rest but technologically stronger as well.

The natural reaction was to delegate power and concentrate resources. The military services and their industrial allies were given unprecedented authority— as much as in World War II—to match the Soviet technological initiative. And the effort of the nation's scientists (and other scholars) was concentrated in equally impressive fashion. None or almost none remained outside. Robert Oppenheimer was excluded, not because he opposed weapons development in general or the hydrogen bomb in particular but because he thought the latter unnecessary and undeliverable. That anyone, on the grounds of principle, should refuse his services to the Pentagon or Dow Chemical was nearly unthinkable. Social scientists also responded eagerly to invitations to spend the summer at RAND. They devoted their winters to seminars on the strategy of defense and deterrence. The only question was whether a man could get a high enough security clearance. The extent of a man's access to secret matters measured his responsibility and influence in public affairs and prestige in the community.

The effect of this concentration of talent was to add to the autonomy and power of the organizations responsible for the effort. Criticism or dissent requires knowledge; the knowledgeable men were nearly all inside. The

Eisenhower Administration affirmed the power of the military by appointing Secretaries of Defense who were largely passive except as they might worry on occasion about the cost. The Democrats, fearing, as always, that they might seem soft on communism, accorded the military more funds and power. The thrust of effort in the Kennedy Administration was principally to make it more efficient.

This enfranchisement of the military power was in a very real sense the result of a democratic decision—it was a widely approved response to the seemingly fearsome forces that surrounded us. With time those who received this unprecedented grant of power came to regard it as a right. Where weapons and military decision were concerned, their authority was meant to be plenary. Men with power have been prone to such error.

Third, secrecy confined knowledge of Soviet weapons and responding American action to those within the public and private bureaucracy. No one else had knowledge, hence no one else was thought qualified to speak. Senior members of the Armed Services, their industrial allies, the scientists, the members of the Armed Services Committees of the Congress were in. It would be hard to imagine a more efficient arrangement for protecting the power of a bureaucracy. In the academic community and especially in Congress there was no small prestige in being a member of this club. And, as the experience of Robert Oppenheimer and other less publicized persons showed, it was possible to exclude the critic or skeptic as a security risk.

Fourth, there was the disciplining effect of personal fear. A nation that was massively alarmed about the unified power of the Communist world was not tolerant of skeptics or those who questioned the only seemingly practical line of response. Numerous scientists, social scientists and public officials had come reluctantly to accept the idea of the Communist threat. This history of reluctance could now involve the danger—real or imagined—that they might be suspected of past association with this all-embracing conspiracy. The late Senator Joseph R. McCarthy and others saw or sensed the opportunity for exploiting national and personal anxiety. The result was further and decisive pressure on anyone who seemed not to concur in the totality of the Communist threat. (McCarthy was broken only when he capriciously attacked the military power.)

Fear provided a further source of immunity and power. Accepted Marxian doctrine holds that a cabal of capitalists and militarists is the cutting edge of capitalist imperialism and the cause of war. Anyone who raised a question about the military-industrial complex thus sounded suspiciously like a Marxist. So it was a topic that was avoided by the circumspect. Heroism in the United States involves an important distinction. It requires a man to stand up fearlessly, at least in principle, to the prospect for nuclear extinction. But it allows him to proceed promptly to cover if there is risk of being called a Communist, a radical, an enemy of the system. Death we must face but not social obloquy or political ostracism. The effect of such discriminating heroism in the fifties or sixties was that most potential critics of the military power were exceptionally reticent.

In 1961, in the last moments before leaving office, as all now know, President Eisenhower gave his famous warning: "In the councils of government we must guard against the acquisition of unwarranted influence, whether sought or unsought, by the military-industrial complex. The potential for the disastrous rise of misplaced power exists and will persist." This warning was to become by a wide margin the most quoted of all Eisenhower statements. It was principally for the flank protection it provided for all who wanted to agree. For many years thereafter anyone (myself included) who spoke to the problem of the military power took the thoughtful precaution of first quoting President Eisenhower. He had shown that there were impeccably conservative precedents for our concern.

Fifth, in the fifties and early sixties, the phrase "domestic priority" had not yet become a cliché. The civilian claim on Federal funds was not, or seemed not, to be overpowering. The great riots in the cities had not yet occurred. The appalling conditions in the urban core that were a cause were still unnoticed. Internal migration had long been under way but millions were yet to come from the rural into the urban slums. Poverty had not yet been placed on the national agenda with the consequence that we would learn how much of it and how abysmal it is. And promises not having been made to end poverty, expectations had not been aroused. The streets of Washington, D.C., were still safer than those of Saigon. Travel by road and commuter train was only just coming to a crawl. Air and water were dirty but not yet lethally so. In this innocent age, in 1964, taxes were reduced because there seemed to be danger of economic stagnation and unemployment from raising more Federal revenue than could quickly be spent. The then Director of the Budget, Kermit Gordon, was persuaded that if an excess of revenue were available the military would latch on to it. Inflation was not a pressing issue. Military expenditures, although no one wished to say so, did sustain employment. Circumstances could not have been better designed, economically speaking, to allow the military a clear run.

Sixth and finally, in these years both liberal and conservative opposition to the military-industrial power were muted.

Nothing could be expected, in principle, to appeal less to conservatives than a vast increase in bureaucratic power at vast cost. In an earlier age the reaction would have been apoplectic. Some conservatives in an older tradition—men genuinely concerned about the Leviathan State—were aroused. Ernest Weir, the head of National Steel and the foe of FDR and the New Deal, Alf M. Landon, the much underestimated man who opposed Roosevelt in 1936, Marriner S. Eccles, banker and longtime head of the Federal Reserve, and a few others did speak out. But for most, it was enough that the Communists—exponents of a yet more powerful state and against private property too—were on the other side. One accepted a lesser danger to fight a greater one. And, as always, when many are moderately aroused, some are extreme. It became a tenet of a more extreme conservatism that civilians should never interfere with the military except to provide more money. Nor would there be any compromise with communism. It must be destroyed. Their military doctrine, as Daniel Bell has said, was "that negotiation with the Communists is impossible, that anyone who discusses the possibility of such negotiation is a tool of the Communists, and that a 'tough policy'—by which, *sotto voce,* is meant a preventive war of a first strike—is the only means of forestalling an eventual communist victory."[1] To an impressive extent, in the fifties and sixties, this new conservatism, guided by retired Air Force generals and the redoubtable Edward Teller, became the voice of all conservatism on defense policy.

The disappearance of liberal criticism was almost as complete—and even more remarkable. An unrestrained association of military and industrial power would have been expected to arouse liberal passion. So also the appropriation of public power for private purpose by defense contractors, some of them defining missions for the Services so as to require what they had to sell. But liberals did not react. Like conservatives, they accepted a lesser threat to liberty to forestall a greater one. Also, it was not easy for a generation that had asked for more executive power for FDR and for Truman and Kennedy over conservative opposition to see danger in bureaucracy. This was a too radical reversal of liberal form.

The liberals who were active in the fifties and sixties had also been scarred by the tactics of the domestic Communists in politics and the trade union movement. And they had seen what had happened to their friends who had committed themselves to the wartime alliance with the Soviets and nailed their colors to its continuation after the war. Stalin had let them down with a brutal and for many a mortal thump. Those that escaped, or many of them, made common cause with the men who were making or deploying weapons to resist communism, urging only, as good liberals, that there was a social dimension to the struggle. And as time passed it was discovered that many good and liberal things—foreign aid, technical assistance, travel grants, fellowships, overseas libraries—could be floated on the Communist threat. Men of goodwill became accomplished in persuading the more retarded to vote for foreign aid legislation, not as a good thing in itself but as an indispensable instrument in the war against communism. Having made this case, one could not then be critical of military spending for the same purpose.

Additionally, in the fifties and sixties American liberals were fighting for a larger Federal budget not for the things it bought but for the unemployment it prevented. Such a budget, with its stabilizing flow of expenditures and supported by personal income taxes which rose and fell with stabilizing effect, was the cornerstone of the New or Keynesian economics. And this economics of high and expanding employment, in turn, was the cornerstone of the liberal position. As noted it was not easy for liberals to admit that defense expenditures were serving this benign social function; when asked thay (i.e., we) always said that spending for education, housing, welfare and civilian public works would serve just as well and be much welcomed as an alternative. But in the absence of strong pressure to spend for these better things, it was not easy to become aroused over an arms policy which had such obviously beneficent effects on the economy.

By the early sixties the liberal position was beginning to change. From comparatively early in the Kennedy Administration—the Bay of Pigs was a major factor in this revelation—many saw that a stand would have to be made against policies urged by the military and its State Department allies. Military intervention in Cuba, military intervention in Laos, military intervention in Vietnam, an all-out fallout shelter program, unrestricted nuclear testing, all of which were urged, would be disastrous for the President as well as for the country and the world. A visible and sometimes sharp division occurred between those who made their alliance with the military power, and those—Robert Kennedy, Adlai Stevenson, Theodore Sorensen, Arthur Schlesinger, Averell Harriman and, though rendering more homage to the organizations of which they were a part, George Ball and Robert McNamara—who saw the dangers of this commitment. With the Johnson Administration this opposition disappeared or was dispersed. The triumph of those who allied themselves with the bureaucracy was the disaster of that Administration.

The opposition, much enlarged, then reappeared in the political theatre. Suspicion of the military power in 1968 was the most important factor uniting the followers of Senators Kennedy, McCarthy, and McGovern. Along with the more specific and more important opposition to the Vietnam conflict, it helped to generate the opposition that persuaded Lyndon Johnson not to run. And the feeling that Vice-President Humphrey was not sufficiently firm on this issue—that he belonged politically to the generation of liberals that was tolerant of the military-industrial power—unquestionably diluted and weakened his support. Conceivably it cost him the election.

FOOTNOTES

[1]Quoted by Ralph E. Lapp in *The Weapons Culture.* New York: Norton, 1968, pp. 27-28.

21. PENTAGON CAPITALISM

Seymour Melman

Seymour Melman, a professor of industrial engineering at Columbia University, has taken the general idea of Galbraith's New Industrial State and applied it with particular force to the Pentagon itself. Thus he shows that the old military-industrial complex of the Eisenhower years has been replaced during the Kennedy-Johnson years by a new state-management which, like one of Galbraith's modern corporations, grows and extends its control because that is its nature and purpose. With great detail he demonstrates how the managers of the Pentagon control a vast enterprise many times larger than the largest private corporation.

In the name of defense, and without announcement or debate, a basic alteration has been effected in the governing institutions of the United States. An industrial management has been installed in the federal government, under the Secretary of Defense, to control the nation's largest network of industrial enterprises. With the characteristic managerial propensity for extending its power, limited only by its allocated share of the national product, the new state-management combines peak economic, political, and military decision-making. Hitherto, this combination of powers in the same hands has been a feature of statist societies—communist, fascist, and others—where individual rights cannot constrain central rule.

Source: Seymour Melman, *Pentagon Capitalism: The Political Economy of War* (New York, 1970), pp. 1-7, 16-17, 20-25, 34.

This new institution of state-managerial control has been the result of actions undertaken for the declared purposes of adding to military power and economic efficiency and of reinforcing civilian, rather than professional, military rule. Its main characteristics are institutionally specific and therefore substantially independent of its chief of the moment. The effects of its operations are independent of the intention of its architects, and may even have been unforeseen by them.

The creation of the state-management marked the transformation of President Dwight Eisenhower's "military-industrial complex," a loose collaboration, mainly through market relations, of senior military officers, industrial managers, and legislators. Robert McNamara, under the direction of President John Kennedy, organized a formal central-management office to administer the military-industrial empire. The market was replaced by a management. In place of the complex, there is now a defined administrative control center that regulates tens of thousands of subordinate managers. In 1968, they directed the production of $44 billion of goods and services for military use. By the measure of the scope and scale of its decision-power, the new state-management is by far the largest and most important single management in the United States. There are about 15,000 men who arrange work assignments to subordinate managers (contract negotiation), and 40,000 who oversee compliance of submanagers of subdivisions with the top management's rules. This is the largest industrial central administrative office in the United States—perhaps in the world.

The state-management has also become the most powerful decision-making unit in the United States government. Thereby, the federal government does not "serve" business or "regulate" business. For the new management is the largest of them all. Government *is* business. That is state capitalism.

The normal operation, including expansion, of the new state-management has been based upon preemption of a lion's share of federal tax revenue and of the nation's finite supply of technical manpower. This use of capital and skill has produced parasitic economic growth—military products which are not part of the level of living and which cannot be used for further production. All this, while the ability to defend the United States, to shield it from external attack, has diminished.

From 1946 to 1969, the United States government spent over $1,000 billion on the military, more than half of this under the Kennedy and Johnson administrations—the period during which the state-management was established as a formal institution. This sum of staggering size (try to visualize a billion of something) does not express the cost of the military establishment to the nation as a whole. The true cost is measured by what has been foregone, by the accumulated deterioration in many facets of life, by the inability to alleviate human wretchedness of long duration.

Here is part of the human inventory of depletion:

1. By 1968, there were 6 million grossly substandard dwellings, mainly in the cities.

2. 10 million Americans suffered from hunger in 1968-1969.

3. The United States ranked 18th at last report (1966) among nations in infant mortality rate (23.7 infant deaths in first year per 1,000 live births). In Sweden (1966) the rate was 12.6.

4. In 1967, 40.7 percent of the young men examined were disqualified for military service (28.5 percent for medical reasons).

5. In 1950, there were 109 physicians in the United States per 100,000 population. By 1966 there were 98.

6. About 30 million Americans are an economically underdeveloped sector of the society.

The human cost of military priority is paralleled by the industrial-technological depletion caused by the concentration of technical manpower and capital on military technology and in military industry. For example:

1. By 1968, United States industry operated the world's oldest stock of metal-working machinery; 64 percent was 10 years old and over.

2. No United States railroad has anything in motion that compares with the Japanese and French fast trains.

3. The United States merchant fleet ranks 23rd in age of vessels. In 1966, world average-age of vessels was 17 years, United States 21, Japan 9.

4. While the United States uses the largest number of research scientists and engineers in the world, key United States industries, such as steel and machine tools, are in trouble in domestic markets: in 1967, for the first time, the United States imported more machine tools than it exported.

As civilian industrial technology deteriorates or fails to advance, productive employment opportunity for Americans diminishes.

All of this only begins to reckon the true cost to America of operating the state military machine. (The cost of the Vietnam war to the Vietnamese people has no reckoning.) Clearly, no mere ideology or desire for individual power can account for the colossal costs of the military machine. A lust for power has been at work here, but it is not explicable in terms of an individual's power drive. Rather, the state-management represents an institutionalized power-lust. A normal thirst for more managerial power within the largest management in the United States gives the new state-management an unprecedented ability and opportunity for building a military-industry empire at home and for using this as an instrument for building an empire abroad. This is the new imperialism.

The magnitude of the decision-power of the Pentagon management has reached that of a state. After all, the fiscal 1970 budget plan of the Department of Defense—*$83 billion*—exceeds the gross national product (GNP) of entire nations: in billions of dollars for 1966—Belgium, $18.1; Italy $61.4; Sweden $21.3. The state-management has become a para-state, a state within a state.

In its beginning, the government of the United States was a political entity. The managing of economic and industrial activity was to be the province of private persons. This division of function was the grand design for American government and society, within which personal and political freedom could flourish alongside of rapid economic growth and technological progress. After 1960, this design was transformed. In the name of ensuring civilian control over the Department of Defense and of obtaining efficiencies of modern management, Secretary of Defense Robert McNamara redesigned the organization of his Department to include, within the office of the Secretary, a central administrative office. This was designed to control operations in thousands of subsidiary industrial enterprises undertaken on behalf of the Department of Defense. Modeled after the central administrative offices of multi-division industrial firms—such as the Ford Motor Company, the General Motors Corporation, and the General Electric Company—the new top management in the Department of Defense was designed to control the activities of subsidiary managements of firms producing, in 1968, $44 billion of goods and services for the Department of Defense.

By the measure of industrial activity governed from one central office, this new management in the Department of Defense is beyond compare the largest industrial management in the United States, perhaps in the world. Never before in American experience has there been such a combination of economic and political decision-power in the same hands. The senior officers of the new state-management are also senior political officers of the government of the United States. Thus, one consequence of the establishment of the new state-management has been the installation, within American society, of an institutional feature of a totalitarian system.

The original design of the American government was oriented toward safeguarding individual political freedom and economic liberties. These safeguards were abridged by the establishment of the new state-management in the Department of Defense. In order to perceive the abridgement of traditional liberties by the operation of the new managerial institution, one must focus on its functional performance. For the official titles of its units sound like just another government bureaucracy: Office of the Secretary of Defense, Defense Supply Agency, etc.

The new industrial management has been created in the name of defending America from its external enemies and preserving a way of life of a free society. It has long been understood, however, that one of the safeguards of individual liberty is the separation of roles of a citizen and of an employee. When an individual relates to the same person both as a citizen and as an employee, then the effect is such—regardless of intention—that the employer-government official has an unprecedented combination of decision-making power over the individual citizen-employee.

In the Soviet Union, the combination of top economic and political decision-power is a formal part of the organization and ideology of that society. In the United States, in contrast, the joining of the economic-managerial and top political power has been done in an unannounced and, in effect, covert fashion.

In addition to the significance of the new state-management with respect to individual liberty in American society, the new organization is significant for its effects in preempting resources and committing the nation to the military operations that the new organization is designed to serve. Finally, the new power center is important because of the self-powered drive toward expansion that is built into the normal operation of an industrial management.

The preemption of resources takes place because of the sheer size of the funds that are wielded by the Department of Defense. Its budget, amounting to over $80 billion in 1969, gives this organization and its industrial-management arm unequalled decision-power over manpower, materials, and industrial production capacity in the United States and abroad. It is, therefore, predictable that this organization will be able to get the people and other resources that it needs whenever it needs them, even if this requires outbidding other industries and other organizations—including other agencies of the federal and other governments.

Regardless of the individual avowals and commitments of the principal officers of the new industrial machine, it is necessarily the case that the increased competence of this organization contributes to the competence of the parent body—the Department of Defense. This competence is a war-making capability. Hence, the very efficiency and success of the new industrial-management, unavoidably and regardless of intention, enhances the war-making capability of the government of the United States. As the war-making department accumulates diverse resources and planning capability, it is able to offer the President blueprint-stage options for responding to all manner of problem situations—while other government agencies look (and are) unready, understaffed, and underequipped. This increases the likelihood of recourse to "solutions" based upon military power.

Finally, the new government management, insofar as it shares the usual characteristics of industrial management, has a built-in propensity for expanding the scope and intensity of its operations—for this expansion is the hallmark of success in management. The chiefs of the new state-management, in order to be successful in their own eyes, strive to maintain and extend their decision-power— by enlarging their activities, the number of their employees, the size of the capital investments which they control, and by gaining control over more and more subsidiary managements. By 1967-1968, the scope of the state-management's control over production had established it as the dominant decision-maker in U.S. industry. The industrial output of $44 billion of goods and services under state-management control in 1968 exceeded by far the reported net sales of American industry's leading firms (in billions of dollars for 1968): A.T.&T., $14.1; Du Pont, $3.4; General Electric, $8.4; General Motors, $22.8; U.S. Steel, $4.6. The giants of United States industry have become small- and medium-sized firms, compared with the new state-management—with its conglomerate industrial base.

The appearance of the new state-managerial machine marks a transformation in the character of the American government and requires us to re-examine our understanding of its behavior. Various classic theories of industrial capitalist society have described government as an essentially political entity, ideally impartial. Other theories depict government as justifiably favoring, or even identifying with, business management, while the theories in the Marxist tradition have depicted government as an arm of business. These theories require revision. . . .

As in other major industrial managements, the state-management shows a propensity in problem-solving to select solutions that also serve to extend its decision-power. Furthermore, this selective preference is a built-in professional-occupational feature that operates with great regularity as a characteristic of people doing their jobs in management organizations. This may be illustrated by the policy preferences shown with respect to questions of the draft, overkill, and the gold reserve of the United States.

In considering the policy options that were selected, it is crucial to recall that the new industrial management is located in the Office of the Secretary of Defense, whose chief is the Secretary of Defense, and that he, in turn, is a Cabinet officer directly responsible to the President of the United States. Therefore, the basic policy decisions of the new state-industrial-management are also the decisions of the principal political officers of the federal government. . . .

In the present case, the drive for improvement of their standing as managers requires them to maintain and enlarge the military-industry and military organizations of the United States; that is precisely what the state-management has done. From 1960 to 1970, the budget of the Department of Defense has been enlarged by 80 percent—from $45 to $83 billion. All large managerial organizations, whether private or governmental, carry on planning and calculate choices among alternatives. When confronted with an array of different ways to solve a particular problem, members of a managerial team are impelled by their particular professional-occupational requirements to select those options that will maintain and extend the decision-power of the managerial group, and improve their own professional standing in the managerial hierarchy. This sort of selective preference by managers is operative in industrial management whether private or public.

An enterprise is private when its top decision-making group is not located in a government office. For this analysis of the Pentagon, what is crucial is whether the top decision-making group is a true management. A management is defined by the performance of a set of definable functions which give management its common character, whether the enterprise is private or public. A management accumulates capital for making investments. Management decides what to produce, how to carry on production, how much to produce, and where to dispose of the product at the acceptable price. It is the performance of these functions by the new organizations in the industrial directorate of the Department of Defense which defines it as a bona fide industrial management. In addition, the operating characteristics of this new management are comparable to those of other industrial managements. The special characteristics of the state-management are associated with its location in the government and its control over military production.

While the industrial-management in the Department of Defense actually owns only a minority part of the industrial capital that is used for military production, it exercises elaborate control over the use of *all* resources in thousands of enterprises. This differentiation between ownership and control is the classic one of the modern industrial corporation. Ever since Berle and Means did their classic study on *The Modern Corporation and Private Property,* it is well understood that the top managers of an industrial corporation do not necessarily wield property rights over the assets used in production, but do control the use of these assets. The differentiation between ownership and control is a central feature of the new state-management.

The Pentagon management also displays the other characteristic features of corporate organization. Management decision-making usually includes a hierarchical organization of the administration group and built-in pressures for expanding the decision-making sphere of the management. Hierarchical organization means the separation of decision-making on production matters from the performance of the work itself, and the investment of final decision-power in the men at the top of the management organization. This sort of organization structure is visible in the Pentagon's organization charts and in the key role played by the Secretary of Defense and his closest aides in controlling the enlargement of nuclear and conventional forces from 1961 to 1969.

Success of management is ordinarily shown by growth in decision-power, measured by size of investment, number of employees, volume of sales, or quantity of goods produced. Such criteria indicate a true competitive gain only when they reflect a differential increase as against other management; thus, what is critical in defining the importance of a management at any one moment is not simply the absolute quantity of sales, but more importantly, the proportion of an industry's activity controlled by the management. Similarly, an increase in the volume of sales or the size of investment or the number of employees is significant only in terms of a proportional increase. In a military organization, for example, if everyone is promoted at the same time by one grade, then no one has been promoted. Similarly, promotion in a hierarchical organization must be relative promotion, and a gain in managerial position must be a relative gain. If we are competitors, then your gain must include my relative loss or you have not gained. This idea of relative gain in managerial position applies not only within a single managerial-hierarchical organization, but also applies *among* managerial organizations.

Within and among managements, the controlling criterion of managerial success is, therefore, competitive gain in decision-making position. From 1960 to

1970, the Defense Department budget rose from $45 to $83 billion, with industrial procurement roughly 50 percent of these amounts. No other management, private or public, has enjoyed such growth. The military-managerial machine is in a class by itself.

I have emphasized here the idea of enlarging decision-power as the occupational imperative, the operative end-in-view of modern corporate management—as against the more traditional idea that profit-making is the avowed central purpose of management. Profit-making, as a step in the recoupment of invested money, has diminished in importance as an independent measure of managerial performance. This stems from the fact that modern industrial operations increasingly involve classes of "fixed" or "regulated" costs, which are subject to substantial managerial control during a given accounting period. For example, a management must decide how it assigns the cost, year by year, of a new factory or a road that it has constructed. There is nothing in the nature of the factory that determines whether its capital investment shall be allocated to the costs of operations in one year, two years, or twenty years, or varied each year according to degree of use. This decision is an entirely arbitrary one, subject to the convenience of the management, within the limits allowed by the tax authorities. Since such assignment of costs is managerially controlled and has substantial effect on the size of profits that remain after costs, profits *per se* have a lessened importance as an autonomous indicator of managerial success. Moreover, there is accumulating evidence that some industrial costs, notably the costs of administration and of selling operations, are enlarged even where that involves reduction in the size of profits that would otherwise be available in a given accounting period. Such reductions in profit are ordinarily made and justified in the name of long-term maintenance or extension of the relative decision-power of the management and its enterprise.

One of the characteristic processes in industrial managements during the twentieth century has been an elaboration in the scope and intensity of managerial controlling. This has been accompanied by growing management costs and a growing ratio of managerial to production employees. All this has meant higher costs and, necessarily, diminished profits. But the choice of options in industrial management has systematically been toward enlarging the scope and intensity of managerial control, rather than toward management methods which would minimize costs and thereby enlarge profits or allow a reduction in prices. The state-management has also been piling on managerial controls, obviously giving priority to the consequent growth in its decision-power, as against possible economies that might be effected in its own central offices or in the operation of subsidiary enterprises of the Pentagon empire.

All this is no mere theoretical exercise for understanding the operation of the state-management. This organization skips over the customary processes of industrial capitalism for enlarging control via an intervening mechanism of investing and recouping money with a gain-profit, then reinvesting more money and, thereby, adding to decision-power. Instead, the state-management, drawing on its unique capital resource—an annual portion of the nation's product—applies this directly to increasing either the scope or the intensity of its decision-power. The usual processes of marketing products and recouping capital are leapfrogged by the state-management.

One of the characteristic features of private industrial management has been a sustained pressure to minimize costs in production. In modern industry, this effort is institutionalized by making it the special province of industrial engineers, cost accountants and others. The state-management . . . includes various professional groups that are identified as acting to control costs. But that does not necessarily produce cost-minimization. For cost control can be focused mainly on controlling the people in various occupations.

The Pentagon record—before, during, and after Robert McNamara—includes obvious cost excesses. Before McNamara, average prices on major weapons systems were 3.2 times their initial cost estimates. Under McNamara, the famous F-111 airplane was costing $12.7 million per plane by December, 1969, as compared to one first cost estimate of $3.9 million—or 3.25 times the initial estimate. Such performance under the well-advertised regime of the state-management's "cost effectiveness" programs was characteristic of this era as well. This pattern of cost excesses during the rule of "cost effectiveness" is explicable, not as aberrant behavior, but as a pattern that is normal to the state-management. The state-management's control system includes monitoring for so-called cost overruns as a regular function. Payment for the cost overruns by the Pentagon has been the functional equivalent of a grant of capital from a central office to a division of its firm, serving to enlarge the assets of the larger enterprise.

Owing to the basic difference between private industrial management and the state-management with respect to the role of conversion of capital through the market place, there is a parallel, distinguishing interest in the stability and instability of industrial operations. Stability means operating within predictable and acceptable limits of variation in output. For private industrial management, this is a highly desirable condition, because this makes possible predictability in the ongoing processes of conversion of money from investment funds to products sold on the market place and to new capital funds for further investment. Where costs, prices, and the value of the dollar in purchasing power are highly unstable, the investment-recoupment process of capital for private management is rendered extremely difficult to operate—it is put "out of control." These limiting conditions are not operative for the administrators of the state-management, for they deal directly with the conversion of capital funds into decision-orders on industrial operations. Also, their products need not be designed to be salable at a price producing a profit which they may accumulate for further investment. Their investment funds have been constantly acquired in the name of defense from a willing Congress and nation. Accordingly, instability in costs, prices, and profits are no major constraint for the managers of the state machine. And so, when military outlays at home and abroad become the traceable cause of danger to the value of the dollar relative to other currencies, it is not a source for alarm among the Pentagon managers. Some measures are taken to slow down the outflow of Treasury gold, but no major policy changes are introduced.

Since its formal organization after 1960 under Robert McNamara, the new state-industrial management has focused attention on military production, its organization and control. At the same time, many Americans, seeing the array of managerial and technical talent deployed in the state-management, have suggested that the same group could apply its talents to organize almost anything—housing, public health, and so forth. Some individuals in the state-management may very well choose to change their employment. Indeed, there has been a sustained turnover, especially in some of the more senior posts of the state-management. Such flexibility does not apply, however, to the organization as an institution. Military organization and military production have special value as a base for the power-extending operations of industrial management.

For a management seeking to enlarge its operations, the military sphere offers the unequaled opportunity to obtain virtually unlimited quantities of fresh capital from the Congress of the United States. This is so because of the "defense" use of this money; the name, Department of Defense, is itself helpful. (Would Congress and the public be equally compliant with a War Department?) Thereby, the state industrial management has an unmatched opportunity for extending its decision-power. This is illustrated in the case of the draft. There are alternative ways of organizing military operations with varying numbers of men being required. There are also alternative ways of obtaining the services of a given number of men. The draft is the one way which not only secures the required number of men, but also guarantees decision-power by the military managers over a fixed proportion of the young people of the society at any given time. This extension of decision power, unprecedented in peacetime in American history, was made possible by the promise of the state-management to perform the service of defending the United States, a promise which cannot be fulfilled. . . .

. . . The Kennedy administration was formally Democratic, but the architect of the present military machine, and its operating chief from 1961 to 1968, was a Republican, Robert McNamara. Support for the plans and the budgets of the state-management have come from both major parties in the Congress. At the same time, there has been a fair amount of turnover in the persons holding key posts at the top of the state-management.

Indeed, the very openness of operations of the state machine is one of its great sources of strength. Thus, no conspiracy, in the ordinary sense of the word, was required to get the American people to accept the myth of the missile gap and the subsequent major capital outlays for an overkill nuclear war program. The American people were sold on the myth and thought they were buying defense. Nor is a conspiracy required to secure fresh capital funds of unprecedented size for further expansion of the state-management. This is agreed to by a Congress and a public that has been taught to believe that all this activity is for defense and that it stimulates the economy of a society that can enjoy both guns and butter. In all of this, the controlling factor is not a political party or a single political theory, not a personality, not a conspiracy: the existence and normal operation of the Pentagon's management-institution dominates and gives continuity of direction.

The government of the United States now includes a self-expanding war machine that uses military power for diverse political operations and is based upon an industrial managment that has priority claims to virtually unlimited capital funds from the federal budget. The state-management is economically parasitic, hence exploitative, in its relation to American society at home. The military-political operations of the Pentagon chieftains abroad, following the pattern of the Vietnam wars program, are parasitic there as well. To the older pattern of exploitative imperialism abroad, there is now added an institutional network that is parasitic at home. This combination is the new imperialism.

22. PENTAGONISM

Juan Bosch

Sometimes our victims know us better than we know ourselves. Juan Bosch, former President of the Dominican Republic, was deposed by a military junta supported by the American military. Central and South America, and the islands of the Carribean, have always been considered by us to be within our peculiar sphere of influence. Nowhere has American imperialism worn a more classic mask than here. Nevertheless Bosch, writing from exile, discovered an important change in the classic form of imperialism, a change which Seymour Melman later called the state-management. Coming from a nation long the victim of American imperialism, Bosch warns Americans that they themselves have now become the colonials and the Pentagon the mother country.

If people in many parts of the world still say that there are imperialist countries and colonialized countries, it is because we have not yet realized that pentagonism has taken the place of imperialism.

In the days when it still existed—a period which lasted until the end of the Second World War—the essence of imperialism was the conquest of colonies in order to invest the surplus capital of the conquering country in them and to take out the raw materials with which to keep the industrial plants of the mother country functioning. At the same time, the colonies were turned into markets for the mother country's industrial production, thereby establishing an endless

Source: Juan Bosch, *Pentagonism: A Substitute for Imperialism* (New York, 1969), pp. 17-29. Reprinted by permission of Grove Press, Inc. Copyright © 1968 by Grove Press, Inc.

chain that fettered the economic life of the colonies through political submissic to the mother country.

As can be seen from this summary description of the phenomenon called imperialism, a colony was both a zone in which capital was invested and a zone in which profits accumulated, for its labor was cheap, its raw materials were bought at low prices, the banking system of the mother country lent very little money, making only short-term loans at a high rate of interest, the transportation of goods to and from the mother country was controlled, and high tariffs were put on what the colonials bought, while the manufactured products of the mother country coming into the colony were high-priced. This situation of economic control, in the final analysis, had one sole purpose: To see to it that the colonial worker received, let us say, ten monetary units per hour of work and had to pay fifty units per hour of work to buy a product that was made in the mother country with the raw material that this same colonial worker—or one from another colony dependent on the same mother country—had produced for five times less money.

Conquering a colony and keeping it a dependent territory called for the use of a military power whose sole purpose was to conquer and keep a hold on a colonial empire. This required funds, arms factories, specialized schools for the training of officials and civil administrators to be sent to the colonies, and poets, musicians, painters, journalists, and orators to create the heroic atmosphere appropriate to wars in the territories destined to be colonies. But this atmosphere has disappeared and children being born now will have to resort to old books and films of other eras to know what colonial armies were like.

Imperialism is now a shadow of the past, yet out of intellectual inertia we keep saying that imperialism still exists and we keep accusing this or that country of being imperialistic. In view of the fact that two-thirds of mankind lives in capitalist societies, and in view of the fact that Lenin indissolubly tied imperialism to capitalism—with its own reason for being, when and where it occurred—by saying that imperialism was the last stage—or the most advanced stage—of capitalism, there are those who think that imperialism still exists because capitalism still exists. But this is an illusion. Imperialism no longer exists and capitalism has survived it.

What is the explanation for what we have just said?

It is that imperialism has been replaced by a superior force. Imperialism has been replaced by pentagonism.

Industrial capitalism began to develop in the hands of technicians, not of scientists, and began to enroll scientists in its service around the end of the nineteenth century. Put in the service of capitalism, science was to open up unsuspected sources of production that were to bring it infinite resources for the accumulation of capital, sources so numerous and so productive that colonial wealth was to appear to be child's play alongside them. Taking advantage of the work of the scientists, industrial capitalism was to evolve rapidly after the First World War in the direction of the unforeseen stage of overdevelopment which it was to reach because of the Second World War. On entering the atomic era, capitalism was to be so different from what the world had known up until 1939 that in terms of historic evolution it was to have more features of the twenty-first century than of the twentieth.

Today's capitalism is overdeveloped capitalism. This new type of capitalism no longer needs to call upon dependent territories to produce cheap raw materials and consume expensive manufactured articles. Overdeveloped capitalism has found within itself the strength necessary to cube the two terms of capitalism that came into play in the imperialist stage. Its formidable industrial plants, operating under conditions created by scientific accumulation, can produce raw materials—once undreamed of—from basic raw materials and at an extremely low cost; these new raw materials, whose quality, volume, consistency, and size are scientifically guaranteed, have allowed production lines to expand until they attain fabulous figures, and have thereby made the subproduct the key to the minimum indispensable profit for maintaining a going industry, so that the profits obtained from the principal products accumulate for the expansion of existing plants or the setting up of new ones, and the final result of this endless process is a very high productivity, unforeseen in the history capitalism. Thanks to this high productivity, overdeveloped capitalism can pay its people very high salaries, thus giving rise to a buying power within its own boundaries that increases at a gallop, and this in turn permits capitalization to an extent that the most impassioned promoter of military expeditions to conquer colonies in the heyday of Victoria, Queen and Empress, would never have suspected.

Now this phenomenon, which necessarily gave rise to new types of relationships between mother countries and their colonies—the granting of independence to their colonies by the British Empire and General de Gaulle—led to a new phenomenon in the country where capitalism is most overdeveloped. This is pentagonism, which has come to occupy the place that imperialism occupied until a short while ago. Imperialism has now disappeared from the globe, and the word which defined it ought to disappear with it. What is taking place at present in Latin America, in Asia, in Africa—in all the underdeveloped areas—is not the old imperialism defined by Lenin as the last stage—or the most advanced stage—of capitalism. It is pentagonism, the product of overdeveloped capitalism.

Pentagonism retains almost all the characteristics of imperialism, especially those that are most destructive and painful, but it is a more advanced form, and bears the same relation to imperialism that today's overdeveloped capitalism bears to the industrial capitalism of the nineteenth century. To state this more graphically, pentagonism resembles imperialism in the nature of its effects, not in its dimensions, just as the cannon used in the Franco-Prussian War of 1870 resembles the atomic bomb dropped on Hiroshima, in that both cause death, but not the same number of deaths.

Pentagonism nonetheless differs from imperialism in that it does not share its most characteristic feature, military conquest of colonial territories and their subsequent economic exploitation. Pentagonism does not exploit colonies: it exploits its own people. This is an absolutely new phenomenon, as new as the overdeveloped capitalism that gave birth to pentagonism.

To succeed in the exploitation of its own people, pentagonism colonizes the mother country; but since the colonization of the mother country must be achieved through the same military process as was used to conquer a colony and since it cannot wage war against its own people, the mother country sends its armies out to make war on other countries. And since sending the army of the mother country out against a foreign territory was what was done in the bygone days of imperialism, people continue to think that imperialism still holds sway. But this is not the case. The fact is that the use of military power has not changed; what has changed is the purpose for which it is used.

The military forces of a pentagonist country are not sent out to conquer colonial territories. War has another purpose; war is waged to conquer positions of power in the pentagonist country, not in some far-off land. What is being sought is not a place to invest surplus capital for profit; what is being sought is access to the generous economic resources being mobilized for industrial war production; what is being sought are profits where arms are manufactured, not where they are employed, and these profits are obtained in the pentagonist mother country, not in the country that is being attacked. A contract for bombers brings in several times more profit, in a much shorter time, than the conquest of the richest mining territory, and the contract is obtained in, and brings money in from, the place where the center of pentagonist power lies. The armies operate a long way away from the pentagonist power, but the planes are built at home, and this is where the fabulous sums produced by the contract are earned. These sums come out of the pockets of the pentagonized people, who are at the same time the mother country and the seat of pentagonist power.

The pentagonized people are exploited as colonies were since they are the ones who pay, through taxes, for the bombers that enrich their manufacturers; the mother country thus turns its own people into its best colony; it is at once a mother country and a colony, in an unforseen symbiosis that requires a new word to define it. It is no longer a classic imperialist power because it does not need colonial territories in order to accumulate profits. It accumulates them at the expense of its own people. A mother country that exploits and an exploited colony no longer exist. There is something else: the "impentagonal" or the "metropo-colony."

What the United States spends in a month of war in Vietnam it could not recoup in five years if it were to devote itself to getting cheap raw materials out of, and at the same time selling expensive manufactured products to, what was formerly Indochina. And what the United States spends there in a year of military operations it could not recoup in half a century even if the two Vietnams—North and South—were covered with a layer of gold half an inch thick. If the diamond mines of the Transvaal were situated in Vietnam, they would not produce in fifty years of intensive exploitation what the United States spent fighting in Vietnam in 1967.

But out of what the United States spends in a year inside its own country on manufacturing arms, warships, fighter planes, clothes, shoes, medicine, and beer for the forces operating in Vietnam, the pentagonists get what is necessary to keep their fabulous industrial plants working and to pay the highest salaries in the world, a sum which in turn is transformed, through increased buying power for those who receive these salaries, into an ultra-rapid formation of capital through profit. The escalation of the war in Vietnam began in May, 1965; and in 1966, according to the Internal Revenue Service, the United States had 164 more millionaires than in 1965.

This capital that has been so rapidly accumulated is not employed in Vietnam, either wholly or partially, to produce more capital, as would have been the case if the war had been a typical imperialist operation to conquer Vietnamese territory in order to submit it to economic exploitation. This capital is used in the United States to produce more war materiel and more consumer goods that will in turn allow the recovery of part of the high salaries received by workers and white collar employees.

Although several studies have been made to prove that United States military expenditures have very little influence on the general economy of the country, the role these expenditures play in the formation and maintenance of pentagonism as a dominant force in American life has been concealed. Beginning in 1951, the military budget of the United States has been higher than the budget of the civilian (federal) government, which in political terms means that military power began to be greater than civilian power since it had more means at its disposal than the latter, and as a consequence civilian power began to depend increasingly on pentagonist expenditures for its stability.

The word "stability," as applied to government, does not have the same meaning in the United States that it has in other countries. In the United States a government is more stable when it has a high percentage of public opinion on its side. And the result is that the expenditures of the Pentagon have become a fundamental factor in obtaining this support. President Johnson recognized this in his "Economic Report of the President Transmitted to the Congress" in January, 1967, when he said that "Furthermore, the expansion of defense spending contributed to a significant change in the climate of opinion. *The Vietnam build-up virtually assured American businessmen that no economic reverse would occur in the near future.*"[1]

When President Johnson affirmed that military expenditures had produced "a significant change in the climate of [public] opinion," he was referring, of course, to a change favorable to the government, not to an unfavorable one; thus the stability of the government was secured, thanks to the military expenditures that were made through the escalation of the war in Vietnam.

Although we are going to continue to quote President Johnson's statements, for the moment we wish to call attention to the key phrase that refers to

American businessmen; we shall return to this later when we study the consequences of pentagonism on the political life of the United States.

The quotation from President Johnson, which we have taken from an official American document, gives the lie to the hired scholars who have attempted to demonstrate, by manipulating statistics with the cleverness of sleight-of-hand artists, that military expenditures have had little influence on the increase in production—and productivity—in the United States. A few lines farther down from the passage we have quoted, President Johnson said: "The increase in defense spending swelled an already strongly rising tide [from the second quarter of 1965 to the first quarter of 1966] of business investment expenditures."[2] Immediately afterward he cited the following figures:

> From the second quarter of 1965 to the first quarter of 1966, business spending for new structures and equipment rose by 9 billions. Defense investment, and social security liberalization, in combination, speeded the growth of disposable income. Consumer spending responded strongly, growing by 29 billions over this three-quarter interval. All in all, GNP advanced at an average of 16 billions a quarter. Real output grew at a phenomenal rate of 7.2 per cent, and industrial production rose at an annual rate of 9.7 per cent.[3]

Although these statements by the President of the United States are important because they categorically give the lie to everything that has been said denying the importance of war expenditures in the growth of the American economy, their political value lies in the phrase that we have referred to, which states that "the Vietnam build-up virtually assured American businessmen that no economic reverse would occur in the near future." These "American businessmen" are the ones who manipulate the pentagonist economy, the ones who share the profits from military contracts; they are the industrialists, the bankers, the shippers, the shopkeepers, and the promoters who, along with the generals and the pentagonist politicians, manipulate the foreign policy of the United States.

It is a known fact that the kind of imperialism which has now disappeared brought profits to the arms manufacturers. But in a sense these profits were marginal, something like commissions advanced on a far-reaching mercantile operation. The profits that the capitalists—and the governments of the imperialist countries—sought were not the immediate profits that came from the sale of military equipment. The profits sought through the conquest of a colonial territory were long-term investments. The expenses of conquest—including, of course, military equipment and mobilization—represented promotion expenses for the establishment of enterprises that would begin to make a profit after the conquest was consolidated and exploitation was organized. It must be realized that all the expenditures, including in them the value of the materiel, occasioned by a colonial army that in the nineteenth century was sent into the heart of Africa or to an Asiatic country, could not begin to equal the enormous figure involved in the cost of production—and production only—of a squadron of B-52 bombers. On the other hand, once expenditures for conquest had been made, the investment of capital to organize the exploitation of the conquered territory began; the installation of equipment such as railroads, mining installations, and ports began. Víctor Raúl Haya de la Torre saw this phenomenon clearly when, commenting on Lenin's thesis concerning imperialism, he said that the Russian leader was right as far as capitalist countries were concerned, but in the colonial territories imperialism stood for the first stage of capitalism, not the last, since it brought these territories capital investments and capitalist techniques of exploitation that they had not known before.

Pentagonism does not operate on the basis of capital investments in a colonial territory. Pentagonism operates with military methods commensurate with or similar to those used by imperialism, but its purpose is different. For to pentagonism the territory that is going to be attacked, or is under attack, is only a place destined to receive expendable material, both mechanical and human. Costly war materiel is going to be consumed in this place: bullets, bombs, medicine, clothes, cement, equipment to build barracks and roads and bridges, food and drink for the soldiers, and also the soldiers themselves, or at least many of them. The attacked country is the final depository of goods that have already been produced and sold and paid for in the mother country.

From a certain point of view, it would not matter to those who accumulate profits through the production of these goods whether they were thrown into the sea or used up in war maneuvers. But in the former case the endless chain of production—high profits, high salaries, greater sales, ultra-rapid accumulation of capital and increase in production once more, and so back to the beginning of the cycle—would be broken, since the production of such expensive and such short-lived equipment could not be justified if it was not meant for war. Moreover, only a state of war—which the pentagonized people accepts as an emergency situation—permits fabulous expenditures and the quick signing of contracts with firms that have at their disposal the prestige, the credit, and the means to produce materiel immediately.

It must be realized that in order to fulfill a production contract for B-52 bombers—to stick to our example—hundreds of millions of dollars must be discounted in one or several banks, and this can be done easily only by those industrialists who are directly or indirectly directors of these banks; that is to say, large contracts must go to established firms which have financial and industrial power beforehand.

As far as business is concerned, pentagonism is man's most fabulous invention and necessarily came into being in the capitalist countries par excellence—the countries of overdeveloped capitalism—since it was there that the capacity for accumulating profit was placed at the top of the scale of social values.

Pentagonism has various advantages over worn-out and now useless imperialism. We can mention two of these, one economic and one moral. The first lies in the fact that pentagonism provides the most rapid and safest means of capitalization conceivable in the world of business, since all of the profits—or almost all—get into the hands of war merchants even before the military equipment has been put to use. In this respect, perhaps only work in the gold mines of California brought such rapid, pure profit, although it was, of course, relatively limited. The second advantage—the moral one—lies in the fact that pentagonism leaves the prestige of the pentagonist country, which is the attacker, intact, because it can say to the world—and to its own people, who are giving the money for the materiel and for the profits of the businessmen and at the same time are providing the soldiers who are going to use this materiel and die while they use it—that it is not making war to conquer colonial territory; that is to say, it is not acting out of imperialist motives.

This last is true, but at the same time it hides the more important truth: that a little group of bankers, industrialists, businessmen, generals, and politicians is making war to obtain rapid and generous profits, which are translated into accumulation of capital and therefore into new investments with which they raise their profits all over again.

The partial truth that serves to hide the fundamental truth is in turn an instrument of propaganda for continuing along the path of pentagonism. Youngsters in the army are easily convinced that their country is not imperialistic, that it is not making war in order to conquer a colonial territory. What is more, they are led to believe that they are going to their deaths to help the attacked country, to save it from an evil. And this is very important, for to lead men to die and to kill it is always necessary to offer them a moral banner to fortify their consciences and justify their actions in their own eyes.

FOOTNOTES

[1]This quotation and those that follow were taken from this report, published by the Government Printing Office, Washington, D.C., 1967. Italics are mine.
[2]*Ibid,* pp. 46-47. The material between brackets follows in the next paragraph.
[3]*Loc. cit.*

23. A CAUSERIE AT THE MILITARY INDUSTRIAL

Paul Goodman

A good deal of the criticism of the military-industrial complex suffers from a certain disparity between the analysis of the problem and the inadequacy of the proposed response. If the situation is as bad as even some of the more sober critics maintain — if the nation has become a garrison state in which most important policy decisions are made in favor of an alliance of military agencies or corporate giants, in which theoretically countervailing institutions such as labor unions, the universities, and the Congress have been bought off with a "piece of the action" — then such extreme conditions would seem to dictate an extreme response.

Yet reaction is seldom extreme. Galbraith, Proxmire, and other liberal critics of the system seem to believe that relatively simple and minor adjustments (although difficult to achieve) will set free countervailing forces and return us to a truly pluralistic society. A few more liberals sent to Congress, a little closer watch over contract negotiations and costs, the banning of classified research from campuses, and such reforms will, it is hoped, bring the system to heel. Paul Goodman, realizing that the military-industrial complex threatens to become a social-industrial complex (to use Michael Harrington's term) as well, took an unlooked for opportunity to "soberly tell them off."

Source: Paul Goodman, "A Causerie at the Military-Industrial," *New York Review of Books,* IX (November 23, 1967), 14-19. Reprinted with permission from *The New York Review of Books.* Copyright © 1967 The New York Review.

The National Security Industrial Association (NSIA) was founded in 1944 by James Forrestal, to maintain and enhance the beautiful wartime communication between the armament industries and the government. At present it comprises 400 members, including of course all the giant aircraft, electronics, motors, oil, and chemical corporations, but also many one would not expect: not only General Dynamics, General Motors, and General Telephone and Electronics, but General Foods and General Learning; not only Sperry Rand, RCA, and Lockheed, but Servco and Otis Elevators. It is a wealthy club. The military budget is $84 billion.

At the recent biennial symposium, held on October 18 and 19 in the State Department auditorium, the theme was "Research and Development in the 1970s." To my not unalloyed pleasure, I was invited to participate as one of the seventeen speakers and assigned the topic "Planning for the Socio-Economic Environment." Naturally I could make the usual speculations about why I was thus "co-opted." I doubt that they expected to pick my brains for any profitable ideas. But it is useful for feeders at the public trough to present an image of wide-ranging discussion. It is comfortable to be able to say, "You see? these far-outniks *are* impractical." And business meetings are dull and I am notoriously stimulating. But the letter of invitation from Henri Busignies of ITT, the chairman of the symposium committee, said only, "Your accomplishments throughout your distinguished career eminently qualify you to speak with authority on the subject."

What is an intellectual man to do in such a case? I agree with the Gandhian principle, always cooperate within the limits of honor, truth, and justice. But how to cooperate with the military industrial club! during the Vietnam war 1967! It was certainly not the time to reason about basic premises, as is my usual approach, so I decided simply to confront them and soberly tell them off.

Fortunately it was the week of the demonstration at the Pentagon, when there would be thousands of my friends in Washington. So I tipped them off and thirty students from Cornell and Harpur drove down early to picket the auditorium, with a good leaflet about the evil environment for youth produced by the military corporations. When they came, the white helmets sprang up, plus the cameras and reporters. In the face of this dangerous invasion, the State Department of the United States was put under security, the doors were bolted, and the industrialists (and I) were not allowed to exit—on the 23rd Street side. Inside, I spoke as follows:

R & D FOR THE SOCIO-ECONOMIC ENVIRONMENT OF THE 1970s

I am astonished that at a conference on planning for the future, you have not invited a single speaker under the age of thirty, the group that is going to live in that future. I am pleased that some of the young people have come to pound on the door anyway, but it is too bad that they aren't allowed to come in.

This is a bad forum for this topic. Your program mentions the "emerging national goals" of urban development, continuing education, and improving the quality of man's environment. I would add another essential goal, reviving American democracy; and at least two indispensable international goals, to rescue the majority of mankind from deepening poverty, and to insure the survival of mankind as a species. These goals indeed require research and experimentation of the highest sophistication, but not by you. You people are unfitted by your commitments, your experience, your customary methods, your recruitment, and your moral disposition. You are the military industrial of the United States, the most dangerous body of men at the present in the world, for you not only implement our disastrous policies but are an overwhelming lobby for them, and you expand and rigidify the wrong use of brains, resources, and labor so that change becomes difficult. Most likely the trends you represent will be interrupted by a shambles of riots, alienation, ecological catastrophes, wars, and revolutions, so that current long-range planning, including this conference, is irrelevant. But if we ask what *are* the technological needs and what ought to be researched in this coming period, in the six areas I have mentioned, the best service that you people could perform is rather rapidly to phase yourselves out, passing on your relevant knowledge to people better qualified, or reorganizing yourselves with entirely different sponsors and commitments, so that you learn to think and feel in a different way. Since you are most of the R & D that there is, we cannot do without you as people, but we cannot do with you as you are.

In aiding technically underdeveloped regions, the need in the foreseeable future is for an intermediate technology, scientifically sophisticated but tailored to their local skills, tribal or other local social organization, plentiful labor force, and available raw materials. The aim is to help them out of starvation, disease, and drudgery without involving them in an international cash nexus of an entirely different order of magnitude. Let them take off at their own pace and in their own style. For models of appropriate technical analyses, I recommend you to E. F. Schumacher, of the British Coal Board, and his associates. Instead, you people—and your counterparts in Europe and Russia—have been imposing your technology, seducing native elites mostly corrupted by Western education, arming them, indeed often using them as a dumping ground for obsolete weapons. As Dr. Busignies pointed out yesterday, your aim must be, while maintaining leadership, to allow very little technical gap, in order to do business. Thus, you have involved these people in a wildly inflationary economy, have driven them into instant urbanization, and increased the amount of disease and destitution. You have disrupted ancient social patterns, debauched their cultures, fomented tribal and other wars, and in Vietnam yourselves engaged in genocide. You have systematically entangled them in Great Power struggles. It is not in your interest, and you do not have the minds or the methods, to take these peoples seriously as people.

The survival of the human species, at least in a civilized state, demands radical disarmament, and there are several feasible political means to achieve this if we willed it. By the same token, we must drastically de-energize the archaic system of nation-states, e.g., by internationalizing space exploration, expanding operations like the International Geophysical Year, de-nationalizing Peace Corps and aid programs, opening scientific information and travel. Instead, you—and your counterparts in Europe, Russia, and China—have rigidified and aggrandized the states with a Maginot-line kind of policy called Deterrence, which has continually escalated rather that stabilized. As Jerome Wiesner has demonstrated, past a certain point your operations have increased insecurity rather than diminished it. But this has been to your interest. Even in the present condition of national rivalry, it has been estimated, by Marc Raskin who sat in on the National Security Council, that the real needs of our defense should cost less than a fourth of the budget you have pork-barreled. You tried, unsuccessfully, to saddle us with the scientifically ludicrous Civil Defense program. You have sabotaged the technology of inspection for disarmament. Now you are saddling us with the anti-missile missiles and the multi-warhead missiles (MIRV). You have corrupted the human adventure of space with programs for armed platforms in orbit. Although we are the most heavily armed and the most naturally protected of the Great Powers, you have seen to it that we spend a vastly greater amount and perhaps a higher proportion of our wealth on armaments than any other nation.

This brings me to your effect on the climate of the economy. The wealth of a nation is to provide useful goods and services, with an emphasis first on necessities and broad-spread comforts, simply as a decent background for un-economic life and culture; an indefinitely expanding economy is a rat-race. There ought to be an even spread regionally, and no group must be allowed to fall outside of society. At present, thanks to the scientific ingenuity and hard work of previous generations, we could in America allow a modest livelihood to everyone as a constitutional right. And on the other hand, as the young have been saying by their style and actions, there is an imperative need to simplify the standard of living, since the affluent standard has become frivolous, tawdry, and distracting from life itself. But you people have distorted the structure of a rational economy. Since 1945, half of new investment has gone into your products, not subject to the market nor even to Congressional check. This year, 86 percent of money for research is for your arms and rockets. You push through the colossally useless Super-Sonic Transport. At least 20 percent of the economy is directly dependent on your enterprises. The profits and salaries of these enterprises are not normally distributed but go heavily to certain groups while others are excluded to the point of being out-caste. Your system is a major factor in producing the riots in Newark. [*At this remark there were indignant protests.*]

Some regions of the country are heavily favored—especially Pasadena and Dallas—and others disadvantaged. Public goods have been neglected. A dispro-portionate share of brains has been drained from more useful invention and development. And worst of all, you have enthusiastically supported an essentially mercantilist economics that measures economic health in terms of abstract Gross National Product and rate of growth, instead of concrete human well-being. Both domestically and internationally, you have been the bell-wether of meaningless expansion, and this has sharpened poverty in our own slums and rural regions and for the majority of mankind. It has been argued that military expenditure, precisely because it is isolated and wasteful, is a stabilizer of an economy, providing employment and investment opportunities when necessary; but your unbridled expansion has been the chief factor of social instability.

Dramatically intervening in education, you have again disrupted the normal structure. Great universities have come to be financed largely for your programs. Faculties have become unbalanced; your kind of people do not fit into the community of scholars. The wandering dialogue of science with the unknown is straitjacketed for petty military projects. You speak increasingly of the need for personal creativity, but this is not to listen to the Creator Spirit for ideas, but to harness it to your ideas. This is blasphemous. There has been secrecy, which is intolerable to true academics and scientists. The political, and morally dubious co-opting of science, engineering, and social science has disgusted and alienated many of the best students. Further, you have warped the method of education, beginning with the primary grades. Your need for narrowly expert personnel has led to processing the young to be test-passers, with a gross exaggeration of credits and grading. You have used the wealth of public and parents to train apprentices for yourselves. Your electronics companies have gone into the "education industries" and tried to palm off teaching machines, audio-visual aids, and programmed lessons in excess of the evidence for their utility. But the educational requirements of our society in the foreseeable future demand a very different spirit and method. Rather than processing the young, the problem is how to help the young grow up free and inventive in a highly scientific and socially complicated world. We do not need professional personnel so much as autonomous professionals who can criticize the programs handed to them and be ethically responsible. Do you encourage criticism of your programs by either the subsidized professors or the students? [*At this, Mr. Charles Herzfeld, the chairman of the session, shouted "Yes!" and there was loud applause for the interruption, yet I doubt that there is much such encouragement.*] We need fewer lessons and tests, and there ought to be much less necessity and prestige attached to mandarin requirements.

Let us turn to urbanism. *Prima facie,* there are parts of urban planning—construction, depollution, the logistics of transportation—where your talents ought to be peculiarly useful. Unfortunately, it is your companies who have oversold the planes and the cars, polluted the air and water, and balked at even trivial remedies, so that I do not see how you can be morally trusted with the job. The chief present and future problems in this field, however, are of a different kind. They are two. The long-range problem is to diminish the urbanization and suburban sprawl altogether, for they are economically unviable and socially harmful. For this, the most direct means, and the one I favor, is to cut down rural emigration and encourage rural return, by means of rural reconstruction and regional cultural development. The aim should be a 20 percent rural ratio instead of the present 5 percent. This is an aspect of using high technology for simplification, increasing real goods but probably diminishing the Gross National Product measured in cash. Such a program is not for you. Your thinking is never to simplify and retrench, but always to devise new equipment to alleviate the mess that you have helped to make with your previous equipment.

Secondly, the immediately urgent urban problem is how to diminish powerlessness, anomie, alienation, and mental disease. For this the best strategy is to decentralize urban administration, in policing, schooling, social welfare, neighborhood renewal, and real-estate and business ownership. Such community development often requires heightening conflict and risking technical inefficiency for intangible gains of initiative and solidarity. This also is obviously not your style. You want to concentrate capital and power. Your systems analyses of social problems always tend toward standardization, centralization, and bureaucratic control, although these are not necessary in the method. You do not like to feed your computers indefinite factors and unknown parameters where spirit, spite, enthusiasm, revenge, invention, etc., will make the difference. To be frank, your programs are usually grounded in puerile theories of social psychology, political science, and moral philosophy. There is a great need for research and trying out in this field, but the likely cast of characters might be small farmers, Negro matriarchs, political activists, long-haired students, and assorted sages. Not you. Let's face it. You are essentially producers of exquisite hardware and good at the logistics of moving objects around, but mostly with the crude aim of destroying things rather than reconstructing or creating anything, which is a harder task. Yet you boldly enter into fields like penology, pedagogy, hospital management, domestic architecture, and planning the next decade—wherever there is a likely budget.

I will use the last heading, improving the quality of man's environment, as a catch-all for some general remarks. In a society that is cluttered, overcentralized, and overadministered, we should aim at simplification, decentralization, and decontrol. These require highly sophisticated research to determine where, how, and how much. Further, for the first time in history, the scale of the artificial and technological has dwarfed the natural landscape. In prudence, we must begin to think of a principled limitation on artifice and to cut back on some of our present gigantic impositions, if only to insure that we do not commit some terrible ecological blunder. But as Dr. Smelt of Lockheed explained to us yesterday, it is the genius of American technology to go very rapidly from R&D to application: in this context, he said, prudence is not a virtue. A particular case is automation: which human functions should be computerized or automated, which should not? This question—it is both an analytic and an empirical one—ought to be critical in the next decade, but I would not trust IBM salesmen to solve it. Another problem is how man can feel free and at home within the technological environment itself. For instance, comprehending a machine and being able to repair it is one thing; being a mere user and in bondage to service systems is another. Also, to feel free, a man must have a rather strong say in the close environment that he must deal with. But these requirements of a technology are not taken into account by you. Despite Dr. Smelt, technology *is* a branch of moral philosophy, subordinate to criteria like prudence, modesty, safety, amenity, flexibility, cheapness, easy comprehension, repairability, and so forth. If such moral criteria became paramount in the work of technologists, the quality of the environment would be more livable.

Still a further problem is how to raise the scientific and technical culture of the whole people, and here your imperialistic grab of the R&D money and of the system of education has done immeasurable damage. You have seen to it that the lion's share has gone to your few giant firms and a few giant universities, although in fact very many, perhaps more than half of, important innovations still come from independents and tiny firms. I was pleased that Dr. Dessauer of Xerox pointed this out this morning. If the money were distributed more widely, there would probably be more discovery and invention, and what is more important, there would be a larger pool of scientific and competent people. You make a fanfare about the spinoff of a few socially useful items, but your whole enterprise is notoriously wasteful—for instance, five billions go down the drain when after a couple of years you change the design of a submarine, sorry about that. When you talk about spinoff, you people remind me of the TV networks who, after twenty years of nothing, boast that they did broadcast the McCarthy hearings and the Kennedy funeral. [*This remark led to free and friendly laughter; I do not know whether at the other industry or at their own hoax.*] Finally, concentrating the grants, you narrow the field of discovery and innovation, creating an illusion of technological determinism, as if we *had* to develop in a certain style. But if we had put our brains and money into electric cars, we would now have electric cars; if we had concentrated on intensive agriculture, we would now find that this is the most efficient, and so forth. And in grabbing the funds, you are not even honest; 90 percent of the R&D money goes in fact to shaping up for production, which as entrepreneurs you should pay out of your own pockets.

No doubt some of these remarks have been unfair and ignorant. [*Frantic applause.*] By and large they are undeniable, and I have not been picking nits.

These remarks have certainly been harsh and moralistic. We are none of us saints, and ordinarily I would be ashamed to use such a tone. But you are the manufacturers of napalm, fragmentation bombs, the planes that destroy rice. Your weapons have killed hundreds of thousands in Vietnam and you will kill other hundreds of thousands in other Vietnams. I am sure that most of you would concede that much of what you do is ugly and harmful, at home and abroad. But you would say that it is necessary for the American way of life, at home and abroad, and therefore you cannot do otherwise. Since we believe, however, that that way of life itself is unnecessary, ugly, and un-American [*Shouts of "Who are we?"*] —we are I and those people outside—we cannot condone your present operations; they should be wiped off the slate.

Most of the 300 in the audience did not applaud these remarks, but there was quite strong applause from a couple of dozen. Afterward these sought me out singly and explained, "Thanks for having the courage" or more significantly, "Those kids outside are right. My son is doing the same thing in Boston—Ohio State—etc."

The chairman of the session, Charles Herzfeld of ITT, felt obliged to exclaim, "The remark about our committing genocide in Vietnam is obscene. He does not say what is really intolerable there, the Viet Cong single out college graduates for extermination."!!

More poignantly, the director of the symposium, a courteous and intelligent man, apologized to the gathering for having exposed them to me, which must have been a wrench for him to say. He had of course seen my text beforehand.

We went out by the exit onto the other avenue, and I was able to rejoin the more amiable company of the young people, who were now sitting with their backs pressed against the auditorium doors, still among the white helmets. I answered their questions about the proceedings and we dispersed. That night NBC-TV showed a picture of the pickets, and next morning I got a story in the Post.

Where is it at? Unquestionably the week of Resistance demonstrations was successful and made its point, that thousands and probably tens of thousands are now willing to go to jail or get their heads broken to stop the Vietnam war. There were no disappointments: Turning in the draft-cards, resistance at the induction centers and staging areas and against the Dow and Navy recruiters, the crowd in Washington and the melee at the Pentagon, all proved strong enough.

We are witnessing a test of legitimacy, and in my opinion the government position is now untenable. Despite a few exotic slogans, there is a groundswell of American populism, including sporadic populist violence as in 1890 or 1933, but mainly solidly secure in the belief that it is itself the democratic voice and LBJ is a usurper. As was not reported in the press, the night vigil on the Pentagon steps on October 22 sang *The Star-Spangled Banner*. It was probably a mistake for the President to have exposed so many troops to the young resisters who were mostly peaceful but obviously spunky and sometimes persuasive.

The climate is beginning to feel like the eve of the French withdrawal from Algeria, including the same coalition of the young, the intellectuals, and the Algerians (Negroes). The question remains, is the American structure so rich and technologically powerful that its government can dispense with legitimacy? I don't know. And while the NLF and the North Vietnamese have been hanging on and continuing to counter-attack (and their people and our people are dying), American opinion has finally begun to veer sharply toward getting out. The hawk spokesmen have become divided and confused.

There is a persistent rumor in Washington that the President (or the hidden government) is about to cast the die and approve the prepared invasion of North Vietnam in December. If so, a hundred thousand youth and many many others will resist non-violently or violently and there will be martial law and concentration camps. I will not speculate further along this atomic line.

But there is evidence that shrewder counsel might prevail; to write off this odious war, adopt a somewhat less adventurous foreign policy, put a little more money into the cities, divert some of the military industrial enterprise into Outer Space and "long-range planning," and come to a solid understanding with the Russians. I think this is the meaning of the rapidly increasing dovishness in Congress and the sudden conversion of the Republicans who threaten to nominate Percy or Gavin. The strategy is similar to the New Deal: when the going gets too rough domestically, accommodate and go on to build a grander corporate structure that is, in some respects, better—temporarily. For this plan, however, Johnson would have to go, since it now seems impossible for him to sound a retreat from Vietnam without getting shot by the irate father of a young man who died in vain. Whether we would then get Robert Kennedy or a moderate Republican is probably unimportant.

Needless to say, this is not the outcome that the radical young are after. They fear, justifiedly, that if we stop the war, most of the Americans will again fall morally and politically asleep. Yet they, like the rest of us, do want to stop the Vietnam war; there are few indeed who are so fanatical for world upheaval as to want that particular evil to continue so that good may come. In my opinion, also, they will have to learn that one is not going to re-structure modern society with a fraction of the 10 percent Negro population, nor even with the "Third World" ruled by Ben Bellas, Nassers, Maos, Nkrumahs, Sukarnos, or their successors. This is not the stuff of new humanism. For instance, those who objected to being processed at Berkeley will have to think seriously about Chairman Mao's little red book. And those who want to make love not war but who also want to imitate Che Guevara in American cities, must ask themselves what adequate guerrilla tactics would be in a high technology, namely to poison the water, wreck the subways, and cause power failures in New York and Chicago; is this what they intend?

But I do not think the young themselves will fall asleep. They have been through remarkable experiences and have found one another. There is the potentiality of a kind of youth international. Most important, the present power-systems of the world are indeed unfit for modern conditions, and this will become increasingly apparent. If the young continue to be in conflict, to try out innovations, and to study professionally what ought to be done with our technology and ecology, mores and authority-structure, and the fact of one world, they will gradually shape for themselves a good inheritance to come into. Considering the tremendous power and complexity of the systems they want to displace, twenty years is a short time to devise something better.

BIBLIOGRAPHY

A complete bibliography of books and articles on the military-industrial complex would be very long indeed. The following list is only a sample of some of the best, or best known, books on various aspects of the problem. An asterisk (*) indicates that the book is available in paperback.

During the early 1960s, three books called attention to the problem Eisenhower had publicized in his Farewell Address. The first was Fred J. Cook, *The Warfare State* (New York, 1962),* which was followed two years later by Tristram Coffin, *The Passion of the Hawks: Militarism in Modern America* (New York, 1964) and Jack Raymond, *Power at the Pentagon* (New York, 1964). All are competent journalistic accounts.

Within the last two years the renewed interest in and concern over the operations of the Pentagon have led to a number of excellent studies. Senator William Proxmire has drawn upon the findings of his congressional committee for *Report from Wasteland: America's Military-Industrial Complex* (New York, 1970). A brief study by two Washington reporters is contained in William McGaffin and Erwin Knoll's *Scandal in the Pentagon: A Challenge to Democracy* (Greenwich, 1969).* A more radical approach is offered by Richard J. Barnet in *The Economy of Death* (New York, 1969).* Barnet is particularly original in his analysis of what he calls "the National Security Managers." Perhaps the best brief survey of the problem is given in Sidney Lens, *The Military-Industrial Complex* (Philadelphia, 1970).* As might be expected from one with Lens' background, his chapter on the involvement of labor unions is particularly good.

Two periodicals deserve particular mention. *The Progressive* devoted an entire issue to "The Power of the Pentagon" [XXXIII (June 1969)]. It is particularly notable because it offers the opinions of many leading congressional liberals. Because of *Newsweek's* mass circulation, its cover story on "The Military Industrial Complex" (June 9, 1969) is also a significant survey of the question.

In addition to these general works, several more specialized are of particular interest. Two books by Ralph E. Lapp, the nuclear physicist and Washington observer, deal pointedly with the weapons aspect of the Pentagon's power: *The Weapons Culture* (Baltimore, 1969)* and *Arms Beyond Doubt: The Tyranny of Weapons Technology* (New York, 1970). Economics is emphasized in Seymour Melman, *Pentagon Capitalism: The Political Economy of War* (New York, 1970).* A good study of one of the most controversial weapons systems of our time is found in Robert J. Art, *The TFX Decision: McNamara and the Military* (Boston, 1968).* A book of major importance, written by a career Air Force officer and dealing with that services goals and tactics, is Perry McCoy Smith, *The Air Force Plans for Peace, 1943-1945* (Baltimore, 1970).

A recent compilation of materials is offered in Herbert I. Schiller and Joseph D. Phillips, eds., *Super-State: Readings in the Military-Industrial Complex* (Urbana, Ill. 1970), which contains papers (critical and favorable) on the armed forces, industry, communications, and science. A more specialized but very useful volume is James L. Clayton, ed., *The Economic Impact of the Cold War: Sources and Readings* (New York, 1970).* Social and cultural aspects are touched upon in Keith L. Nelson, *The Impact of War on Life: The Twentieth-Century Experience* (New York, 1971).* The bibliography of the Nelson book is particularly excellent.

Two collections especially useful to activists are *The University-Military-Police Complex: A Directory and Related Documents* (New York, 1970),* compiled by Michael Klare and published by The North American Congress on Latin America, and *War Incorporated: The Complete Picture of the Congressional-Military-Industrial-University Complex* (Berkeley, n.d.),* published by the Student Research Facility. Another volume containing excellent essays and useful appendices is Leonard S. Rodberg and Derek Shearer, eds., *The Pentagon Watchers: Students Report on the National Security State* (Garden City, N.Y., 1970).*

The export of arms is covered in George Thayer, *The War Business: The International Trade in Armaments* (New York, 1969).* A case study of corruption and incompetence is told in Berkeley Rice, *The C-5A Scandal: An Inside Story of the Military-Industrial Complex* (Boston, 1971). Among the books written by participants or firsthand observers are J. William Fulbright, *The Pentagon Propaganda Machine* (New York, 1970),* which documents the charges made famous by the CBS News special, "The Selling of the Pentagon." Adam Yarmolinsky, one of the original McNamara team, has written *The Military Establishment: Its Impact on American Society* (New York, 1971).* Two former Pentagon employees, Alain C. Enthoven and K. Wayne Smith, look back over the Kennedy-Johnson years in *How Much Is Enough? Shaping the Defense Program, 1961-1969* (New York, 1971). Richard F. Kaufman, a staff member of the Joint Economic Committee of the Congress has provided a popular account of the Proxmire findings in *The War Profiteers* (Indianapolis, 1970).

APPENDICES

APPENDIX 1
THE 100 LARGEST INDUSTRIAL CORPORATIONS IN THE UNITED STATES RANKED BY SALES IN 1970

1.	General Motors Corp.	38.	Firestone Tire & Rubber Co.
2.	Standard Oil Co. (N.J.)	39.	Phillips Petroleum Co.
3.	Ford Motor Co.	40.	Occidental Petroleum Corp.
4.	General Electric Co.	41.	General Dynamics Corp.
5.	International Business Machines Corp.	42.	Caterpillar Tractor Co.
6.	Mobil Oil Corp.	43.	Singer Co.
7.	Chrysler Corp.	44.	McDonnell Douglas Corp.
8	International Telephone	45.	General Foods Corp.
	& Telegraph Corp.	46.	Continental Can Co., Inc.
9.	Texaco Inc.	47.	Monsanto Co.
10.	Western Electric Co., Inc.	48.	Sun Oil Co.
11.	Gulf Oil Corp.	49.	Honeywell, Inc.
12.	United States Steel Corp.	50.	Grace (W.R.) & Co.
13.	Westinghouse Electric Corp.	51.	Dow Chemical Co.
14.	Standard Oil of California	52.	International Paper Co.
15.	Ling-Temco-Vought, Inc.	53.	American Can Co.
16.	Standard Oil (Indiana)	54.	Borden, Inc.
17.	Boeing Co.	55.	Rapid-American Corp.
18.	Du Pont (E.I.) de Nemours & Co.	56.	Burlington Industries, Inc.
19.	Shell Oil Co.	57.	Union Oil of California
20.	General Telephone & Electronics	58.	R.J. Reynolds Industries, Inc.
21.	RCA Corp.	59.	Sperry Rand
22.	Goodyear Tire & Rubber Co.	60.	Xerox Corp.
23.	Swift and Co.	61.	Boise Cascade Corp.
24.	United Carbide Corp.	62.	Cities Service Co.
25.	Procter & Gamble Co.	63.	Minnesota Mining &
26.	Bethlehem Steel Corp.		Manufacturing Co.
27.	Eastman Kodak Co.	64.	Consolidated Foods Corp.
28.	Kraftco Corp.	65.	Gulf & Western Industries, Inc.
29.	Greyhound Corp.	66.	Textron, Inc.
30.	Atlantic Richfield Co.	67.	Coca-Cola Co.
31.	Continental Oil Co.	68.	TRW Inc.
32.	International Harvester Co.	69.	Armco Steel Corp.
33.	Lockheed Aircraft Corp.	70.	Beatrice Foods Co.
34.	Tenneco Inc.	71.	Ralston Purina Co.
35.	North American Rockwell Corp.	72.	Uniroyal, Inc.
36.	Litton Industries, Inc.	73.	Aluminum Co. of America
37.	United Aircraft Corp.	74.	American Brands, Inc.

APPENDIX 1 (con't)

75.	Bendix Corp.	88.	Raytheon Co.
76.	National Cash Register Co.	89.	Warner-Lambert Co.
77.	American Standard Inc.	90.	Genesco Inc.
78.	Signal Companies, Inc.	91.	Allied Chemical Corp.
79.	Ashland Oil Inc.	92.	National Steel Corp.
80.	Owens-Illinois Inc.	93.	Weyerhaeuser Co.
81.	United Brands Co.	94.	U.S. Industries, Inc.
82.	CPC International Inc.	95.	Getty Oil Co.
83.	Standard Oil (Ohio)	96.	Teledyne, Inc.
84.	Republic Steel Corp.	97.	Colgate-Palmolive Co.
85.	U.S. Plywood-Champion Papers, Inc.	98.	B.F. Goodrich Co.
86.	FMC Corp.	99.	Georgia-Pacific Corp.
87.	American Home Products Corp.	100.	Whirlpool Corp.

Source: Economics Division, Congressional Research Service, Library of Congress, *The 100 Largest Industrial Corporations in the U.S. Ranked by Sales in 1970* (May 24, 1971).

APPENDIX 2
PRINCIPAL INDUSTRIAL CONTRACTORS WITH THE OFFICE OF SCIENTIFIC RESEARCH AND DEVELOPMENT DURING WORLD WAR II

Western Electric Company	94	$17,091,819.00
Research Construction Company	2	13,950,000.00
General Electric Company	58	8,077,047.14
Radio Corporation of America	54	5,783,498.13
E. I. du Pont de Nemours and Company	59	5,704,146.54
Westinghouse Electric Manufacturing Corporation	54	5,122,722.26
Remington Rand, Incorporated	3	4,675,050.00
Eastman Kodak Company	29	4,509,200.00
Monsanto Chemical Company	8	4,222,044.00
Zenith Radio Corporation	3	4,175,000.00
Standard Oil Development Company	14	3,453,000.00
Hygrade Sylvania (Sylvania Electric Company)	17	3,093,451.16
Erwood Sound Company	1	2,875,000.00
Douglas Aircraft Company	3	2,592,500.00
M. W. Kellogg Company	2	1,915,000.00
Budd Wheel Company	2	1,655,000.00
Gulf Research and Development Company	9	1,601,450.00
Delta Star Electric Company	1	1,464,850.00
Emerson Radio and Phonograph Corporation	5	1,333,500.00
Ford, Bacon and Davis, Inc.	2	1,300,000.00
Globe-Union, Incorporated	2	1,275,000.00
Federal Telephone and Radio Corporation	13	1,211,390.00
Bowen and Company	1	1,160,000.00
National Carbon Company	4	1,076,000.00
Galvin Manufacturing Corporation	7	1,041,950.00

Source: James Phinney Baxter 3rd, *Scientists Against Time* (Boston: Atlantic-Little Brown, 1946), pp. 456-457.

APPENDIX 3
TOP 100 SPACE CONTRACTORS (NATIONAL AERONAUTICS
AND SPACE ADMINISTRATION) FOR FISCAL YEAR 1967

Rank	Companies	Thousands of dollars
	Total Awards to Business	$3,864,133
1.	North American Aviation, Inc.	983,814
2.	Grumman Aircraft Engineering Corp.	481,137
3.	Boeing Co.	273,514
4.	McDonnell Douglas Corp.	243,913
5.	International Business Machines Corp.	186,355
6.	General Electric Co.	179,261
7.	Bendix Corp.	120,028
8.	Aerojet-General Corp.	95,691
9.	Chrysler Corp.	76,602
10.	General Motors Corp.	65,222
11.	General Dynamics Corp.	60,990
12.	Radio Corp. of America	57,512
13.	TRW Inc.	52,551
14.	LTV, Aerospace Corp.	46,326
15.	Lockheed Aircraft Corp.	42,036
16.	United Aircraft Corp.	39,989
17.	Sperry Rand Corp.	38,666
18.	Philco-Ford Corp.	32,059
19.	Trans World Airlines, Inc.	25,091
20.	General Precision, Inc.	24,987
21.	Honeywell, Inc.	22,647
22.	Hughes Aircraft Co.	19,850
23.	Brown Engineering Co., Inc.	16,713
24.	Martin Marietta Corp.	12,828
25.	Union Carbide Corp.	12,648
26.	Federal Electric Corp.	12,305
27.	Computer Sciences Corp.	11,796
28.	Air Products & Chemicals, Inc.	11,788
29.	Thiokol Chemical Corp.	11,455
30.	Mason-Rust	11,213
31.	Catalytic Construction Co.	11,051
32.	Westinghouse Electric Corp.	10,388
33.	Brown & Root Co./Northrop Corp. (Joint Venture)	10,000
34.	Fairchild Hiller Corp.	9,794
35.	Bellcom, Inc.	9,318
36.	Garrett Corp.	9,293
37.	Bechtel Corp.	9,198
38.	Vitro Corp. of America	8,988
39.	Bell Aerospace Corp.	8,877
40.	Northrop Corp.	8,815
41.	Hayes International Corp.	7,289
42.	Control Data Corp.	7,111
43.	Graham Engineering Co., Inc.	7,109
44.	Scientific Data Systems	7,080
45.	Spaco, Inc.	6,785
46.	Ball Brothers Research Corp.	6,648
47.	Dow Chemical Co.	6,471
48.	ILC Industries, Inc.	6,336
49.	Documentation, Inc.	5,880
50.	Warrior Constructors, Inc./Notkin, Inc./National Constructors, Inc.	5,776

APPENDIX 3 (con't)

Rank	Companies	Thousands of dollars
51.	Sanders Associates, Inc.	$5,626
52.	Zia Co.	5,096
53.	Space-General Corp.	5,007
54.	Management Services, Inc.	4,745
55.	Basic Construction Co.	4,737
56.	Allis-Chalmers Manufacturing Co.	4,731
57.	Southern Bell Telephone Co.	4,432
58.	American Telephone & Telegraph Co.	4,397
59.	American Science & Engineering, Inc.	4,175
60.	Aero Spacelines, Inc.	3,631
61.	Gillmore-Olson Co.	3,602
62.	Perkin-Elmer Corp.	3,546
63.	Western Union Telegraph Co.	3,472
64.	Computer Application, Inc.	3,461
65.	Wolf Research & Development Corp.	3,360
66.	Computing & Software, Inc.	3,337
67.	Electronic Associates, Inc.	3,312
68.	Pacific Crane & Rigging Co.	3,234
69.	Lawrence, J. H. Co.	3,226
70.	Ampex Corp.	3,176
71.	Avco Corp.	3,049
72.	Electro Optical Systems, Inc.	2,896
73.	Air Reduction Co.	2,754
74.	Communications Satellite Corp.	2,745
75.	International Telephone & Telegraph Corp.	2,651
76.	Melpar, Inc.	2,640
77.	Radiation, Inc.	2,506
78.	Texas Instruments, Inc.	2,440
79.	Consolidated Electrodynamics Corp.	2,405
80.	Systems Engineering Laboratory, Inc.	2,360
81.	GCA Corp.	2,342
82.	New Orleans Public Service, Inc.	2,312
83.	Western Electric Co.	2,282
84.	Motorola, Inc.	2,219
85.	Dynalectron Corp.	2,162
86.	Keltec Industries, Inc.	2,098
87.	Virginia Electric Power Co.	2,053
88.	Kaiser Industries Corp.	2,032
89.	Goodyear Aerospace Corp.	1,997
90.	Greenhut Construction, Inc.	1,960
91.	Electro-Mechanical Research, Inc.	1,945
92.	Kollsman Instrument Corp.	1,939
93.	Minnesota Mining & Manufacturing Co.	1,935
94.	Sylvania Electric Products, Inc.	1,880
95.	Pearce DeMoss King, Inc.	1,858
96.	Hazeltine Corp.	1,807
97.	Cleveland Electric Illuminating Co.	1,790
98.	ITT World Communication, Inc.	1,764
99.	Marquardt Corp.	1,758
100.	Western Union International, Inc.	1,742
	Other	286,315

Source: *Competition in Defense Procurement.* Hearings before the Subcommittee on Antitrust and Monopoly of the Committee on the Judiciary, U.S. Senate, 90th Cong., 2d sess. (1968), pp. 874-876.

APPENDIX 4
TOP 100 DEFENSE CONTRACTORS LISTED ACCORDING TO NET VALUE
OF MILITARY PRIME CONTRACT, FISCAL YEAR 1969, CONTRACTS TO
SUBSIDIARIES INCLUDED (in thousands of dollars)

1.	Lockheed Aircraft Corp.	$2,040,236
2.	General Electric Co.	1,620,775
3.	General Dynamics Corp.	1,243,055
4.	McDonnell Douglas Corp.	1,069,743
5.	United Aircraft Corp.	997,380
6.	American Telephone & Telegraph Co.	
	(including Western Electric Co.)	914,579
7.	Ling Temco Vought, Inc.	914,114
8.	North American Rockwell Corp.	674,175
9.	Boeing Co.	653,638
10.	General Motors Corp.	584,439
11.	Raytheon Co.	546,772
12.	Sperry Rand Corp.	467,861
13.	Avco Corp.	456,054
14.	Hughes Aircraft Co.	439,016
15.	Westinghouse Electric Corp.	429,558
16.	Textron, Inc.	428,290
17.	Grumman Aircraft Engineering Corp.	417,052
18.	Honeywell, Inc.	405,575
19.	Ford Motor Co.	396,333
20.	Olin Matheison Chemical Corp.	354,359
21.	Litton Industries, Inc.	317,102
22.	Teledyne, Inc.	308,455
23.	RCA Corp.	298,992
24.	Standard Oil Co. (N.J.)	291,053
25.	Martin Marietta Corp.	264,279
26.	General Tire & Rubber Co.	263,501
27.	International Business Machines Corp.	256,623
28.	Raymond Morrison	254,000
29.	International Telephone & Telegraph Corp.	238,267
30.	Tenneco, Inc.	236,679
31.	Du Pont (E.I.) de Nemours & Co.	211,965
32.	FMC Corp.	195,625
33.	Norris Industries	187,553
34.	Bendix Corp.	184,437
35.	Hercules, Inc.	179,622
36.	Northrop Corp.	178,907
37.	Uniroyal, Inc.	174,088
38.	TRW, Inc.	170,379
39.	Pan American World Airways, Inc.	167,437
40.	Asiatic Petroleum Corp.	155,583
41.	Mobil Oil Corp.	151,515
42.	Standard Oil Co. of California	148,773
43.	Fairchild Hiller Corp.	148,586
44.	Collins Radio Co.	145,751
45.	Kaiser Industries Corp.	142,398
46.	General Telephone & Electronics Corp.	140,476
47.	Day & Zimmerman, Inc.	137,793
48.	Texas Instruments, Inc.	132,483
49.	Federal Cartridge Corp.	131,901
50.	Magnavox Co.	130,282

APPENDIX 4 (con't)

51.	Thiokol Chemical Corp.	$128,070
52.	Texaco, Inc.	123,973
53.	Chrysler Corp.	121,816
54.	Pacific Architects & Engineers, Inc.	120,959
55.	Sanders Associates, Inc.	118,482
56.	U.S. Steel Corp.	117,798
57.	Goodyear Tire & Rubber Co.	116,460
58.	Singer Co.	116,242
59.	Chamberlain Mfg. Corp.	115,925
60.	Lear Siegler, Inc.	115,753
61.	American Machine & Foundry Co.	115,266
62.	Colt Industries, Inc.	114,425
63.	Eastman Kodak Co.	109,848
64.	City Investing Co.	109,199
65.	Whittaker Corp.	107,688
66.	American Mfg. Co. of Texas	106,745
67.	Massachusetts Institute of Technology	100,519
68.	Gulf Oil Corp.	95,942
69.	National Presto Industries, Inc.	94,908
70.	Kidde Walter & Co., Inc.	91,921
71.	Signal Companies, Inc.	91,265
72.	Curtiss Wright Corp.	91,171
73.	Harvey Aluminum Inc.	90,458
74.	States Marine Lines, Inc.	87,059
75.	Reynolds (R.J.) Industries, Inc.	84,929
76.	Aerospace Corp.	76,245
77.	Motorola Inc.	73,164
78.	Automation Industries, Inc.	73,112
79.	Talley Industries, Inc.	72,470
80.	Harris-Intertype Corp.	71,606
81.	Firestone Tire & Rubber Co.	66,656
82.	Seatrain Lines, Inc.	64,572
83.	Aluminum Co. of America	64,458
84.	Hughes Tool Co.	63,693
85.	National Gypsum Co.	63,214
86.	Hazeltine Corp.	60,553
87.	Western Union Telegraph Co.	57,686
88.	Control Data Corp.	56,913
89.	White Motor Corp.	56,284
90.	Continental Airlines, Inc.	55,242
91.	World Airways, Inc.	54,930
92.	Atlantic Richfield Co.	54,311
93.	Tumpane Co., Inc.	53,963
94.	Cessna Aircraft Co.	53,417
95.	Smith Investment Co.	51,701
96.	Sverdrup & Parcel & Associates, Inc.	50,247
97.	Dynalectron Corp.	50,049
98.	Letourneau R. G., Inc.	49,903
99.	Flying Tiger Line, Inc.	48,261
100.	Southern Airways, Inc.	48,260

Source: "Top 100 Defense Contractors Announced," *Defense Industry Bulletin*, 5 (December, 1969), 13-16. Original lists subsidiaries separately.

APPENDIX 5
PRIME MILITARY CONTRACT AWARDS 1960-1967 TO U.S. COMPANIES FOR FIRMS TOTALING
MORE THAN $1 BILLION IN THIS 7-YEAR PERIOD (dollar amounts in millions)

Fiscal year	1961	1962	1963	1964	1965	1966	1967	7-yr total	Percent of total sales
1. Lockheed Aircraft	1,175	1,419	1,517	1,455	1,715	1,531	1,807	10,619	88
2. General Dynamics	1,460	1,197	1,033	987	1,179	1,136	1,832	8,824	67
3. McDonnell Douglas	527	779	863	1,360	1,026	1,001	2,125	7,681	75
4. Boeing Co.	920	1,133	1,356	1,365	583	914	912	7,183	54
5. General Electric	875	976	1,021	893	824	1,187	1,290	7,066	19
6. No. American-Rockwell	1,197	1,032	1,062	1,019	746	520	689	6,265	57
7. United Aircraft	625	663	530	625	632	1,139	1,097	5,311	57
8. American Tel. & Tel.	551	468	579	636	588	672	673	4,167	9
9. Martin-Marietta	692	803	767	476	316	338	290	3,682	62
10. Sperry-Rand	408	466	446	374	318	427	484	2,923	35
11. General Motors	282	449	444	256	254	508	625	2,818	2
12. Grumman Aircraft	238	304	390	396	353	323	488	2,492	67
13. General Tire	290	366	425	364	302	327	273	2,347	37
14. Raytheon	305	407	295	253	293	368	403	2,324	55
15. AVCO	251	323	253	279	234	506	449	2,295	75
16. Hughes	331	234	312	289	278	337	419	2,200	u
17. Westinghouse Electric	308	246	323	237	261	349	453	2,177	13
18. Ford (Philco)	200	269	228	211	312	440	404	2,064	3
19. RCA	392	340	329	234	214	242	268	2,019	16
20. Bendix	269	286	290	257	235	282	296	1,915	42
21. Textron	66	117	151	216	196	555	497	1,798	36
22. Ling-Temco-Vought	47	133	206	247	265	311	535	1,744	70
23. Internat. Tel. & Tel.	202	244	266	256	207	220	255	1,650	19
24. I.B.M.	330	155	203	332	186	182	195	1,583	7
25. Raymond International	46	61	84	196	71	548	462	1,568	u
26. Newport News Shipbuilding	290	185	221	400	185	51	188	1,520	90+
27. Northrop	156	152	223	165	256	276	306	1,434	61
28. Thiokol	210	178	239	254	136	111	173	1,301	96
29. Std. Oil of N.J.	168	180	155	161	164	214	235	1,277	2
30. Kaiser Industries	—	87	49	152	219	441	306	1,255	45

31. Honeywell	86	127	170	107	82	251	306	1,129	24
32. General Tel.	61	116	162	229	232	196	138	1,124	25
33. Collins Radio	94	150	144	129	141	245	202	1,105	65
34. Chrysler	158	181	186	170	81	150	165	1,091	4
35. Litton	–	88	198	210	190	219	180	1,085	25
36. Pan. Am. World Air.	127	147	155	164	158	170	115	1,046	44
37. F.M.C.	88	160	199	141	124	163	170	1,045	21
38. Hercules	117	182	183	137	101	120	195	1,035	31

u—unavailable.
[1]Includes Morrison-Knudsen, Brown & Root, and J. A. Jones Construction Co.

Source: *Competition in Defense Procurement*. Hearings before the Subcommittee on Antitrust and Monopoly of the Committee on the Judiciary, U.S. Senate, 90th Cong., 2d sess. (1968), pp. 868-869.

APPENDIX 6
NATIONAL DEFENSE AND TOTAL BUDGET OUTLAYS: 1940-1970

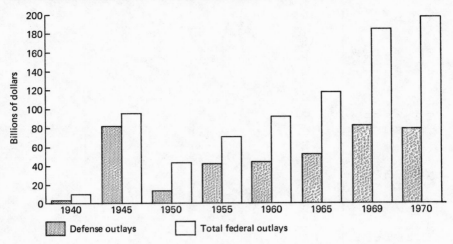

Source: U.S. Department of Commerce, *Statistical Abstract of the United States, 1970* (Washington, D.C., 1970), p. 244.

APPENDIX 7
SOCIAL WELFARE EXPENDITURES UNDER SELECTED PUBLIC PROGRAMS: 1940-1969

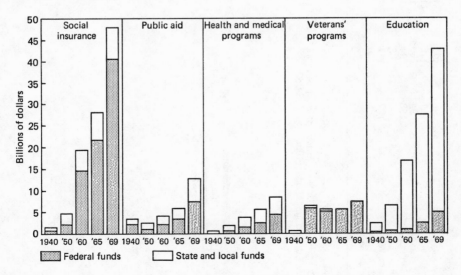

Source: U.S. Department of Commerce, *Statistical Abstract of the United States, 1970* (Washington, D.C., 1970), p. 272.

APPENDIX 8
CHANGING COMPOSITION OF FEDERAL BUDGET OUTLAYS, FISCAL YEARS 1959-1969 (dollar amounts in billions)

Functional categories	Outlays 1959	Outlays 1964	Outlays 1969	Percentage distribution 1959	Percentage distribution 1964	Percentage distribution 1969	Change 1959-69
National defense:							
DOD, military	$41.5	$49.6	$77.8	45.0	41.8	41.9	$36.3
Military assistance (MAP)	2.2	1.2	.6	2.4	1.0	.3	-1.6
Subtotal, military and MAP	43.7	50.8	78.4	47.4	42.8	42.2	34.7
Support of Southeast Asia operations	–	–	(28.8)	–	–	(15.5)	(28.8)
Other	2.9	2.8	2.6	3.2	2.4	1.4	-.3
Subtotal, national defense	46.6	53.6	81.0	50.6	45.2	43.6	34.4
Civilian programs:							
International affairs and finance	3.3	4.1	4.0	3.5	3.5	2.1	.7
Space	.1	4.2	4.2	.2	3.5	2.3	4.1
Agriculture and natural resources	6.6	7.2	9.0	7.1	6.0	4.9	2.4
Human resources programs	19.6	28.4	58.1	21.3	24.0	31.3	38.5
Veterans	5.4	5.7	7.7	5.9	4.8	4.2	2.3
Other civilian programs	5.6	8.5	11.0	6.1	7.2	5.9	5.4
Subtotal, civilian programs	40.6	58.1	94.1	44.1	49.0	50.7	53.4
Interest	7.1	9.8	15.6	7.7	8.3	8.4	8.5
Undistributed intragovernmental transactions	-2.2	-2.9	-5.1	-2.4	-2.5	-2.8	-2.9
Total	92.1	118.6	185.6	100.0	100.0	100.0	93.5

Note: Detail will not necessarily add to totals because of rounding.

Source: *The Military Budget and National Economic Priorities.* Hearings before the Subcommittee on Economy in Government of the Joint Economic Committee, 91st Cong., 1st sess. (June 3-24, 1969), Part 2, p. 672.

APPENDIX 9
MILITARY OUTLAYS, FEDERAL OUTLAYS, AND GNP RELATIONSHIPS, 1939-1970 (dollar amounts in billions)

Fiscal years:	Deflator:[1] 1958=100	Deflator:[2] 1964=100	Military outlays in 1964 dollars	GNP[3]	Net total[4]	Military[5]	Other[6]	Offsets[7]	Total	Military	Other	Military outlays as percent of Federal budget[9]
1939	40.8	36.4	$3.2	$87.6	$8.8	$1.2	$7.7	[10]	10.1	1.3	8.8	13.2
1940	40.2	35.8	4.4	95.0	9.6	1.6	8.8	[10]	10.1	1.6	8.5	16.3
1941	46.6	41.5	14.6	109.4	14.0	6.1	7.9	[10]	12.8	5.5	7.2	43.4
1942	52.5	46.8	50.4	139.2	34.5	23.6	10.9	[10]	24.8	16.9	7.9	68.3
1943	54.9	48.9	129.0	177.5	78.9	63.1	15.8	[10]	44.5	35.5	8.9	80.0
1944	53.8	48.0	158.5	201.9	94.0	76.1	17.9	[10]	46.5	37.7	8.9	81.0
1945	53.1	47.3	168.9	216.8	95.2	79.9	15.3	[10]	43.9	36.8	7.1	83.9
1946	57.3	51.1	82.2	201.6	61.7	42.0	19.7	[10]	30.6	20.8	9.8	68.1
1947	65.6	58.5	23.6	219.8	36.9	13.8	23.1	[10]	16.8	6.3	10.5	37.4
1948	69.8	62.2	17.8	243.5	36.5	11.1	25.4	[10]	15.0	4.6	10.4	30.4
1949	73.0	65.1	18.4	260.0	40.6	12.0	28.6	[10]	15.6	4.6	11.0	29.6
1950	72.9	65.0	18.4	263.3	43.1	11.9	31.2	[10]	16.4	4.5	11.9	27.9
1951	79.4	70.8	29.2	310.5	45.8	20.7	25.1	[10]	14.7	6.7	8.1	45.7
1952	81.2	72.4	57.1	337.2	68.0	41.4	26.6	[10]	20.2	12.3	7.9	60.2
1953	81.4	72.5	65.1	358.9	76.8	47.7	29.1	[10]	21.4	13.3	8.1	62.1
1954	83.5	74.4	58.6	362.1	71.1	43.6	28.5	-$1.2	19.6	12.0	7.9	61.5
1955	86.9	77.5	48.2	378.6	68.5	37.4	32.4	-1.2	18.1	9.9	8.6	54.5
1956	91.7	81.7	46.2	409.4	70.5	37.7	34.2	-1.5	17.2	9.2	8.3	53.6
1957	95.8	85.4	47.1	431.3	76.7	40.2	38.4	-1.9	17.8	9.3	8.9	52.4
1958	100.0	89.1	46.5	440.3	82.6	41.4	43.1	-1.9	18.8	9.4	9.8	50.1
1959	102.2	91.1	48.0	469.1	92.1	43.7	50.6	-2.2	19.6	9.3	10.8	46.3
1960	104.2	92.9	46.4	495.2	92.2	43.1	51.4	-2.3	18.6	8.7	10.4	45.6
1961	105.2	93.8	47.6	506.5	97.8	44.6	55.7	-2.5	19.3	8.8	11.0	44.5
1962	105.6	94.1	51.3	542.1	106.8	48.3	61.1	-2.6	19.7	8.9	11.3	44.2
1963	108.0	96.3	51.5	573.4	111.3	49.5	64.5	-2.7	19.4	8.6	11.2	43.4
1964	112.2	100.0	50.8	612.2	118.6	50.8	70.7	-2.9	19.4	8.3	11.5	41.8
1965	115.5	102.9	45.8	654.2	118.4	47.1	74.5	-3.2	18.1	7.2	11.4	38.7
1966	118.8	105.9	52.1	720.7	134.7	55.2	82.9	-3.4	18.7	7.7	11.5	40.0
1967	121.2	108.0	63.3	766.5	158.4	68.3	94.1	-4.0	20.7	8.9	12.3	42.1
1968	126.1	112.4	69.4	822.6	178.9	78.0	105.5	-4.6	21.7	9.5	12.8	42.5

1969	131.8	117.5	66.7	893.0	185.6	78.4	112.3	−5.1	20.8	8.8	12.6	41.1
1970	134.2	119.6	65.1	960.0	190.1	77.9	117.9	−5.7	19.8	8.1	12.3	39.8
1970R[11]	137.9	122.9	65.1	960.0	192.9	80.0	118.6	−5.7	20.1	8.3	12.4	40.3

[1]Economic Report of the President, January 1969, p. 231 through 1968; 1969 and 1970 figures are based on the next column at 112.2 to 100 (see note[2]).

[2]1970 figure estimated. Details are presented in attachments to Table 2 of the statement furnished to the Joint Economic Committee on June 6, 1969. 1968 and earlier figures are based on the deflator with 1958 = 100, coverting at 112.2:100 (see note[1]); 1969 figure is interpolated between 1968 and 1970.

[3]Budget of the United States, 1970, Special Analyses, p. 17, fiscal year 1939 data are derived by averaging 1938 and 1939 calendar year data from the 1969 Economic Report of the President, p. 227. Fiscal year 1970 data are derived from the chart in the fiscal year 1970 budget, p. 29.

[4]Source: 1939-68—The Budget of the United States, 1970, Table 20, p. 533. 1969-70, revised estimates, Bureau of the Budget.

[5]Source: 1939-53—OASD(C), FAD-236, May 1, 1969. 1954-58—Data provided by Treasury Department to reflect outlays on same basis as published in Annual Report of the Secretary of the Treasury, June 30, 1968, Statistical Annex, p. 17. 1959-68—The Budget of the United States, 1970, Table 17, p. 527. 1969-70—OASD(C), Table 3, May 21, 1969. Includes "Defense-Military" and "Military assistance."

[6]The offsets are added to the net total to produce the agency total; that is, the total amounts that are reflected in the budgets of various agencies before deduction of Government-wide offsets. The military total is deducted from this agency total to derive the total for other agencies.

[7]Through fiscal year 1968, the source is: Statistical Appendix to Annual Report of the Secretary of the Treasury, June 30, 1968, p. 17. Amounts are undistributed, intragovernmental transactions deducted from Government-wide totals under new concepts. Includes Government contribution for employee retirement and interest received by trust funds. For fiscal year 1969 and fiscal year 1970, the source is the fiscal year 1970 budget, p. 530.

[8]Figures do not add to total for 1954 and later because of intragovernmental transactions.

[9]For 1954 and later, this is the military percentage of the agency totals, before deducting intragovernmental transactions.

[10]Not available.

[11]This line reflects data resulting from inclusion of the Government-wide pay raise effective July 1, 1969. In the 1970 President's budget, the pay raise was excluded from DOD estimates for 1970 but included elsewhere as a separate item covering all Government agencies.

Source: The Military Budget and National Economic Priorities. Hearings before the Subcommittee on Economy in Government of the Joint Economic Committee, 91st Cong., 1st sess. (June 3-24, 1969), Part 1, pp. 374-375.

APPENDIX 10
DISTRIBUTION OF U.S. MILITARY PRIME CONTRACT AWARDS, 1940-1965

Period	Percentage of total accounted for by			
	Largest 100	Largest 50	51-100	Small business
June 1940-Sept. 1944 (WWII)[1]	67.2	57.6	9.6	
July 1950-June 1953 (Korean War)	64.0	56.3	7.7	
Jan. 1955-June 1957	67.4	59.5	7.9	
FY 1957	68.4	59.8	8.6	19.8
FY 1958	74.2	66.9	7.3	17.1
FY 1959	73.8	65.3	8.5	16.6
FY 1960	73.4	64.8	8.6	16.1
FY 1961	74.2	65.8	8.4	15.9
FY 1962	72.3	63.4	8.9	17.7
FY 1963	73.9	65.6	8.3	15.8[2]
FY 1964	73.4	65.8	7.6	17.2[2]
FY 1965	68.9	61.2	7.7	19.6[2]

Sources: For World War II, Smaller War Plants Corporation, *Report to U.S. Senate Special Committee to Study Problems of American Small Business, Economic Concentration and World War II* (Washington: Government Printing Office, 1946), pp. 30-31.
For the Korean War, U.S. Congress, Senate Committee on Armed Services, Preparedness Investigating Subcommittee, *Investigation of the Preparedness Program, Second Report, Report on Concentration of Defense Contracts* (Washington: Government Printing Office, 1955), pp. 8-14.
For FY 1957-65, OSD, *100 Companies and Their Subsidiaries Listed According to Net Value of Military Prime Contract Awards,* various years; OSD, *Military Prime Contract Awards and Subcontract Payments, July 1964-June 1965,* p. 12.
[1]The figure for World War II is based on prime contracts of $50,000 or more and excludes procurement of food. The more recent series are based on contracts of $10,000 or more, including food procurement. Thus, neither coverage nor base are strictly comparable.
[2]Because of a change in reporting coverage, the ratios starting with FY 1963 are not comparable with those for prior years. On a comparable basis, the FY 1963 ratio is 16.5 percent; those for FY 1964 and FY 1965 are not available.

Source: William L. Baldwin, *The Structure of the Defense Market, 1955-1964* (Durham, N.C.: Duke University Press, 1967), p. 9.

APPENDIX 11
AFTER-TAX FINANCIAL RATES OF RETURN FOR PUBLICLY OWNED,
PROFIT-SEEKING FIRMS AMONG THE 50 LARGEST PRIME CONTRACTORS,
BY DEGREE OF SPECIALIZATION IN DEFENSE SALES, 1957 AND 1962

Percentage of total sales for defense	Average rate of return on			Over-all rate of return on		
	Assets	Owners' equity	Sales	Assets	Owners' equity	Sales
1957: 90-100	7.32	16.20	2.98	8.10	18.01	2.71
80-89	7.19	13.88	3.08	8.69	18.04	3.38
70-79	7.42	15.99	3.72	6.18	13.91	3.09
60-69	6.60	11.32	3.96	6.16	10.69	3.91
50-59	7.42	12.03	3.61	7.42	12.03	3.61
40-49	5.62	8.90	4.12	5.46	8.47	4.26
30-39	8.42	13.61	6.77	8.48	13.67	6.82
20-29	7.57	13.63	5.97	9.56	17.45	6.51
10-19	6.69	10.12	4.68	6.24	9.35	4.40
1-9	7.75	11.56	9.27	8.01	12.02	8.97
1962: 90-100	6.28	11.22	2.93	6.48	12.80	2.72
80-89	6.86	15.08	2.88	6.27	12.08	2.54
70-79	6.42	11.56	3.34	6.07	11.32	3.29
60-69	6.96	11.58	3.48	7.49	12.43	3.70
50-59	6.62	12.21	4.13	6.64	11.75	4.07
40-49	5.44	7.18	3.88	4.78	6.52	3.46
30-39	5.84	8.73	5.10	5.93	8.96	4.55
20-29	6.95	10.20	4.57	7.78	11.79	5.01
10-19	7.47	12.19	8.90	8.00	13.75	8.72
1-9	7.46	10.63	9.27	8.22	12.14	10.61

Source: William L. Baldwin, *The Structure of the Defense Market, 1955-1964* (Durham, N.C.: Duke University Press, 1967), p. 190.

APPENDIX 12

DEFENSE-ORIENTED INDUSTRIES—EMPLOYEES, VALUE ADDED, AND SHIPMENTS AND RECEIPTS, 1963-1967, AND BY INDUSTRY, 1967 (Value in millions of dollars. Coverage varies; for 1967 covers approximately 7,078 establishments accounting for 85-90 percent of all shipments and receipts in these industries. "N.e.c." means not elsewhere classified.)

Standard industrial classification code	Year and industry	Employees (1,000)	Value added by manufacture	Value of shipments and receipts		
				Total	Government[1]	Non-government
(X)	1963	1,933	22,326	79,626	37,364	42,263
(X)	1965	3,859	54,577	105,987	28,785	77,202
(X)	1966	4,262	60,984	122,531	35,368	87,164
(X)	1967, total	4,507	66,848	134,391	41,216	93,185
19	Ordnance, except complete guided missiles	160	1,730	3,958	3,421	536
28	Chemicals and allied products[2]	102	2,142	3,951	1,195	2,756
2819	Inorganic chemicals, n.e.c.	66	1,702	3,187	698	2,489
2911	Petroleum refining	103	4,540	20,000	781	19,219
3069	Rubber products, n.e.c.	117	1,423	2,560	268	2,292
33	Primary metal industries[2]	342	5,108	12,827	1,718	11,108
3323	Steel foundries	64	719	1,117	93	1,023
3351	Copper rolling and drawing	38	672	2,105	223	1,881
3352	Aluminum rolling and drawing	56	856	2,840	438	2,402
3357	Nonferrous wire drawing, etc.	72	1,308	3,480	285	3,195
34	Fabricated metal products[2]	291	3,937	7,447	778	6,669
3441	Fabricated structural steel	60	681	1,686	138	1,548
3443	Boiler shop products	58	850	1,643	172	1,472
3452	Bolts, nuts, rivets, and washers	55	784	1,307	152	1,155
3494	Valves and pipe fittings	85	1,190	2,026	181	1,845
35	Machinery, except electrical[2]	696	10,481	19,716	2,175	17,543
3519	Internal combustion engines	65	1,008	2,133	408	1,725
3531	Construction machinery	110	1,673	3,486	304	3,182
3541	Metalcutting machine tools	66	1,032	1,672	116	1,556
3561	Pumps and compressors	70	1,036	1,937	131	1,808
3562	Ball and roller bearings	58	813	1,327	144	1,184
3573	Electrical computing equipment	108	1,954	3,831	467	3,364
3574	Calculating and accounting machines	18	207	295	70	225
36	Electrical machinery[2]	1,269	16,039	27,170	8,848	18,324
3613	Switchgear and switchboards	58	846	1,362	76	1,286
3621	Motors and generators	105	1,267	2,220	308	1,912
3661	Telephone, telegraph apparatus	116	1,537	2,643	161	2,482
3662	Radio, TV, communications equipment	376	4,687	7,838	6,143	1,696
3679	Electronic components, n.e.c.	198	2,178	4,152	808	3,345
3694	Engine electrical equipment	50	677	1,206	101	1,105
37	Transportation equipment[2]	1,104	15,519	28,032	19,685	8,350
3721	Aircraft	398	5,804	11,330	7,433	3,897
1925	Complete guided missiles	164	2,588	4,033	3,876	157
3722	Aircraft engines and parts	197	2,952	5,340	3,978	1,362
3723, 3729	Aircraft propellers and parts, and equipment, n.e.c.	181	2,450	4,004	2,736	1,270
3731	Shipbuilding and repairing	127	1,329	2,348	1,491	857

Source: U.S. Department of Commerce, *Statistical Abstract of the United States, 1970* (Washington, D.C., 1970), p. 254.

APPENDIX 12   (con't)

Standard industrial classifica- tion code	Year and industry	Em- ployees (1,000)	Value added by manu- facture	Value of shipments and receipts		
				Total	Gov- ern- ment[1]	Non- govern- ment
38	Instruments and related products[2]	265	4,672	7,199	1,163	6,037
3821	Mechanical measuring devices	59	775	1,182	131	1,051
3861	Photographic equipment	81	2,288	3,336	388	2,950
(X)	Miscellaneous industries	57	1,253	1,532	1,183	349

X Not applicable.
[1]Comprises products shipped to, or receipts for work done for, Federal agencies, their contractors, subcontractors, and suppliers.
[2]Includes industries not shown separately.

APPENDIX 13
CONCENTRATION RATIOS IN THE MILITARY MARKET,
FISCAL YEAR 1967 (dollar amounts in millions)

Market category	Size	Percent of contracts	
		Top 4 firms	Top 8 firms
Surveillance and detection satellites	$ 236	100	100
Nuclear submarines	211	99	99
Space boosters	263	97	100
Fighter aircraft	2,164	97	100
Attack aircraft	570	97	100
Missile inertial guidance systems	539	97	99
Inertial navigation systems	201	96	99
Missile reentry vehicles	278	95	99
Aircraft fire control systems	414	95	98
Transport and tanker aircraft	1,003	94	99
Helicopters	1,208	93	99
Jet aircraft engines	1,892	93	99
Data processing systems	336	83	93
Missile solid rocket propulsion systems	356	81	90
Combat vehicles	256	74	91
Ships and parts	1,391	67	77
Surface based sonar systems	278	63	82
Countermeasures systems	209	63	76
Surface radar systems	215	62	81
Missile systems	2,119	59	82
Drones	224	59	72
Communications systems	224	56	81
Navy power systems	877	50	59
Administrative and management services	1,458	37	65
Artillery fuse systems	497	35	52
Aircraft ground handling and service systems	287	25	40
Heavy artillery	1,255	25	38

Source: *Competition in Defense Procurement*. Hearings before the Subcommittee on Antitrust and Monopoly of the Committee on the Judiciary, U.S. Senate, 90th Cong., 2d sess. (1968), p. 21.

APPENDIX 14
DEFENSE CONTRACT AWARDS AND PAYROLLS—STATES: 1967-1969 (In millions of dollars. For years ending June 30.
Data for contracts refer to awards made in fiscal year specified; expenditures relating to those awards may extend over several years.)

State	1967 Contract awards[1]	1967 Estimated annual payroll Military personnel[2]	1967 Estimated annual payroll Civilians[3]	1968 Contract awards[1]	1968 Estimated annual payroll Military personnel[2]	1968 Estimated annual payroll Civilians[3]	1969 Contract awards[1]	1969 Estimated annual payroll Military personnel[2]	1969 Estimated annual payroll Civilians[3]
Total	41,817	9,350	8,044	41,241	9,378	8,570	39,310	10,125	9,712
Alabama	297	184	233	409	182	212	408	190	238
Alaska	86	166	56	107	155	50	91	165	58
Arizona	250	139	61	287	155	67	344	156	76
Arkansas	127	58	33	121	52	31	117	53	40
California	6,689	1,150	1,328	6,470	1,256	1,437	6,825	1,315	1,561
Colorado	210	223	116	263	256	131	244	285	150
Connecticut	1,936	20	32	2,355	23	36	1,715	25	43
Delaware	52	50	10	43	48	12	47	45	15
District of Columbia	358	186	209	350	205	202	321	242	287
Florida	799	384	213	976	388	256	964	420	277
Georgia	1,148	532	287	964	529	337	933	583	367
Hawaii	65	176	171	96	195	179	115	184	213
Idaho	15	22	4	17	21	5	16	27	7
Illinois	1,064	304	221	932	283	235	933	322	272
Indiana	898	52	116	1,108	45	136	1,059	53	161
Iowa	279	9	6	261	9	6	202	4	9
Kansas	399	179	40	292	152	44	350	229	54
Kentucky	124	289	109	60	299	127	59	312	146
Louisiana	656	199	57	461	195	63	390	199	70
Maine	57	61	13	75	51	15	53	39	15
Maryland	870	327	366	704	298	393	731	310	462
Massachusetts	1,422	139	193	1,619	145	180	1,550	152	195
Michigan	1,034	104	103	796	91	105	683	92	124

State									
Minnesota	651	26	18	620	23	16	741	25	23
Mississippi	115	143	50	369	111	54	218	139	67
Missouri	2,278	178	166	1,357	183	176	1,095	205	212
Montana	78	57	10	20	49	10	22	39	12
Nebraska	103	83	30	120	77	26	102	81	33
Nevada	29	37	19	18	41	21	27	53	26
New Hampshire	163	29	65	156	25	76	102	27	82
New Jersey	1,235	227	243	1,108	300	234	1,270	313	275
New Mexico	80	96	88	87	81	87	96	99	100
New York	3,262	168	313	3,484	156	255	3,074	156	280
North Carolina	448	439	87	487	481	103	515	510	119
North Dakota	17	76	9	68	67	11	36	71	12
Ohio	1,603	135	354	1,641	146	318	1,533	156	340
Oklahoma	157	210	226	165	230	279	173	213	292
Oregon	99	20	25	120	19	29	86	19	32
Pennsylvania	1,649	77	528	1,727	79	527	1,700	87	613
Rhode Island	198	44	71	126	34	75	119	39	85
South Carolina	181	243	130	133	292	151	173	289	164
South Dakota	9	38	10	34	30	8	3	32	10
Tennessee	538	90	49	542	95	50	486	93	59
Texas	3,547	1,068	515	4,087	943	584	3,525	1,094	644
Utah	179	28	203	131	26	218	157	28	234
Vermont	100	1	1	105	1	1	86	1	2
Virginia	665	590	623	693	530	757	711	584	875
Washington	606	250	197	530	291	217	575	336	240
West Virginia	140	3	9	132	3	9	67	2	11
Wisconsin	384	17	23	406	11	16	394	10	25
Wyoming	33	24	5	15	21	3	13	22	5
Undistributed	4,435	—	—	3,994	—	—	4,061	—	—

Source: U.S. Department of Commerce, *Statistical Abstract of the United States, 1970* (Washington, D.C., 1970), p. 251.

— Represents zero.

[1] Awards of $10,000 or more for supplies, services, and construction. Figures reflect impact of prime-contracting on State distribution of defense work. Often the State in which a prime contractor is located is not the State in which the subcontracted work is done.

[2] For shore-based personnel only.

[3] Direct hire employees only.

APPENDIX 15
SMALL BUSINESS SHARE OF MILITARY PURCHASING,
FISCAL YEAR 1968 (percentage of total awards to business)

Category	Percent
Construction	64
Textiles and clothing	61
Subsistence	56
Procurements of less than $10,000	50
Miscellaneous hard goods	39
Services	26
Fuels and lubricants	22
Ordnance weapons	17
Tanks and automotive vehicles	14
Ships	12
Ammunition	11
Electronics and communication equipment	11
Aircraft	3
Missiles and military space systems	2

Source: *Economics of Military Procurement*. Hearings before the Subcommittee on Economy in Government of the Joint Economic Committee, 90th Cong., 2d sess. (1969), Part 1, p. 51.

APPENDIX 16
PERCENT OF SALES TO GOVERNMENT (NAVY AND ARMY) TO COMPANIES' TOTAL SALES, 1927-1933

Company	Percent government sales to companies' total sales
Boeing Airplane Co.	59
Chance Vought Corp.	75
Consolidated Aircraft Co.	79
Curtiss Aeroplane and Motor Co.	76
Douglas Aircraft Co.	91
Glenn Martin Co.	100
Great Lakes Aircraft Co.	73
Grumman Aircraft Engineering Corp.	75
Keystone Aircraft Corp.	77
Pratt & Whitney Aircraft Co.	64
Wright Aeronautical Co.	58

Source: Reprinted by permission of the publisher, The Vanguard Press, from *The Aviation Business: From Kitty Hawk to Wall Street* by Elsbeth E. Freudenthal. Copyright, 1940, by Elsbeth E. Freudenthal.

APPENDIX 17
COST OF EMERGENCY FACILITIES EXPANSION, AIRCRAFT
INDUSTRY, WORLD WAR II AND KOREAN WAR (millions of dollars)

Total expansion	Total	Privately financed	Federally financed
1940-1945*	$3,894	$ 420	$3,474
1950-1953	3,528[1]	1,204[2]	2,324[1]
Structures			
1940-1945	1,556	212	1,344
1950-1953	1,085[1]	805[3]	280[1]
Equipment			
1940-1945	2,338	208	2,130
1950-1953	2,443[1]	399[4]	2,044[1]

Source: G. R. Simonson, ed., *The History of the American Aircraft Industry* (Cambridge, Mass.: MIT Press, 1968), p. 213.
*Cost of manufacturing facilities authorized July 1940-June 1945.
[1]Estimate by Aircraft Industries Association of Air Force and Navy obligations since Korea (excludes funds for guided missiles, electronics, and Air Force Heavy Press Program).
[2]Total Tax Amortization Certificates processed by the National Production Authority Aircraft Division as of March 1, 1953.
[3]Totals of Tax Amortization Certificates for land, building, facilities, and miscellaneous processed by National Production Authority Aircraft Division as of March 1, 1953.
[4]Total of Tax Amortization Certificates for plant equipment, machine tools, etc., processed by National Production Authority Aircraft Division as of March 1, 1953.

APPENDIX 18
TOTAL INVESTMENT OF GOVERNMENT AND PRIVATE FUNDS IN
FACILITIES USED BY CERTAIN AIRCRAFT COMPANIES DURING 1955

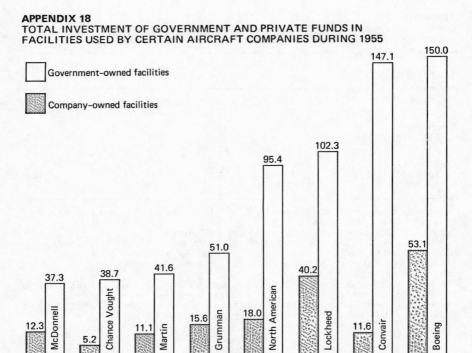

Source: G. R. Simonson, ed., *The History of American Aircraft Industry* (Cambridge, Mass..
MIT Press, 1968), p. 221.

APPENDIX 19
AIRBORNE WEAPON SYSTEMS—PERFORMANCE AGAINST
ORIGINAL SPECIFICATIONS, 1950s-1960s

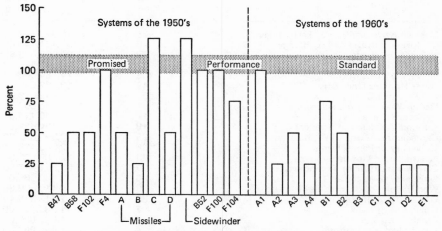

Letter designations are for systems which cannot be identified for security reasons

Source: *The Military Budget and National Economic Priorities*. Hearings before the Subcommittee on Economy in Government of the Joint Economic Committee, 91st Cong., 1st sess. (June 3-24, 1969), Part 1, p. 97.

APPENDIX 20
PRINCIPAL NONINDUSTRIAL CONTRACTORS WITH THE OFFICE OF
SCIENTIFIC RESEARCH AND DEVELOPMENT DURING WORLD WAR II

	Number of contracts	Total dollar value of contracts
Massachusetts Institute of Technology	75	$116,941,352.05
California Institute of Technology	48	83,451,746.45
Harvard University	79	30,963,478.80
Columbia University	73	28,521,412.63
University of California	106	14,384,506.98
Johns Hopkins University	49	10,572,642.61
University of Chicago	53	6,742,070.64
George Washington University	2	6,561,650.00
Princeton University	17	3,593,446.51
National Academy of Sciences	19	3,164,531.14
Carnegie Institution of Washington	26	2,999,035.00
University of Pennsylvania	36	2,960,438.31
Northwestern University	29	2,568,628.00
Carnegie Institute of Technology	20	2,511,675.00
University of Michigan	30	2,159,035.00
Woods Hole Oceanographic Institute	5	2,110,000.00
University of Illinois	30	2,013,525.49
University of Iowa	7	1,933,350.00
Franklin Institute	13	1,923,025.00
Evans Memorial Hospital	4	1,920,960.00
University of Rochester	35	1,859,863.57
Duke University	11	1,210,579.50
Cornell University	31	1,147,836.50
University of New Mexico	9	1,141,550.00
Battelle Memorial Institute	15	1,141,500.00

Source: James Phinney Baxter 3rd, *Scientists Against Time* (Boston: Little Brown, 1946), p. 456.

APPENDIX 21
OBLIGATIONS BY THE DEPARTMENT OF DEFENSE FOR R & D AT
100 UNIVERSITIES AND COLLEGES RECEIVING THE LARGEST
AMOUNTS, 1964 (dollar amounts in thousands)

Institution Name	State	Rank	DOD	Army	Navy	Air Force	Def. Agency
Mass. Inst. of Technology	Mass.	1	46,819	3,965	18,807	21,928	2,119
University of Michigan	Mich.	2	14,736	5,413	1,284	4,966	3,073
Stanford University	Cal.	3	12,815	1,824	5,214	4,573	1,204
Columbia University	N.Y.	4	9,194	1,489	4,459	3,184	36
University of Illinois	Ill.	5	7,612	2,524	1,704	1,343	2,041
U. of Cal. Los Angeles	Cal.	6	6,871	397	5,221	1,106	147
U. of Cal. Berkeley	Cal.	7	5,424	439	3,140	1,592	253
Univ. of Pennsylvania	Pa.	8	5,304	1,473	673	961	2,197
University of Texas	Tex.	9	5,281	571	3,502	1,208	0
Ohio State University	Ohio	10	5,256	466	253	4,185	0
University of Chicago	Ill.	11	4,615	774	1,702	1,374	765
Harvard University	Mass.	12	4,539	705	1,425	1,010	1,399
Carnegie Inst. Technology	Pa.	13	4,519	130	334	340	3,668
Cornell University	N.Y.	14	4,358	510	680	452	2,570
California Inst. of Tech.	Cal.	15	4,232	348	1,673	2,211	0
New York University	N.Y.	16	4,019	1,750	1,239	1,030	0
Illinois Inst. of Tech.	Ill.	17	3,852	2,069	352	1,431	0
University of Denver	Colo.	18	3,773	488	81	3,204	0
Johns Hopkins University	Md.	19	3,732	1,098	757	1,867	0
Princeton University	N.J.	20	3,709	561	1,863	1,285	0
Northwestern University	Ill.	21	3,461	332	843	722	1,564
Polytechnic Inst. Brooklyn	N.Y.	22	3,254	113	1,411	1,730	0
University of Maryland	Md.	23	3,089	1,001	210	1,324	514
Duke University	N.C.	24	2,946	2,341	169	436	0
Brown University	R.I.	25	2,746	325	647	389	1,385
University of Colorado	Colo.	26	2,709	2,163	152	394	0
University of Dayton	Ohio	27	2,643	0	0	2,643	0
U. of Cal. San Diego	Cal.	28	2,455	0	29	2,426	0
University of Miami	Fla.	29	2,174	467	1,605	102	0
New Mexico State Univ.	N.M.	30	2,157	1,546	343	268	0
University of Pittsburgh	Pa.	31	2,080	886	340	680	100
Syracuse University	N.Y.	32	2,046	337	382	1,327	0
University of Washington	Wash.	33	1,986	199	1,381	406	0
Purdue University	Ind.	34	1,981	477	10	694	800
Yale University	Conn.	35	1,813	274	530	1,009	0
Northeastern University	Mass.	36	1,685	98	12	1,575	0
Univ. of Southern California	Cal.	37	1,617	121	462	1,034	0
George Washington Univ.	D.C.	38	1,526	395	926	205	0
Univ. of N.C. at Chapel Hill	N.C.	39	1,441	211	74	605	551
Pennsylvania State Univ.	Pa.	40	1,214	381	89	744	0
Texas A. & M. University	Tex.	41	1,204	233	808	163	0
University of New Mexico	N.M.	42	1,199	0	150	1,049	0
University of Oklahoma	Okla.	43	1,193	533	36	624	0
U. of Wis. Madison	Wisc.	44	1,102	358	278	466	0
University of Iowa	Iowa	45	1,077	0	947	55	75
U. of Minn. Mnpls.-St. Paul	Minn.	46	1,076	0	764	312	0
Indiana University	Ind.	47	1,075	153	342	580	0
University of Virginia	Va.	48	1,030	295	643	92	0
Tufts University	Mass.	49	1,021	303	88	630	0
University of Utah	Utah	50	1,020	333	69	618	0

APPENDIX 21   (con't)

Institution Name	State	Rank	DOD	Army	Navy	Air Force	Def. Agency
Wentworth Institute	Mass.	51	979	0	0	979	0
Univ. of Minn. All Campuses	Minn.	52	967	0	0	967	0
University of Florida	Fla.	53	958	352	143	308	0
Okla. St. U. Agric. & App. Sci.	Okla.	54	924	119	111	694	0
Oregon State University	Oreg.	55	887	46	453	388	0
University of Rochester	N.Y.	56	877	314	152	411	0
Univ. of Rhode Island	R.I.	57	857	1	751	105	0
Texas Western College	Tex.	58	846	781	0	65	'
Stevens Institute of Tech.	N.J.	59	839	247	350	242	0
American University	D.C.	60	834	780	54	0	0
Lowell Technological Inst.	Mass.	61	748	79	0	669	0
University of Arizona	Ariz.	62	725	213	199	172	27
Western Reserve Univ.	Ohio	63	720	417	126	177	0
Utah State University	Utah	64	713	100	0	613	0
Georgia Institute of Tech.	Ga.	65	710	419	214	77	0
Catholic Univ. of America	D.C.	66	679	110	228	155	186
Boston College	Mass.	67	661	25	0	636	0
Georgetown University	D.C.	68	658	550	33	75	0
University of Cincinnati	Ohio	69	648	134	0	474	40
University of Hawaii	Hawaii	70	612	103	253	256	0
Florida State University	Fla.	71	607	81	134	392	0
Case Inst. of Technology	Ohio	72	594	71	197	326	0
N. Mex. Inst. Mining & Tech.	N.M.	73	554	0	540	14	0
Washington University	Mo.	74	552	235	160	157	0
Arizona State University	Ariz.	75	532	65	54	413	0
University of Puerto Rico	P.R.	76	531	562	29	0	0
University of Delaware	Del.	77	502	198	109	195	0
Rensselaer Poly. Institute	N.Y.	78	500	149	212	139	0
University of Missouri	Mo.	79	494	369	76	49	0
University of Connecticut	Conn.	80	469	340	0	129	0
Colorado State University	Colo.	81	446	297	95	54	0
Michigan State University	Mich.	82	428	145	71	89	0
Iowa St. U. of Sci. & Tech.	Iowa	83	424	213	0	151	0
Brandeis University	Mass.	84	422	253	30	139	0
University of Alaska	Alaska	85	402	80	74	248	0
Medical Col. of Virginia	Va.	86	386	157	45	0	184
Boston University	Mass.	87	383	150	32	201	0
Rutgers—The State Univ.	N.J.	88	379	158	89	132	0
St. Univ. N.Y. All Inst.	N.Y.	89	370	0	0	370	0
Tulane Univ. of Louisiana	La.	90	369	248	30	75	0
Ohio University	Ohio	91	368	0	15	353	0
Dartmouth College	N.H.	92	364	173	76	115	0
Yeshiva University	N.Y.	93	364	115	10	239	0
St. Louis University	Mo.	94	361	114	15	232	0
Univ. of N.C. St. at Raleigh	N.C.	95	344	113	67	164	0
U. of Cal. San Francisco	Cal.	96	343	297	46	0	0
University of Georgia	Ga.	97	327	0	13	134	0
University of Louisville	Ky.	98	325	315	10	0	0
U. of Cal. Riverside	Cal.	99	319	62	0	257	0
Emmanuel College	Mass.	100	312	0	0	312	0

Source: *Competition in Defense Procurement.* Hearings before the Subcommittee on Antitrust and Monopoly of the Committee on the Judiciary, U.S. Senate, 90th Cong., 2d sess. (1968), pp. 878-879.

APPENDIX 22
FEDERAL GOVERNMENT R & D CONDUCT EXPENDITURES
BY FUNCTIONAL FIELD, 1961 AND 1969 (percent of total)

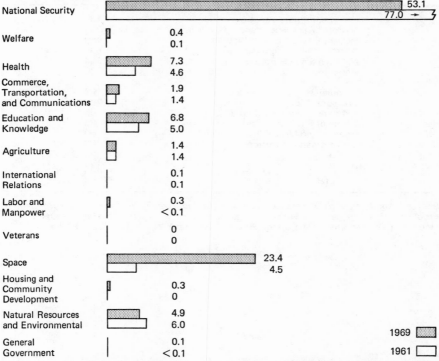

	1969	1961
National Security	53.1	77.0 →
Welfare	0.4	0.1
Health	7.3	4.6
Commerce, Transportation, and Communications	1.9	1.4
Education and Knowledge	6.8	5.0
Agriculture	1.4	1.4
International Relations	0.1	0.1
Labor and Manpower	0.3	<0.1
Veterans	0	0
Space	23.4	4.5
Housing and Community Development	0.3	0
Natural Resources and Environmental	4.9	6.0
General Government	0.1	<0.1

Source: National Security Industrial Association, *A Bi-Ennial Symposium on Federal Research and Development in the 70's—Its Need and Scope* (June 11-12, 1969), p. 10.

APPENDIX 23
CONDUCT OF R & D BY GOVERNMENT AGENCY,
FISCAL YEAR 1971 (dollar amounts in millions)

Defense, military functions	$7,762
National Aeronautics and Space Administration	3,354
Health, Education, and Welfare	1,459
Atomic Energy Commission	1,559
National Science Foundation	384
Agriculture	306
Interior	271
Commerce	99
Transportation	226
Veterans' Administration	65
Office of Economic Opportunity	90
Housing and Urban Development	60
Smithsonian Institution	20
Justice	29
All other	124
Total	15,808

Source: *Application of Aerospace and Defense Industry Technology to Environmental Problems.* Hearings before a Subcommittee of the Committee on Government Operations, House of Representatives, 91st Cong., 2d sess. (November 23-24, 1970), p. 197.